THE WY CAMPING GUIDE

Marc Smith

Open Space Publications
Casper, Wyoming

Copyright © 2021 by Open Space Publications, LLC
All rights reserved. No part of this book may be reproduced in any form by any means without the express consent of the publisher.

All inquiries, corrections, or feedback should be directed to:
Open Space Publications, LLC
PO Box 50133
Casper, WY 82605-0133

www.openspacepublications.com

ISBN: 978-1-7322271-1-8

Printed in the United States of America
Fifth Edition

All photos by author unless otherwise credited. The color photographs of Yellowstone's Old Faithful and Lower Falls were taken by Nadine Cownover.

Edited by Judith Savala-Wright.
Cover design by Julie Cornia of Black Dog Design, LLC.

CAUTION

Camping and outdoor recreation are potentially dangerous activities that pose risks. The author and publisher assume no responsibility or liability for any damages, losses, accidents, or injuries incurred from using this book. It is the reader's responsibility to be aware of all risks and take the necessary precautions to handle those risks.

While the author has made considerable attempts to make this book as accurate as possible, errors may exist. Campground information, roads, and recreational facilities can and do change. All maps and distances are for general reference only and should not be relied on for actual navigation.

Contents

Wyoming Regions 10
Map Legend 10

Introduction 11
Define: Wyoming 12
Geography 12
History 12
Flora 13
Weather 14
Wildlife 16
Camping Options 19
Camping Suggestions 20
Outdoor Ethics 21
Outdoor Safety 21
Roads and Driving 24
Backcountry Navigation 26
Using this Guide 26

Northwest 29
Privately-owned Campgrounds
and RV Dump Stations 31

Area 1: Yellowstone Country 32
Pebble Creek Campground 36
Slough Creek Campground 37
Tower Fall Campground 38
Mammoth Campground 39
Indian Creek Campground 41
Canyon Campground 42
Norris Campground 44
Madison Campground 45
Baker's Hole Campground 46
Fishing Bridge RV Park 47
Bridge Bay Campground 49
Grant Village Campground 51
Lewis Lake Campground 52
Snake River Recreation Area 54
Sheffield Creek Campground 55
Headwaters Campground (Flagg Ranch) 56
Cave Falls Campground 57

Area 2: Grand Teton National Park
and Surrounding Mountains 59
Lizard Creek Campground 62

Colter Bay Campground and RV Park........................ 63
Pacific Creek Campground.. 64
Signal Mountain Campground.................................... 65
Jenny Lake Campground 67
Gros Ventre Campground 69
Atherton Creek Campground..................................... 71
Crystal Creek Campground 72
Curtis Canyon Campground 73
Trail Creek Campground 74
Reunion Flats Campground....................................... 75
Teton Canyon Campground 76
Kozy Campground.. 77
Granite Creek Campground 78
Hoback Campground... 80

Area 3: Northern Absaroka Range and Beartooth Mountains...82
Island Lake Campground 84
Beartooth Lake Campground 86
Lily Lake Camping Area 88
Crazy Creek Campground... 89
Fox Creek Campground 91
Montana Campgrounds near Yellowstone 92
Lake Creek Campground 93
Hunter Peak Campground... 94
Dead Indian Campground 95
Little Sunlight Campground 97
Sunlight WHMA 98
Hogan and Luce 98

Area 4: Buffalo Bill Cody Country................................99
Buffalo Bill State Park.. 102
Big Game Campground... 104
Wapiti Campground.. 105
Elk Fork Campground.. 106
Clearwater Campground 108
Rex Hale Campground 109
Newton Creek Campground 110
Eagle Creek Campground 111
Three Mile Campground.. 112

Area 5: Southeastern Absaroka Range......................114
Deer Creek Campground 116
Jack Creek Campground... 117
Wood River Campground 119
Brown Mountain Campground................................. 120

Area 6: The Togwotee Trail 121
Spence/Moriarity WHMA 124
Kirk Inberg/Kevin Roy WHMA 124
Whiskey Basin WHMA 125
Horse Creek Campground 126
Double Cabin Campground 127
Falls Campground 128
Pinnacles Campground 129
Brooks Lake Campground 130
Turpin Meadows Campground 132
Hatchet Campground 133

North - Northeast 135
Privately-owned Campgrounds
and RV Dump Stations 137

Area 1: Northern Bighorn Mountains 138
Connor Battlefield State Park & Historic Site 142
Amsden Creek WHMA 143
Sibley Lake Campground 143
Prune Creek Campground 145
Pine Island Group Picnic Area & Campground 146
North Tongue Campground 147
Bald Mountain Campground 148
Porcupine Campground 149
Five Springs Falls Campground 151
Bighorn Canyon National Recreation Area 152
Yellowtail WHMA 154
Owen Creek Campground 154
Tie Flume Campground 155
Dead Swede Campground 156
Ranger Creek Campground 157
East Fork Campground 158
Little Goose Campground 160
Cross Creek Campground 161
Shell Creek Campground 163
Ranger Creek Campground 164
Medicine Lodge Lake Campground 165
Lower Paint Rock Lake Campground 167

Area 2: Southern Bighorn Mountains 168
Mikesell-Potts Recreation Area (DeSmet Lake) 171
Hunter Campground 172
Middle Fork Campground 173
Hettinger Group Campground 174

Circle Park Campground 175
Tie Hack Campground.. 176
South Fork Campground 178
Lost Cabin Campground... 180
Doyle Campground.. 181
Lakeview Campground... 182
Sitting Bull Campground... 183
Willow Park Group Campground............................. 184
Boulder Park Campground 186
Island Park Campground.. 187
Deer Park Campground.. 187
West Tensleep Lake Campground.......................... 188
Leigh Creek Campground 190
Medicine Lodge Archaeological Site 191
Castle Gardens Campground................................. 193

Area 3: Black Hills and Northeastern Lowlands..........194
Sand Creek Public Access Area.............................. 196
Bearlodge Campground 197
Cook Lake Campground.. 198
Sundance Horse Campground................................ 199
Reuter Campground.. 200
Belle Fourche Campground
(Devils Tower National Monument) 201
Keyhole State Park.. 203

Central 205
Privately-owned Campgrounds
and RV Dump Stations.. 207

Area 1: Wind River Country 208
Boysen State Park... 211
Dickinson Creek Campground................................. 215
Ocean Lake WHMA... 216
Sinks Canyon State Park... 217
Sinks Canyon Campground..................................... 218
Worthen Meadows Campground.............................. 220
Fiddlers Lake Campground 221
Little Popo Agie Campground.................................. 222
Louis Lake Campground 223
Big Atlantic Gulch Campground 225
Atlantic City Campground.. 226

Area 2: Hole-in-the-Wall Hideouts 228
Outlaw Cave Campground...................................... 231
Middle Fork Campground 233

Grave Springs Campground 234
Buffalo Creek Campground 234

Area 3: Central Mountains and Reservoirs 236
Casper Mountain Campgrounds 239
Lodgepole Campground 241
Rim Campground 242
Alcova Reservoir 243
Pathfinder Reservoir 246
Cottonwood Campground (Green Mountain) 249
Prior Flat Campground 250
Seminoe State Park 251
Dugway Campground 253

Area 4: Eastern Reservoirs and Laramie Range 254
Hawk Springs State Park 257
Grayrocks Reservoir WHMA 258
Guernsey State Park 258
Glendo State Park 262
Ayres Natural Bridge Campground 265
Esterbrook Campground 266
Friend Park Campground 267
Curtis Gulch Campground 268
Campbell Creek Campground 269
Tom Thorne/Beth Williams WHMA 270

Southwest 271
Privately-owned Campgrounds
and RV Dump Stations 273

Area 1: Snake River Range 274
East Table Creek Campground 276
Station Creek Campground 277
Wolf Creek Campground 278
Little Cottonwood Group Campground 279
Alpine Campground 280
McCoy Creek Campground 280

Area 2: Western Ranges 281
Sacajawea Campground 283
Middle Piney Lake Campground 284
Murphy Creek Campground 286
Moose Flat Campground 287
Forest Park Campground 289
Hobble Creek Campground 290

Hams Fork Campground 292
Swift Creek Campground 293
Lake Viva Naughton Campground 293
Cottonwood Lake Campground 295
Allred Flat Campground 296

Area 3: Wind River Range 297
Sweetwater Guard Station Campground 300
Sweetwater Bridge Campground 301
Big Sandy Wilderness Campground 302
Scab Creek Campground 304
Boulder Lake Campground 305
North Boulder Lake Campground 306
Fremont Lake Campground 307
Half Moon Lake 308
Trails End Campground 309
Willow Lake Campground 310
Soda Lake WHMA 311
New Fork Lake Campground 311
Narrows Campground 312
Whiskey Grove Campground 314
Green River Lake Campground 315
Warren Bridge Recreation Area 317
Warren Bridge Campground 319

Area 4: Southwestern Desert and Mountains 320
New Fork River Campground 322
Big Sandy Recreation Area 323
Fontenelle Creek Campground 324
Fontenelle Reservoir Campgrounds 325
Three Patches Campground 328
Buckboard Crossing Campground 329
Firehole Campground 331
Utah Campgrounds at the Flaming Gorge NRA 333
Deadhorse Trailhead Campground 334
Meeks Cabin Campground 336

South - Southeast 337
Privately-owned Campgrounds
and RV Dump Stations 339

Area 1: Sierra Madre Range 340
Encampment River Campground 343
Bottle Creek Campground 344
Hog Park Campground 345

Lost Creek Campground 347
Jack Creek Campground..348
Teton Reservoir Recreation Site 349

Area 2: Medicine Bow Mountains 350
Laramie Plains Lakes 353
Wick/Beumee WHMA 354
Bow River Campground 354
Deep Creek Campground... 355
Aspen Campground... 356
Pine Campground... 357
Willow Campground 358
Spruce Campground 359
North Fork Campground... 360
Nash Fork Campground 361
Brooklyn Lake Campground..................................... 362
Sugarloaf Campground 364
Silver Lake Campground... 365
Ryan Park Campground... 367
South Brush Creek Campground 368
Lincoln Park Campground.. 369
Lake Owen Campground.. 370
Rob Roy Campground.. 372
French Creek Campground...................................... 373
Corral Creek Campground 374
Bennett Peak Campground 375
Pickaroon Campground.. 376
Miller Lake Dispersed Camping Area....................... 377
Pelton Creek Campground....................................... 377
Six Mile Campground 378

Area 3: Vedauwoo and Vicinity 379
Curt Gowdy State Park... 381
Vedauwoo Campground... 384
Vedauwoo Designated Dispersed Camping Zone.... 385
Yellow Pine Campground.. 386
Tie City Campground.. 387

Contacts 388
Index 392
Acknowledgments and Afterword 397
About the Author/Open Space Publications 398

Wyoming Regions

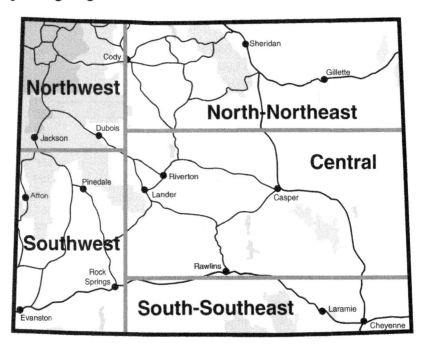

Map Legend

INTRODUCTION
What to know before you go

Welcome to Wyoming! Whether you picked up this book to help guide you on your next camping vacation or to use as a reference for your weekend excursions, you're in for a good time. With this guidebook, you'll spend more time camping and enjoying outdoor activities and less time racing to find a campsite.

This guide contains the details that outdoor folks care about. Details such as parking spur lengths, elevations, camping seasons, trail distances, fishing holes and the types of fish that swim them. You'll discover the best scenic drives, dispersed camping areas, and places to go boating. You'll learn where to watch for wildlife and where to go rock climbing… where to go four-wheeling or where to find solitude. It's all here. Now grab your gear and go.

Define: Wyoming

Wyoming is a blend of rugged mountain ranges, forests, grasslands, desert bluffs, and sagebrush expanses that spread to each corner of the horizon. It's where the wilderness is still wild—something lost in many other parts of the country. It's a state where people prize wide-open spaces, unpopulated mountain backcountry, the spirit of the Old West, and a strong sense of independence. It's also a state prized for its tremendous outdoor recreation value.

Geography

Simply described by some as one of those "big square states out West," Wyoming is indeed a large state—the ninth largest in the country. It's also a high state. With a mean elevation of 6,700 feet, it's surpassed by Colorado, the nation's highest, by only a hundred feet. The lowest elevation of just 3,099 feet is located in the state's northeast corner. The highest point is found in the Wind River Range on the summit of Gannett Peak, 13,804 feet.

Roughly a third of the state is considered mountainous, and at least one range is usually visible anywhere in the state. These mountains have cores of granite, limestone, and metamorphic or volcanic rock. Unlike neighboring states in the Rocky Mountain Region, most of Wyoming's mountain ranges—over a dozen of them—are not continuous, but rather stand divided by huge basins. The gap between the ranges on the southern border and those around the Yellowstone area is what separates the southern Rocky Mountains from the Northern Rockies.

The Continental Divide, which naturally directs river flows to either the Atlantic Ocean or the Pacific Ocean, runs a south central to northwest course through the state. In Wyoming's Red Desert, the Divide splits around an area called the Great Divide Basin. The scant precipitation that falls in this basin either evaporates or soaks into the ground, never making it to a river.

History

Wyoming's history reflects many different time periods. The state is known worldwide for its archeological dig sites where dinosaur bones and fossils have been uncovered. Indian tribes such as the Crow, Shoshone, and Sioux lived off the land long before explorers and trappers arrived looking for adventure and a better life. Then came the wagon trains and the railroads, all before the state was established in 1890.

Travel anywhere in Wyoming and you'll experience its history. While development continues to change Wyoming, much of the state must look the way it did to those early travelers who came to mine, homestead, or push through to greener pastures. Simply seeing land as it existed hundreds of years ago is like stepping into a history book.

Those looking for tangible remnants of the state's history won't be disappointed. There are dinosaur tracks, petroglyphs, forts, old mines and cabins. The Oregon Trail—just one of over a dozen historic routes that passed through the state—can still be seen in surprising clarity in some areas.

Wyoming has a broad selection of excellent history books. This isn't one of them. While you'll occasionally find bits of history worked into these pages, those who are interested should pick up a copy of "Roadside History of Wyoming" by Candy Moulton or the intriguing "Wyoming Place Names" by Mae Urbanek.

Flora

Wyoming's plant life includes over 2,000 species across numerous plant communities including sagebrush-grassland prairie, foothills, forested mountains, and alpine settings. The plants that grow in these communities vary by elevation, as shown in the following illustration.

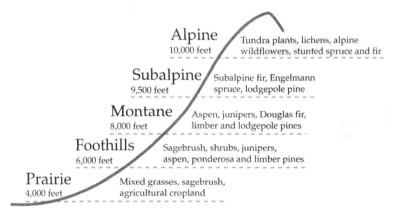

Alpine — 10,000 feet — Tundra plants, lichens, alpine wildflowers, stunted spruce and fir

Subalpine — 9,500 feet — Subalpine fir, Engelmann spruce, lodgepole pine

Montane — 8,000 feet — Aspen, junipers, Douglas fir, limber and lodgepole pines

Foothills — 6,000 feet — Sagebrush, shrubs, junipers, aspen, ponderosa and limber pines

Prairie — 4,000 feet — Mixed grasses, sagebrush, agricultural cropland

Nearly 60% of the state is shortgrass prairie. Common types of grass include wild rye, green needle grass, bluebunch wheatgrass, and cheatgrass. In the driest parts of the state, especially the central and southwest regions, sagebrush carpets the ground. It may not look like much, but biologists have identified 87 mammals, 297 birds, and 63 reptiles that are supported by this plant community.

The soil is dry and shallow in the foothills, which are often comprised of rocky, shallow-soiled slopes and canyons. Acting as a transition zone between the grasslands and the forested mountains, the foothills consist of sagebrush, shrubs, and short juniper evergreens.

The montane and subalpine plant communities consist of mostly coniferous forests, which are found in roughly a fifth of the state. Drier mountain ranges, such as the Black Hills and Laramie Range, are robed in ponderosa pine. Where precipitation is greater, evergreens such as lodgepole pine, whitebark pine, limber pine, subalpine fir, Douglas fir, and Engelmann spruce are common. Deciduous trees are also found in the forests, though their numbers are less widespread. Cottonwoods flourish along riverbanks, and aspens are found throughout the state.

The alpine zone in Wyoming, those areas above treeline, occurs around 11,500 feet in the southern part of the state and around 9,800 feet in the northern mountains. The hardy plants that grow in these environments include stunted shrub-like spruce and fir, lichens, wildflowers, and tiny tundra plants.

Although all plant communities serve as critical wildlife habitat, it is Wyoming's riparian areas that play the largest role. It is estimated that drainages and wetlands support 80% of the state's wildlife species by providing water, forage, and protective cover. Common plants in these areas include planeleaf willow as well as a variety of sedges and grasses like elephanthead, alpine timothy, and tufted hairgrass.

Weather

Wyoming weather is just like its terrain—varied. While it could be blistering hot in the desert basins, a blizzard could be pounding the high country. Conversely, the plains could be getting hammered with a thunderstorm while the mountains remain mild and sunny. You can soak up a 65°F day in January or shiver through a 20°F day in July—you just never know. While all states in the Rocky Mountain region experience this volatility, Wyoming is known for its extremes. When recreating, be prepared for any weather during any season and consider the following conditions:

Temperatures—Though Wyoming's temperature extremes have ranged from -66°F to 114°F, the averages are between 12°F and 87°F. Average summer temperatures in the mountains range between 40-70°F. Temperatures during the same season at lower elevations range between 50-90°F. These numbers vary by elevation and location, of course, and it is not unusual to have daily fluctuations of 30 or 40 degrees.

Wind—The wind blows in Wyoming, and hard. Areas that seem to get especially harsh wind include the Interstate corridors as well as central Wyoming. So just how windy is it? Of the ten windiest places in the United States, four of them (Casper, Rawlins, Cheyenne, and Laramie) are located in Wyoming. It's something of which to be mindful when driving a large RV through the state. Fortunately, the wind slows considerably during the summer months and is never even noticed by many campers.

When recreating in the backcountry, remember that cold breezes are not just uncomfortable, they are deadly when combined with wetness. A layer of windproof clothing is a wise acquisition. Keep in mind that a mild wind in the trees may be brutal at the top of the mountain. In general, wind speeds at the bottom of a valley are twice as high on the top of a ridge.

Sunburn—The dangers from sun exposure in Wyoming are compounded by altitude and a general absence of cloud cover. The hazard is multiplied even further if there is snow on the ground, which acts like a giant mirror.

Keep your skin covered or use sunscreen. Remember that your eyes are also at risk of being burned. Sunglasses are in order.

Precipitation—Precipitation amounts vary wildly throughout Wyoming. While much of the state receives less than 14 inches annually, parts of the Teton Range receive over 70 inches a year.

Summers are generally terrific in Wyoming's mountains although the potential for wet weather always exists. A typical day in the forests usually includes a clear sun-saturated morning, followed by a build up of clouds in the afternoon (which may or may not involve precipitation), then a clearing in the evening. Most storms are brief, but others can settle in for a day or longer. Clouds that build rapidly or turn from white to gray hold the most promise for producing precipitation. While rain is the most expected form of precipitation during the warm weather months, be prepared to handle sleet, hail, or horizontally-driven snow. I've seen August snow in Yellowstone and was snowed out of a four-wheeling trip in the Bighorns on a 4th of July weekend.

Wyoming flash floods have proven to be deadly. Be wary of recreating in tight canyons during rainy weather and avoid camping in a basin or near a watercourse in such weather.

Lightning—Thunderstorms assault the mountains during late spring and summer. Lightning is not just a threat on the high peaks; all areas are susceptible to strikes.

In a lightning storm, the old advice of avoiding tall objects and lone trees is still key. If reaching suitable shelter (a building or vehicle) is not possible, prepare to wait out the storm. Distance yourself from tent poles, hiking poles, and other potential conductors that you may be handling or carrying on your pack. Squat down on the balls of your feet, keeping the feet together, and cover your ears with your hands.

Other suggestions to consider:

- Watch the clouds as they are building; dark, flat bottoms are indicative of a thunderstorm. Plan hikes so you are off high and exposed ridges before these storms build, particularly during the afternoon hours. Seek out the protection of a dense forest with trees of uniform height.

- Remember that once lightning contacts the ground, the electrical current follows the path of least resistance (like water). Avoid small caves, overhangs, and unenclosed shelters.

- When planning an outing, check the weather forecast in the area, by visiting a weather website such as www.weather.gov.

Wildlife

Wyoming is known for its abundant wildlife, and surveys have shown that wildlife viewing is one of the state's most popular outdoor activities. The list of animals that you may see is extensive. While you will surely find a variety of birds and small mammals, most campers look for larger animals. Information regarding the most popular animals is shown in the following table.

Animal	Male Female Young	Characteristics	Habitat
Bighorn Sheep	Ram Ewe Kid	Brownish-gray coat, white rump patch, adult rams have large curled horns, 75–275 pounds	Cliffs, rocky slopes in the high country with light timber or brush
Bear	Boar Sow Cub	Black: Black, brown, or blonde color, taller ears, 135–400 pounds, Grizzly: Black, brown, or blonde color, shoulder hump, dished face, longer claws, 225–1000 pounds	Black: dense forests and open slopes across the state Grizzly: Open valleys and forests in the state's northwest region
Pronghorn Antelope		Tan coat with white markings and white rump, 70–130 pounds	Plains, open sagebrush grasslands, and rolling desert areas
Deer	Buck Doe Fawn	Mule: Brownish-gray coat, 100–400 pounds Whitetailed: Reddish-gray coat, white tail, 125–200 pounds	Mule: desert shrubs, prairie rivers, forests Whitetailed: river bottoms, dense forest
Moose		Dark brown to black coat, long legs, 600–1200 pounds, antlers are "paddle" shaped	Willow flats, swamps, wilderness areas with marshes
Elk	Bull Cow Calf	Light brown with dark neck, 500–1000 pounds	High plains, foothills, mountain meadows, open woodlands
Bison		Dark brown coat, huge head and shoulder hump, 1200–2000 pounds	Meadows and grasslands in the northwest corner of state

Viewing Wildlife
There are several ways you can increase your chances of viewing wildlife:
- Get up early and stay out late. Most animals are most active during the cooler parts of the day. This is usually from sunrise to 10:00 a.m. and from 4:00 p.m. till dark. Animals are also more active during cooler, cloudy days but less active during periods of rain or snow.
- When you are in likely habitat, use binoculars or a spotting scope to "glass" the area. In many cases, animals will be bedded down and may be hard to find. Look for dark spots or specific parts of an animal, such as antlers, just above the grass or brush.
- If you spot wildlife, stay quiet, avoid sudden movements, and try not to disturb the animals. Wildlife that feels threatened or bothered by your presence will quickly move out of the area. If you have a pet, keep it in the vehicle. A barking dog can be a great liability when you are near wild animals.
- Zoom in or use a telephoto lens to capture a closer picture instead of approaching an animal. Never honk, yell, or throw anything to get an animal's attention. While this may yield a better picture, it is senseless to try to alter the animal's behavior and may motivate it to move further away.

Avoiding Close Encounters
While many animals portray a lethargic or uninterested demeanor, they know of your presence. To remain safe, keep your distance and don't approach wildlife. If you intrude on an animal's circle of comfort, all predictability is lost. The animal may leave, which may be considered wildlife harassment (this is a violation punishable by fine in Wyoming's national parks). If the animal doesn't leave, it may choose to deal with the threat—that is to attack you. While all wildlife should be considered dangerous, the following animals deserve specific words of caution.

Ungulates—Although bears are the most suspected, it is moose, elk, bison, and even deer that are responsible for the majority of injuries. These animals will protect their young and their space when they feel threatened.

Mountain Lions—These large cats—also called pumas, panthers, and cougars—are predatory animals that are occasionally involved in attacks across the West. Although these nocturnal creatures are typically very shy around humans and sleep throughout much of the day, they still pose a risk, especially to children. In the unlikely event that you encounter a mountain lion, it is important that you do not act like prey. Increase your height by standing on a log or rock to appear more intimidating. If you have a child, pick him or her up. If you have a jacket on, you can fan the sides out to look wider. Wave, throw stones, and make noise. The effort will usually send the lion running away. If you are attacked, fight back under all circumstances using anything and everything that you have. People have survived mountain lion attacks by fighting back with their bare hands, by using rocks, or a small pocketknife.

Bears—There are two types of bears found in Wyoming. The smaller of the two is the black bear, which has a strong statewide population. The larger and more feared grizzly inhabits the greater Yellowstone area including the Wind River Range. Since these animals know no boundaries, assume that you are in bear country even if you are miles away from known habitat. Take the following precautions to help prevent bear encounters:

- Separate cooking and sleeping areas and keep your camp free of odor, scraps, and food containers. Burn your trash or put it in a bear-proof trash container. Place your food, coolers, and any odorous items in a bear box, hard-sided camper, or vehicle. If you are in the backcountry, hang everything that has a smell—including food, toiletries, and the clothes you cooked in—at least 10 feet off of the ground.
- Hike in groups during daylight hours. While hiking, nearly every expert agrees that making noise, such as clapping or talking loudly, is an effective technique to let bears know that you are in the area. Bears will almost always leave when they hear humans approaching.
- Avoid areas that show bear sign (tree markings, scat, or dig sites). Also, if you see a carcass, leave the area and report it to a ranger.
- Carry bear spray. Pepper spray designed specifically for use on bears has proved its ability to deter attacks or to reduce the ferocity of an attack. Only use the spray during a serious bear encounter, never as a repellent (which would only add seasoning to the bear's next meal).

Most bear encounters end with the bear running in the opposite direction. However, bears that are injured, surprised, feeling threatened, or protecting their cubs or food source may attack. If you encounter a bear, do not run! Instead, slowly back away and talk softly. If the bear is approaching you, consider dropping an item (not food) to possibly redirect the bear's attention. If you are wearing a pack, do not take it off; it'll help protect your back in an attack. While you want to be facing the bear, avoid direct eye contact. If the bear should charge, know that grizzlies are known to "bluff charge," that is to veer off to one side at the last moment. On the other hand, if you are knocked down, heed the old advice to play dead. The best position for this is to lock your hands behind your neck and lay face down. If the bear rolls you over, try to flip back over to your stomach.

While attacks at night in camp are rare, they have occurred. Since this is considered a predatory attack, the advice changes. If a bear is in your camp, most experts suggest that you make noise to let the bear know that you are there. If it enters your tent, fight back with everything you have as the bear may be considering you as a source of food. This isn't always the case, however. "Kelty," a Yellowstone bear, was named for its habit of collapsing tents, apparently for the fun of it.

Other Animals and Pests—Here are additional precautions for dealing with wildlife and other critters:
- Do not feed wildlife. This is especially true with bears. It is said that a fed bear is a dead bear. This rule also applies to smaller animals such as birds, squirrels, and other campground roamers.
- Do not approach wildlife. No matter how tolerant an animal may appear, remember that it is wild and unpredictable.
- Stay alert for rattlesnakes in the lower regions of the state. If you are bitten, remain calm. Clean and bandage the bite area and seek medical attention as soon as possible. Your odds of a full recovery are good.
- Take precautions to avoid ticks and mosquitoes. Deer ticks can transmit very serious diseases to humans if they are attached to the skin for longer than a day or two. Mosquitoes can carry a disease called West Nile Virus. The best way to deter these pests is to use a repellent and wear long sleeves and pants. Check yourself periodically. If you find a tick that's lodged, pull it straight out with tweezers, getting as close to its head as possible, then wash and cover the area.

Camping Options

With eight national forests, two national parks, a handful of state parks, and millions of acres of public land, Wyoming has an abundance of camping opportunities. When looking for a place to camp, you have three primary choices that range from primitive to borderline luxurious.

Public Campgrounds—This book includes all of Wyoming's developed public campgrounds. These camps are maintained by one of several government agencies including the National Park Service, USDA Forest Service, Bureau of Land Management (BLM), Wyoming Game & Fish, and city or county governments. Except for a handful, public campgrounds do not offer the hookups or services like those found at a privately-owned campground. Most of them do offer potable water, pit toilets, picnic tables, fire rings, and trash containers. Many Forest Service campgrounds have on-site hosts between Memorial Day and Labor Day to help maintain the campground and aid campers as needed.

Public campgrounds require campers to follow a few reasonable campground rules and regulations. These rules include a designated quiet time (usually between 10:00 p.m. and 6:00 a.m.), keeping your pets leashed or under control, and storing your camping gear and food properly. In addition, riding ATVs on campground roads is not allowed unless used for egress. Check the campground's fee board for local rules and regulations.

Dispersed Camping—Dispersed camping is nothing more than finding an area you like on public land and setting up camp. By doing so, you'll carry the responsibility of properly handling your trash and human waste as well as preserving the general condition of the land. Dispersed campsites are frequently found along Forest Service roads and are easily spotted by looking for tire tracks and crudely-constructed rock fire rings. Many of these dispersed camping areas are mentioned in this book.

Certain rules apply when dispersed camping. Though restrictions vary by area, you are generally permitted to drive within 100 yards of an open road to set up camp if you can do so without damaging the land. The length of stay is usually limited to between 14 to 21 days at the campsite and immediate vicinity. After that time, you must move a minimum of five air miles away. You may return to the original site after 14 days have passed. Before you decide to pick a dispersed camping spot, check with the governing authority for regulations and campfire restrictions.

No charge or permit is required to disperse camp, but keep in mind that you cannot use the services or facilities of a nearby public campground. If you choose to camp in this manner, please do so with a low-impact attitude and respect paying campers who are in developed campgrounds.

Privately-owned Campgrounds—Privately-owned campgrounds, such as RV parks, are generally within city limits or are within close proximity to a town. Although the most costly, these types of campgrounds are great for campers with large RVs and trailers who prefer to have full hookups including water, electricity, and sewer. Some offer cable TV and wireless Internet. Most camps also have a small store, showers, and other amenities such as swimming pools. If you are traveling through Wyoming in a motor home and towing a secondary vehicle, a private camp may be your best option.

Since privately-owned campgrounds change management, change names, are competitive, and always want to be presented as the very best, you won't find specific ones listed in this book. What you will find, however, are the towns where the camps and RV parks are located. For a specific list of current camps, check the Wyoming Office of Tourism campground directory at travelwyoming.com.

Camping Suggestions

Here are a few simple suggestions to make your campout more enjoyable.
- Plan on arriving in the early afternoon to secure a site at most campgrounds. For more popular camps, arrive in the early morning.
- Take your own cooking grate if you plan on cooking over a campfire as not all campgrounds have grates over the fire rings.
- Take a grill or cooking stove in case there are fire restrictions in the area where you are camping. Campfires are often prohibited in late summer or in drought years when dry conditions advance the fire danger.
- If feasible, gather your firewood from the local forest if you are planning to have a campfire. Trying to scavenge for wood in campgrounds that are already stripped clean of all deadfall is usually a futile effort. Many campground hosts sell firewood by the bundle (or offer it for free).

Outdoor Ethics

Outdoor recreationists can leave the land as they found it and minimize the signs of use by embracing low-impact techniques. With increasing numbers of visitors on public lands, it is simply vital that we all do our part. Unfortunately, some regard low-impact techniques as nothing more than a political movement from "environmental-whackos" or "tree-huggers." But ignoring common sense strategies to minimize impact to our land does not hurt the environmental movement; it hurts the very sport that causes the damage. Those who go four-wheeling and mountain biking should take special precautions to avoid trail damage and conflicts with others.

Techniques to reduce the impact to our land vary slightly depending on their source, but the basic concepts are listed here.

- Find a campsite instead of making one. Camp on durable surfaces such as rock, gravel, dry grass, or snow. Leave rocks, plants, and other natural objects as you found them. Do not build structures or dig trenches around tents.

- In the backcountry, travel single file along designated trails. Travel in small groups of four to six people to reduce the impact on a given area. Yield to people you meet on the trail and step to the downhill side if you encounter pack stock.

- Dispose of your waste properly. This means you pack out what you packed in—including waste, food, and litter. Human waste should be buried 6-8 inches underground and at least 200 feet away from water sources. Toilet paper needs to be packed out or burned.

- When making a campfire, keep it reasonably sized. Unless you are using an established fire ring, use a stove to do your cooking. If you make a campfire in a dispersed area, burn all the fuel thoroughly and scatter the cool ashes afterwards.

- Respect wildlife. Watch wildlife from a distance and don't approach them. Never feed wildlife and be sure to keep your pets under control.

- Be considerate to others. Keep voices and noises to a minimum and be courteous to other outdoor enthusiasts.

- When four-wheeling, stay on designated roads and trails and do not take shortcuts. Travel during dry weather; going mud-bogging or damaging resources during wet conditions only increases area restrictions and closures.

Outdoor Safety

Outdoor activities are inherently dangerous. You can dramatically reduce your risk of injury or mishap by being prepared, being aware, and using common sense.

- **Be prepared.** Cellular phones, GPS devices, and personal locator beacons certainly save lives, but they don't bring immediate help. Being on a search and rescue team, I've learned firsthand that it can take many hours (if not a day) to reach a scene even if we know exactly where it is. It can then take many more hours to complete a rescue. To come away from a crisis with a story that has a happy ending, prepare yourself with reliable equipment, practiced outdoor skills, and the ability to deal with unexpected conditions or circumstances.
- **Be aware.** This is perhaps the most repeated statement made by safety experts. Situational awareness will allow you to take action before it is too late. Noticing building storm clouds in the morning is better than being alarmed when you first hear a clap of thunder. Noting the mileage on a remote backcountry road is better than suddenly realizing that you have more miles than fuel.
- **Use common sense.** Many unfortunate and tragic situations could have been avoided with a little forethought. For example, check the trees above you before pitching your tent. Little missteps in the woods can have big consequences.

Of course, there are a number of specific dangers that are worth mentioning. These topics, or their suggestions, are not conclusive and you are encouraged to learn more on your own.

First Aid—Anybody who recreates in the outdoors should be able to administer general first aid properly. The backcountry is a minefield of potential injuries and dangers. Professional medical services can be hours or even a day or more away depending on conditions and your location. Do you know how to treat an allergic reaction to a sting? How do you handle a sprained or broken ankle? Take the time to customize a first aid kit and learn CPR. At the very least, toss a small first aid guide into your pack.

Altitude Sickness—It is widely said that the air is thin in the high country. Technically, this is true as an increase in altitude results in a decrease in air pressure and oxygen density. The risk of quickly ascending into the mountains by automobile and recreating at higher elevations is experiencing altitude sickness. Symptoms include headache, fatigue, nausea, dizziness, and vomiting. A more severe condition, known as High Altitude Pulmonary Edema (HAPE), is characterized by the same symptoms in addition to coughing, rapid pulse, pink froth at the mouth, and bluish skin.

Most of Wyoming's recreation areas are between 7,000 and 10,000 feet. This altitude doesn't present a problem for most visitors, especially those from neighboring states. However, exceptions do occur, and those visiting from lower elevations should take precautions.

To prevent getting sick, give your body time to acclimate to higher elevations and drink plenty of water. In general, don't gain more than 7,000 feet of elevation on the first day or two of your trip.

Curing altitude sickness in its early phases is simple. Descend from the current elevation, preferably at least 2,000 feet, as soon as symptoms occur. Once lowered, the condition should quickly improve.

Hypothermia—This potentially fatal condition occurs when the body's core temperature falls below its normal temperature of 98.6°F. As the body loses heat, hypothermia disables bodily functions and deteriorates mental awareness. This can happen even when the ambient air temperature is well above freezing, when temperatures are in the 40s and 50s (common summertime temperatures in the mountains). These temperatures, wind, and wetness (from sweating, a precipitation, or falling in water) are independent ingredients of the hypothermia recipe.

The best way to combat hypothermia is to practice prevention. The cardinal rule is to stay dry. If you are out on a day hike, adjust your clothing so you do not sweat. Wet skin or clothing increases heat loss exponentially. You also don't want to hike while sick, injured, or after consuming alcohol—all of which weaken the body's ability to maintain heat. Carry the proper equipment for the conditions you could encounter; this includes windproof and waterproof clothing to protect against the elements and synthetic clothing that insulates better than cotton. Lastly, but just as important, stay hydrated and well fed.

Mild hypothermia (just below 98°F) can be recognized by shivering or feeling chilled. As hypothermia progresses, the victim loses muscular coordination and may begin shivering violently. In this phase, it is important to drink liquids (preferably warm), start a fire, and change into warm and dry clothing, or slip into a sleeping bag.

As the temperature continues to drop, shivering becomes violently intense and speech becomes impaired. The victim may also become agitated with denial, confused, less coordinated, and unable to function normally. This is a critical point for reversing hypothermia before it enters more severe stages.

With severe hypothermia, muscles become rigid, vital functions slow, and shivering ceases. The victim may actually begin to feel warmer at this point and mistakenly try to remove clothing. Left untreated, unconsciousness will precede a shutdown in respiratory and cardiac systems. This can all happen with shocking rapidity.

A person suffering from a severe case of hypothermia needs to receive immediate medical attention. If that is not possible, try to stabilize the condition by carefully moving the victim to a dry shelter and following the same suggestions for treating mild hypothermia until medical services can be utilized. It is important to note that suddenly re-warming a severely hypothermic person can be fatal if cold blood reaches the heart.

Frostbite—Frostbite is a condition where the flesh becomes frozen and can ultimately lead to loss of that tissue (such as toes). Unless you are winter camping, you generally don't have much to worry about. The important things are to keep your extremities warm by drinking and eating properly, staying well-rested, and wearing proper clothing to protect you from the elements. If your skin starts to feel very painful or go numb, re-warm it using a warmer part of your (or somebody else's) body. If you have access to indoor plumbing, run warm (not hot) water over the area until feeling returns. If you experience severe frostbite, do not try to thaw the frozen area—leave it frozen and seek medical attention.

Drinking Water—Most campgrounds have hand-pump wells or piped water. However, some of these water systems are quite dated and can spit out a pretty suspicious-looking liquid (though they are tested often). To be on the safe side, carry a supply of water with you.

Use special precautions when looking for water in the backcountry. Water from the seemingly purest of sources may pose a risk to your health. The culprits are a variety of bacteria, viruses, parasites and pollutants. The most commonly reported ailment is Giardiasis, the result of consuming the Giardia parasite, which causes intense diarrhea, vomiting, and cramps. Suitable methods for purifying water include:

- Bring the water to a boil to kill harmful microorganisms. This is undoubtedly the most effective way to treat your drinking water.
- Use iodine tablets. For clear or warm water, use one tablet and wait 10 minutes before drinking. Use two tablets and wait 45 minutes if the water is cold or cloudy. Although simple to use, these tablets lose effectiveness in cold weather and give the water a foul taste.
- Use a water filter or purifier unit. Note that these devices may not neutralize all threats that may be contaminating the water.

Roads and Driving

Wyoming is one of the best places to take a good ol' road trip. While other states suffer from clogged Interstates and highway systems, Wyoming's open roadways beg for the throttle. Words can't describe the pleasure of roving through miles of open space bridled only by your sense of adventure and the size of your gas tank.

Wyoming has fifteen scenic highways and designated byways. Of these, five are backcountry backways that explore some of the most unpopulated regions of the state. Though many agree that Wyoming's vast open areas contribute to the state's appeal, some find themselves a little uneasy in such big, rural country. The following tips will help ensure safe travel:

- Keep your vehicle maintained and be sure to have plenty of fuel.
- Keep alert for ATVs, especially on curvy mountain roads.
- Watch for domestic livestock on the roadway. These animals are stubborn and they typically won't clear the way like other animals. Also, watch for wildlife. If you want to watch a wild animal, use a designated turnout or pull completely off the road. Driving excessively slow or stopping in the lane is an invitation for problems.

- Drive responsibly in poor weather. The wind in Wyoming creates dangerous conditions for high-profile vehicles and light trailers. In the winter, the wind causes whiteout conditions and drifting snow.
- Dirt roads can become impassable after a rainstorm. If you are caught on such a road, stay put and let the sun come out for a couple of hours. Attempting to negotiate these troughs of mud during wet conditions can cause you to get stuck or slide off the road. Most storms are short-lived and will quickly pass through the area.
- Snowdrifts keep roads closed at higher elevations well into the summer. It's advisable to wait until the snow recedes completely before attempting to blast through a drift, which often conceals a slick layer of ice on the ground. I've pulled a number of people out of these drifts after they had extended the capabilities of their four-wheel drive SUVs and pickups. Remember, 4x4s are great, but they aren't tanks.
- Most campgrounds and trailheads can be accessed on good gravel or paved roads, but there are a few that utilize four-wheel-drive (4WD) routes. You can expect rocks, snowdrifts, ruts, potholes, puddles, and an occasional ford or log on these roads. High clearance is a must.
- Towns are many a mile apart in Wyoming. You can make a 100-mile drive without passing a gas station or food stop. Fortunately, as a camper you will already be equipped with supplies such as extra clothing, food, and water. Worth tossing into a bag are jumper cables, towrope, and shovel. A compact air compressor and tire repair kit can also be trip savers.

Off-Road Driving—Driving off-road vehicles (ORVs) such as ATVs is permitted and popular on BLM and Forest Service roads. In most areas, operators must be 14 years of age with a permit or 16 years old with a driver's license to drive on signed roads. All ORVs must be equipped with mufflers, functional brakes, and are required to have a current registration decal. Lights must be used when driving a half hour after sunset until a half hour before sunrise. Travel restrictions vary widely; off-road travel may be completely prohibited or permitted without limitation. Some areas allow driving 300 feet off signed roads for firewood gathering, game retrieval, or camping if no damage is caused. When in doubt, check with the land management agency for the area you will be traveling in. Irresponsible off-roading only leads to more road closures and restrictions.

Road Conditions/Emergencies—Refer to the Wyoming Department of Transportation for road conditions. Their website includes web cameras for dozens of statewide roads. You can also download the Wyoming 511 app onto your phone for road notifications. For emergencies, dial 911.

Wyoming Department of Transportation
http://www.wyoroad.info
511 (within Wyoming)
888-WYO-ROAD (nationwide)

Wyoming Highway Patrol
911
800-442-9090

Backcountry Navigation

If you plan on venturing into the backcountry, a map and compass need to be on your equipment checklist. Even if you're never lost, reading a map is useful for discovering the name of a peak, determining how much farther it is to a fishing lake, or showing a less fortunate person the way.

U.S. Geological Survey (USGS) "quad" topographic maps should be used for backcountry navigation. These maps are highly detailed, showing features like terrain and elevation and distinguishing between wooded lands and open areas. These maps are available in print and digital formats, or you can use a software application such as those offered by Garmin and National Geographic. These programs are great for planning trips and printing customized segments of a quad.

If you get lost, stop and think about your last known destination. If it is getting dark and further travel is hazardous, it may be better to set up camp for the night. Remember that trekking downhill will usually place you at a stream, which often leads to a road. Also remember that three sounds, such as three whistle blasts or gunshots, serves as a distress signal.

Using this Guide

The campgrounds in this book are separated into five chapters, one for each Wyoming region. Each region is further separated into smaller areas. Within each area, campgrounds are generally listed from north to south or from east to west, although they are sometimes grouped in the order that you are likely to drive past them. Each camp write-up has this format:

Location/Map—This section offers a general description of the campground's location in relation to the nearest large town or city. It also shows the page number where you will find a map.

GPS Coordinates—GPS coordinates are provided for each campground in the degrees, decimal minutes format.

Sites/Spur Length—This section states the number of campsites at a campground as well as an average length of the parking spurs to help you determine if your RV or trailer will fit at the site. In most cases with a trailer, the tow vehicle will have to be unhitched in order to fit. The lengths are defined as follows:

- Short: RVs under 20 feet (pickup campers, pop-up trailers, vans)
- Medium: RVs between 20-30 feet (average motor homes and trailers)
- Long: RVs over 30 feet (large motor homes and fifth-wheel trailers)

Cost—Campground rates range from nothing to more than $80 at privately-owned campgrounds. These costs are always changing—increasing and even decreasing—depending on services provided. On average, expect to pay $10-30 a night at public campgrounds. Some agencies charge $5 or more for additional vehicles at a site.

If you are staying in a privately-owned campground, inquire about long-term or seasonal rates.

If you are 62 or older, you qualify for a National Parks and Federal Recreational Lands – Lifetime Senior Pass. After paying a one-time $80 fee, this license permits free entrance to any federal recreation area in the United States. It is also good for a 50% discount at most recreation sites like campgrounds. The free Access Pass has similar benefits and is offered to permanently disabled U.S. citizens. You can get these passes at federal recreation sites and offices, by calling 888-275-8747, or visiting store.usgs.gov.

Facilities/Services—Campgrounds offer varying facilities such as fire rings, grills, picnic tables, pit toilets, restrooms, bear boxes (for food storage), playgrounds, RV dump stations, laundry, and showers. Services include trash removal, water, and cellular phone coverage. It's important to note that these are not always reliable services. Trash pickup may not be available every year. Likewise, the availability of potable water is even more unpredictable as a campground's water well may be shut down if the water doesn't meet health standards, the weather is cold, or the system needs maintenance. Consider carrying a few gallons of water with you. Cellular service varies greatly by carrier, phone, and campsite. Cell service is only listed if a signal was obtained by at least one carrier, typically Verizon. This signal may be limited to only voice calls and may not always be usable.

Managing Agency—Agencies that maintain Wyoming's public campgrounds include the National Park Service, USDA Forest Service, Bureau of Land Management, Wyoming Game & Fish Department, Wyoming State Parks, and a number of county and city governments. Some campgrounds have a volunteer host who maintains the camp facilities. Hosts can vary by year, but this section notes if one is often present.

Reservations—This section includes reservation information, if applicable. The primary agencies that accept reservations are:
- National Park Service (Yellowstone): Call 866-439-7375 or visit yellowstonenationalparklodges.com
- National Park Service (Grand Teton): Call 307-543-3100
- Wyoming State Parks: Call 877-996-7275 or visit wyoparks.state.wy.us
- USDA Forest Service: Call 877-444-6777 or visit www.recreation.gov

Most campgrounds in Wyoming operate on a first-come, first-served basis. Your best chance for getting a good campsite is to arrive at the campground between 11:00 a.m. and 3:00 p.m. Popular campgrounds often fill by Friday morning on busy holiday weekends.

Season/Usage—This section gives a campground's normal operating season. Many of Wyoming's campgrounds are open between Memorial Day weekend and Labor Day weekend. There may be a great departure from this time frame depending on a campground's location, elevation, and the season's weather. Cold temperatures and lingering snowpack can keep a campground closed for weeks after the planned opening date. For this reason, among others, you'll find campgrounds at higher elevations often do not open until well into June or even July.

While you will be able to get into some campgrounds during the off-season, many are barricaded by lock and gate. If you are planning an off-season camping trip, check with the governing agency to confirm that you'll have access to the area. If you do, you'll enjoy several benefits of off-season camping. For one, unless it's hunting season, you'll be able to take the site of your choice. Second, fire restrictions from the dry, hot summer months are usually lifted in the spring and fall. Third, by staying in a campground that hasn't been officially opened (or has closed) for the season and doesn't yet offer services, you will usually not be required to pay the campground fee. Just remember to take plenty of water, pack out your own trash, and leave your site as you found it.

The usage section gauges a campground's popularity, a determination that is highly variable. A campground that normally sees little use can have higher visitation due to weather, holidays, road construction, local events, or closures of neighboring campgrounds. Conversely, a high-use campground may be found nearly empty for reasons ranging from forest fires to an economic recession.

Directions—This section includes driving directions for each campground. US and Wyoming highways are abbreviated as "HWY." Interstates are abbreviated with an "I" and "FR" and "CR" refer to Forest Road and County Road respectively. Bureau of Land Management roads use the "BLM" abbreviation. Mileage reported on your tripometer may vary slightly from the directions. Also be aware that road signs may be missing or vandalized.

The maps shown in this book are intended for general navigation only. You'll find them helpful for locating campgrounds, but use more detailed maps for other recreation purposes. Depending on your activities, you may need several different maps; dozens were used to find all the attractions included in this book.

Good choices for general statewide navigation, including BLM roads, is the DeLorme Wyoming Atlas & Gazetteer or the Wyoming Road and Recreation Atlas by Benchmark Maps. Detailed maps of national and state parks are available at their entrance stations. National Forests sell their own detailed maps, which are worth buying.

Description—Each campground write-up describes campsites with information relating to privacy, room, shade, and features. This section also describes each campground's opportunities for outdoor recreation such as hiking, fishing, boating, rock climbing, floating, scenic driving, and wildlife viewing. For ease of reference, recreational information has been duplicated for each campground in which it pertains. For example, if there is a hiking trail near three different campgrounds, the same trail description is shown for each campground.

Field Notes—The Field Notes section has additional information about a campground or particular area and may include my opinion, field observations, or other general notes.

NORTHWEST
The greater Yellowstone area

The attractions in northwest Wyoming are what characterize the state in the minds of millions of people. Neighboring neatly in the corner near Montana and Idaho are the state's greatest assets: Yellowstone National Park and Grand Teton National Park. Yet the greatness of these two parks spills over their political boundaries into some of the wildest areas in the Lower 48.

Each year millions of travelers come to this region, over four million just to Yellowstone itself. While many focus only on the attractions promoted by the national park system, others have discovered their own in places like the Shoshone National Forest, the spirit-lifting Beartooth Mountains, or the unspoiled Teton Wilderness.

In this part of the state, there are more attractions than time to see them. The possibilities for outdoor recreation are countless. Hike in a canyon between Teton peaks. Walk along a boardwalk beside bubbling pools of colored water. Gaze out over dozens of miles from one of the scenic highway overlooks. Just be prepared to leave your heart here when you return home.

Northwest Areas

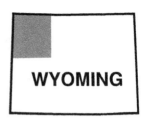

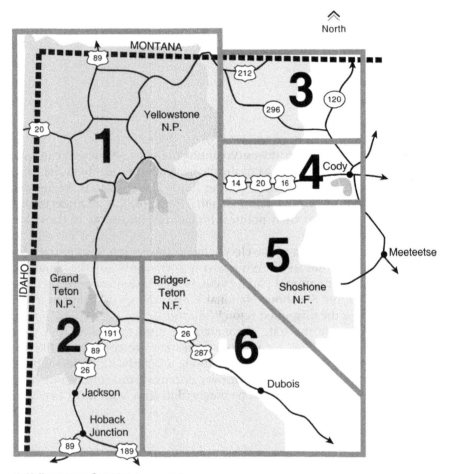

1. **Yellowstone Country** (page 32)
2. **Grand Teton National Park and Surrounding Mountains** (page 59)
3. **Northern Absaroka Range and Beartooth Mountains** (page 82)
4. **Buffalo Bill Cody Country** (page 99)
5. **Southeastern Absaroka Range** (page 114)
6. **The Togwotee Trail** (page 121)

Privately-owned Campgrounds and RV Dump Stations

This section includes the general locations of privately-owned RV parks. For contact information and addresses for these businesses, look online or check out the campground directory on the Wyoming Office of Tourism website at travelwyoming.com.

Area 1: Yellowstone Country
Private campgrounds are located in Gardiner, Montana (north entrance) and West Yellowstone, Montana (west entrance). Flagg Ranch, located a few miles from the park's south entrance, is one of the most popular private campgrounds in the area. Call 800-443-2311 or visit www.gtlc.com.

Area 2: Grand Teton National Park and Surrounding Mountains
Jackson is home to about half a dozen private campgrounds. Further north, there is a large camp several miles east of Moran on HWY 287/26. There is also an RV park next to Colter Bay Campground.

Area 3: Northern Absaroka Range and Beartooth Mountains
There are no private campgrounds in this area, but there are some in nearby Powell and Cody. Powell has a pair of campgrounds owned by the city and county. Both camps offer economical city camping.

Area 4: Buffalo Bill Cody Country
If you need a private campground east of Yellowstone, look no further than Cody. Nearly a dozen camps are found in this authentic western town.

Area 5: Southeastern Absaroka Range
The tiny western town of Meeteetse has a private campground. For more options, you'll need to travel a half-hour north to Cody.

Area 6: The Togwotee Trail
A number of private campgrounds can be found a few miles east of Dubois on HWY 26/287. There is also a terrific KOA right in town. Further west, there is a large RV camp just several miles east of Moran.

RV Dump Stations
The locations below include public RV dump stations. Additional dump stations can often be found at private campgrounds and large gas stations.
- Buffalo Bill State Park
- Cody RV Dump Station - west of airport on Lt. Childers St, Cody, WY
- Homesteader Park, Powell, WY
- Yellowstone National Park: Bridge Bay Campground, Fishing Bridge Campground, Grant Village Campground, Madison Campground
- Grand Teton National Park: Colter Bay Campground, Gros Ventre Campground, Signal Mountain Campground

AREA 1 NORTHWEST
Yellowstone Country

Yellowstone National Park is what puts Wyoming on the map. Take away this national treasure, and some might relegate the state to nothing more than a bland mix of forest and open expanse. But with geysers that burst through the earth's crust, prized wildlife, deep canyons, tall waterfalls, and colored pools that rival the best kaleidoscopes, Yellowstone is unique indeed.

Aside from the park's enchanting attractions, Yellowstone's underlying beauty lies in its natural state; it's a land where nature manages and balances itself—and we observe. Visiting such a place shows how forest fires regenerate life, not destroy it. It illustrates the grisly reality of how the food chain really works. It's a living example of how nature functions when we aren't bent on developing it.

Yellowstone is a very accessible national park with a good road system. The paved Grand Loop Road forms a large figure 8 and connects peripheral roads to the park's five entrances. Most park roads are closed from early November to early May, though construction projects can close sections during the summer.

When recreating in Yellowstone country, allow yourself some time to appreciate and respect the area's incalculable natural value. It's easy to get caught up in gift shops, lodges, restaurants, and interpretive signs. For some, this development is the only part of Yellowstone that they'll truly see and remember. But beyond Yellowstone's narrow corridors of civilization is a ruthless natural world where everything revolves around survival. While the National Park Service has made Yellowstone inviting and family-friendly on the surface, the qualities (and dangers) that inherently belong to wilderness must never be forgotten.

What to Expect: Camping in Yellowstone can be quite special, a place where you can build lasting memories and capture postcard-worthy photographs. Or, without the proper planning, it can be stressful and hurried. To make your stay easier, make reservations for the Madison, Fishing Bridge, Bridge Bay, Grant Village, and Canyon campgrounds. For the other campgrounds that operate on a first-come, first-served basis, arrive early in the morning and claim a site before taking in the park's attractions. These type of campsites are usually occupied by early afternoon.

Interpretive, ranger-led programs are often held at those campgrounds that have amphitheaters. Firewood can be purchased from on-site staff. Food, showers, and general stores can be found near many of the camps.

Campgrounds just outside of the park receive far less use and offer a more rustic camping experience. Regardless of where you stay, all of these camps are in bear country—both black and grizzly—and you must properly store your food. Fortunately, many of the campgrounds have bear-proof boxes where you can lock away your food and cooking supplies.

Yellowstone Lake has 110 miles of shoreline —NPS Photo by J. Schmidt

Area 1: Yellowstone Country

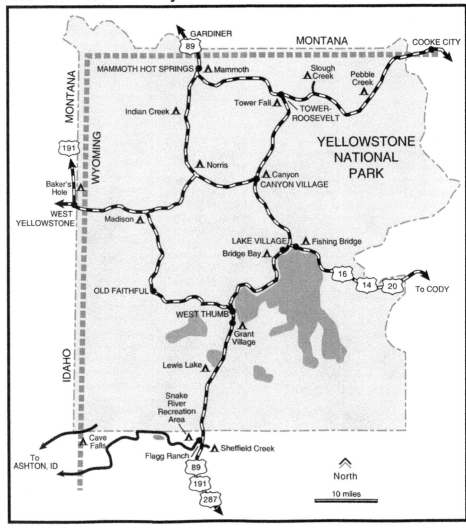

Campgrounds

Campgrounds	Sites	Cost	Average Spur Length	Electrical Hookups	Cellular Service (varies by carrier/site)	Reservations Accepted	Page Number
Pebble Creek Campground	27	$15	M				36
Slough Creek Campground	16	$15	M		📶		37
Tower Fall Campground	31	$15	M				38
Mammoth Campground	85	$20	L		📶		39
Indian Creek Campground	70	$15	L				41
Canyon Campground	273	$32	M		📶	✔	42
Norris Campground	111	$20	M				44
Madison Campground	278	$27	M			✔	45
Baker's Hole Campground (MT)	73	$28	L	✔			46
Fishing Bridge RV Park	346	$79	L	✔	📶	✔	47
Bridge Bay Campground	432	$27	M		📶	✔	49
Grant Village Campground	430	$32	M		📶	✔	51
Lewis Lake Campground	84	$15	S				52
Snake River Recreation Area	14	Free	M				54
Sheffield Creek Campground	5	$10	L				55
Headwaters Campground at Flagg Ranch	175	$42-84	L	✔		✔	56
Cave Falls Campground	23	$10	L				57

Average Spur Length: S = Short (under 30 feet), M = Medium (+-30 feet), L = Long (+-40 feet)
Cellular Service: 1 bar = weak/unreliable signal, 2 bars = low usable signal, 3+ bars = reliable signal for most users

*At the time of this writing, cellular service upgrades were being made to improve and expand coverage in developed areas of Yellowstone and Grand Teton National Park.

Pebble Creek Campground

6,850 feet

Location/Map	Northeast Yellowstone; Page 34
GPS Coordinates	N44° 55.01' W110° 6.83'
Sites/Spur Length	27 sites; Short to medium spurs—under 30 feet
Cost	$15
Facilities/Services	Fire rings, picnic tables, water, pit toilets, trash and recycling containers, bear boxes
Managing Agency	National Park Service (Yellowstone National Park)
Reservations	Not accepted—first come, first served
Season/Usage	Open June through late September; High use

Directions: From Yellowstone's northeast entrance, drive 9 miles to the campground. It's about 80 miles from Red Lodge, Montana.

Description: This compact camp in Yellowstone's remote northeast corner is isolated from the conveniences of stores and restaurants found at many of the other campgrounds in the park. Most of the parking spurs are short (there are a few long pull-throughs) and a good number of sites are designated for tent campers. Mature evergreen trees don't offer much shade, but they do permit unobstructed views of the surrounding mountains. Pebble Creek flows beside the campground and attracts anglers and hikers alike. Generators are not allowed. Sites often fill by noon so arrive early to claim a spot.

Wildlife Viewing: The Lamar Valley, about 10 miles farther into the park, is a popular area for bison, grizzly bears, and wolves. There are numerous pullouts that attract professional, determined photographers with high-end optics. The friendlier ones may offer you an up-close glimpse of their subjects through a telephoto lens.

Fishing: Pebble Creek makes a good fly-fishing stream for cutthroat trout. The upper regions of the creek near the Montana border promise the best fishing. Remember that a park permit is required to fish in Yellowstone.

Trails: An easy 2-mile loop that circles Trout Lake is located just over a mile to the south of the campground. The Pebble Creek Trail, which has two access points near the campground, offers a more strenuous and scenic route into Yellowstone's beautiful backcountry. This trail follows Pebble Creek for most of its 12-mile length; approximately 5 miles of the path are located in Montana. The trail ends at Warm Creek Trailhead near Yellowstone's northeast entrance.

Field Notes: After spending a day at Yellowstone's crowded attractions, it can sometimes feel like this is the park's secret hideaway. If you don't mind "roughing it," you'll fit in nicely at this less-developed campground.

Slough Creek Campground

6,250 feet

Location/Map	Northeast Yellowstone; Page 34
GPS Coordinates	N44° 56.92' W110° 18.4'
Sites/Spur Length	16 sites; Short to medium spurs—under 30 feet
Cost	$15
Facilities/Services	Fire rings, picnic tables, water, pit toilets, trash and recycling containers, bear boxes, cellular service
Managing Agency	National Park Service (Yellowstone National Park)
Reservations	Not accepted—first come, first served
Season/Usage	Open late May through late October; High use

Directions: From Yellowstone's northeast entrance, drive 24 miles. Turn north on the signed gravel road and drive 2.5 miles.

Description: A good distance from the main road, this "out-of-the-way" camp is primitive by Yellowstone standards. Slough Creek flanks the west and north side of the camp. Some sites are among the open sagebrush, others are shaded along the creek, and the rest are snuggled under pine trees. A few of the spots along the creek are walk-in sites. Plan on using the food storage boxes because wild animals do frequent the campground. Generators are not allowed.

Wildlife Viewing: I've seen more bears (grizzly and black) near this campground than anywhere else in Yellowstone. In fact, one morning in late spring yielded six separate bear sightings in the area. The Lamar Valley, located east of the camp, is a popular area for bison, grizzly bears, and wolves.

Fishing: Slough Creek is a favorite for anglers, and the stream receives heavy fishing traffic as a result. The preferred fishing areas are in meadows located between 3 to 8 miles from the campground. A hardy hike is required, but reports of enormous cutthroat trout are said to make the trip worth the effort. Remember that a park permit is required to fish in Yellowstone.

Trails: The trailhead for the Slough Creek Trail is located just south of the campground. The route follows an old wagon road that is still used by the Silver Tip Ranch located north of the park. The first mile climbs at a fair grade, but then moderates by 2 miles where the trail reaches a meadow along Slough Creek. After an intersection for the Buffalo Plateau Trail, the route continues to the northeast for a number of miles, passing meadows well known for their beauty and fishing.

Field Notes: On one visit, I watched a coyote wandering about as if it were a family pet. A short time later, a scraggly black bear scampered down a sage hill toward the camp. I notified an on-site ranger who then jumped on a bike to warn campers. The bear never came into the camp and had seemingly snuck away. As I was leaving, the bear emerged in the road and stopped to watch me. A prolonged stare-off ensued before the animal ran off toward a group of hikers who had just started up the trail.

Tower Fall Campground
6,600 feet

Location/Map	Northeast Yellowstone; Page 34
GPS Coordinates	N44° 53.4' W110° 23.37'
Sites/Spur Length	31 sites; Short to medium spurs—under 30 feet
Cost	$15
Facilities/Services	Fire rings, picnic tables, water, pit toilets, trash and recycling containers, bear boxes, supply store
Managing Agency	National Park Service (Yellowstone National Park)
Reservations	Not accepted—first come, first served
Season/Usage	Open mid-May through late September; High use

Directions: From Yellowstone's northeast entrance, drive 29 miles to Tower-Roosevelt Junction. Turn south and continue 2.5 miles to the campground road, which is a moderately steep one-way drive with a tight curve.

Description: This campground is located near an impressive waterfall that is often overlooked by the larger falls near Canyon Campground. Even so, this small and popular camp fills early in the day. The camp occupies the side of a semi-open hill where you'll be perfectly positioned for sunsets. Sites are arranged around a single loop. Only a few of these can accommodate shorter RVs or trailers so tent campers have the best options. Generators are not allowed.

Natural Attractions: Tower Fall, near the area's general store, plummets 132 feet before flowing into the larger Yellowstone River. Another nearby natural feature is a petrified tree, really a stump, which is located 1.5 miles west of Tower Junction.

Tower Fall Campground

Scenic Driving/Wildlife Viewing: Drive west from Tower Junction toward Mammoth and you'll find spectacular overlooks and waterfalls. There is also a 7-mile, one-way gravel road that traverses the Blacktail Deer Plateau. Drive it early or late to improve your odds of spotting bears.

Drive south toward Canyon Village and you'll traverse Dunraven Pass where the stripped trunks of the burned forest yield impressive views to the west. Bears and bighorn sheep can sometimes be spotted near the pass.

Trails: There are a few short trails around the Tower Fall area that are best located by watching for signs. One of these is a half-mile route that leads to the Tower Fall overlook before switchbacking a half mile to the base of the cascade.

The Lost Lake Trail is a backcountry route that leaves from the campground and heads northwest for 2 miles to intersect another trail. Turn west at this junction to visit Lost Creek Falls, then Lost Lake at 1.25 miles. A shorter and more popular route to the lake and 40-foot falls can be found behind Roosevelt Lodge, north of the campground.

The summit of Mt. Washburn (10,243 feet) is likely the most popular hiking destination in the park. There are two routes to the top, but the main trail starts 11 miles south of the campground at Dunraven Pass (the other is farther north at the Chittenden parking area). The 3-mile route switchbacks to the windy summit of the mountain where an enclosed observation station is located. Grand panoramic views of the park and Grand Canyon of the Yellowstone can be seen.

Field Notes: If you tire of your camp food and want a hot meal, consider stopping by Roosevelt Lodge located north of the campground. The lodge and restaurant have a genuine western feel to them, not the touristy flavor that other Yellowstone facilities have. Horseback and stagecoach rides can also be arranged at the lodge.

Mammoth Campground

6,000 feet

Location/Map	North Yellowstone; Page 34
GPS Coordinates	N44° 58.37' W110° 41.61'
Sites/Spur Length	85 sites; Medium to long spurs—over 30 feet
Cost	$20
Facilities/Services	Fire rings, picnic tables, water, restrooms, trash and recycling containers, cellular service
Managing Agency	National Park Service (Yellowstone National Park)
Reservations	Not accepted—first come, first served
Season/Usage	Open all year; High use

Directions: From Yellowstone's north entrance near Gardiner, Montana, travel south for 5 miles.

Boardwalks cross the terraces at Mammoth Hot Springs

Description: This campground is in a dry mountain valley on the northern edge of Yellowstone where sagebrush outnumbers trees and the smell of sulfur permeates the air. Sites have no privacy, no significant shade, and no real appeal. Even so, the campground is packed during the tourism season. The reason? For one, no reservations are needed to get into one of these level pull-through sites. For another, there are a slew of nearby attractions including Mammoth Hot Springs, the Albright Visitor Center, and Yellowstone's Park Headquarters—its lawns often occupied by elk. Couple these attractions with the close proximity to civilization (there are restaurants in Mammoth and nearby Gardiner), and you have the recipe for a complete summer vacation.

Natural Attractions/Walking: Mammoth Hot Springs are remarkable stone terraces built from cascading mineral-laden hot water that contains calcium carbonate. Boardwalks allow you to walk around the terraces.

Scenic Driving: Yellowstone has several tumbling waterfalls and a few worthwhile overlooks along its northern road between Mammoth and Tower-Roosevelt. For a closer drive off the beaten path (on gravel), take the 4-mile, one way Old Gardiner Road. This route starts behind the Old Mammoth Hotel and ends at the park's northern entrance near Gardiner.

Fishing: Fly-fishing for various trout species is excellent in the Gardner River around Mammoth. The best fishing starts when the water clears in early July. Remember that a park permit is required to fish in Yellowstone.

Trails: The Lava Creek Trail begins across the road from the campground. The route follows a creek of the same name through a canyon and eventually, after about 7 miles, reaches the Grand Loop Road near Blacktail Pond.

An easier walking path along the Gardner River can be found north of the campground at an easily seen parking area.

Closer to town, the Sepulcher-Beaver Ponds Trailhead is found just north of the hot spring terraces. Here, the Sepulcher Mountain Trail makes a full 10-mile loop while topping a 9,646-foot summit at 4 miles. The 5-mile Beaver Ponds Loop Trail is an easier route that is well suited for family hiking.

Field Notes: Of all the campgrounds in Yellowstone, this one feels the most hurried and "in the way." Having a busy highway wrap around three sides of the camp certainly contributes to this feeling. Of course, this is more of the case during the summer. My wife and I stayed a night here in December and were the only ones in the campground. On that trip, we expected frigid conditions and brought our best winter sleeping bags. Instead, we encountered mild temperatures that never dropped below freezing and had a fairly miserable night trying to sleep in -30 degree bags when the temperature was near 40!

Indian Creek Campground
7,300 feet

Location/Map	Northwest Yellowstone; Page 34
GPS Coordinates	N44° 53.19' W110° 44.1'
Sites/Spur Length	70 sites; Long spurs—over 30 feet
Cost	$15
Facilities/Services	Fire rings, picnic tables, water, pit toilets, trash and recycling containers
Managing Agency	National Park Service (Yellowstone National Park)
Reservations	Not accepted—first come, first served
Season/Usage	Open early June through mid-September; High use

Directions: From Mammoth Hot Springs, head south for 8.5 miles.

Description: This appealing camp has a good selection of campsites. While many are best suited for tents, over half of them will fit longer trailers or RVs. There are pull-through sites as well as a couple that are reserved for motorcycles or bicyclists. Compared to other Yellowstone campgrounds, this one has more trees, more privacy, and is slower to fill. Generators are not allowed. Evidence of the 1988 wildfire can be seen in the surrounding mountains and Indian Creek, adjacent to the camp, is very photogenic.

Natural Attractions/Picnicking: The Sheepeater Cliff Picnic Area is directly north of the campground and deserves a visit. The rock cliff is composed of columns of blocks where yellow-bellied marmots can be found.

Scenic Driving/Wildlife Viewing: The stretch of road between Mammoth and Madison offers incredible scenery including lush meadows and snowcapped peaks in the Gallatin Range. Grizzly sightings are common along the route.

Fishing: Three tributaries (Panther Creek, Indian Creek, and Obsidian Creek) flow into the Gardner River near the campground. These waters hold pan-sided brook trout. Remember that a park permit is required to fish in Yellowstone.

Trails: A trailhead for Bunsen Peak is just 3.5 miles north of the campground. The trail climbs 1,300 feet in just 2.1 miles to reach the panorama-yielding summit at 8,564 feet. If you continue down the other side of the peak, you'll find a junction where you can hike to Osprey Falls (4.6 miles) or trek north to Mammoth Hot Springs (5.2 miles).

Grizzly Lake Trailhead is found 6.5 miles south of the campground. The trail here travels west through a burned forest for 2 miles to reach the northern tip of the lake. There is a mild climb of a few hundred feet at the beginning of the hike and a similar descent near the lake.

Field Notes: This is one of my favorite Yellowstone campgrounds. There are no nearby stores, restaurants, or visitor centers, so it feels more remote and has less drive-by traffic than other camps. Campsites have a little more room here.

Canyon Campground
8,000 feet

Location/Map	Central Yellowstone; Page 34
GPS Coordinates	N44° 44.16' W110° 29.31'
Sites/Spur Length	273 sites; Short to medium spurs—20 to 30 feet
Cost	$32
Facilities/Services	Fire rings, picnic tables, water, restrooms, trash and recycling containers, showers, laundry facility, dump station, supply store, limited cellular service
Managing Agency	National Park Service (Yellowstone National Park)
Reservations	Call 866-439-7375 or visit www.YellowstoneNationalParkLodges.com
Season/Usage	Open early June through early September; High use

Directions: From Yellowstone's east entrance, travel 27 miles to Fishing Bridge Junction. Turn north and proceed 16 miles. The campground is just east of Canyon Junction.

Description: With nearby overlooks named like Lookout Point, Grand View, Inspiration Point, and Artist Point, it's clear that Canyon Campground is located in a very scenic area of Yellowstone. In fact, the deep canyon and tall waterfalls found here attract visitors from all over the world. In the large campground, you'll discover a dizzying assortment of sites situated around nearly a dozen loops. Campsites are shaded by a forest of skinny lodgepole pines and favor tent and car campers over RVs or trailers. This isn't a camp where you'll be driving around looking for the best site; they all look pretty much the same.

If you don't make reservations, plan on arriving at this campground early so you can claim a morning vacancy. Canyon Village is within walking distance of the campground and offers supplies, groceries, and restaurants.

Natural Attractions: The campground is located just minutes from one of the most well-known waterfalls in the world, the 308-foot drop known as Yellowstone's Lower Falls. A one-way road takes you to numerous viewing points and paved walkways along the colorful Grand Canyon of the Yellowstone. It is this canyon where you'll find the Lower Falls as well as the shorter Upper Falls.

Scenic Driving/Wildlife Viewing: Drive north from Canyon Village and you'll traverse Dunraven Pass where the burned forest yields impressive views to the west. Bears and bighorn sheep can sometimes be spotted near the pass. A southern drive takes you through gorgeous Hayden Valley where bison herds and bird life are often seen.

Trails: The summit of Mt. Washburn (10,243 feet) is likely the most popular hiking destination in the park. There are two routes to the top, but the main trail starts north of the campground at Dunraven Pass (the other is farther north at the Chittenden parking area). The 3-mile route switchbacks to the windy summit of the mountain where an enclosed observation station is located. Grand panoramic views of the park can be expected.

Canyon Campground

The Cascade Creek Trailhead can be found just a quarter mile west of Canyon Junction. This 2.5-mile route has minimal elevation change as it leads to Cascade Lake.

If you're looking for a trail with fewer people, drive 3.5 miles west of Canyon Junction to the Grebe Lake Trailhead. The trail here follows an old fire road through partially burned tracts of forest for 3 miles to the lake. Another trail can be picked up at the lake that travels east and west. Read the trail description for Norris Campground for more details.

Field Notes: This camp often looks deserted during the day making it hard to believe that it's full. Come evening, the place comes alive with campers as they return from touring the park.

Norris Campground   7,550 feet

Location/Map	West Yellowstone; Page 34
GPS Coordinates	N44° 44.26' W110° 41.64'
Sites/Spur Length	111 sites; Short to medium spurs—20 to 30 feet
Cost	$20
Facilities/Services	Fire rings, picnic tables, water, restrooms, trash and recycling containers, pay phone
Managing Agency	National Park Service (Yellowstone National Park)
Reservations	Not accepted—first come, first served
Season/Usage	Open late May through late September; High use

Directions: From Mammoth, head south for 20 miles. If traveling from West Yellowstone, head east to Madison, then northeast to Norris Junction. The campground is just north of this intersection.

Description: Norris has roomy sites along three nicely wooded loops. The first loop has a few walk-in sites for tent campers. Other loops contain a few sites that are reserved for 30 to 50-foot units, but most parking spurs only accommodate the smallest of rigs and many are unlevel. Campground perks include the Museum of the National Park Ranger, a concession station that offers firewood and ice, and evening presentations held at the Norris Campfire Circle near Loop C. Perhaps the best thing about this campground is the beautiful surrounding scenery. The best sites overlook a sprawling verdant meadow where the Gibbon River flows.

Natural Attractions/Walking: Norris Geyser Basin, located south of the campground, is home to Steamboat, the world's tallest geyser. Boardwalks guide you through the basin to various viewing platforms. As an alternative to driving, you can get to the basin by taking the 1-mile path that begins near the campground entrance.

Scenic Driving: The stretch of road between Mammoth and Madison offers incredible scenery including lush meadows and snowcapped peaks in the Gallatin Range.

Wildlife Viewing: Look in the meadows north and south of the campground for bison and elk. Patient observers can often spy roaming grizzly bears in these same areas.

Trails: The Solfatara Creek Trail begins at the campground area and heads northward to intersect with the Ice Lake trail. You can continue north at the junction and follow a powerline for 2.5 miles to Whiterock Springs. If you bear right, you can travel over 3 miles to Ice Lake and have your pick of other destinations such as Wolf Lake, Grebe Lake, and Cascade Lake.

Families looking for a brief taste of Yellowstone's backcountry should check out the shorter .3-mile route to Ice Lake. The trailhead for the shorter trail is 3.5 miles east of Norris.

Another short trip is to Grizzly Lake via a trail that is 5.5 miles north of the campground. The path travels west for 2 miles to reach the northern tip of the lake.

Picnicking: There is a picnic area just west of Norris Junction.

Field Notes: You don't hear much about the Norris area of the park, but consider staying here. The campground is conveniently located in the middle of Yellowstone's Grand Loop Road, a "figure 8," which makes for shorter drives to most of the park's attractions.

Madison Campground

6,850 feet

Location/Map	West Yellowstone; Page 34
GPS Coordinates	N44° 38.74' W110° 51.66'
Sites/Spur Length	278 sites; Short to medium spurs—20 to 30 feet
Cost	$27
Facilities/Services	Fire rings, picnic tables, water, restrooms, trash and recycling containers, pay phone, dump station
Managing Agency	National Park Service (Yellowstone National Park)
Reservations	Call 866-439-7375 or visit www.YellowstoneNationalParkLodges.com
Season/Usage	Open early May through late October; High use

Directions: From Yellowstone's west entrance, head east for 13.5 miles to the campground. The campground is 16 miles north of Old Faithful.

Description: This attractive camp has ten loops on a bench above the Madison River. The two loops closest to the river are reserved for tent campers. The other loops will hold smaller RVs and trailers and even a few longer ones (call for a reservation if you have a long camper).

Skinny pines create plenty of shade, but do little to offer privacy—not a major concern for Yellowstone campers. To find out more about the park, you can get your fill of knowledge from the nearby information center and bookstore. If that's not enough, you can supplement your reading by attending one of the nightly presentations held at the camp's amphitheater.

Natural Attractions/Walking: Fountain Paint Pot, Midway Geyser Basin, Biscuit Basin, Black Sand Basin, and Old Faithful all have interpretive trails (boardwalks) where you can observe and learn about some of Yellowstone's most intriguing natural attractions. These areas are located between 8 and 16 miles south of the campground. Old Faithful, the world's most famous geyser, erupts every 74 minutes on average (18 to 21 times per day). The eruption reaches an average height of 130 feet. (See page 50 for more information on Old Faithful.)

Scenic Driving/Wildlife Viewing: The road between West Yellowstone and Madison Junction hugs the Madison River as it travels through a scenic canyon. Much of the drive shows the dramatic impact of the 1988 fire season. Watch for bald eagles and bison along the river course.

Heading south from Madison Junction, you'll travel through a region of thermal activity, which includes notorious attractions such as Old Faithful and the Fountain Paint Pots. The one-way Firehole Canyon Drive is also a worthwhile side trip.

Fishing: The Madison River is open to fly-fishing. Anglers will find rainbow and brown trout as well as grayling and whitefish. Remember that a park permit is required to fish in Yellowstone.

Picnicking: A picnic area is located at the campground near the bookstore. There are also numerous picnic areas east, west, and south of the campground.

Field Notes: Although Madison Campground is close to Yellowstone's geyser basins, it is also a good choice if you are planning to spend time in the small town of West Yellowstone. The town is home to the Yellowstone Giant Screen Theatre and Grizzly & Wolf Discovery Center. The latter is a great place to watch and learn more about Yellowstone's most intriguing predators. As a bonus, kids are allowed to hide food for the bears and then watch the bruins turn over rocks and stumps as they sniff out the scraps.

Baker's Hole Campground (Custer Gallatin National Forest, Montana)

Baker's Hole is a gorgeous camp located on the banks of the Madison River where it flows out of Yellowstone National Park. There are 73 spacious sites with long and level parking spurs; nearly half of these have electrical service. You can choose a shaded spot in the pines or a sunny patch near the river where bison commonly roam. These first-come, first-served sites cost between $20-28 a night. A host is often present. To reach the camp from West Yellowstone, take HWY 191 north for 3 miles.

Fishing Bridge RV Park

7,800 feet

Location/Map	Central Yellowstone; Page 34
GPS Coordinates	N44° 33.82' W110° 22.17'
Sites/Spur Length	346 sites; Long spurs—over 30 feet
Cost	$79
Facilities/Services	Hookups, restrooms, trash and recycling containers, pay phone, showers, limited picnic tables, laundry facility, dump station, supply store, cellular service
Managing Agency	National Park Service (Yellowstone National Park)
Reservations	Call 866-439-7375 or visit www.YellowstoneNationalParkLodges.com
Season/Usage	Open early May through late October; High use

Directions: From Yellowstone's east entrance, head west for 25 miles. The camp is located 1 mile east of Fishing Bridge Junction.

Description: Though expensive and cramped, Fishing Bridge Campground's full facilities and central location on the north side of Yellowstone Lake make it a popular destination. Hundreds of back-in sites are squeezed along straight rows and you'll have almost no privacy unless the shades are closed in the RV next to you. You also won't have a fire ring (campfires are prohibited) and many sites don't have picnic tables. However, a recent renovation made improvements by adding larger pull-through sites to the upper loop. Many of the older facilities were also updated and expanded. If you're interested in staying here, make reservations up to a year in advance. Bears are active in the area, so only hard-sided camping units are allowed.

Natural Attractions: Yellowstone Lake is North America's largest mountain lake. It has 110 miles of shoreline and a maximum depth of 400 feet.

The odd mud volcanoes are worth a look and are located 6 miles north of Fishing Bridge Junction. A trail provides access to the various features in this fascinating area, including one called Dragon's Mouth.

Scenic Driving: Fishing Bridge's central location offers access to a trio of scenic drives. A northern drive takes you through gorgeous Hayden Valley where bison herds and bird life are often seen. If you decide to head south, you'll find a scenic road that hugs the west shoreline of Yellowstone Lake. Drive east from the campground, and you'll skirt the northern shore of Yellowstone Lake where grizzlies are often spotted, particularly during the spring spawning season. A great overlook of the lake can be found 1 mile east of where the road leaves the lakeshore. Past the lake, the road climbs to a high point of 8,530 feet at Sylvan Pass.

Fishing: Despite the historic images of fishing off Yellowstone's famous "Fishing Bridge," this practice is no longer allowed. However, fishing for cutthroat trout in Yellowstone Lake is allowed (with restrictions). Remember that a park permit is required to fish in Yellowstone.

Trails: Pelican Creek is a short 1-mile loop that travels through the forest to the shoreline of Yellowstone Lake. The trail is located just 1 mile east of Fishing Bridge. For a longer hike, drive 3 miles east of Fishing Bridge. The 2.5-mile Storm Point Loop near Indian Pond travels to a rocky bluff that overlooks Yellowstone Lake and the surrounding mountain ranges.

The longer Howard Eaton Trail can be found west of the campground, but is not shown on many maps.

Field Notes: You don't have to stay at the RV park to take advantage of the facilities. Fishing Bridge is a good place to get a shower, wash some laundry, and re-supply. The nearby Fishing Bridge Visitor Center and Trailside Museum is the place to learn more about Yellowstone's bird life. There is also a bookstore there.

Visitors may see grizzly bears in Yellowstone National Park —NPS Photo

Bridge Bay Campground

7,750 feet

Location/Map	Central Yellowstone; Page 34
GPS Coordinates	N44° 32.07' W110° 26.22'
Sites/Spur Length	432 sites; Group sites; Short to medium spurs—up to 30 feet
Cost	$27
Facilities/Services	Fire rings, picnic tables, water, restrooms, trash and recycling containers, bear boxes, dump station, marina, boat ramp, limited cellular service
Managing Agency	National Park Service (Yellowstone National Park)
Reservations	Call 866-439-7375 or visit www.YellowstoneNationalParkLodges.com
Season/Usage	Open late May through mid-September; High use

Directions: From Yellowstone's east entrance, drive west for 27 miles. At Fishing Bridge Junction, turn south and drive 3.5 miles.

Description: This huge campground is found next to a Yellowstone Lake inlet where a full-service marina is operated. It is comprised of ten very different loops and the campsites vary greatly giving you many different choices. Sites in loops A through D sit in a mostly open area, whereas the upper loops are tucked into a coniferous forest (and have tighter sites if you're backing in an RV or trailer). Loops E, F, and G have views of Yellowstone Lake. The J Loop is designated for tents.

Natural Attractions: Yellowstone Lake is North America's largest mountain lake. It has 110 miles of shoreline and a maximum depth of 400 feet.

Scenic Driving: The lake-hugging road north and south of the campground has numerous pullouts where you can stop and admire spectacular views of Yellowstone Lake and the Absaroka Range to the southeast.

Fishing: Yellowstone Lake is the area's most popular fishery. Populated by cutthroat, but threatened by displaced lake trout, the lake is controlled by several fishing restrictions so educate yourself before casting a line. If you want to fish from a boat, inquire about guided fishing trips at the marina. Remember that a park permit is required to fish in Yellowstone.

Trails: The short 1.5-mile Natural Bridge Trail starts at the marina parking lot, then joins an old road that leads to a rocky bridge along Bridge Creek.

Hikers looking for a more laborious trek should check out the Elephant Back Mountain Trail. This 3.5-mile loop climbs 800 feet to the crest of a lava flow where you can experience a sweeping view of nearby Yellowstone Lake. The trailhead is located 2.3 miles north of the campground, just a mile south of Fishing Bridge Junction. Bears frequent both of these trails.

Boating: Boat tours of the lake leave from a marina located next to the campground. The tour offers a thrilling dash across the northern part of the

Bridge Bay Campground

lake to Stevenson Island. Tour reservations can be made at any Yellowstone concessionaire desk. Boat rentals are also available at the marina.

If you have your own boat, you'll find four boat ramps situated along the southern and western shoreline of Yellowstone Lake and another on Frank Island. Boating is limited to 5 mph in the South and Southeast Arms except for the lower parts of the Arms where only hand-propelled crafts are permitted.

Picnicking: You'll find a picnic area between the road and the marina.

Field Notes: The sites and loops here are tight and best suited for the smallest trailers, vans, and pickup campers. Lake Village, 2 miles to the north, will fill your need for gifts, groceries, and camping supplies. You'll also find a post office there.

Old Faithful: A Yellowstone Icon
If only a single feature represents Yellowstone, it's Old Faithful. This cone geyser is named for its consistent and frequent eruptions, which occur every 60-110 minutes. An eruption spews thousands of gallons of scorching water at least a hundred feet into the air and sometimes nearly 200 feet. Though each burst lasts only a few minutes, each one often attracts hundreds of spectators during the days of summer. The geyser even has its own web camera so you can watch it from anywhere at any time of the year. The Old Faithful area has a historic inn, post office, lodging, stores, and restaurants. Old Faithful is located in southwestern Yellowstone, 37 miles from the south entrance and 27 miles from the west entrance.

Grant Village Campground

7,800 feet

Location/Map	South-central Yellowstone; Page 34
GPS Coordinates	N44° 23.66' W110° 33.81'
Sites/Spur Length	430 sites, group sites; Short to medium spurs—up to 30 feet
Cost	$32
Facilities/Services	Fire rings, picnic tables, water, restrooms, trash and recycling containers, dump station, limited cellular service
Managing Agency	National Park Service (Yellowstone National Park)
Reservations	Call 866-439-7375 or visit www.YellowstoneNationalParkLodges.com
Season/Usage	Open late May through mid-September; High use

Directions: From Yellowstone's south entrance, head north for 20 miles. At the Grant Village sign, turn east and drive another mile.

Description: This massive, sprawling campground consists of eleven loops along Yellowstone Lake's West Thumb. Three of the loops are designated for tents. Average-sized trailers and motor homes will fit in the other loops, but smaller units hold the advantage. While you'll find a few back-in spurs, most of the squished sites you'll find here are pull-offs, which make for easier parking. A forest of skinny pines offers shade, but the trees provide little to no sense of separation between campers.

At Grant Village, a small community next to the campground, you'll find modern conveniences including a laundry facility, showers, restaurant, visitor center, gas station, amphitheater, and post office.

Natural Attractions: Yellowstone Lake is North America's largest mountain lake. It has 110 miles of shoreline and a maximum depth of 400 feet.

Natural Attractions/Walking: The West Thumb Geyser Basin, less than 2 miles north of the campground, has an interpretive boardwalk trail that tours colorful hot springs and dormant geysers.

Scenic Driving: This is Yellowstone, so no matter where you drive, you'll find scenic mountain grandeur. Turn south and you'll drive through an ever-changing landscape of canyon land, green forest, burned slopes, and lush meadows. Head north and you'll drive around scenic Yellowstone Lake. Drive west and you'll cross over Craig Pass to Old Faithful. You can't lose!

Fishing: Yellowstone Lake is the area's most popular fishery. Populated by cutthroat, but threatened by displaced lake trout, the lake is controlled by several fishing restrictions so educate yourself before casting a line. Remember that a park permit is required to fish in Yellowstone.

Trails: The 2-mile Lake Overlook Loop departs from the West Thumb Geyser Basin parking lot and gains 400 feet to an overlook. An even shorter hike is to Duck Lake, which starts from a separate trailhead in the same area.

Looking for a longer, more remote excursion? The 2.5-mile Riddle Lake Trail can be found 2.5 miles south of the campground, near the Continental Divide sign. Another option is the 3-mile trail along DeLacy Creek to Shoshone Lake. The trailhead is 8.8 miles west of West Thumb Junction.

Boating: There are four boat ramps (including one near the campground) along the southern and western shoreline of Yellowstone Lake and another on Frank Island. Boating is limited to 5 mph in the South and Southeast Arms except for the lower parts of the Arms where only hand-propelled crafts are permitted. Boat tours and rentals are available at a marina located near Bridge Bay Campground.

Field Notes: Though it has been over three decades, I still have vivid memories of my first camping trip to Yellowstone, which was here at Grant Village. It's a good family campground and the nearby stores and facilities take the rough edges off camping. Just know that this is often a busy, packed camp.

Lewis Lake Campground
7,800 feet

Location/Map	South Yellowstone; Page 34
GPS Coordinates	N44° 16.93' W110° 37.66'
Sites/Spur Length	84 sites; Short spurs—up to 25 feet
Cost	$15
Facilities/Services	Fire rings, picnic tables, water, pit toilets, trash and recycling containers, boat ramp
Managing Agency	National Park Service (Yellowstone National Park)
Reservations	Not accepted—first come, first served
Season/Usage	Open mid-May through early November; High use

Directions: From Yellowstone's south entrance, drive north for 11 miles.

Description: Lewis Lake is the first Yellowstone campground you'll reach when traveling north from Grand Teton National Park. The nicely wooded and more primitive camp appeals to avid outdoors folks more than once-a-year campers. Anglers, paddlers with canoes, or anyone looking to explore some of Yellowstone's backcountry trails will find this campground to be a good fit. Short and unlevel parking spurs along three loops are best suited for tents, vans, or truck campers. A few walk-in sites are also available. The campsites have good privacy and shade, especially compared to other camps in the park. This is one of the slowest campgrounds in the park to fill, but you'll still want to arrive early to get a spot. Generators are not allowed.

Scenic Driving/Wildlife Viewing: Drive south of the campground and you'll find scenic Lewis Falls as well as a deep gorge that runs through land that was parched by the 1988 forest fires. Even further south, toward the southern entrance, there are meadows that sustain moose and other wildlife.

Fishing: Lewis Lake holds various trout species. The stream that connects it to Shoshone Lake is said to be an excellent fishery. Remember that a park permit is required to fish in Yellowstone.

Trails: Three backcountry trails can be found 3 miles north of the campground. The first heads east almost 7 miles to Heart Lake. The other two trails, DeLacy Creek and Dogshead, depart from the west side of the road and travel northwest to Lewis River and Shoshone Lake. The names of the trails vary depending on the map.

South of the campground, the Pitchstone Trail leaves a roadside trailhead and heads west. This trail travels nearly 20 miles into Yellowstone's southwest "Cascade Corner," known for its many waterfalls. The trail eventually reaches Grassy Lake Road south of Yellowstone.

Boating: Motorized boats are permitted on Lewis Lake except for a posted area near the outlet bay. A boat ramp is located at the campground on the south side of the lake.

Picnicking: There is a picnic area near the lake.

Field Notes: In my opinion, this is Yellowstone's best camp if you're looking for privacy, shade, and less traffic. It also feels more like a wilderness encampment than a touristy vacation destination. There are downsides, of course. The camp roads are unlevel and cramped (not RV or trailer friendly) and the mosquitoes are thick and relentless.

A boater skims across Lewis Lake in Yellowstone

Snake River Recreation Area

6,800 feet

Location/Map	South of Yellowstone; Page 34
GPS Coordinates	N44° 5.35' W110° 41.76'
Sites/Spur Length	14 sites; Short to medium spurs—up to 30 feet
Cost	Free
Facilities/Services	Fire rings, picnic tables, pit toilets
Managing Agency	USDA Forest Service (Bridger-Teton National Forest)
Reservations	Not accepted—first come, first served
Season/Usage	Open late May through mid-September; Moderate use

Directions: From Moran, head north for 25 miles on HWY 89/191/287 to Flagg Ranch. Turn onto Grassy Lake Road, also called Ashton-Flagg Ranch Road, and drive 1 to 18 miles to the various campsites. The road deteriorates the further you travel.

Description: This is a camping area of a different variety. There are more than a dozen semi-dispersed campsites strung along Grassy Lake Road. The camping areas closer to Flagg Ranch are aligned along the Snake River making them the most popular and scenic. Many of the sites further down the road sit in dark timber and lack the views of the Teton Range afforded near the river. Campsites are clustered together in a single parking area and offer almost no privacy if other campers are present. If you're looking for solitude, keep driving until you find a parking area that only has one site. While most sites are located within the first five miles, the last two are found at mile 13 and mile 18.

Fishing: Anglers can fish for brown and cutthroat trout in the Snake River.

Trails: The Glade Creek Trailhead is found at mile 4 on Grassy Lake Road. A fairly level path heads south here and begins to parallel the Snake River after 2 miles. At 4.5 miles, the trail splits at a junction. Continue south for a couple of miles and you'll round Harem Hill (7,326 feet) to reach Jackson Lake. Make a west turn and you'll be exploring true wilderness where the trail intersects a multitude of other routes.

Further west on Grassy Lake Road is the small 11,000-acre Winegar Hole Wilderness, an obscure tract of low-laying wetlands. It is noted for its tremendous elk, moose, and bear habitat. Designated by Congress in 1984, the wilderness is rarely visited and consists of terrain that is not conducive to backcountry travel. Only two trails exist in the wilderness: Calf Creek and Fish Lake; both are accessed from Yellowstone's South Boundary Trail or from Grassy Lake Road.

Field Notes: Want to escape the national park crowds? Continue west on Grassy Lake Road toward Idaho to find boggy lakes and remote wilderness. A 53-mile drive will get you to some very cool waterfalls at Cave Falls Campground (see page 57).

Sheffield Creek Campground

6,900 feet

Location/Map	South of Yellowstone; Page 34
GPS Coordinates	N44° 5.57' W110° 39.78'
Sites/Spur Length	5 sites; Long spurs—over 30 feet
Cost	$10
Facilities/Services	Fire rings, picnic tables, pit toilets, bear boxes
Managing Agency	USDA Forest Service (Bridger-Teton National Forest)
Reservations	Not accepted—first come, first served
Season/Usage	Open late May through late September; Low use

Directions: From Moran, head north for 24 miles on HWY 89/191/287 to the Sheffield Creek turnoff (about 3 miles south of Yellowstone's south entrance). Turn east onto the gravel road and follow it a half mile to the campground. Before you get there, you'll ford Sheffield Creek, which may be flowing high depending on seasonal snowpack and the time of year you visit. A concrete structure is in place to make this crossing easier, but as of this writing it was damaged and only made the ford rougher. A high clearance vehicle is suggested. Larger rigs may also have trouble with tree branches that crowd the roadway.

Description: Though this trailhead camp is just a few minutes from Yellowstone National Park, it's a sleepy recreation site that bears no resemblance to the bustling campgrounds to the north. The camp occupies a clearing surrounded by a young pine forest that is regenerating thickly from a 1988 wildfire. Hundreds of old snags still rise above the shorter trees on the facing hillside known as Huckleberry Ridge. The sites themselves have few trees and you'll get plenty of sunshine here. The parking spurs are long and level, perfect for horse trailers. You'll need to bring your own water and pack out your trash.

Fishing: Anglers can fish for brown and cutthroat trout in the Snake River, which is just north of the campground's entrance road. Sheffield Creek, which runs west of the camp (the one that was forded to get to the camp) is a tributary to the Snake River and likely holds the same fish.

Trails: The trailhead at the campground serves as one of several access points to the western side of the Teton Wilderness. (Other nearby trails that lead into the wilderness are Arizona Creek and Pilgrim Creek, both of which are passed on the main highway). The Sheffield Creek Trail here at the campground leads to the top of Huckleberry Mountain (9,615 feet) where there is a lookout tower on an outcropping that overlooks the region. It's a little over 5 miles to get there so count on a nearly 11-mile round trip. This is considered a steep and difficult hike through rough, burned-out terrain.

Field Notes: On my visits, I've found this camp empty, but the trailhead area does receive moderate daytime traffic from both trail users and rangers.

Headwaters Campground (Flagg Ranch)   6,800 feet

Location/Map	Between Yellowstone and Grand Teton National Parks; Page 34
GPS Coordinates	N44° 7.87' W110° 0.89'
Sites/Spur Length	175 sites; Long spurs—over 30 feet
Cost	$42 (tents), $84 (RVs)
Facilities/Services	Hookups, fire rings, picnic tables, water, restrooms, trash and recycling containers, showers, laundry facility, supply store, dump station, future cellular service (under construction at the time of this writing)
Managing Agency	Flagg Ranch Company (National Park Service concessionaire)
Reservations	Call 800-443-2311 or visit gtlc.com
Season/Usage	Open mid-May through mid-September; High use

Directions: From Moran, head north for 25 miles on HWY 89/191/287 to Flagg Ranch.

Description: Though this is technically a private campground, it's treated as a camp for Grand Teton National Park. It's actually sandwiched between the boundaries of Grand Teton and Yellowstone, making it a terrific base if you're going to be visiting both parks.

Here, you'll find sites lined among a pine forest, though many of them are in the open. The views of the Snake River, which is within walking distance, and the northern reaches of the Teton Range, are hard to beat. You'll find both tent sites and pull-through sites with full hookups for RVs.

Snake River near Flagg Ranch

Flagg Ranch itself is a comfortable place to spend a vacation. Aside from the campground, there is a steakhouse, saloon, gift shop, and supply store. Cabins can be rented and outdoor adventures can be reserved, such as rafting, fishing, horseback riding, and national park touring.

Fishing: Anglers can fish for brown and cutthroat trout in the Snake River.

Trails: There are at least two trails that can be started from Grassy Lake Road at the ranch. The first is the Polecat Creek Loop Trail, an easy 2.5-mile path that travels through the forest and above a marsh. The second is the Flagg Canyon Trail, which starts on the northeast side of the Polecat loop, about a half mile from the starting point on the road. This easy 4-mile route gives you scenic views of the Snake River.

Field Notes: The ranch's location seems surreal, like something out of a western movie. Towering peaks, mountain rivers, and dense forests, all next door to two outstanding national parks, make this a worthy destination, though some campers take issue with the cost and road dust.

Cave Falls Campground
6,200 feet

Location/Map	Southwest of Yellowstone; Page 34
GPS Coordinates	N44° 7.87' W110° 0.89'
Sites/Spur Length	23 sites; Long spurs—over 30 feet
Cost	$10
Facilities/Services	Fire rings, grills, picnic tables, water, pit toilets, trash containers, bear boxes
Managing Agency	USDA Forest Service (Caribou-Targhee National Forest)
Reservations	Not accepted—first come, first served
Season/Usage	Open June through mid-September; Moderate use

Directions: From Ashton, Idaho take HWY 47 east for over 5 miles and watch for the Cave Falls sign. Turn right at the sign and continue a little over 19 miles to the campground. The last 14 miles of roadway have a good gravel surface.

Description: Cave Falls is a little-known Wyoming campground accessible only from Idaho. The camp is wonderful and undoubtedly it is the "secret place" for some vacationers. Spacious and well-treed sites, mostly pull-throughs, are lined along the banks of the wide Falls River. While weekends see increased traffic from the locals, you won't find as many campers here during the middle of the week. Numerous signs warn of bear activity, but it's mostly black bears that inhabit the area. The more feared grizzly, while still considered to reside in the area, tends to stay in the higher elevations of the Yellowstone ecosystem.

Natural Attractions: Cave Falls is located just over a mile northeast of the campground inside Yellowstone's boundary. This beautiful roaring cascade flows over a broad shelf, making it quite unique.

Fishing: If your paradise is defined by a wide, clear mountain stream teeming with trout, the Falls River is it. The drainage holds mostly rainbow trout, with a few cutthroat. Remember that a park permit is required to fish inside the Yellowstone boundary.

Trails: The Bechler Area, the region around Cave Falls, has some great trails for day hiking. A brochure at the picnic area includes a map and trail descriptions. Among the best is a 3-mile trail to Bechler Falls. The level route rounds a bend of the Falls River before following the banks of Bechler River. It's then over 1 more mile to the falls.

There are also plenty of longer trails of 18 miles or more. These trails begin from the Bechler Ranger Station, which is located a few miles northwest of the campground. Watch for signs along the incoming road.

Picnicking: You can find perfect picnic spots at both the campground and near the waterfalls.

Field Notes: It can take several hours to get to this campground from the main Yellowstone area. Save yourself the trip unless you want to see a really cool and unique waterfall or just want to explore a quiet corner of Yellowstone.

Cave Falls flows over a ledge on the Falls River

NORTHWEST AREA 2
Grand Teton National Park and Surrounding Mountains

Grand Teton National Park and its surrounding mountain ranges comprise Wyoming's most renowned peaks and landscapes. These mountains enclose Jackson Hole, a broad valley in western Wyoming. The jagged peaks of the Teton Range rise sharply from the west side of the valley floor, impressing those who pass below them. Nothing short of spectacular, these mountains are frequently seen in calendars, paintings, and photographs. The rugged Absaroka and Gros Ventre Mountains close in from the east and north, while the Salt River Range seals the valley's southern edge. Gathering its water just south of Yellowstone, the popular Snake River flows into Jackson Lake, a large reservoir, and then southward through the valley.

The area is rich with wildlife. Bison, grizzly bears, black bears, moose, osprey, and bald eagles are just a few animals that live in the region. Some 4,000 elk also live in Grand Teton National Park. These, and thousands more, migrate to the National Elk Refuge near Jackson for the winter.

Jackson Hole is known for its world-class recreation. Famous for its skiing in the winter, the area also attracts masses of campers, hikers, and mountaineers during the summer. Boating and floating the river are other common pursuits.

With the grand scenery, abundant wildlife, and vast recreational activities, the area can't be a secret—and it's not. Of all the regions in this book, this one certainly feels like Wyoming's busiest–and it just might be. Grand Teton National Park is not only a destination in and of itself, but it also serves as a major gateway to Yellowstone.

A description of this area would be incomplete without mentioning Jackson, one of the most recognized communities in the Rocky Mountain West. The town is looked upon with mixed attitudes, especially from Wyoming residents. Some savor Jackson's culture, affluence, and sophistication, as well as the fact that it is home to a handful of Hollywood celebrities, at least for part of the year. But Jackson is also a liberal bastion within the nation's most right-leaning state. Aside from stirring up a bit of political ire, some also see the town as a perversion to Wyoming's rugged and unpolished way of living. Differences aside, all can agree that Jackson contributes to the state's social diversity.

What to Expect: Grand Teton National Park offers some of the best camping this nation has to offer—this is simply a place you will not forget. Aside from Jenny Lake, you might be surprised to learn that these camps fill a little slower than those in Yellowstone. Even so, you'll still need to arrive early to get a site. There are usually sites available at Gros Ventre Campground and the handful of Forest Service camps just outside of the park see lighter use. At the time of this writing, the construction of numerous cell phone towers in the park were to be constructed. Once completed, cell signals will be significantly stronger and widespread.

Area 2: Grand Teton National Park and Surrounding Mountains

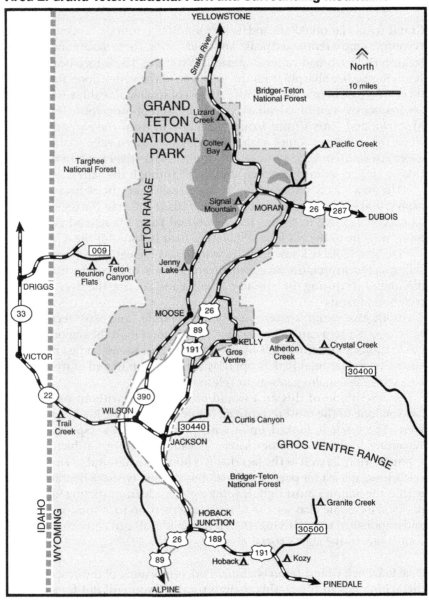

Campgrounds

Campgrounds	Sites	Cost	Average Spur Length	Electrical Hookups	Cellular Service (varies by carrier/site)	Reservations Accepted	Page Number
Lizard Creek Campground	60	$29	M				62
Colter Bay Campground/RV	350/112	$30-68	L	✔	▪▫▫	✔	63
Pacific Creek Campground	8	$10	L				64
Signal Mountain Campground	88	$31-50	L		▪▫▫		65
Jenny Lake Campground	59	$28	Tent		▪▫▫		67
Gros Ventre Campground	350	$28	L		▪▫▫		69
Atherton Creek Campground	20	$18-25	M		▪▫▫		71
Crystal Creek Campground	6	$12	M		▪▫▫		72
Curtis Canyon Campground	12	$15	M				73
Trail Creek Campground	11	$12	M			✔	74
Reunion Flats Campground (group camp)	8	$12-100	L			✔	75
Teton Canyon Campground	20	$12-24	L			✔	76
Kozy Campground	8	$15	M				77
Granite Creek Campground	51	$15	L				78
Hoback Campground	14	$15	L				80

Average Spur Length: S = Short (under 30 feet), M = Medium (+-30 feet), L = Long (+-40 feet)
Cellular Service: 1 bar = weak/unreliable signal, 2 bars = low usable signal, 3+ bars = reliable signal for most users

*At the time of this writing, cellular service upgrades were being made to improve and expand coverage in developed areas of Yellowstone and Grand Teton National Park.

Lizard Creek Campground

6,800 feet

Location/Map	North Grand Teton National Park; Page 60
GPS Coordinates	N44° 0.4' W110° 41.06'
Sites/Spur Length	60 sites; Medium spurs—up to 30 feet
Cost	$29, $11 for hikers/bicyclists
Facilities/Services	Fire rings, picnic tables, water, restrooms, trash and recycling containers
Managing Agency	National Park Service (Grand Teton National Park)
Reservations	Not accepted—first come, first served
Season/Usage	Open June through early September; High use

Directions: From Moran, head north on HWY 89/191/287 for 17.5 miles. If traveling from Jackson, drive north toward Yellowstone for 47 miles.

Description: Banked on the north side of scenic Jackson Lake, this campground is wrapped in a dense forest that nicely separates the sites. It's also much smaller and doesn't give the same crowded feeling that you get in the other national park camps. There is an RV loop that will hold short trailers and RVs and a tent loop; over a dozen of the sites are walk-ins for tent campers. If you arrive early enough, you'll increase the likelihood of getting one of the prime sites—those that have a view of the lake and adjacent Teton Range. It's not uncommon to find a couple open sites here, but you'll want to arrive early to get one.

Scenic Driving/Wildlife Viewing: The drive through Grand Teton National Park is simply spectacular. The sudden rise of the jagged Teton Range, the winding beauty of the Snake River, and the awe of its wild animals go unparalleled. The northern area of the park, where the campground is located, boasts of incredible scenery where the high peaks of the Tetons dramatically tower over Jackson Lake. The area is also a wildlife catchall. You may find bears, moose, elk, deer, bison, and a variety of small animals and bird life.

Fishing: Scenic Jackson Lake harbors mostly cutthroat and lake trout. Most fish pulled from these waters are less than 18 inches in length, but the occasional trophy fish has been snatched.

Trails: Not many established trails are found in this area, but an old roadbed and trail do parallel Arizona Creek about 5 miles north of the campground. Warning: the bears are thick and dangerous in this particular drainage. If you go, take pepper spray and a good number of loud-talking buddies.

Picnicking: A picnic area is located 3 miles south of the camp entrance.

Field Notes: On one visit to this campground, we watched a blonde bear scour the brush near the lake's shoreline before it came straight at us and brushed alongside our vehicle. Remember to use caution in this country as some of these bears have long lost their fear of humans.

Colter Bay Campground and RV Park   6,800 feet

Location/Map	North Grand Teton National Park; Page 60
GPS Coordinates	N43° 54.7' W110° 37.8'
Sites/Spur Length	Campground: 350 sites, 11 group sites; Long spurs—over 30 feet RV Park: 112 sites; Long spurs—up to 40 feet
Cost	Campground: $30, RV Park: $68
Facilities/Services	Campground: Fire rings, picnic tables, water, restrooms, trash and recycling containers, pay phones, showers, laundry facility, supply store, dump station, propane, boat ramp, limited cellular service RV Park: Hookups, restrooms, trash and recycling containers, picnic tables, showers, laundry facility, limited cellular service
Managing Agency	National Park Service (Grand Teton National Park)
Reservations	Campground: Not accepted—first come, first served RV Park/Group sites: Call 800-628-9988
Season/Usage	Open late May through early September; High use

Directions: From Moran, head north on HWY 89/191/287 for 9.5 miles. If driving from Jackson, head north toward Yellowstone for 40 miles.

Description: Colter Bay is a great family-friendly campground that offers amazing views, accessible paved roads, and a long list of campground features and facilities. You won't be roughing it here. Nearby Colter Bay Village has a visitor center, restaurant, grocery store, gift shop, museum, and a gas station. Burrowed into a forest of evergreen trees, the camp contains rows upon rows of sites that include a varied mix of back-ins and pull-throughs. They are surprisingly spacious and private. Rows F and G are set aside for tents. Rows A–G restrict the use of generators.

The Colter Bay RV Park here is similar, except that it offers full hookups and pull-through sites with almost no privacy. Campfires and tents are not allowed in the RV park area.

Aside from the two campgrounds, Colter Bay has a unique tent-cabin area where you can stay in a hybrid shelter composed of two log walls and two canvas walls. Inside, you'll find pull-down bunks (cots are available) and a heating stove. If you prefer a more durable shelter, you can get a cabin—there are a multitude of sizes available, from sleeping two to ten.

With all the available options, you're sure to find a site to fit your liking. Oh, there's one more camping option if winter is your season. You can pitch a tent in the snowy parking lot next to the visitor center for $5 a night.

Scenic Driving/Wildlife Viewing: The drive through Grand Teton National Park is simply spectacular. The sudden rise of the jagged Teton Range, the winding beauty of the Snake River, and the awe of its wild animals go unparalleled. Jackson Lake Dam, 7 miles to the south on the Teton Park Road, attracts birders who come to watch swans, spotted sandpipers, and other fauna. The forest south of the dam is home to bison, elk, and moose.

Fishing: Scenic Jackson Lake harbors mostly cutthroat and lake trout. Most fish pulled from these waters are less than 18 inches in length, but the occasional trophy fish has been snatched.

Trails: The Hermitage Point Trailhead is located just south of the Colter Bay Visitor Center (near the marina) and offers short, level trails suitable for family outings. Popular destinations include Swan Lake at .7 miles, Heron Pond at 1 mile, and Hermitage Point at 4.4 miles. Watch for waterfowl and moose around the ponds. The 2-mile Lakeshore Trail forms a figure 8 as it explores the shoreline of a small peninsula off Jackson Lake. You could easily log a dozen miles or more on these interconnected loops. The trails are shown on the Grand Teton brochure available at any entrance station.

Boating: Boat rentals and scenic boat tours (highly recommended) are available from the Colter Bay Village Marina. Boat ramps are available here and at Leeks Village, just over a mile to the north.

Picnicking: A picnic area—complemented with views of Jackson Lake and the Tetons—is found near the visitor center. Another picnic area is located 2 miles north of Colter Bay Village.

Field Notes: Mornings are busy with people leaving and incoming campers arriving to claim the fresh vacancies. Though it gets busy and crowded, this camp is among my favorites. It's a great place for families to walk, bike, boat, and soak in the amazing scenery. It's expensive, but comfortable.

Pacific Creek Campground
7,000 feet

Location/Map GPS Coordinates	East of Grand Teton National Park; Page 60 N43° 56.35' W110° 26.57'
Sites/Spur Length	8 sites; Long spurs—over 30 feet
Cost	$10
Facilities/Services	Fire rings, picnic tables, pit toilets, bear boxes
Managing Agency	USDA Forest Service (Bridger-Teton National Forest)
Reservations	Not accepted—first come, first served
Season/Usage	Open late May through early September; Low use

Directions: From Moran, go north on HWY 89/191/287 for 1 mile and turn right onto Pacific Creek Road. Follow this paved road for 2 miles staying right at the fork for Two Ocean Lake, then left at the next fork. Travel another 6 miles on a rougher gravel road to reach the campground.

Description: If you like camping in gorgeous, remote and wild country, this one is for you. Edged up against the Teton Wilderness boundary, Pacific Creek Campground borders one of the wildest areas of the country. The beautiful camp is found in a diverse mix of light deciduous and evergreen trees and is most popular with hunters in the fall. Sites are spacious and quiet, but the adjacent trailhead does get some traffic. Bears frequent the area so use the bear boxes and the hanging racks to prevent undesired removal of food and game meat.

Wildlife Viewing: Wildlife is abundant around Pacific Creek and Two Ocean Lake. Elk are commonly seen, but there are plenty of other animals as well. Read the Field Notes below for animals that we've seen in the area.

Fishing: Pacific Creek, found for several miles along the incoming road, camp area, and ensuing trail, is considered a good fly-fishing stream for cutthroat trout.

Trails: The Pacific Creek Trailhead, located at the campground, offers access to a multitude of remote trails in the Teton Wilderness. A pack route, named the Atlantic Pacific Creek Trail (this is Continental Divide country after all), follows Pacific Creek uphill until it crosses the stream at 5 miles and again a mile later. After 11 miles, the path intersects a major junction with the Enos Lake Trail where the lake can be reached by turning north and traveling 1.5 miles. There are all sorts of intersecting backcountry routes in this area so be sure to have a good map and proper wilderness skills.

Two Ocean Lake, an absolutely gorgeous lake that is accessed from Pacific Creek Road, has a varied assortment of foot trails. The simplest trip is an easy 7-mile loop around the lake. There is also the option of making a 12-mile loop around nearby Emma Matilda Lake. To really get the views, you can climb 500 feet to the top of Grand View Point (7,327 feet). A trip to the top and back is roughly 9 miles from the parking area.

Field Notes: If you enjoy looking for wildlife, I strongly recommend this area. On one evening drive from Two Ocean Lake to the campground, we spotted a coyote, moose, and three herds of elk. We also found a pile of bear scat, which didn't come as a surprise because this area is well known for its high density of black and grizzly bears. If you travel into the backcountry, carry pepper spray and make noise. Numerous maulings have occurred on this side of the Teton Wilderness.

Signal Mountain Campground

6,800 feet

Location/Map	Central Grand Teton National Park; Page 60
GPS Coordinates	N43° 50.52' W110° 36.63'
Sites/Spur Length	86 sites; Long spurs—over 30 feet
Cost	$31 or $50 with electric hookups
Facilities/Services	Fire rings, picnic tables, water, restrooms, trash and recycling containers, bear boxes, dump station, supply store, boat ramp, cellular service
Managing Agency	National Park Service (Grand Teton National Park)
Reservations	Not accepted—first come, first served
Season/Usage	Open mid-May through early October; High use

Signal Mountain Campground

Directions: From Jackson, head north on HWY 26/89/191 for 12 miles. At Moose Junction, turn west onto Teton Park Road and drive another 17 miles. If traveling from Moran, head north for 4 miles to Jackson Lake Junction. Turn onto Teton Park Road and drive 3 miles to the campground entrance.

Description: This is one of the most scenic campgrounds in the state of Wyoming. The sites edge into a hillside next to Jackson Lake and offer terrific views of Mount Moran (12,605 feet) and other skyscraping crags of the Teton Range. Sites are roomy enough for modest-sized trailers or RVs, while others are designated specifically for tents. The timber here is thin, and some sites have better cover and privacy than others. Overall, it's a win-win situation: the more open the site, the better the views.

Scenic Driving/Wildlife Viewing: The drive through Grand Teton National Park is spectacular. The sudden rise of the jagged Teton Range, the winding beauty of the Snake River, and the awe of its wild animals is truly special.

The 20-mile Teton Park Road between Moose Junction and Jackson Lake Junction takes you up close to the Tetons. You'll pass by numerous interpretive turnouts, trailheads, picnic areas, and the Jenny Lake Visitor Center. An abundance of wildlife can be observed along the road, including elk, which are commonly seen grazing in the sage flats.

Another worthwhile drive is Signal Mountain Summit Road. Drive a mile south of the campground and turn east. The paved road climbs 800 feet in 5 miles to an unsurpassable overlook near 7,600 feet. We spent an evening at the top watching and listening to the valley's elk. A black bear sighting on the way back down topped it off.

Fishing: Scenic Jackson Lake harbors mostly cutthroat and lake trout. Most fish pulled from these waters are less than 18 inches in length, but the occasional trophy fish has been snatched.

Trails: Strong hikers can hike to Signal Mountain's summit, rather than drive to the top. The best place to park is at the Signal Mountain Lodge. From the parking lot, walk back to the main road and turn south for a short distance to the trailhead sign. It's about 8 miles to the summit from this point.

Boating: A marina near the campground offers a boat ramp. Further south, a boat shuttle and rentals can be found at the Jenny Lake recreation area.

4WD Routes: There is a very scenic 15-mile four-wheel drive road near the campground where you can parallel the Snake River and Teton Range. The route is relatively easy and can be completed by any vehicle with high clearance. To begin the drive, head south from the campground for 1.4 miles and watch for the unsigned dirt road on the left. The route ends where it rejoins Teton Park Road, 4 miles south of Jenny Lake.

Picnicking: There are two picnic areas between the campground and Jackson Lake Dam.

Field Notes: Some people have told me that they are absolutely enthralled by the Grand Tetons. If you'd say the same of yourself, you should stay at this campground. Waking on a crisp morning to watch the rising sun illuminate the eastern face of the Teton Range is something you won't soon forget.

Jenny Lake Campground

6,800 feet

Location/Map	Central Grand Teton National Park; Page 60
GPS Coordinates	N43° 45.22' W110° 43.25'
Sites/Spur Length	59 tent sites; Short spurs—up to 20 feet
Cost	$28, $13 for hikers/bicyclists
Facilities/Services	Fire rings, picnic tables, water, restrooms, trash and recycling containers, bear boxes, cellular service
Managing Agency	National Park Service (Grand Teton National Park)
Reservations	Not accepted—first come, first served
Season/Usage	Open mid-May through early October; High use

Directions: From Jackson, head north on HWY 26/89/191 for 12 miles. At Moose Junction, turn west on Teton Park Road and drive another 7.5 miles to the campground's entrance at South Jenny Lake Junction.

Description: Without a doubt, the most popular campground in Wyoming is Jenny Lake. The campground often fills by 8:00 in the morning so be ready for strong competition. Only tent campers are permitted and stay is limited to 7 days. Ten sites are reserved for hikers and bicyclists without vehicles. The sites are spread throughout a stand of dark timber and are not exceptionally private, but some do offer close-up views of the Teton Range. This is prime wildlife habitat and bears frequent the camp so food must be stored in vehicles or bear boxes.

Scenic Driving/Wildlife Viewing: The drive through Grand Teton National Park is spectacular. The sudden rise of the jagged Teton Range, the winding beauty of the Snake River, and the awe of its wild animals is truly special.

The 20-mile Teton Park Road between Moose Junction and Jackson Lake Junction takes you up close to the Tetons. You'll pass by numerous interpretive turnouts, trailheads, picnic areas, and the Jenny Lake Visitor Center. An abundance of wildlife can be observed along the road, including elk, which are commonly seen grazing in the sage flats.

A pleasant drive can be made by driving north on Teton Park Road to North Jenny Lake Junction (about 4 miles from the campground). Turn left and follow the one-way road back to the campground.

Fishing: Jenny Lake holds cutthroat and lake trout, but go elsewhere if you're looking for solitude. The lake receives heavy traffic both on its waters and around its shores.

Trails: The Jenny Lake area is a major starting point for many of the park's backcountry trails and mountain climbs. Two popular destinations are found at the mouth of Cascade Canyon near the western shore of Jenny Lake. A short half-mile hike up the canyon takes you to stunning Hidden Falls. Inspiration Point, a scenic overlook just a half-mile farther, requires more of a climb but can be attained with little additional effort.

More serious hikers can continue 4 more miles up the spectacular canyon to reach a fork with the South and North Fork Trails. You can add 2 miles to any of these destinations by hiking around the south half of Jenny Lake rather than taking the fee-based shuttle boat. Of course, if you get too enamored by the glacially carved lake, you can always continue along the shoreline trail to form a 6-mile loop.

Boating: Jenny Lake is a great destination to launch your canoe. Rentals are available near the lakeside trailhead. There is also a shuttle boat that transfers visitors, mostly hikers, to the other side of the lake to a trailhead. It's a fun ride, even if you don't plan on doing any trekking.

Mountaineering/Rock Climbing: Mountaineers of all skill levels come to scale the jagged peaks of the Teton Range. The most skilled often climb on their own, but there are also Jackson-based climbing guides that can be hired to help with an ascent. If you're interesting in getting started in the sport, stop by the Jenny Lake Ranger Station and inquire about the rock-climbing classes.

Jenny Lake

Field Notes: Many tent campers consider Jenny Lake to be the best camping destination Wyoming has to offer. Towering mountains that can be seen over the highest evergreens, a large mountain lake, and world-class outdoor activities are just a few reasons people come here. If these reasons appeal to you, get to the camp extra early to claim a site.

Gros Ventre Campground
6,500 feet

Location/Map	Southeast Grand Teton National Park; Page 60
GPS Coordinates	N43° 36.99' W110° 40.02'
Sites/Spur Length	350 sites, 5 group sites; Long spurs—over 30 feet
Cost	$28
Facilities/Services	Fire rings, picnic tables, water, restrooms, trash and recycling containers, pay phones, dump station, cellular service
Managing Agency	National Park Service (Grand Teton National Park)
Reservations	Single sites: Not accepted—first come, first served Group sites: Call 800-628-9988
Season/Usage	Open May through mid-October; High use

Directions: From Jackson, head north on HWY 26/89/191 for 6.5 miles. Turn east on Gros Ventre Road and drive 4.5 miles to the campground.

Description: Gros Ventre, an Arapahoe Indian term pronounced "gro-vont," is a large campground on the southern edge of Grand Teton National Park. While it's the furthest from the main attractions, it's very accessible and is a good choice if you have a larger trailer or RV. The vast majority of campsites are strung through a sprawling stand of cottonwood trees along the Gros Ventre River. Other sites are on the more open sagebrush-covered valley floor. The northern loops hold tents, trailers, and RVs while the sites in the more heavily-vegetated southern loops are for tent campers. Overall, these sites are stretched across a mile and a half of river frontage.

Nature Programs: Naturalists from the National Park Service often conduct campfire talks at the campground's amphitheater. Far too few campers take advantage of these outstanding presentations!

Natural Attractions/Scenic Driving: While the crowds gather at the attractions along the base of the Teton Range, the scenic area west of the campground goes virtually unnoticed. To start exploring, drive east from the campground to the small settlement of Kelly. Drive north for a mile, and then turn east onto Gros Ventre Road. The road surface gets bumpy as it climbs 5 miles to Lower Slide Lake. This area is known for a tremendous landslide in 1923 that followed a wet spring and days of heavy rain. The slide's debris dammed the Gros Ventre River for two years before breaking apart and flooding the area, taking six human lives in the event. You can continue west along the road through a scenic land of red hills to find another mountain lake and a few more campgrounds.

Fishing: The Gros Ventre River gathers its water from the high country east of the campground and flows into the Snake River near Jackson. Cutthroat is the most popular fish, though rainbows also exist. Lower Slide Lake, described above, can also be fished.

Gros Ventre Campground

Field Notes: This camp has an "out of the way" feeling that can be very welcoming after a busy day around Jackson. This is the last park campground to reach capacity and there are often a few open sites even during the height of the tourist season.

Atherton Creek Campground
7,000 feet

Location/Map	Northeast of Jackson; Page 60
GPS Coordinates	N43° 38.31' W110° 31.32'
Sites/Spur Length	20 sites; Long spurs—over 30 feet
Cost	$18 ($25 for double sites)
Facilities/Services	Fire rings, picnic tables, water, pit toilets, trash containers, boat ramp, cellular service
Managing Agency	USDA Forest Service (Bridger-Teton National Forest); A host is often present
Reservations	Not accepted—first come, first served
Season/Usage	Open late May through late September; Moderate use

Directions: From Jackson, head north on HWY 26/89/191 for 6.5 miles. Turn east and take this road 8 miles to a junction north of Kelly. Turn east again onto Gros Ventre Road and travel 6 miles.

Description: In 1923, after many days of heavy rain, a slope on Sheep Mountain tumbled down and dammed the Gros Ventre River, forming a lake. Two years later the water burst through the dam and flooded the area. Six lives were lost. A sizable portion of the dammed water, now named Lower Slide Lake, remains to this day and Atherton Creek Campground is planted on its northern shore. (Don't let the name mislead you; this is not a shady camp along a creek, it's a bright lakeside destination.)

With a stretched view of the Teton Range on the horizon, this camp is a nice choice if you want to be in the Teton region without the crowds. The camp offers paved access, generous parking spurs, and wheelchair accessibility. Roomy sites are on a sunny hillside amidst a light aspen forest.

Natural Attractions: Check out the interpretive overlook and short trail just west of the camp to learn more about the Gros Ventre slide and its geology.

Fishing/Boating: Cutthroat trout dominate Lower Slide Lake, but small numbers of rainbow and whitefish can also be expected. There is a boat ramp next to the campground.

Trails: The .8-mile (round trip) Gros Ventre Slide Interpretive Trail is located west of the camp at the slide overlook. Longer backcountry trails are found further east near the Red Hills and Crystal Creek campgrounds.

Picnicking: A picnic area is located at the campground near the boat ramp.

Field Notes: This is a terrific alternative to the national park campgrounds; it's cheaper, quieter, and more spacious.

Crystal Creek Campground

7,000 feet

Location/Map	Northeast of Jackson; Page 60
GPS Coordinates	N43° 36.62' W110° 25.77'
Sites/Spur Length	6 sites, 2 group sites; Medium spurs—up to 30 feet
Cost	$12
Facilities/Services	Fire rings, picnic tables, water, pit toilets, bear boxes
Managing Agency	USDA Forest Service (Bridger-Teton National Forest)
Reservations	Not accepted—first come, first served
Season/Usage	Open late May through early September; Low use

Directions: From Jackson, head north on HWY 26/89/191 for 6.5 miles. Turn east and take this road 8 miles to a junction north of Kelly. Turn east again onto Gros Ventre Road and travel a final 11.8 miles. The last stretch of this road is bumpy.

Description: This is a delightful camp along the Gros Ventre River that resonates with a feeling of remoteness. Red bluffs stand stark against the western sky. Mix in the light shades of sagebrush and darker evergreen forests and you have an incredibly beautiful place to spend the weekend. Sites are well-shaded and will suit tent campers best, though there are a couple of spurs here that will fit a moderately-sized trailer or RV. A large overflow park with two single sites and two group sites is located across the road.

Lower Slide Lake and the Red Hills area east of Grand Teton National Park

Fishing: As with nearby Lower Slide Lake, anglers will find whitefish, cutthroat, and rainbow trout in the Gros Ventre River.

Trails: A trailhead west of camp provides access to the lower slopes of Sheep Mountain, which can be seen by looking southwest. The main route has minimal elevation gain, but many fluctuations, as it heads toward Grizzly Lake, 4 miles to the west. The trail intersects the West Miner Creek Trail at 1.5 miles and the Blue Minor Lake Trail soon after. Blue Minor is the more strenuous route as it climbs 2,400 feet to a cradled pool below a steep ridge. The trailhead sign shows that it is 7.5 miles to the lake.

4WD/ATV Routes: Just over a mile to the east, you'll find a dirt road that leads to the Slate Creek Trailhead at the river's edge. On the other side of the river—a ford is required—you'll find nearly 20 miles of ATV trails including FT 4215, a 12-mile loop that travels along flourishing creek bottoms. The loop itself can only be ridden in its entirety from July 1 to September 9, but the other trails are open through November.

Further east, you'll find FR 30410 and FR 30415 on the east side of Upper Slide Lake. This is a 9-mile 4WD route that climbs 2,000 feet to Gunsight Pass. A few other tracks and ATV trails connect to this route.

Field Notes: Half of this small campground remains unusable due to a river washout in 2017. However, a few sites remain open, as well as the overflow sites on the other side of the road.

Curtis Canyon Campground 7,050 feet

Location/Map	Northeast of Jackson; Page 60
GPS Coordinates	N43° 30.82' W110° 39.66'
Sites/Spur Length	12 sites; Medium spurs—up to 30 feet
Cost	$15
Facilities/Services	Fire rings, picnic tables, water, pit toilets, trash containers, bear boxes, cellular service
Managing Agency	USDA Forest Service (Bridger-Teton National Forest); A host is often present
Reservations	Not accepted—first come, first served
Season/Usage	Open late May through mid-September; Moderate use

Directions: From E. Broadway Street in Jackson, head east and follow the campground signs along the southern edge of the National Elk Refuge. After 5 miles, turn east onto a rough, washboarded road and drive 3 more miles. The last stretch of this drive is also narrow and steep.

Description: This campground gets its name from a gorge to the south that is not visible from the camp. It is in no way descriptive of the wooded perch the camp occupies on the side of a mountain. For many campers, the location is ideal: close to town and above a broad valley overlooking the entire Teton Range. The campsites themselves are nestled below mature Douglas fir trees. The incoming road has sections that are rough and steep; tents, pickup campers, and camper vans are the best choice for these compact sites.

Natural Attractions: Across the road from the campground, you'll find the Curtis Canyon Overlook—a vantage point of the Teton Range and Jackson Hole valley that is commonly missed by tourists.

Trails: There is a nature trail across the road from the National Elk Refuge. Watch for the sign on your way to the campground. Don't count on seeing too many elk if you visit during the summer though, as these animals reside at the refuge between October and May.

Picnicking: The campground is open to picnicking, but sites are rarely open.

Field Notes: A decade ago, this camp was often found empty. On my last visit, each site was taken and there was even a campground host. This place is no longer a local secret. It was only a matter of time before Jackson's closest public campground was discovered.

Trail Creek Campground
6,950 feet

Location/Map	West of Jackson; Page 60
GPS Coordinates	N43° 32.47' W111° 2.47'
Sites/Spur Length	11 sites; Medium spurs—up to 30 feet
Cost	$12
Facilities/Services	Fire rings, grills, picnic tables, water, pit toilets, trash containers, bear boxes
Managing Agency	USDA Forest Service (Caribou-Targhee National Forest); A host is often present
Reservations	Call 877-444-6777 or visit www.recreation.gov
Season/Usage	Open late May through mid-September; Moderate use

Directions: From Jackson, take HWY 22 west over Teton Pass for 17 miles. This is no road for timid drivers—Teton Pass has a 10 percent grade and can be a little crazy when commuter traffic is heavy.

Description: If it were located anywhere else, this campground would be top-notch with its beautifully mixed conifer forest and placid clear creek. Unfortunately, the frenzy from the neighboring highway permeates the campground, giving it a hurried feeling. The road noise is perpetual.

On a positive note, campsites are relatively private, roomy, and don't face each other. One side of the camp is nicely timbered while the other side is sunnier. A few pull-throughs are available, but these are tight quarters, so only smaller trailers and RVs will get much use from them.

Scenic Driving: A trip over Teton Pass (8,431 feet) is far from being a leisurely mountain drive, but it's certainly scenic. A steep switchbacking grade, coupled with speeding drivers who use this road to commute to Jackson from Idaho, make this a treacherous stretch of highway. However, you will find a few turnouts where you can pull off.

Trails: The Coal Creek Trail System can be found 3 miles east of the campground. The uphill trail here wastes no time or distance; it gets you up into the Teton high country in short order. You'll find Coal Creek Meadows at 2.2 miles and then a junction 1.5 miles later. Continue north to reach Moose Meadows or take the east fork to travel over Phillips Pass (8,932 feet). Both destinations are over 4 miles from the trailhead.

Trail Creek Trailhead is located 10 miles east of the campground (and 2 miles west of Wilson) on Trail Creek Road. You can use this trailhead as a starting point to access the 10-mile Black Canyon Loop. From the trailhead, the trail makes a west-bearing semicircle through the northern Snake River Range and emerges nearly 2,000 feet higher on Teton Pass. You can use the Old Pass Road to descend back to the trailhead.

Field Notes: This is a nice camp that shouldn't be overlooked if it's along your travel route. If it's not, I'd skip it. Another option is Mike Harris Campground, located a short distance to the west in Idaho. If your destination is Grand Teton National Park, choose a camp further east.

Reunion Flats Campground

6,850 feet

Location/Map	East of Driggs, Idaho; Page 60
GPS Coordinates	N43° 45.45' W110° 57.01'
Sites/Spur Length	5 sites, 3 group sites; Long spurs—over 30 feet
Cost	$12, $50 for up to 65 people, $100 for groups of 66-150 people
Facilities/Services	Fire rings, picnic tables, water, pit toilets, trash containers
Managing Agency	USDA Forest Service (Caribou-Targhee National Forest); A host is often present
Reservations	Call 877-444-6777 or visit www.recreation.gov
Season/Usage	Open June through mid-September; Moderate use

Directions: In Driggs, Idaho, turn at the Targhee National Recreation Area sign and follow the paved road for 7 miles to a junction. Bear right onto smooth FR 009 and drive 2.5 miles to the campground.

Description: This campground has two group areas that can accommodate up to 65 people each and a third that can hold up to 150 people. In addition, there are five single sites that have an eight-person occupancy limit. Individuals can use the single sites if no groups are present. Campsites are roomy, level, and generally open though the campground itself is surrounded by a dense evergreen forest. Large gravel parking areas make it easy to maneuver trailers and RVs into position. The tops of the mighty Tetons are visible on the eastern horizon.

Fishing: Teton Creek runs along the camp and holds brook and Yellowstone cutthroat trout.

Trails: Trailheads are located at nearby Teton Canyon Campground, just a short distance to the east.

Field Notes: This is the perfect campground for group events such as church campouts or large family reunions. It's clean, modern, and handicap accessible.

Teton Canyon Campground   6,700 feet

Location/Map	East of Driggs, Idaho; Page 60
GPS Coordinates	N43° 45.41' W110° 55.25'
Sites/Spur Length	25 sites; Long spurs—over 30 feet
Cost	$12 ($24 for double sites)
Facilities/Services	Fire rings, grills, picnic tables, water, pit toilets, trash containers, bear boxes, corrals
Managing Agency	USDA Forest Service (Caribou-Targhee National Forest); A host is often present
Reservations	Call 877-444-6777 or visit www.recreation.gov
Season/Usage	Open mid-May through mid-September; High use

Directions: In Driggs, Idaho, turn east at the Targhee National Recreation Area sign and follow the paved road for 7 miles to a junction. Bear right onto smooth FR 009 and drive 4.3 miles to the campground.

Description: Much of the enjoyment of being at this campground is just experiencing this lesser-visited side of the Teton Range. Although you're approaching the Tetons from the west where they are largely obstructed by more elevated terrain, the summits still jut impressively into the sky. The peaks themselves cannot be seen from the campground, but don't let that divert you from this appealing area.

A good number of sites sit exposed in the open, but others are tucked into rather dense forest along Teton Creek. This area is popular with tent campers, but a few spurs will fit longer trailers and RVs. Two of the sites are for campers with horses. Though the campground sees moderate overnight use, the area as a whole sees heavy daytime traffic, though considerably less than the eastern front of the Teton Range.

Fishing: Teton Creek runs along the camp and holds brook and Yellowstone cutthroat trout.

Trails: A number of backcountry trails depart from area trailheads. You can use these trails to explore the Jedediah Smith Wilderness as well as Grand

Teton National Park. There are multiple routes that traverse this spectacular country so be sure to get a trail map before beginning an excursion.

One scenic route travels 7 miles to an amazing area named the Alaska Basin. Another option is to travel the strenuous Table Mountain Trail. This route heads to the mountain's summit by ascending approximately 4,000 feet over the course of 6 miles (the trailhead sign shows the distance as being 8.1 miles). A rock scramble is required to reach the summit, but the glorious views make it a worthwhile effort. For the best conditions, hike this trail late in the season, but always be prepared for poor weather.

Field Notes: This camp sees plenty of sun, but I often find it cloudy and wet. Expect plenty of storms here as the weather builds over the mighty Tetons.

Kozy Campground

6,350 feet

Location/Map	Southeast of Jackson; Page 60
GPS Coordinates	N43° 16.22' W110° 31.01'
Sites/Spur Length	8 sites; Medium spurs—up to 30 feet
Cost	$15
Facilities/Services	Fire rings, grills, picnic tables, pit toilets, trash containers
Managing Agency	USDA Forest Service (Bridger-Teton National Forest)
Reservations	Not accepted—first come, first served
Season/Usage	Open late May through early September; Moderate use

Directions: From Jackson, drive south 11 miles to Hoback Junction. Turn east on HWY 189/191 for 13 miles.

Hoback River near Kozy Campground

Description: This convenient, paved campground is located immediately off the highway in Hoback Canyon. As might be expected, the camp is mostly used for single nights by travelers working their way toward or from Grand Teton and Yellowstone National Parks. The tall evergreen trees are patchy, but the lack of forest opens up wonderful views. Large foothills surround the camp and the Hoback River rumbles along one side. The paved parking spurs are spacious and will fit an average-sized trailer, but they are unlevel.

Scenic Driving: The 20-mile stretch between Bondurant and Hoback Junction (south of Jackson) is not a designated scenic byway, but it certainly qualifies to be one. Highlights along this beautiful drive include the tall peaks of the Hoback, Snake River, and Grow Ventre Ranges as well as the Hoback River as it gushes through a winding canyon.

Fishing: Cutthroat trout swim the waters of the Hoback River. Fishing in the drainage often improves as summer progresses.

Trails: The Shoal Creek Trailhead is located a half mile west of the campground. A sign at the trailhead shows two destinations: 1 mile to Shoal Creek and 22 miles to Shoal Creek Lake.

Field Notes: The paved access is perfect if you don't want to drive down a dusty, bumpy Wyoming backroad. There are usually a couple of sites that remain open during the evening.

Granite Creek Campground   6,900 feet

Location/Map	Southeast of Jackson; Page 60
GPS Coordinates	N43° 21.56' W110° 26.8'
Sites/Spur Length	51 sites; Long spurs—over 30 feet
Cost	$15
Facilities/Services	Fire rings, grills, picnic tables, water, restrooms, pit toilets, trash containers, bear boxes
Managing Agency	USDA Forest Service (Bridger-Teton National Forest); A host is often present
Reservations	Not accepted—first come, first served
Season/Usage	Open June through mid-September; High use

Directions: From Jackson, drive south 11 miles to Hoback Junction. Turn east on HWY 189/191 and proceed 11 miles. Turn north onto washboarded FR 30500 and drive a bumpy (but very scenic) 9 miles.

Description: The Granite Creek area has a lot to offer a vacationer and I consider the campground to be one of the most scenic in the state. It starts with the drive to the camp. Impressive peaks from the Gros Ventre Wilderness dominate much of the view as the road parallels Granite Creek. You can also see evidence of a recent forest fire, and the ensuing recovery.

In camp you'll find roomy, fairly private sites among three loops. Most campers use tents or medium-sized trailers, but a good number of the parking spurs will hold long units. Many of the sites overlook Granite Creek and the nearby mountain peaks.

Hot Springs: A developed hot spring with a changing cabin and a 45x75-foot pool is located at the end of FR 30500. Hours are from 10:00 a.m. to dusk unless off-season conditions make the road impassable. The melting spring snow mixes with the pool's water supply and cools the spring to approximately 80 degrees. It gradually warms after the snow thaw to reach its high temperature of about 110 degrees by midwinter.

Just 50 yards downstream on the eastern side of the creek are a number of hot springs that go relatively unnoticed. These springs offer free wading and soaking with no restrictions. You can reach the hot springs by fording the creek (which may not be possible) or by following a foot trail down from the developed pool.

Natural Attractions: The scenic Granite Creek waterfall can be found just a short distance north of the campground.

Wildlife Viewing: Watch the hillsides to the east of the creek at dawn and dusk to spot animals as they make their way down to the water. Moose are common in the area.

Fishing: There are cutthroat trout in Granite Creek and the Hoback River.

The view from Granite Creek Campground

Trails: Hikers and backpackers will find many trails in the area. The main trailhead is just south of the campground. Look for the dirt road that crosses the creek and accesses the trailhead parking area. From here, one trail follows Granite Creek upstream to reach Turquoise Lake and to join other trails in the Gros Ventre Wilderness. There are also two trails that head east from the trailhead. The more northern route follows Swift Creek. The other route travels 6 miles to Shoal Falls. Both of these trails eventually intersect to form a nearly 20-mile loop.

Dispersed Camping: There are a few dispersed campsites along the incoming road, FR 30500.

Field Notes: The Forest Service used to conduct nature presentations on Friday nights at a primitive amphitheater. On one visit, the topic was black bears and their uncommon presence in the campground. Coincidently, a bear came into camp and threatened a man for his pot of chili just a week later. Bears aren't the only animals that can be seen in camp. A pair of moose stampeded through our site—in alarmingly close proximity—during the dusk hour. Then, long after the sun had set, we heard the eerie cries of a large mountain cat.

Hoback Campground

6,200 feet

Location/Map	Southeast of Jackson; Page 60
GPS Coordinates	N43° 16.79' W110° 35.86'
Sites/Spur Length	14 sites; Long spurs—over 30 feet
Cost	$15
Facilities/Services	Fire rings, grills, picnic tables, pit toilets, trash containers
Managing Agency	USDA Forest Service (Bridger-Teton National Forest); A host is often present
Reservations	Not accepted—first come, first served
Season/Usage	Open June through mid-September; High use

Directions: From Jackson, drive south 11 miles to Hoback Junction. Turn east on HWY 189/191 and drive 8 miles.

Description: This is a great stopover campground if you are heading to or from Grand Teton National Park and want to stay out of the touristy bustle. It's about 30 miles to the park, which makes it just shy of an hour's drive. The short access road from the highway is paved, along with the parking spurs themselves (no mud or dust). Some sites abut the Hoback River, which emits a constant, soothing sound as it flows through the forested canyon.

Scenic Driving: The 20-mile stretch between Bondurant and Hoback Junction (south of Jackson) is not a designated scenic byway, but it certainly qualifies to be one. Highlights along this beautiful drive include the tall peaks of the Hoback, Snake River, and Gros Ventre ranges as well as the Hoback River as it gushes through a winding canyon.

Fishing: Cutthroat trout swim the waters of the Hoback River. Fishing in the drainage often improves as summer progresses.

Trails: A number of nearby backcountry trails can be accessed from Willow Creek Trailhead. From the campground, drive west for 3.5 miles and turn south on a dirt road. Follow this road past Camp Davis for 1.5 miles to the trailhead. The trail starts by climbing to a junction at 1.2 miles. An unsigned trail on the right leads to Ann's Ridge (7,444 feet), just .4 miles to the northwest. The other trail turns south and soon splits into the Alder Creek Trail, Willow Creek-Wyoming Range National Recreation Trail, and the Elk Ridge Trail—all of which offer long trips into the Hoback Range.

Rock Climbing: Limestone slabs on the north side of HWY 189/191 provide climbers with several roadside routes. To reach a popular wall known as Hoback Shield, head east on the highway for 3 miles to a pulloff on the right. The climbing area is on the opposite side of the road.

Picnicking: A picnic area at Hoback Campground makes an inviting and scenic lunchtime stop.

Field Notes: Easy in, easy out. You'll find quite a bit of turnover here each day with latecomers arriving around sunset.

Hoback Campground

AREA 3 | NORTHWEST
Northern Absaroka Range and Beartooth Mountains

Wyoming's northern Absaroka and Beartooth Mountains contain what is often said to be the wildest country remaining in the continental United States. The Absarokas (named after the Crow Indians) abut Yellowstone's eastern and southern boundary. The range supplements the national park's critical elk and grizzly bear habitat. The Beartooth Mountains, east of the Absaroka Range, straddle the Wyoming-Montana border and are known for their gorgeous alpine country.

Due in part to the North Absaroka Wilderness, Absaroka-Beartooth Wilderness, and Beartooth High Lakes Wilderness Study Area, the mountains in this part of the state are largely protected from development. Roads in these mountains are scarce and good hiking trails aren't very common either. Many trails are primarily used only by very experienced backpackers or those on horseback. The land is rough and the drainages are huge. In many places, the backcountry is simply impenetrable. There are exceptions, of course, and the two highest campgrounds in the Beartooths have some excellent hiking trails that traverse the mountain grandeur.

The two paved roads that cross this region are designated scenic routes. The Chief Joseph Scenic Highway, Wyoming Highway 296 northwest of Cody, winds a nearly 50-mile course between the Absaroka Range and the Beartooth Mountains. The road offers incredible overlooks of Sunlight Basin and Clarks Fork Canyon. Equally impressive, if not more so, is the roughly 70-mile Beartooth Scenic Byway (US Highway 212). The road is one of the nation's highest as it climbs over 10,000 feet to cross the Beartooth Plateau, a broad shelf of alpine splendor. Deep snow keeps the highway closed for much of the year, and even when it opens—often by Memorial Day Weekend—cars pass under walls of snow commonly over a dozen feet high. During the brief period when the snow has receded, you'll discover a world of alpine tarns and a tundra-covered landscape adorned by wildflowers and photogenic peaks.

What to Expect: Camping in this part of the state is a delight and you'll find the campgrounds right along the highway to be popular. Expect to find only a handful of empty sites by the evening rush. Other things that you can count on here are early afternoon thunderstorms, summer snow (both old snowdrifts and new falling snow), and bear activity. Also, remember that this is huge country, mind-boggling huge country. You'll find steep grades over many miles of roads. Be prepared for the remoteness and plan to make a lot of scenic stops. Whether you camp here or just drive through, have extra memory available for your camera, adequate clothing for higher elevations, and enough fuel to get you where you are going.

Area 3: Northern Absaroka Range and Beartooth Mountains

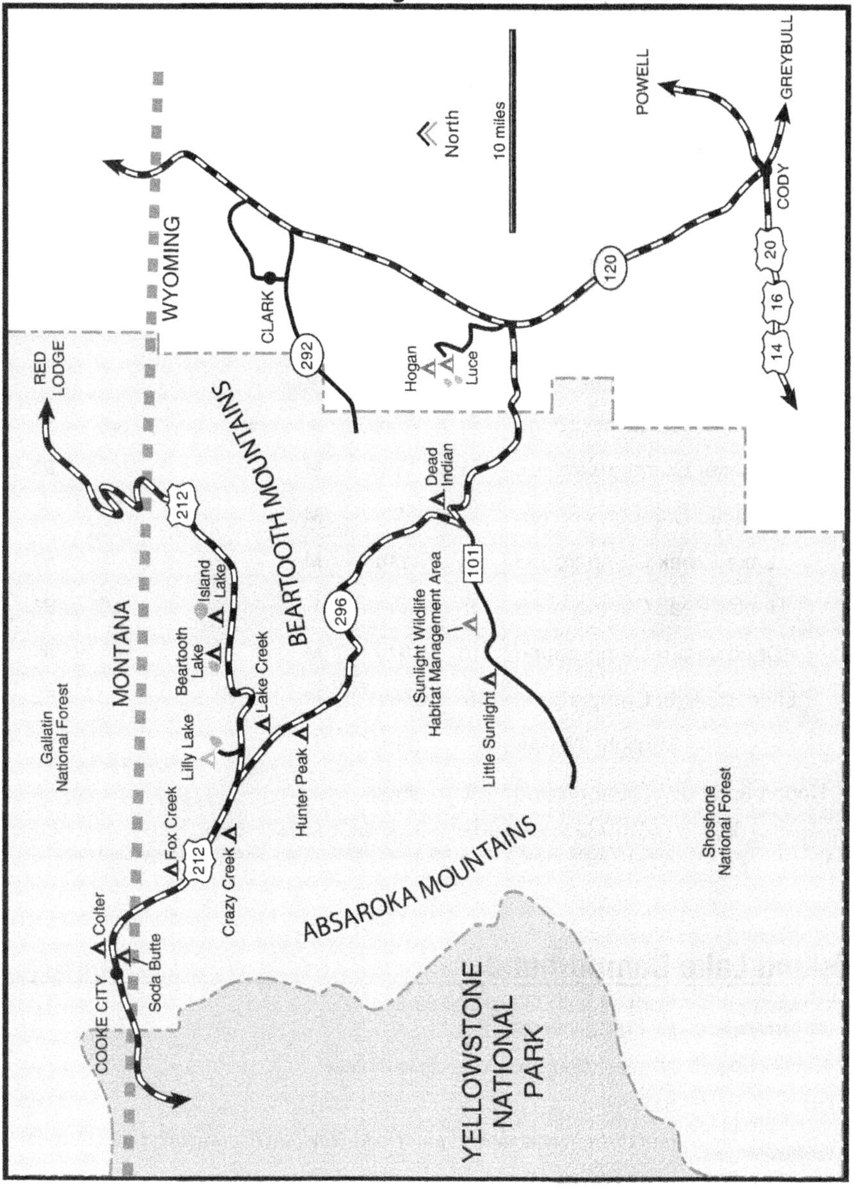

Campgrounds	Sites	Cost	Average Spur Length	Electrical Hookups	Cellular Service (varies by carrier/site)	Reservations Accepted	Page Number
Island Lake Campground	20	$15	M				84
Beartooth Lake Campground	21	$15	M				86
Lily Lake Camping Area	8	Free	S				88
Crazy Creek Campground	16	$10	L				89
Fox Creek Campground	34	$15-60	L	✔		✔	91
Colter Campground (MT)	23	$8	M				92
Soda Butte Campground (MT)	27	$9	M				92
Lake Creek Campground	6	$10	M				93
Hunter Peak Campground	9	$15	L			✔	94
Dead Indian Campground	10	$10	M				95
Little Sunlight Campground	5	Free	M				97
Sunlight WHMA	-	Free	L				98
Hogan and Luce Campground	5	Free	L				98

Average Spur Length: S = Short (under 30 feet), M = Medium (+-30 feet), L = Long (+-40 feet)
Cellular Service: 1 bar = weak/unreliable signal, 2 bars = low usable signal, 3+ bars = reliable signal for most users

Island Lake Campground

9,550 feet

Location/Map	Northwest of Cody; Page 83
GPS Coordinates	N44° 56.24' W109° 32.2'
Sites/Spur Length	20 sites; Medium spurs—up to 30 feet
Cost	$15
Facilities/Services	Fire rings, picnic tables, water, pit toilets, trash containers, bear boxes, boat ramp
Managing Agency	USDA Forest Service (Shoshone National Forest); A host is often present
Reservations	Not accepted—first come, first served
Season/Usage	Open July through early September; High use

Directions: From Cody, take HWY 120 north for 17 miles. Turn left onto HWY 296 and drive 47 miles. Turn east on HWY 212 and drive just short of 13 miles.

Beartooth Scenic Byway

Description: Beautiful Island Lake—capped by the snow-dotted peaks of the Beartooth Mountains—easily ranks within the top most scenic campgrounds in the state. This is high country and the recess from snow is very brief, forcing the popular campground into a stunted two-month operating season. There are several nicely-developed loops inside a mature, but stunted sub-alpine forest that is punctuated with boulders and rock slabs. Campers fortunate enough to get a site in Loop C will have a view of the lake. Bear rules are in effect here, so be sure to properly store your food.

Scenic Driving: HWY 212, the Beartooth Scenic Byway, is among the most scenic drives in America. The 70-mile road traverses Beartooth Pass (10,947 feet) as it connects Red Lodge, Montana to Yellowstone's northeast entrance. The spectacular route ascends from the grassy prairie to the alpine tundra, where you'll find panoramic views of wildflowers, glacial lakes, and snowcapped peaks. The top of Beartooth Pass is roughly 7 miles east of the campground. There is good cellular service near the top.

Fishing/Boating: Fishing for brook trout can be tricky here; the beautiful mountain scenery makes it nearly impossible to concentrate on the bobber at the end of a line. A boat ramp is available.

Trails: A popular trail located at the campground explores the alpine beauty of the Beartooth High Lakes Wilderness Study Area. The route begins by traveling north along a string of scenic gems such as Night Lake and a number of unnamed ponds. The path intersects Beauty Lake Trail at 3 miles. In this case, all routes lead to Beartooth Lake Campground. The left trail is the shortest route to the campground. The right fork is the longer option and intersects a trail that leads into Montana.

4WD Routes: Two four-wheel drive routes can be started near the campground. The shorter one, FR 149, begins a quarter mile east of the campground and travels less than 4 miles past a number of alpine lakes to end at Sawtooth Lake. This route can be done with a stock 4WD vehicle.

The longer 4WD route can be found 1.8 miles east of the campground. This route, FR 120 (Morrison 4WD Road), is one of Wyoming's most challenging backroads. The road descends from the Beartooth Mountains and loses 5,200 feet of elevation over the course of 22 miles. Most of this elevation loss occurs after mile 14 where the road drops steeply to the bottom of Clark's Fork Canyon using over two dozen extremely tight switchbacks. This stretch is only wide enough for ATVs and narrower 4WD vehicles. Once the road reaches the river, it is a beautiful, but very rocky, drive out of the canyon toward the small settlement of Clark.

Field Notes: More times than not, I've found the weather here to be overcast and cool, especially in the afternoons when thunderstorms rumble across the Beartooth Mountains. Be prepared for wind, rain, and even snow. Arrive early to get a site and bring bug spray for the mosquitoes, too.

Beartooth Lake Campground   8,950 feet

Location/Map	Northwest of Cody; Page 83
GPS Coordinates	N44° 56.52' W109° 35.77'
Sites/Spur Length	21 sites; Medium spurs—up to 30 feet
Cost	$15
Facilities/Services	Fire rings, picnic tables, water, pit toilets, trash containers, bear boxes, boat ramp
Managing Agency	USDA Forest Service (Shoshone National Forest); A host is often present
Reservations	Not accepted—first come, first served
Season/Usage	Open July through early September; High use

Directions: From Cody, take HWY 120 north for 17 miles. Turn left onto HWY 296 and drive 47 miles. Turn east on HWY 212 and drive just short of 10 miles.

Description: It's hard to think of a more attractive location for a campground. Hidden off the highway between Yellowstone and one of the most scenic roadways in North America, the camp is perched on a shelf above Beartooth Lake. Reflected in the lake is beautiful Beartooth Butte. Sites are divided between three loops in a thin evergreen forest. While spacious, they are not necessarily private. Check out sites in Loop B if you're pulling

Beartooth Lake

a longer trailer or driving an RV. Tent campers will do better in the smaller C loop. This is bear country and you'll want to use the bear boxes that are available.

Scenic Driving: HWY 212, the Beartooth Scenic Byway, is among the most scenic drives in America. The 70-mile road traverses Beartooth Pass (10,947 feet) as it connects Red Lodge, Montana to Yellowstone's northeast entrance. The spectacular route ascends from the grassy prairie to the alpine tundra, where you'll find panoramic views of wildflowers, glacial lakes, and snowcapped peaks. Two nearby viewing points to the west include the Clay Butte Fire Lookout (accessible from a short forest road) and Pilot Index Overlook.

Fishing/Boating: Anglers will love this scenic mountain lake as they can fish for various trout, mackinaw, and grayling. There is a boat ramp.

Trails: A stunningly beautiful trail leaves the campground and explores the Beartooth High Lakes Wilderness Study Area. A nice 7-mile loop can be hiked by following the trail around the eastern side of Beartooth Lake and Beartooth Butte (10,514 feet) to a junction. Bear right at the junction (around 2.5 miles in) and head southeast toward Beauty Lake. At 5 miles, you'll reach another junction. Turn right to return to Beartooth Lake Campground. If you keep left at the intersection, you'll visit a string of beautiful lakes and end at Island Lake Campground, 3 miles away.

Picnicking: There is a picnic area and pit toilet next to the boat ramp.

Field Notes: This campground (as well as nearby Island Lake Campground) receives my highest recommendation. It is a terrific place to spend a weekend or even a week. It's easier to find a campsite here than at Island Lake, but you'll need to arrive early in the day to claim your site of choice. Don't get too worked up if you don't; even the last sites to fill are good ones. One drawback: mosquitoes!

Lily Lake Camping Area   7,700 feet

Location/Map	Northwest of Cody; Page 83
GPS Coordinates	N44° 56.67' W109° 42.86'
Sites/Spur Length	8 sites; Short spurs—up to 20 feet
Cost	Free
Facilities/Services	Picnic tables, pit toilets, bear boxes, boat ramp
Managing Agency	USDA Forest Service (Shoshone National Forest)
Reservations	Not accepted—first come, first served
Season/Usage	Open June through late October; High use

Directions: From Cody, take HWY 120 north for 17 miles. Turn left onto HWY 296 and drive 47 miles. Turn east on HWY 212, go less than a mile and turn left on FR 128. Follow this rough, narrow road for 1.5 miles to the top of the steep hill. From the junction at the top, bear right onto a lesser track (high clearance recommended) and drive a half mile more to the camp and lake.

Description: This is a primitive camping area along the western shoreline of Lily Lake. It's a compact area that often feels crowded with even a couple of occupied campsites. Although there are 8 sites (roughly), only a handful of these have picnic tables and there are just three bear boxes. The terrain here is uneven and nicely wooded with pine trees.

4WD/ATV Routes: Back at the top of the hill (along the incoming road), you'll find the Crazy Lakes Jeep Road, which bears northwest for 4 miles. This track makes an outstanding backcountry drive that constantly varies with the terrain. There are steep sections and a creek ford as well as gentle stretches through the timber and beside marshes. The road ends at the Absaroka Beartooth Wilderness boundary. A short hike from this point gets you to Ivy Lake.

Scenic Driving: HWY 212, the Beartooth Scenic Byway, is among the most scenic drives in America. The 70-mile road traverses Beartooth Pass (10,947 feet) as it connects Red Lodge, Montana to Yellowstone's northeast entrance. The spectacular route ascends from the grassy prairie to the alpine tundra, where you'll find panoramic views of wildflowers, glacial lakes, and snowcapped peaks. A remarkable scenic overlook is located east of the campground.

Fishing/Boating: Lily Lake holds rainbow and brook trout as well as grayling. There is a primitive boat ramp, but only non-motorized use is allowed.

Field Notes: Even though you'll be tucked away at this location, expect heavy traffic throughout the day (everything from cars to ATVs). Campsites that are closest to the lake also serve as a lakeside parking lot, so keep that in mind. Also, remember to bring your own water, maybe a portable table, and pack out your trash.

Crazy Creek Campground

6,900 feet

Location/Map	Northwest of Cody; Page 83
GPS Coordinates	N44° 56.53' W109° 46.36'
Sites/Spur Length	16 sites; Long spurs—over 30 feet
Cost	$10
Facilities/Services	Fire rings, picnic tables, pit toilets, trash containers, bear boxes
Managing Agency	USDA Forest Service (Shoshone National Forest); A host is often present
Reservations	Not accepted—first come, first served
Season/Usage	Open June through mid-September; Moderate use

Directions: From Cody, take HWY 120 north for 17 miles. Turn left onto HWY 296 and drive 47 miles. Turn west on HWY 212 and go 2.5 miles.

Description: With a lower elevation, you'll find this campground to be a bit warmer and less exposed than those on the Beartooth Plateau. The camp offers sizable and attractive sites. Your camping options are varied: a few parking spurs (and pull-throughs) are shadowed by a coniferous forest while others sit on a sage-lined bench and face an eastern front of the Absaroka Range. You can walk up this hill for a panoramic view of the area. Hunter Peak, at 9,034 feet, and a trio of other summits can be seen 7 miles to the southeast while Pilot Peak is found to the northwest.

Natural Attractions: A rushing waterfall is found across the road from camp.

Scenic Driving: HWY 212, the Beartooth Scenic Byway, is among the most scenic drives in America. The 70-mile road traverses Beartooth Pass (10,947 feet) as it connects Red Lodge, Montana to Yellowstone's northeast entrance. The spectacular route ascends from the grassy prairie to the alpine tundra, where you'll find panoramic views of wildflowers, glacial lakes, and snowcapped peaks. A remarkable scenic overlook is located east of the campground.

Fishing: Expect excellent fly-fishing out of the Clark's Fork of the Yellowstone River, just south of the campground. Trout species include brook, cutthroat, and rainbow.

Trails: A trail departs from the highway directly across from the campground. The path works uphill a short distance to an impressive waterfall and then continues into the North Absaroka Wilderness for 5 miles to Crazy Lakes, a cluster of sizable fishing lakes along the Wyoming-Montana border. Remember that you need a Montana fishing license if you fish the lakes on the other side of the state line.

Field Notes: This camp (or any in this area for that matter), is worth a day or two. Our most recent stay included daily visits by a curious albino fox. The mosquitoes are relentless in July.

Pilot Peak spears the sky above the Clark's Fork of the Yellowstone River

Fox Creek Campground

7,050 feet

Location/Map	Northwest of Cody; Page 83
GPS Coordinates	N44° 58.45' W109° 50.01'
Sites/Spur Length	34 sites; Long spurs—over 30 feet
Cost	$15, $20 with electric hookups; $60 for group sites
Facilities/Services	Electric hookups, fire rings, picnic tables, water, pit toilets, trash containers, bear boxes
Managing Agency	USDA Forest Service (Shoshone National Forest)
Reservations	Call 877-444-6777 or visit www.recreation.gov
Season/Usage	Open June through late September; Moderate use

Directions: From Cody, take HWY 120 north for 17 miles. Turn left onto HWY 296 and drive 47 miles. Turn west on HWY 212 and go 6.5 miles.

Description: Fox Creek is the most RV-friendly camp in this area. Long, spacious, and private sites with electric hookups are tucked into two heavily wooded loops. Some sites are on the Clark's Fork of the Yellowstone River. There is also a pair of triple sites (also with electric hookups) to accommodate larger groups. This is known grizzly country so keep a clean camp and store your food properly.

Scenic Driving: HWY 212, the Beartooth Scenic Byway, is among the most scenic drives in America. The 70-mile road traverses Beartooth Pass (10,947 feet) as it connects Red Lodge, Montana to Yellowstone's northeast entrance. The spectacular route ascends from the grassy prairie to the alpine tundra, where you'll find panoramic views of wildflowers, glacial lakes, and snowcapped peaks.

Fishing: Expect excellent fly-fishing out of the Clark's Fork of the Yellowstone River. Trout species include brook, cutthroat, and rainbow.

Trails: Look for the Pilot Creek Trailhead 1.5 miles southeast of the campground. The trail here is sometimes indistinct as it follows Pilot Creek through a burned forest of dead snags for 7 miles, passing one waterfall and ending at another. It's 4 miles to the North Absaroka Wilderness boundary.

Field Notes: Welcome to the future. As more feature-rich travel trailers and RVs hit the road, the public is demanding more public campgrounds like this one with electric hookups. I've always prided myself in being a rugged camper that can endure any season with a simple tent. But after my last stay here in a trailer, I have to admit that I thoroughly enjoyed running the furnace through the chilly September night.

Montana Campgrounds near Yellowstone (Gallatin National Forest)

There are two campgrounds along the Beartooth Scenic Highway (HWY 212) just east of Cooke City, Montana. These are good camps within the Gallatin National Forest near Yellowstone National Park's northeast entrance. While Yellowstone campgrounds fill quickly to capacity, the camps in the adjacent national forests, including this duo, almost always have at least a few vacancies. For reasons ranging from cost to better scenery, many campers actually prefer to avoid the park, which is only a few minutes down the road.

Both of these camps have similar facilities and services: fire rings, picnic tables, water, pit toilets, trash containers, and bear boxes. No reservations are accepted. Also, at the time of this writing, only hard-sided campers were allowed due to grizzly bear activity. Campers need to be careful and take precautions when handling and storing food. Remember to keep a clean site and store your food in a bear box or hard-sided vehicle.

Take note that the Chief Joseph campground that was also in this area was closed by the Forest Service. The campground is still shown on many maps, literature, and websites.

Colter Campground

Located 1.7 miles east of Cooke City, Montana, this camp has 23 spacious sites among an interior loop and an outer road. Medium-sized parking spurs hold average trailers or RVs, but some of these are unlevel. The camp has a tight turnaround that is not suitable for larger camping units. A fire swept through this area in the past and the coniferous forest is now regenerating. The fee is $8 a night. The camp is open from early to mid-July through September.

Soda Butte Campground

Roughly a half mile east of Cooke City, Montana, Soda Butte has 27 sites with medium-sized parking spurs. Campsites are stretched throughout an evergreen forest where you'll enjoy impressive mountain views. The fee is $9 a night. The camp is open from July through September.

This campground is the reason why the area's camps are only open to hard-sided campers. In 2008, a grizzly bear bit a camper here in the hand. Two years later, a grizzly killed one camper and left two others injured in the middle of the night.

Lake Creek Campground   6,900 feet

Location/Map	Northwest of Cody; Page 83
GPS Coordinates	N44° 55.26' W109° 42.43'
Sites/Spur Length	6 sites; Medium spurs—up to 30 feet
Cost	$10
Facilities/Services	Fire rings, picnic tables, pit toilets, bear boxes
Managing Agency	USDA Forest Service (Shoshone National Forest)
Reservations	Not accepted—first come, first served
Season/Usage	Open June through September; Moderate use

Directions: From Cody, take HWY 120 north for 17 miles. Turn left onto HWY 296 and drive 45 miles. If you are coming from the Beartooth Highway, turn onto HWY 296 and travel south for just over 1 mile.

Description: It's easy to blast right by this compact campground on the way to other destinations. The camp is immured in the foliage of the Lake Creek drainage where a mountain stream carves a course through the trees. Sites are best suited for tents, vans, and pickup campers, but drivers do fit trailers and RVs into a few of the more level spurs.

Scenic Driving: HWY 212, the Beartooth Scenic Byway, is among the most scenic drives in America. The 70-mile road traverses Beartooth Pass (10,947 feet) as it connects Red Lodge, Montana to Yellowstone's northeast entrance. The spectacular route ascends from the grassy prairie to the alpine tundra, where you'll find panoramic views of wildflowers, glacial lakes, and snowcapped peaks.

The Chief Joseph Scenic Byway, HWY 296, rolls through the mountain countryside for 47 miles between the Beartooth Mountains and the Absaroka Mountains. The road passes over Wyoming's highest bridge where it spans Sunlight Creek Gorge. Be sure to stop at the Dead Indian Summit Overlook, too. It is often called the most scenic overlook in the state.

Wildlife Viewing: Look for elk on the slopes and ridges that surround HWY 296. Bears sometimes roam near the roadway, but a sighting would be lucky. Also, watch for dusky grouse, trumpeter swans, and mule deer.

Fishing: Though Lake Creek flanks the campground, it is far too swift to be fished. The best fly-fishing is on the Clark's Fork of the Yellowstone River. The river meanders around much of HWY 212 (to the northwest) and HWY 296 (to the south). Trout species include brook, cutthroat, and rainbow.

Picnicking: Reef Creek Picnic Area is 11 miles to the south on HWY 296.

Field Notes: This camp is often overlooked as people head to Yellowstone or Beartooth Pass. For photographers and sightseers, its location couldn't be better as it sits at the intersection of two designated scenic highways.

Hunter Peak Campground

6,500 feet

Location/Map	Northwest of Cody; Page 83
GPS Coordinates	N44° 53.16' W109° 39.32'
Sites/Spur Length	9 sites; Long spurs—over 30 feet
Cost	$15
Facilities/Services	Fire rings, picnic tables, water, pit toilets, trash containers, bear boxes
Managing Agency	USDA Forest Service (Shoshone National Forest); A host is often present
Reservations	Call 877-444-6777 or visit www.recreation.gov
Season/Usage	Open all year; Moderate use

Directions: From Cody, take HWY 120 north for 17 miles. Turn left onto HWY 296 and drive for 41.5 miles. If you are coming from the Beartooth Highway, turn onto HWY 296 and travel south for 5 miles.

Description: Named after the nearby 9,034-foot mountain, Hunter Peak Campground is situated in mature timber along the Clark's Fork of the Yellowstone River. Sites are roomy and wide, helping to accommodate longer trailers, though you may have to park your towing vehicle at the extra parking area near the campground's entrance. The camp is open all year and is popular during the hunting season.

Scenic Driving: HWY 212, the Beartooth Scenic Byway, is among the most scenic drives in America. The 70-mile road traverses Beartooth Pass (10,947 feet) as it connects Red Lodge, Montana to Yellowstone's northeast entrance. The spectacular route ascends from the grassy prairie to the alpine tundra, where you'll find panoramic views of wildflowers, glacial lakes, and snowcapped peaks.

The Chief Joseph Scenic Byway, HWY 296, rolls through the mountain countryside for 47 miles between the Beartooth Mountains and the Absaroka Mountains. The road passes over Wyoming's highest bridge where it spans Sunlight Creek Gorge. Be sure to stop at the Dead Indian Summit Overlook, too. It is often called the most scenic overlook in the state.

Wildlife Viewing: Look for elk on the slopes and ridges that surround HWY 296. Bears sometimes roam near the roadway, but a sighting would be lucky. Also, watch for dusky grouse, trumpeter swans, and mule deer.

Fishing: There is excellent fly-fishing in the Clark's Fork of the Yellowstone River. The river flows next to the camp and meanders around much of HWY 212 to the north. Trout species include brook, cutthroat, and rainbow.

Trails: The Clark's Fork Trailhead, located across the road from the campground, provides access to the Lewis and Clark Trail, a long course that explores the north side of the Clark's Fork of the Yellowstone River. It is 2.5 miles to Beartooth Creek, 8 miles to the main river, and nearly 20 miles before the trail meets the Morrison 4WD road. Consider the trail strenuous as it crosses through numerous side drainages (there are at least seven) that may be impassable depending on water levels. The trail is open to horse and foot traffic.

The North Crandall Trailhead, 3 miles to the south, offers access to the North Absaroka Wilderness—wild country that is often visited only by horseback during the fall hunting season. The Crandall area consists of nearly impossible fords and burned snags. If those obstacles are not enough to dissuade you, consider this: Yellowstone's problem bears are sometimes relocated to this area.

Picnicking: The Reef Creek Picnic Area is 7 miles to the south on HWY 296.

Field Notes: Whenever I visited this camp, I'd see campers relaxing in camp chairs and hammocks looking especially content. It appeared to be a great place to enjoy the Rocky Mountains. After a decade of passing it up, I finally stayed here and confirmed my suspicion. Despite paralleling a highway, this is one of the quietest, most peaceful camps in which I have ever stayed.

Dead Indian Campground

6,000 feet

Location/Map	Northwest of Cody; Page 83
GPS Coordinates	N44° 45.18' W109° 25.02'
Sites/Spur Length	10 sites; Medium spurs—up to 30 feet
Cost	$10
Facilities/Services	Fire rings, picnic tables, pit toilets, trash containers, bear boxes
Managing Agency	USDA Forest Service (Shoshone National Forest); A host is often present
Reservations	Not accepted—first come, first served
Season/Usage	Open all year; Moderate use

Directions: From Cody, take HWY 296 north for 17 miles, and then turn left onto HWY 296 and drive 21 miles. The campground has two entrances.

Description: Dead Indian Campground sits in a small wooded area at the bottom of a broad valley. Surrounding the camp is an impressive round of mountain views. Relatively level sites are found in two separate loops on opposite sides of Dead Indian Creek. While some sites are nicely shaded, others are not, though there is a dense curtain of streambank flora.

The "Dead Indian" name belongs to many local features in the area including a hill, a pass, a creek, and, of course, the campground. The roots of the reference are not completely certain. One account tells of a Bannock who was wounded by the US Army in 1878. After being discovered, he was killed and the body was hidden under rocks. Other accounts describe an Indian body that was propped up to trick the Cavalry when Chief Joseph led his people through this country.

Scenic Driving: The Chief Joseph Scenic Byway, HWY 296, rolls through the mountain countryside for 47 miles between the Beartooth Mountains and the Absaroka Mountains. The road passes over Wyoming's highest bridge where it spans Sunlight Creek Gorge. Be sure to stop at the Dead Indian Summit Overlook, too. To get off the beaten path, take the gravel Sunlight Basin road west of the campground; the scenery will not disappoint you.

Wildlife Viewing: Look for elk on the slopes and ridges that surround HWY 296. Bears sometimes roam near the roadway, but a sighting would be lucky. Also, watch for dusky grouse, trumpeter swans, and mule deer.

Fishing: You can flyfish for brook, cutthroat, and rainbow trout in Dead Indian Creek.

Trails: The Dead Indian Creek Trailhead, complete with corrals, can be found across the highway from the campground. One route here travels over a dozen miles through the Shoshone National Forest and emerges at a trailhead near the Sunlight Ranger Station. Two other routes lead to destinations inside the eastern finger of the North Absaroka Wilderness: Dead Indian Meadows at 8 miles and Trout Peak (12,244 feet) at 20 miles. Be sure to obtain a map before traveling through this rugged country.

The Dead Indian Trail (actually a segment of the Nez Perce National Historic Trail) is located a half-mile east of the campground at the end of an unmarked road. The trail has two destinations: an observation point at 2 miles and the Clark's Fork of the Yellowstone River at 5 miles (the trailhead sign shows 4 miles). The trek to the observation point is suitable

Dead Indian Campground

for family hiking and rewards visitors with grand views of towering cliffs and a waterfall. Hikers choosing to reach the river will find the last mile to be a steep, precarious descent to the bottom of Clark's Fork Canyon.

Field Notes: This camp receives a lot of drive-through traffic from the highway. It also seems to be a place where people go to hang out for an afternoon. If you're looking for a camp with lighter visitation, check out the campgrounds further north.

Little Sunlight Campground

6,900 feet

Location/Map	Northwest of Cody; Page 83
GPS Coordinates	N44° 43.14' W109° 35.36'
Sites/Spur Length	5 sites; Medium spurs—up to 30 feet
Cost	Free
Facilities/Services	Fire rings, picnic tables, pit toilets, bear boxes
Managing Agency	USDA Forest Service (Shoshone National Forest)
Reservations	Not accepted—first come, first served
Season/Usage	Open June until snow closure; Moderate use

Directions: From Cody, take HWY 120 north for 17 miles. Turn left onto Wyoming HWY 296 and drive 23 miles. Turn onto Sunlight Road (CR 7GQ and FR 101) and continue 12 miles through the gorgeous countryside.

Description: Here's your opportunity to secure a campsite in some of the wildest country in the Lower 48. Surrounding this camp, especially to the west, are miles upon miles of unspoiled wilderness with few roads and trails. The Absaroka Mountains envelop the area, but the wider views are blocked by a towering, picturesque cliff band. A small creek of the same name runs through the camp. There are only a handful of sites in this nicely shaded nook, but dispersed camping is available nearby if needed. Grizzly bears are common in this area.

4WD Route: Continue west of the campground and you'll find a road that gradually deteriorates as the terrain becomes more dramatic and impressive. If you don't have a 4WD vehicle, you'll likely want to turn around after 4 miles as there are fords of Gas Creek and Spring Creek. This last stretch of road is only open from mid-July through September. Another 8 miles (and staying right at the junction) will lead you through swift Sunlight Creek to Lee City, an old mining area where a few ruins still exist. The track continues westward from this point, but it's challenging terrain that should only be tackled by experienced off-road drivers.

Fishing: Sunlight Creek—the larger tributary that parallels the road—will delight anglers with large brook trout. Other local fishing spots are Dead Indian Creek and Clark's Fork of the Yellowstone River.

Sunlight Creek near Little Sunlight Campground

Trails: There are several wild backcountry trails in this grizzly bear area. The Little Sunlight Trailhead, with corrals, is located at the campground. The trail here follows Little Sunlight Creek upstream for 2.7 miles while gaining 500 feet of elevation.

Another trail leaves the nearby Sunlight Ranger Station, makes a large sweep through the Shoshone National Forest, and emerges at a trailhead at Dead Indian Campground over a dozen miles away.

Field Notes: This isn't the quiet spot it used to be as visitation has increased over the years. Expect a steady flow of traffic, including ATVs and UTVs.

Sunlight Wildlife Habitat Management Area (Wyoming Game & Fish)

This 1,414-acre area offers primitive camping along FR 101 in Sunlight Basin. Located a little over 4 miles east of Little Sunlight Campground, you'll find an open parking lot and dispersed sites with some fire rings and a pit toilet. Trails here access Trail Creek, Painter Gulch, Windy Mountain (10,262 feet), and Marguerite Draw. All of these lead into the Shoshone National Forest and a few connect to HWY 296 to the north.

Hogan and Luce Campground/Bald Ridge Trailhead (BLM)

This camp has six sites and open parking on the shoreline of Hogan Reservoir, which is just a quarter mile from Luce Reservoir. There are picnic tables, fire rings, horse facilities, and a pit toilet. Fishing is said to be good at both reservoirs. From Cody, drive north on HWY 120 for 18 miles and turn left onto CR 7RP. Drive 4.7 miles and turn left onto the 1-mile access road.

NORTHWEST AREA 4
Buffalo Bill Cody Country

It's impossible to travel through this area without seeing the name Buffalo Bill Cody. A civil war scout, showman, and hunter, Buffalo Bill is said to have killed nearly 4,300 bison in just 18 months. Today, his name is intertwined along the North Fork of the Shoshone River where he had a hunting lodge. Even the roadway here is named after him. The North Fork shares its course with the Buffalo Bill Cody Scenic Highway (US HWY 14/16/20) between Cody and Yellowstone's east entrance.

From Yellowstone, the North Fork flows downstream toward Cody for over 50 miles before being dammed at Buffalo Bill Reservoir. The river's course is a scenic one, with beautiful canyon walls and rock pinnacles. Theodore Roosevelt once called this the most scenic 50 miles in the nation. One could only speculate the praise he might have doled out had he traveled on some of Wyoming's newer scenic highways.

Driving the highway, you may notice that many of the evergreens are dead. These are trees affected by a widespread beetle infestation. Mild winters, a prolonged drought, and the stress of the 1988 fire season made the forest more susceptible to disease and damaging insects. The Forest Service estimates 70% of the trees in the North Fork drainage will eventually die from the infestation. Of course, the forest will regenerate itself over time, and recent fires here have begun accelerating the process, but it'll be many years before nature completes this cycle.

In terms of wildlife, the corridor supports animals such as grizzly bears, elk, bighorn sheep, and moose. The river itself is managed as a wild fishery—a highly-rated one—and holds a variety of sizable trout like rainbow, cutthroat, brook, and lake. Mountain whitefish can also be found. The lower sections have public access areas that are managed by the Wyoming Game and Fish Department. Higher stretches are managed by the Shoshone National Forest, which provides public access for many miles between Wapiti and Yellowstone.

There are eight Forest Service campgrounds along the highway, as well as Buffalo Bill State Park, which has two camps of its own. One might think the campgrounds closer to Yellowstone would be the busiest, but just the opposite holds true. Many campers stay closer to Cody to experience the town's unique western culture, which includes attractions like the Buffalo Bill Historical Center and a nightly rodeo during the summer.

What to Expect: This string of campgrounds is very accessible and you'll enjoy the option of taking the scenic drive into Yellowstone or zipping down to Cody. The camps are located at relatively low elevations, so you'll have milder temperatures than you'd encounter at campgrounds to the north in the Beartooths or to the south near Togwotee Pass. These lower elevations can also be advantageous to those who have health conditions that are exacerbated by higher altitudes.

Visitation along the North Fork of the Shoshone River is curiously sporadic during the summer. On some weekends, you'll find several of the camps to be full. On others, you'll have no trouble finding the campsite of your choice.

This area routinely sees troublesome grizzly bears that have become habituated to human food, trash, or livestock. When camping, use the bear boxes and follow the posted bear rules. When hiking, be sure to travel in groups and make noise as you go. Also, keep in mind that there is a lot of wildlife along this river corridor; drive safely, especially at night.

Shoshone Canyon from the Buffalo Bill Reservoir Dam

Area 4: Buffalo Bill Cody Country

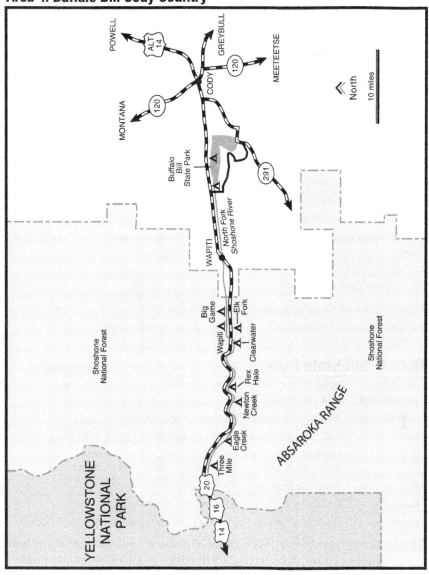

Campgrounds	Sites	Cost	Average Spur Length	Electrical Hookups	Cellular Service (varies by carrier/site)	Reservations Accepted	Page Number
Buffalo Bill State Park	99	$15-25	L	✔	▪▫▫	✔	102
Big Game Campground	16	$10	L			✔	104
Wapiti Campground	40	$15-40	L	✔		✔	105
Elk Fork Campground	13	$15	M				106
Clearwater Campground	10	$10-60	Tent			✔	108
Rex Hale Campground	30	$15-20	L	✔		✔	109
Newton Creek Campground	31	$15	L				110
Eagle Creek Campground	20	$15	L				111
Three Mile Campground	21	$15	L			✔	112

Average Spur Length: S = Short (under 30 feet), M = Medium (+-30 feet), L = Long (+-40 feet)
Cellular Service: 1 bar = weak/unreliable signal, 2 bars = low usable signal, 3+ bars = reliable signal for most users

Buffalo Bill State Park

5,400 feet

Location/Map	West of Cody; Page 101, 103
GPS Coordinates	N44° 30.04' W109° 11.28'
Sites/Spur Length	99 sites, 1 group site; Long spurs—over 30 feet
Cost	$15 state residents, $25 nonresidents (includes $6 or $9 day-use fee)
Facilities/Services	Hookups, fire rings, grills, picnic tables, water, restrooms, playground, pit toilets, showers, trash containers, dump station, boat ramps
Managing Agency	Wyoming State Parks, Historic Sites & Trails
Reservations	Call 877-996-7275 or visit wyoparks.state.wy.us
Season/Usage	Open May through September (reservoir open all year); Moderate use

Directions: From Cody, take HWY 14/16/20 west for 9 miles to the North Shore Campground or 12.5 miles to the North Fork-Trout Creek Campground.

Description: Buffalo Bill State Park, just west of Cody, is the gateway to beautiful western Wyoming. Being just 40 miles east of Yellowstone's east entrance, the state park finds favor with those who like to take advantage of Cody's conveniences while making daytrips into the national park.

Buffalo Bill Reservoir, the park's main feature, is surrounded by the dry eastern slopes of the Absaroka Mountains. You won't find much shade here during the hot summer months, but cooler temperatures can be found just up the road in the Shoshone National Forest.

Buffalo Bill State Park

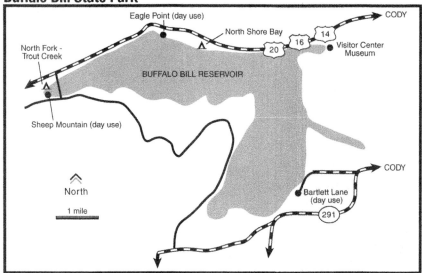

There are two developed campgrounds in the state park. Both are large enough to accommodate the mass of campers who travel through the area to visit Yellowstone country. The first, North Shore Bay Campground, has 37 sites including some pull-throughs and five designated tent sites. The second campground, North Fork, has 62 sites, hookups, pay showers, and a playground. All sites are pull-throughs with the exception of six tent spots.

The Trout Creek group camping area is located within the North Fork camp. It has a group shelter, picnic tables, a grill, and room for tents, trailers, and RVs. The group area must be reserved at a cost of $50 per day in addition to a deposit and the park's normal day-use fee.

Visitor Center: A visitor center at the east end of the reservoir has a museum where you can learn more about the area's history and dam. You can also walk across the dam and peer into the deep gorge of Shoshone Canyon.

Fishing/Boating: Anglers will find mackinaw and various types of trout in Buffalo Bill Reservoir. Three boat ramps are provided for boaters. The reservoir is also the most popular place in the state to windsurf.

Trails: The Trout Creek Natural Trail is a .25-mile route that explores the wetlands around the group camping area. There is also a short handicap-accessible trail at the Eagle Point day-use area.

Picnicking: The park has numerous picnic areas around the shoreline. There is also a reservable group picnic area at the Sheep Mountain day use area.

Field Notes: Bring plenty of sunscreen and a hat. Insect repellent is also a good idea although a perpetual breeze helps keep the bugs away.

North Shore Bay Campground at Buffalo Bill State Park

Big Game Campground — 5,900 feet

Location/Map	West of Cody; Page 101
GPS Coordinates	N44° 27.68' W109° 36.45'
Sites/Spur Length	16 sites; Long spurs—over 30 feet
Cost	$10
Facilities/Services	Fire rings, picnic tables, pit toilets, trash containers, bear boxes
Managing Agency	USDA Forest Service (Shoshone National Forest)
Reservations	Call 877-444-6777 or visit www.recreation.gov
Season/Usage	Open early June until early September; High use

Directions: From Cody, take HWY 14/16/20 west for 26 miles.

Description: This is the first of many Forest Service campgrounds along the stretch between Cody and Yellowstone. Interesting sandstone rock walls and thick vegetation along the North Fork of Shoshone River make this an attractive campground. Campsites are very roomy and have such dense brush that there is almost complete privacy between them. A couple of large pull-through sites are available for larger RVs or trailers. Each campground this side of Cody is regarded as bear country so keep a clean camp. Take note that there is no water here, so you'll have to bring your own.

Scenic Driving/Wildlife Viewing: The Buffalo Bill Cody Scenic Byway begins at the Shoshone National Forest boundary and travels 27 miles through the

Wapiti Valley to the east entrance of Yellowstone. In the lower valley, you'll find fascinating rock pinnacles and spires along the North Fork. The upper region, closer to the national park, is home to an abundance of wildlife. Watch for moose, bighorn sheep, and grizzly bears along the drive.

Fishing: The scenic North Fork of Shoshone River is a wild trout fishery containing rainbows and cutthroats. Everything upstream from the forest boundary is open to the public.

Trails: A paved interpretive trail that follows the river can be found east of the campground.

Picnicking: Horse Creek Picnic Area is located just over a mile to the east of the campground.

Field Notes: This is a nice base camp for the region. A small Forest Service visitor center is a little over a quarter of a mile to the west.

Wapiti Campground

6,000 feet

Location/Map	West of Cody; Page 101
GPS Coordinates	N44° 27.86' W109° 37.45'
Sites/Spur Length	40 sites (including double sites); Long spurs—over 30 feet
Cost	$15 or $20 with electric hookups ($30-$40 for double sites)
Facilities/Services	Electric hookups, fire rings, picnic tables, water, pit toilets, trash containers, bear boxes
Managing Agency	USDA Forest Service (Shoshone National Forest); A host is often present
Reservations	Call 877-444-6777 or visit www.recreation.gov
Season/Usage	Open mid-May through September; High use

Directions: From Cody, take HWY 14/16/20 west for 29 miles.

Description: Wapiti is a Shawnee Indian word for "elk," which you may see in Yellowstone if that is your eventual destination. Although there probably won't be any elk around this camp, you're sure to be intrigued by the rock formations and red canyon walls that rise above the North Fork of the Shoshone River. Level sites are spacious with decent privacy and shade is provided from cottonwood trees. Half of the campground has electric hookups and double sites are also available.

Scenic Driving/Wildlife Viewing: The Buffalo Bill Cody Scenic Byway begins at the Shoshone National Forest boundary and travels 27 miles through the Wapiti Valley to the east entrance of Yellowstone. In the lower valley, you'll find fascinating rock pinnacles and spires along the North Fork. The upper region, closer to the national park, is home to an abundance of wildlife. Watch for moose, bighorn sheep, and grizzly bears along the drive.

Fishing: The scenic North Fork of Shoshone River is a wild trout fishery containing rainbows and cutthroats. The water upstream from the forest boundary is open to the public.

Trails: A trailhead is located across the road at Elk Fork Campground. A trail here leads several miles into the Washakie Wilderness.

Picnicking: Horse Creek Picnic Area is 2 miles east of the campground.

Field Notes: This campground is a favorite for many campers who come to Cody each year. The spacious sites and electric hookups are big hits. A small Forest Service visitor center is a half-mile to the east.

Elk Fork Campground
6,000 feet

Location/Map	West of Cody; Page 101
GPS Coordinates	N44° 27.88' W109° 37.61'
Sites/Spur Length	13 sites (including double sites); Medium spurs—up to 30 feet
Cost	$10
Facilities/Services	Fire rings, picnic tables, pit toilets, trash containers, bear boxes
Managing Agency	USDA Forest Service (Shoshone National Forest); A host is often present
Reservations	Not accepted—first come, first served
Season/Usage	Open mid-May through October; Moderate use

Directions: From Cody, take HWY 14/16/20 west for 30 miles.

Description: Located across the highway from Wapiti Campground, this camp is situated along the Elk Fork drainage, which is a tributary to the North Fork of Shoshone River. Sites are roomy and will fit most RVs and trailers. Willows and mature cottonwood trees line the camp, although the foliage isn't enough to block noise from the busy highway. A few of the campsites on the creek side have great views of snowy rock caps in the adjacent wilderness. A trailhead at the back of the campground adds to drive-through traffic during the day.

Scenic Driving/Wildlife Viewing: The Buffalo Bill Cody Scenic Byway begins at the Shoshone National Forest boundary and travels 27 miles through the Wapiti Valley to the east entrance of Yellowstone. In the lower valley, you'll find fascinating rock pinnacles and spires along the North Fork. The upper region, closer to the national park, is home to an abundance of wildlife. Watch for moose, bighorn sheep, and grizzly bears along the drive.

Fishing: The scenic North Fork of the Shoshone River is a wild trout fishery containing rainbows and cutthroats. The water upstream from the forest boundary is open to the public. Elk Fork Creek, next to the campground, offers decent fishing for smaller brook, rainbow, and cutthroat.

Elk Fork Campground

Trails: The Elk Creek Trailhead is located behind the campground and includes a horse corral and large parking area. The Elk Fork Trail travels over two dozen miles through the high country of the Washakie Wilderness and onwards into the Teton Wilderness. Don't take an excursion here lightly; this is some of the wildest backcountry in the Lower 48.

Picnicking: Two group picnic sites are available 2 miles to the west at Clearwater Campground. In addition, Horse Creek Picnic Area is located 2 miles east of the campground.

Field Notes: This is a nice camp that's worth checking out, but with a trailhead here and another campground located across the road, this area feels a little "bunched up." You'll find quieter and more private sites at the other campgrounds if those are factors that you consider. Also take note that there is no potable water here.

Clearwater Campground

6,000 feet

Location/Map	West of Cody; Page 101
GPS Coordinates	N44° 27.75' W109° 40.1'
Sites/Spur Length	10 sites, 1 group site; Walk-in tent sites only
Cost	$10, $60 group site
Facilities/Services	Fire rings, picnic tables, pit toilets, trash containers, bear boxes
Managing Agency	USDA Forest Service (Shoshone National Forest)
Reservations	Call 877-444-6777 or visit www.recreation.gov (group site only)
Season/Usage	Open mid-May through late September; Moderate use

Directions: From Cody, take HWY 14/16/20 west for 32 miles.

Description: A stark red canyon wall creates a beautiful backdrop at this riverside campground. There are nearly a dozen walk-in tent sites that sit on the open banks of the North Fork of the Shoshone River. Three sites on the east side of the camp create a single group area that can be reserved for up to 50 people. If you camp in a tent, be aware that most of the remaining uphill camps closer to Yellowstone (Newton Creek, Eagle Creek, and Three Mile) have restrictions on tent camping. Be sure to pack your own water to this camp.

Scenic Driving/Wildlife Viewing: The Buffalo Bill Cody Scenic Byway begins at the Shoshone National Forest boundary and travels 27 miles through the Wapiti Valley to the east entrance of Yellowstone. In the lower valley, you'll find fascinating rock pinnacles and spires along the North Fork. The upper region, closer to the national park, is home to an abundance of wildlife. Watch for moose, bighorn sheep, and grizzly bears along the drive.

Fishing: The scenic North Fork of the Shoshone River is a wild trout fishery containing rainbows and cutthroats. The water upstream from the forest boundary is open to the public.

Trails: The Elk Creek Trailhead is located 2 miles to the east at Elk Fork Campground and includes a horse corral and a large parking area. The Elk Fork Trail travels over two-dozen miles into the high country of the Absaroka Mountains before intersecting with other trails in the Teton Wilderness. Don't take an excursion here lightly; this is some of the wildest backcountry in the Lower 48.

Picnicking: Two group picnic sites are located in the campground.

Field Notes: It's not quite Sedona, but the red walls here do have a flavor of that intriguing Arizona scenery. It is less than 20 miles to Yellowstone from this camp.

Rex Hale Campground

6,150 feet

Location/Map	West of Cody; Page 101
GPS Coordinates	N44° 27.35' W109° 43.71'
Sites/Spur Length	30 sites; Long spurs—over 30 feet
Cost	$15 or $20 with electric hookups
Facilities/Services	Electric hookups, fire rings, picnic tables, water, pit toilets, trash containers, bear boxes
Managing Agency	USDA Forest Service (Shoshone National Forest)
Reservations	Call 877-444-6777 or visit www.recreation.gov
Season/Usage	Open mid-May through late September; Moderate use

Directions: From Cody, take HWY 14/16/20 west for 36 miles.

Description: Pinched between the highway and the North Fork, this camp offers little to no privacy, but that doesn't prevent people from taking advantage of the easily accessible camp with electric hookups (not all sites have hookups). In fact, those with RVs and trailers seem to prefer it. The spacious campsites include lowland foliage such as sagebrush, shrubs, and a few lonely coniferous trees.

Scenic Driving/Wildlife Viewing: The Buffalo Bill Cody Scenic Byway begins at the Shoshone National Forest boundary and travels 27 miles through the Wapiti Valley to the east entrance of Yellowstone. In the lower valley, you'll find fascinating rock pinnacles and spires along the North Fork. The upper region, closer to the national park, is home to an abundance of wildlife. Watch for moose, bighorn sheep, and grizzly bears along the drive.

Fishing: The scenic North Fork of the Shoshone River is a wild trout fishery containing rainbows and cutthroats. The water upstream from the forest boundary is open to the public.

Trails: A deadly forest fire killed 15 firefighters and injured 39 more in this area in 1937. The Blackwater National Recreation Trail travels 4 miles to a memorial near Clayton Mountain (10,219 feet). A longer option is to follow the trail to a fork that leads to Blackwater Natural Bridge (14 miles round-trip). To find the trailhead, travel west from the campground for a mile and park along FR 435. The trail starts at the end of this 4WD road.

Picnicking: There are two nearby picnic areas: Blackwater Pond is located directly to the west of the campground and Newton Spring is 2 miles to the west.

Field Notes: While summers along the North Fork are often hot and dry, it's worth preparing for worse. I've seen it snow here in early June and late August. The fast-moving June weather especially caught campers by surprise as it was bright and sunny just minutes before the snowstorm hit.

Newton Creek Campground

6,200 feet

Location/Map	West of Cody; Page 101
GPS Coordinates	N44° 27.23' W109° 45.55'
Sites/Spur Length	31 sites; Long spurs—over 30 feet (only hard-sided units allowed)
Cost	$15
Facilities/Services	Fire rings, picnic tables, water, pit toilets, trash containers, bear boxes
Managing Agency	USDA Forest Service (Shoshone National Forest)
Reservations	Not accepted—first come, first served
Season/Usage	Open mid-May through late September; Moderate use

Directions: From Cody, take HWY 14/16/20 west for 37.5 miles.

Description: Just 15 minutes from Yellowstone, this camp is situated directly off the highway within an appealing mature forest. While not the most private, there are two loops with roomy and shady sites. Check out the more open east loop if you are looking for river frontage. Steep cliffs rise above the river to make a scenic backdrop. Newton Creek flows through camp and empties into the North Fork. Due to grizzly bear activity along Newton Creek, only hard-sided camping units (no tents or canvas pop-ups) can be used.

Scenic Driving/Wildlife Viewing: The Buffalo Bill Cody Scenic Byway begins at the Shoshone National Forest boundary and travels 27 miles through the Wapiti Valley to the east entrance of Yellowstone. In the lower valley, you'll find fascinating rock pinnacles and spires along the North Fork. The upper region, closer to the national park, is home to an abundance of wildlife. Watch for moose, bighorn sheep, and grizzly bears along the drive.

Fishing: The scenic North Fork of the Shoshone River is a wild trout fishery containing rainbows and cutthroats. The water upstream from the forest boundary is open to the public. Newton Creek flows through the campground and may offer a shot at decent fishing.

Trails: A deadly forest fire killed 15 firefighters and injured 39 more in this area in 1937. The Blackwater National Recreation Trail travels 4 miles to a memorial near Clayton Mountain (10,219 feet). A longer option is to follow the trail to a fork that leads to Blackwater Natural Bridge (14 miles round-trip). To find the trailhead, drive east from the camp for about a mile to a roadside memorial next to FR 435. The trail starts at the end of this 1.7-mile dirt road.

Picnicking: There are two nearby picnic areas: Newton Spring, directly east of the campground, and Blackwater Pond, just a short distance further.

Field Notes: If there is a defining point in the transition between the open hills around Cody and the deep forests of Yellowstone, this is it. This campground and the two to the west do not have the "foothills" feeling of the camps closer to Cody.

North Fork of the Shoshone River

Eagle Creek Campground

6,500 feet

Location/Map	West of Cody; Page 101
GPS Coordinates	N44° 28.33' W109° 53.3'
Sites/Spur Length	20 sites; Long spurs—over 30 feet (only hard-sided units allowed)
Cost	$15
Facilities/Services	Fire rings, picnic tables, water, pit toilets, trash containers, bear boxes
Managing Agency	USDA Forest Service (Shoshone National Forest)
Reservations	Not accepted—first come, first served
Season/Usage	Open mid-May until mid-September; Moderate use

Directions: From Cody, take HWY 14/16/20 west for 45 miles.

Description: This campground once boasted nicely timbered sites, but a thinning project has since exposed some of the parking spurs and significantly reduced privacy. Even so, Eagle Creek is still an attractive place to stay. There are a number of pull-throughs and you'll find the other sites to be long and accommodating. A gravel path runs along the North Fork of the Shoshone River and a footbridge spans the water. This is grizzly bear country and only hard-sided camping units are permitted.

Guest Ranches: Looking for a hot meal or horseback ride into the wilderness? Watch for signs along the highway for local guest ranches that can get you packing for a trip you won't soon forget.

Scenic Driving/Wildlife Viewing: The Buffalo Bill Cody Scenic Byway begins at the Shoshone National Forest boundary and travels 27 miles through the Wapiti Valley to the east entrance of Yellowstone. In the lower valley, you'll find fascinating rock pinnacles and spires along the North Fork. The upper region, closer to the national park, is home to an abundance of wildlife. Watch for moose, bighorn sheep, and grizzly bears along the drive.

Fishing: The scenic North Fork of the Shoshone River is a wild trout fishery containing rainbows and cutthroats. The water upstream from the forest boundary is open to the public. Nearby Eagle Creek is said to be a good fishery for cutthroat and brook trout.

Trails: There are two trailheads in the vicinity. The Eagle Creek Trailhead is located east of the campground and has a metal corral for pack animals. Fish Hawk, a trailhead that accesses two separate trails and has corrals and water, is located 1.5 miles east of the campground. All three routes follow creeks as they ascend into the Washakie Wilderness.

Picnicking: The Sleeping Giant Picnic Area (once a campground) is 3 miles west of the campground.

Field Notes: If you are heading west and the day is growing old, you may want to grab a site here or at nearby Three Mile campground. After Three Mile, it's over 30 miles, and at least an hour, to the closest Yellowstone campground and it has a good chance of being full.

Three Mile Campground
6,600 feet

Location/Map	West of Cody; Page 101
GPS Coordinates	N44° 29.78' W109° 56.84'
Sites/Spur Length	21 sites; Long spurs—over 30 feet (only hard-sided units allowed)
Cost	$15 ($30 for double sites)
Facilities/Services	Fire rings, picnic tables, water, pit toilets, trash containers, bear boxes
Managing Agency	USDA Forest Service (Shoshone National Forest); A host is often present
Reservations	Call 877-444-6777 or visit www.recreation.gov
Season/Usage	Open June until early-September; Moderate use

Directions: From Cody, take HWY 14/16/20 west for 49 miles.

Description: This well-kept and attractive campground is your last camping option before Yellowstone National Park, which is only 3 miles to the west (hence the name). However, the closest Yellowstone campground that may have an open site is still 30 miles away. Sites here are shaded under a mix of evergreens along the banks of the North Fork river. There are several extra long pull-through sites and each picnic table has a lantern hook. Due to grizzly bear activity, only hard-sided camping units are permitted.

There is a small community called Pahaska Tepee just up the road that consists mostly of a lodge, gift shop, and convenience store. Buffalo Bill Cody built the lodge in 1901 to host his hunting guests.

Scenic Driving/Wildlife Viewing: The Buffalo Bill Cody Scenic Byway begins at the Shoshone National Forest boundary and travels 27 miles through the Wapiti Valley to the east entrance of Yellowstone. In the lower valley, you'll find fascinating rock pinnacles and spires along the North Fork. The upper region, closer to the national park, is home to an abundance of wildlife. Watch for moose, bighorn sheep, and grizzly bears along this drive.

Fishing: The scenic North Fork of the Shoshone River is a wild trout fishery containing rainbows and cutthroats. The water upstream from the forest boundary is open to the public. Any fishing that you do in Yellowstone requires a special park permit.

Trails: The Pahaska Trailhead is on the north side of the highway. The trail here travels north for several miles to intersect a handful of other backcountry routes in the North Absaroka Wilderness.

Picnicking: Several picnic tables at the campground are available for day use. In addition, the Sleeping Giant Picnic Area is located 1 mile to the east.

Field Notes: I spotted my first grizzly near this campground along the banks of the river. Bear encounters—some that ended badly—have occurred in this area in recent years. If you are headed into the backcountry, be sure to make plenty of noise and carry pepper spray.

North Fork of the Shoshone River from Three Mile Campground

AREA 5 | NORTHWEST
Southeastern Absaroka Range

The Absaroka Range occupies a large swath across northwestern Wyoming. These mountains serve as a buffer between Yellowstone and the Bighorn Basin of north-central Wyoming. Without a region like this, it is likely that Yellowstone, and its wildlife, would be much more threatened by a human presence.

The east face of the Absaroka area provides crucial habitat for elk, bighorn sheep, mountain goats, and other large animals. In recent years, grizzlies and wolves from the Yellowstone ecosystem have reoccupied the mountains west of Meeteetse. As these predators expand their range, they find themselves increasingly at odds with the locals—ranchers who have livestock at stake.

Vast segments of these mountains are managed as federally protected wilderness and have no roads or other developments. Access into this area of the Absarokas is limited. Aside from a few 4WD roads on the eastern front, the only other way to access the mountains is by foot or horse. A number of backcountry trails enter the Washakie Wilderness, which covers a significant portion of the range.

Meeteetse, between Thermopolis and Cody, typifies an old town of the Wild West. Instead of zipping through this small, rugged community, consider spending some time here. There is an excellent museum along the highway where you can take a step back into history. Among the most interesting exhibits is "Little Wab"—the second largest grizzly bear known to exist in the greater Yellowstone area. The nearly 900-pound bear was terminated by officials after years of killing and feeding off cattle.

What to Expect: There are only a handful of campgrounds in this area and half of them are underutilized. These camps are not found "in the mountains" per se, but rather at the eastern base of the range where sagebrush meets the forest.

Staying at any of these camps during the middle of a week will give you a healthy dose of solitude. While it's the locals that you'll find most often in the area, outsiders occasionally wander into camp. Weekend traffic picks up a bit and you'll likely encounter some ATV riders or horsepackers. Backpackers, too, utilize the area's trailheads to launch into some of this nation's most pristine and wild backcountry.

Parts like these demand that you be self-sufficient and staying in these campgrounds is no different. You'll usually need to bring your own water and take your own trash. What you won't need is money. As of this writing, all of these campgrounds were free.

Area 5: Southeastern Absaroka Range

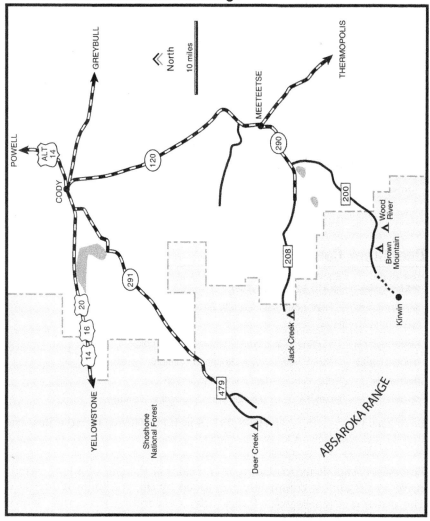

Campgrounds	Sites	Cost	Average Spur Length	Electrical Hookups	Cellular Service (varies by carrier/site)	Reservations Accepted	Page Number
Deer Creek Campground	6	Free	S				116
Jack Creek Campground	7	Free	M				117
Wood River Campground	5	Free	M				119
Brown Mountain Campground	7	Free	M				120

Average Spur Length: S = Short (under 30 feet), M = Medium (+-30 feet), L = Long (+-40 feet)
Cellular Service: 1 bar = weak/unreliable signal, 2 bars = low usable signal, 3+ bars = reliable signal for most users

Deer Creek Campground
6,500 feet

Location/Map	Southwest of Cody; Page 115
GPS Coordinates	N44° 9.52' W109° 37.24'
Sites/Spur Length	6 sites; Short spurs—up to 20 feet
Cost	Free
Facilities/Services	Fire rings, picnic tables, pit toilets, bear boxes
Managing Agency	USDA Forest Service (Shoshone National Forest)
Reservations	Not accepted—first come, first served
Season/Usage	Open mid-June through early September; Low use

Directions: From Cody, take HWY 291 (South Fork Road) for 40 miles. The first 33 miles are paved.

Description: This dusty roadside camp resides at the end of a long, scenic drive and is almost completely enveloped by the Washakie Wilderness. The peaks of the Absaroka Range offer outstanding panoramic views. Level pull-through sites are divided along both sides of the road, so any passing traffic can make things quite dusty. A small brook from Deer Creek trickles along one side of the road as it flows toward the larger South Fork of the Shoshone River. This is bear country—use the bear boxes to store food and supplies.

Fishing: Fishing for brook and brown trout is limited due to access and river flows. If you're determined to fish this tributary, you can find public access by driving to the end of the South Fork Road and hiking the trail a mile to the west.

Trails: There are several lengthy trails here that lead into the nearby wilderness areas. From Cody, you'll find five trailheads along the South

Fork Road: Twin Creek Trailhead at 24 miles, Bobcat Trailhead at 27 miles, Ishawooa Trailhead at 31 miles, Ishawooa Mesa Trailhead at 32 miles, and the Deer Creek Trailhead at 39 miles. In addition, the Boulder Basin Trailhead can be found at the end of FR 480, a parallel road to the south of the campground.

These trailheads are setup for pack animals and most have a corral. The trails are not well documented in guidebooks, but a few are shown on maps. All trails travel through the Washakie Wilderness, while the Ishawooa and Deer Creek trails continue further west into the Teton Wilderness. The Boulder Basin Trail travels southeast for nearly 25 miles to Jack Creek Campground. Be sure to contact the Forest Service for more information on these routes before making an excursion.

Field Notes: This campground also makes a good place for a Sunday picnic. Beautiful scenery, an easily driven road, and a peaceful mountain brook make it very appealing.

Jack Creek Campground

7,600 feet

Location/Map	West of Meeteetse; Page 115
GPS Coordinates	N44° 6.59' W109° 21.05'
Sites/Spur Length	7 sites; Medium spurs—up to 30 feet
Cost	Free
Facilities/Services	Fire rings, picnic tables, pit toilets, bear boxes
Managing Agency	USDA Forest Service (Shoshone National Forest)
Reservations	Not accepted—first come, first served
Season/Usage	Open all year; Low use

Directions: From Meeteetse, go west on HWY 290 for 11 miles. Turn right onto CR 41X (Pitchfork Ranch Road) and follow the Jack Creek signs past a series of forks for 17 additional miles.

Description: While this campground along the Greybull River goes virtually unused, the adjacent trailhead receives plenty of traffic. Campsites are overgrown and show little use. In fact, you may have to poke around in the weeds to even find some of the parking spurs. A little shade—none really—is offered from sparse aspen and willows, but the lack of thick timber opens up views of the rugged countryside.

Fishing: The Greybull River flows eastward from the Absaroka Mountains, right along the campground. Anglers will find trout in this tributary. Remember that bears often roam through the brush that lines the riverbanks.

Trails: The trailhead here offers a trio of pack trails that cover vast swaths of rarely visited country. The Jack Creek Trail heads south toward Haymaker

Jack Creek Campground

Pass and Jacks Peak (11,202 feet) while the Piney Trail heads north toward Piney Pass. The Greybull Trail follows the banks of the Greybull River and works southward for 22 miles to the historical ghost town of Kirwin.

4WD Route: The steep four-wheel drive road that goes up Phelps Mountain offers outstanding views of the Absaroka Mountains. Actually, that's an understatement. The views from the top are among the best you'll find in the state! The road is rough (rocky and steep) at first, but improves up high to reveal top-of-the-world scenery. To find the road, watch for the Phelps Mountain sign near a drill site a few miles east of the campground.

Field Notes: Carter Mountain, the large mountain ridge to the north of the campground, was once devoid of grizzlies, but now hosts a growing population of the large bear. Tom Reed illustrated how the re-emergence of grizzlies impacts this area in his fascinating book titled "Great Wyoming Bear Stories." It's a must read for anybody who has in interest in this animal.

Wood River Campground

7,300 feet

Location/Map	Southwest of Meeteetse; Page 115
GPS Coordinates	N43° 55.92' W109° 7.88'
Sites/Spur Length	5 sites; Medium spurs—up to 30 feet
Cost	Free
Facilities/Services	Fire rings, picnic tables, pit toilets
Managing Agency	USDA Forest Service (Shoshone National Forest)
Reservations	Not accepted—first come, first served
Season/Usage	Open May through September; Low use

Directions: From Meeteetse, take HWY 290 for 7 miles and turn left onto Wood River Road. Drive 16.3 miles to the campground.

Description: Wood River is a miniature camp near the banks of a river with the same name. It is one of two campgrounds that share this scenic mountain valley in the Absaroka Range. The level sites are quickly taken, leaving latecomers with sloping spurs. There is enough shade to thwart complaining, but not a great deal of privacy—none really.

Fishing: Cutthroat and brook trout can be found in Wood River, but the fishing is generally said to be of poor quality. The Sunshine Reservoirs offer better fishing for cutthroat and are easily accessed from HWY 290 just west of the Wood River Road intersection.

Kirwin: Absaroka Ghost Town

Kirwin is a gold-mining ghost town located at 9,200 feet. By 1906, there were more than 200 people living and working there. Then disaster struck.

After nine days of snowfall in the winter of 1907, a massive avalanche rumbled off Brown Mountain, the towering 12,161-foot mountain that stands to the northwest. Three people died in the slide, which proved to be too much for the town. When spring came, the residents left.

Kirwin is reached by driving west of Brown Mountain Campground for 8.5 miles. This is a rough road with some rocky terrain and multiple river fords. The trip can be made in any 4WD vehicle, but only when the creeks are safe enough to cross (usually by mid-summer).

At the townsite, you can tour the old structures by crossing a footbridge near the parking area. If you want to see more, consider walking up the closed road (past a locked gate) to reach the Dollar Cabin and the foundation of Amelia Earhart's home, which was never completed.

Trails: There are two trailheads located on both sides of the campground: the South Fork Wood River Trailhead and the Wood River Trailhead. The trails at both trailheads lead into the Washakie Wilderness. Corrals are provided for pack animals.

4WD Route: A four-wheel drive road to the abandoned town of Kirwin can be found further west at Brown Mountain Campground.

Field Notes: If you camp here and you're not from the Meeteetse area, be prepared to feel like the villain walking through the door of an old western saloon. Well, it may not be quite that extreme, but you certainly get the feeling that all eyes are on you! Admittedly, this only happened once on a busy weekend. Other visits found the camp to be empty.

Brown Mountain Campground

7,600 feet

Location/Map	Southwest of Meeteetse; Page 115
GPS Coordinates	N43° 56.15' W109° 10.75'
Sites/Spur Length	7 sites; Medium spurs—up to 30 feet
Cost	Free
Facilities/Services	Fire rings, picnic tables, pit toilets
Managing Agency	USDA Forest Service (Shoshone National Forest)
Reservations	Not accepted—first come, first served
Season/Usage	Open late May through October; Low to moderate use

Directions: From Meeteetse, take HWY 290 for 7 miles and turn left onto Wood River Road. Drive 18.5 miles to the campground.

Description: This scenic camp features sites that boast of better quality and a little more privacy than its closest neighbor, Wood River Campground. Just like that camp, this one also sits on the banks of Wood River.

Only a couple campsites have good shade, but they all have great views of the surrounding peaks—the highest being Franc's Peak at 13,158 feet. This peak, and a handful of 12,000-footers, create a stunning horizon. Anyone willing to drive an RV or trailer to this remote part of the state will find level campsites and there are a few that are long enough to fit larger rigs.

Fishing: Cutthroat and brook trout can be found in Wood River, but the fishing is generally said to be of poor quality. The Sunshine Reservoirs, easily accessed from HWY 290 just west of the Wood River Road intersection, offer better fishing for cutthroat.

Trails: The Kirwin Trailhead, located 8.5 miles to the west on a 4WD road, offers access to an assortment of trails in the Washakie Wilderness. There are also two trailheads just a few miles east near Wood River Campground.

4WD Route: Follow the Wood River Road west for 8.5 miles to reach Kirwin, an old mining ghost town (see side bar on previous page for more information).

Field Notes: If you appreciate rugged and incredibly wild mountains, this camp at the foot of the Absaroka Range is for you. It's a personal favorite of mine and I'm always reminded that these mountains have yet to be tamed. On my last stay here, the camp's only occupant, I heard animals throughout the night. It was deer and moose that I saw on the riverbanks at dusk, but there were other critters, unknown ones, that were bumping around the campsite in the dark hours.

NORTHWEST AREA 6
The Togwotee Trail

Topographically, the small western town of Dubois (pronounced "dew-boys") is found in an area of transition. The community is located between colorful badlands and towering, glaciated mountains. In the lower elevations, the upper Wind River adds a lush green hue to a semi-arid landscape. Further west, the terrain changes rapidly as dense forests and peaks take hold. In the high country, a band of rocky pinnacles and buttes, called Pinnacle Buttes and Breccia Cliffs, are sure to capture your attention near Togwotee Pass.

Experiencing the geographical change described above is as easy as traveling Wyoming's Centennial Scenic Byway (US Highway 287). Nearly 40 miles in length, the road climbs over Togwotee Pass and crosses the Continental Divide at 9,544 feet. From its apex, the highway descends to Moran near Grand Teton National Park. The state heavily advertises this stretch of road as the Togwotee Trail, named after an Indian subchief who guided expeditions over the pass.

Like much of northwestern Wyoming, this region is rich with wildlife and provides important habitat for big game, especially elk. The grizzly bear is very much at home in this part of the state. Whiskey Mountain, south of Dubois, is home to North America's largest herd of Rocky Mountain bighorn sheep. The National Bighorn Sheep Interpretive Center in town is an excellent place to learn more about these animals.

Any one of the campgrounds along the Togwotee Trail is capable of landing on your list of favorites. From the beautiful Brooks Lake to the incredible scenery surrounding Double Cabin, the campgrounds are radically different but share impressive scenery. If you are traveling through the Dubois area en route to Yellowstone or Grand Teton National Park, consider a stay at one of these campgrounds; disappointed you will not be.

What to Expect: The scenery surrounding these campgrounds is hard to beat and their vicinity to the Tetons and Yellowstone make them even more enticing. Surprisingly, the handful of campgrounds closest to Grand Teton National Park are lightly visited and often overgrown. In this area, the popular camps are those near Togwotee Pass. Grabbing a campsite in one of these gems is usually not a problem, but getting a prime site requires an early arrival and a little bit of luck. Whereas many campgrounds surrounding the national parks are only used for a single night, these camps can, and do, serve as the chief destination. It's not uncommon to have campers pull in for several days or even a week.

If you're planning a stay in the three camps near Togwotee Pass, you should be prepared for cool (cold) nights. At these elevations, it's possible to drop below freezing even during the summer. Nights are typically crisp in these mountains, but stay here much into September and you raise the chances of getting socked by a snowstorm. While on the topic of September, know that most of these camps have their water turned off and trash collection suspended after the Labor Day weekend. Most will then stay open for the hunting season, free of charge, until they are no longer accessible due to snow.

Waterfall at Falls Campground with the Pinnacle Buttes in the background

Area 6: The Togwotee Trail

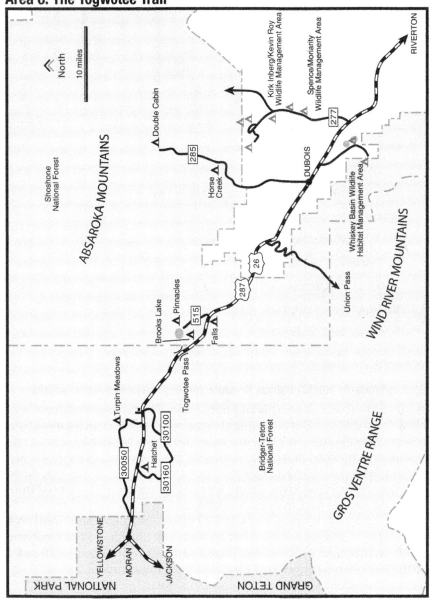

Campgrounds	Sites	Cost	Average Spur Length	Electrical Hookups	Cellular Service (varies by carrier/site)	Reservations Accepted	Page Number
Spence/Moriarity WHMA	-	Free	L				124
Kirk Inberg/Keven Roy WHMA	-	Free	L				124
Whiskey Basin WHMA	-	Free	L				125
Horse Creek Campground	9	$15	M				126
Double Cabin Campground	14	$15	L				127
Falls Campground	54	$15-20	L			✔	129
Pinnacles Campground	21	$15	M				129
Brooks Lake Campground	13	$10	M				130
Turpin Meadows Campground	18	$12	M				132
Hatchet Campground	8	$12	M		▁▃▅		133

Average Spur Length: S = Short (under 30 feet), M = Medium (+-30 feet), L = Long (+-40 feet)
Cellular Service: 1 bar = weak/unreliable signal, 2 bars = low usable signal, 3+ bars = reliable signal for most users

Spence/Moriarity Wildlife Habitat Management Area (Wyoming Game & Fish)

With nearly 40,000 acres, this area northwest of Dubois serves primarily as elk habitat, though all of Wyoming's big game animals (except the mountain goat) can be found here. There are three rivers that hold various trout and mountain whitefish. Two of the three primitive campgrounds—really just parking lots—are found along the larger drainage, the cottonwood-lined East Fork of the Wind River. Except for river access, the area is closed from December to mid-May to protect wildlife.

To reach the camping areas from Dubois, head southeast on HWY 26/287 for 10.5 miles and turn left on East Fork Road (CR 277). Continue north on this road; it's 4 miles to the turnoff for the first camp or 10 miles to the last. There are signs that have area information and maps.

Kirk Inberg/Kevin Roy Wildlife Habitat Management Area (Wyoming Game & Fish)

This large wildlife area is between the Spence/Moriarity Wildlife Management Area (to the south) and the Shoshone National Forest (to the north). This is the doorstep of the Absaroka Mountains where sagebrush grasslands meld with rugged mountain shrublands pocketed with conifer stands. Impressive cottonwood stands flank Bear Creek and Wiggins Fork River, both of which are pretty, photogenic drainages.

Most Game & Fish campgrounds are just gravel parking lots, but the three camps you'll find here resemble true campgrounds. The enveloping beauty and solitude of this backcountry make these appealing choices.

The Lower Bear Creek Campground has four sites in a cottonwood stand along the creek. Along with spacious parking areas, you'll find bear boxes, stone fire rings, a corral, meat-hanging poles, and a pit toilet. Big open parks and foothills surround this shady encampment. Further west, on a rougher road, is the slightly more primitive Wiggins Fork Campground. This site sits in a spruce forest near the creek of the same name. Near the northern boundary at the elk winter headquarters, you'll find the larger Upper Campground. This one has roughly 15 sites with stone fire rings, bear boxes, a corral, pit toilet, and lots of shade from a mixed forest. There is a lot of room to move about here, especially nice if you're bringing a horse trailer.

To reach the camping areas from Dubois, head southeast on HWY 26/287 for 10.5 miles and turn left on East Fork Road (CR 277). Continue north on this road for nearly 10 miles and bear left along Bear Creek. Follow this narrow lane for 3.5 miles to the turnoff for the lower camp or about 6 miles to the upper camp. The turnoff for the Wiggins Fork camp is found between these two—watch for an uphill track on the left and follow it for 2 miles. There are signs that have area information and maps. The area is closed from December to mid-May to protect wildlife.

Whiskey Basin Wildlife Habitat Management Area (Wyoming Game & Fish)

This popular 12,181-acre area supports around 1,000 bighorn sheep, the largest herd in the U.S. and possibly the world (depending on the source). These animals can best be viewed here from late November through April. While the management area is closed to vehicles from December to mid-May, the main road remains open all year.

The management area can be divided into two halves. The lower east side includes sagebrush grasslands, creeks, and a string of glacial lakes that are open to fishing and boating—these include Torrey Lake, Ring Lake, and Trail Lake. The rugged area west of the road rolls up into the Shoshone National Forest. There are Indian petroglyphs on the rocks west of the road (across from the lakes); posts along the road indicate where some of these carvings can be found.

There are five primitive campgrounds here, all of which are open, unshaded parking lots. The first three are located next to the lakes and the last two are located further west near the road's end. You'll find a few stone fire rings, pit toilets, and an occasional table.

To reach Whiskey Basin from Dubois, head southeast on HWY 26/287 for 4 miles to Trail Lake Road (CR 411). Follow this gravel road to reach the camping area of your choice. The road ends at 8.5 miles at a trailhead next to the last camping area.

Horse Creek Campground

7,700 feet

Location/Map	North of Dubois; Page 123
GPS Coordinates	N43° 39.93' W109° 38.17'
Sites/Spur Length	9 sites; Medium spurs—up to 30 feet
Cost	$15
Facilities/Services	Fire rings, picnic tables, water, pit toilets, trash containers, bear boxes
Managing Agency	USDA Forest Service (Shoshone National Forest); A host is often present
Reservations	Not accepted—first come, first served
Season/Usage	Open June until snow closure; Moderate use

Directions: From Dubois, head north on FR 285 (Horse Creek Road) for 11 miles.

Description: This campground is situated along a creek in the scenic foothills of the Absaroka Range. Although it doesn't share the sense of remoteness that Double Cabin Campground possesses (16 miles to the north), it is much easier to reach. Shade from a coniferous forest exists, but the camp has a predominately open feel to it. Most camping rigs can fit in the long, level parking spurs and a few vacancies can be expected. This is grizzly bear country.

4WD Routes: The surrounding area has several worthwhile 4WD roads that explore the badlands to the east (FR 506), the lower mountains to the west (FR 511), and a few very cool lakes to the north (FR 510 and FR 504). Getting a Shoshone National Forest map is a good idea. I also detail these routes in my Wyoming Backroads book.

Fishing: Horse Creek is adjacent to the campground. Another option—great for kids—is tiny Scott's Pond, a few miles south on FR 285.

Picnicking: A picnic area is located at the campground. There are also nice spots along the creek.

Field Notes: You can expect some decent traffic in and around this camp throughout the day as Horse Creek Road is a major trunk route into these mountains. The setting along the creek is hard to beat. September is a nice time to stay, but be aware that the water is turned off and trash is no longer collected. As with most other camps that remain open with no services, no nightly fee is required.

Double Cabin Campground

8,000 feet

Location/Map	North of Dubois; Page 123
GPS Coordinates	N43° 48.48' W109° 33.66'
Sites/Spur Length	14 sites; Long spurs—over 30 feet (32-foot or shorter is suggested)
Cost	$15
Facilities/Services	Fire rings, picnic tables, water, pit toilets, trash containers, bear boxes
Managing Agency	USDA Forest Service (Shoshone National Forest); A host is often present
Reservations	Not accepted—first come, first served
Season/Usage	Open June until snow closure; Moderate use

Directions: From Dubois, head north on FR 285 (Horse Creek Road) for 27 miles. The last half of this drive is narrow and bumpy.

Description: Double Cabin is prized for its wild character. The campground is located over two-dozen miles from the nearest highway and is surrounded on three sides by some of the wildest country in the Lower 48. The panoramic views of the Absaroka Range that ring this valley are nothing short of spectacular. The campsites, some being pull-throughs, are roomy and reside in an evergreen forest near the confluence of Wiggins Creek and Frontier Creek. So what are the drawbacks? First, many of the trees in the area have died. Second, it's a long, bumpy drive that you may not want to tow a trailer over (though many do). While some of the spurs are longer, the Forest Service does not suggest units over 32 feet. Remember that this is grizzly bear country.

Towering mounts and wide creeks at Double Cabin Campground

Fishing: Anglers can flyfish both the Wiggins Creek and Frontier Creek drainages.

Trails: A wilderness trailhead is located in the meadow north of the campground. The Frontier Creek Trail and Wiggins Fork Trail lead into the Washakie Wilderness, following creeks of the same names while taking opposing sides of a large mountain. Conversely, the Indian Point Trail heads south through the Shoshone National Forest toward Bear Pass. This is beautiful and big country, but hard to cover by foot. Horsepacking is popular in these wild parts as these animals can handle the labor that is required to traverse such expansive country.

Dispersed Camping: The primitive campsites in the adjacent meadow often hold more campers than the campground itself.

Field Notes: This is a special place in the Rocky Mountains. If you like to escape into the backcountry and put some space between yourself and the modernized world, look no further than this out-of-the-way secret.

Falls Campground

8,300 feet

Location/Map	Northwest of Dubois; Page 123
GPS Coordinates	N43° 42.52' W109° 58.33'
Sites/Spur Length	54 sites; Long spurs—over 30 feet
Cost	$15 or $20 with electric hookups
Facilities/Services	Fire rings, picnic tables, water, pit toilets, trash containers, bear boxes
Managing Agency	USDA Forest Service (Shoshone National Forest); A host is often present
Reservations	Not accepted—first come, first served
Season/Usage	Open June until mid-September; Moderate use

Directions: From Dubois, take HWY 26/287 northwest for 23 miles to the camp on the left.

Description: Most tourists speed past this area as they zip over Togwotee Pass to get to Wyoming's name-brand attractions. What a mistake. This camp is a gem that deserves an overnight stay, or at the very least, a visit to stop and stretch your legs. Long, level, and shady sites sit along two nicely wooded loops. Some sites have electric service and a few of these are double sites. The campground derives its name from an impressive waterfall that tumbles down a steep slope near the camp's entrance.

Natural Attractions: The Breccia Cliffs are an awesome display of nature. An interpretive sign near the campground's entrance explains these rocky pinnacles. You'll also find a short trail that edges a steep cliff to overlook a tall waterfall. Follow the path to its end, and you'll be rewarded with a magnificent overlook of western Wyoming.

Scenic driving: HWY 26/287, between Grand Teton National Park to a point west of Dubois, is designated as Wyoming's Centennial Scenic Byway. This 39-mile paved route crosses the Continental Divide with an overlook near Togwotee Pass (9,658 feet). Most of the mountain scenery north of the road belongs to the Teton and Washakie wilderness areas, and to the south, the Gros Ventre Range.

Fishing: Brooks Lake Creek, the stream flowing over the waterfall, is said to provide fly-fishing opportunities though access is minimal here.

Field Notes: Considering scenery, ease of access, and campsite facilities, I place this camp among Wyoming's best. It was late summer when I last stayed here and I was awakened by the sound of elk bugling. It was just 23 degrees the next morning.

Pinnacles Campground
9,050 feet

Location/Map	Northwest of Dubois; Page 123
GPS Coordinates	N43° 45.13' W109° 59.73'
Sites/Spur Length	21 sites; Medium spurs—up to 30 feet (only hard-sided units allowed)
Cost	$15
Facilities/Services	Fire rings, picnic tables, water, pit toilets, trash containers, bear boxes
Managing Agency	USDA Forest Service (Shoshone National Forest); A host is often present
Reservations	Not accepted—first come, first served
Season/Usage	Open mid-June through September; High use

Directions: From Dubois, head west on HWY 26/287 for 23 miles to FR 515. Follow signs along the washboarded road for anther 5 miles to the camp on the right.

Description: The photogenic pinnacles that dominate this area's landscape are often seen in Wyoming's tourism publications and for good reason. These buttes are well deserving of all the pictures you'll surely take of them. Add some summer foliage, early-morning fog, and a steady lake, and you're bound to produce a stunning photograph of postcard quality.

The camp sits above the shores of Brooks Lake, just a short distance from another campground here that shares the lake's name. You'll find a mix of both back-in and pull-through sites in a forest of light, thinned evergreens. Grizzly bears frequent this area, so only hard-sided camping units—no tents or canvas pop-ups—are allowed. Bring your own supply of water as it is sometimes not available.

Scenic driving: HWY 26/287 between Grand Teton National Park to a point west of Dubois, is designated as Wyoming's Centennial Scenic Byway. This 39-mile paved route crosses the Continental Divide, with an overlook near Togwotee Pass (9,658 feet). Most of the mountain scenery north of the road belongs to the Teton and Washakie wilderness areas, and to the south, the Gros Ventre Range.

Fishing/Boating: There are few better places in Wyoming to paddle a canoe than the scenic waters of Brooks Lake. A boat ramp is located near Brooks Lake Campground. The lake holds rainbow trout, mackinaw, and splake.

Trails: A trailhead is located at nearby Brooks Lake Campground.

Picnicking: A picnic area is located at the campground.

Field Notes: The prime sites are those that overlook the lake, but they also catch more wind. The last time I was here, a camp host told me that they had at least 9 grizzlies in the campground that season.

Brooks Lake Campground — 9,050 feet

Location/Map	Northwest of Dubois; Page 123
GPS Coordinates	N43° 45.02' W110° 0.31'
Sites/Spur Length	13 sites; Medium spurs—up to 30 feet (only hard-sided units allowed)
Cost	$10
Facilities/Services	Fire rings, picnic tables, pit toilets, trash containers, bear boxes, boat ramp
Managing Agency	USDA Forest Service (Shoshone National Forest)
Reservations	Not accepted—first come, first served
Season/Usage	Open mid-June through September; High use

Directions: From Dubois, head west on HWY 26/287 for 23 miles to FR 515. Follow signs along the washboarded road for another 5 miles to the camp on the left.

Description: This compact campground is just a short jaunt from Pinnacles Campground and shares the same lake and stunning views. It's worth looking at both camps to get a broader range of site choices. Due to grizzly bear activity, only hard-sided camping units are allowed. The mature evergreens that used to cover this scenic encampment were removed due to a widespread spruce beetle infestation so you'll get plenty of welcome sunshine. At over 9,000 feet in elevation, the summer temperatures at this mountain lake stay cool and the nights are chilly.

Scenic driving: HWY 26/287, between Grand Teton National Park to a point west of Dubois, is designated as Wyoming's Centennial Scenic Byway. This 39-mile paved route crosses the Continental Divide, with an overlook near Togwotee Pass (9,658 feet). Most of the mountain scenery north of the road belongs to the Teton and Washakie wilderness areas, and to the south, the Gros Ventre Range.

Fishing/Boating: Anglers will find rainbow trout, mackinaw, and splake. There are few better places in Wyoming to paddle a canoe than the scenic waters of Brooks Lake. A boat ramp is located at the camp.

Trails: Pinnacle Trailhead is found on the southern shoreline of the lake near the camp. From the trailhead, a path rounds the western shoreline of the lake before splitting into multiple routes. The left fork leads about a mile to Upper and Lower Jade Lakes. The right fork will take you to a junction within a half-mile. Stay north and you'll follow the drainage roughly 2 miles to Bear Cub Pass and Upper Brooks Lakes. If you take the east-bearing fork, you'll be on the Dunoir Trail, which travels over Bonneville Pass and across many miles through the Absaroka Mountains.

A separate trail that leads to Bonneville Pass can be started from a trailhead that is located on a spur road just off of FR 515.

Picnicking: There is a picnic area here along the lake's shoreline.

Pinnacle Buttes near Brooks Lake and Pinnacles Campground

Field Notes: You can't visit this campground without noticing the huge log cabin complex next door. It's the Brooks Lake Lodge, an upscale guest ranch that offers everything that a typical guest ranch does... and more. For the price to stay there just one night, you could stay in the campground for over a month.

Turpin Meadows Campground

6,930 feet

Location/Map	East of Grand Teton National Park; Page 123
GPS Coordinates	N43° 51.39' W110° 15.91'
Sites/Spur Length	18 sites; Medium spurs—up to 30 feet (only hard-sided units allowed)
Cost	$12
Facilities/Services	Fire rings, picnic tables, water, pit toilets, trash containers, bear boxes
Managing Agency	USDA Forest Service (Bridger-Teton National Forest); A host is often present
Reservations	Not accepted—first come, first served
Season/Usage	Open late May through September (or later); Moderate use

Directions: From Moran, go east on HWY 26/287 for 3.5 miles and turn north onto Buffalo Valley Road. Follow this paved road for 10 miles to the campground's short access road.

If traveling from Dubois, go west on HWY 26/287 for 42 miles to Fourmile Meadow. Turn north onto FR 30050 and drive 4.5 miles to the campground's access road.

Turpin Meadows Campground

Description: This is the place to go if you have horses and want to explore the Teton Wilderness. The campground has few trees but is surrounded by dense forest. Open grassy sites and extended parking areas help accommodate stock trailers. There are hitching posts at each site. The area sees modest use during the summer, as well as in the fall when hunters hope to catch the elk migrating from Yellowstone to the National Elk Refuge.

Fishing: Buffalo Fork is considered to be a good fly-fishing stream for cutthroat trout.

Trails: The two main routes departing from the Turpin Meadows area include the Clear Creek Trail and North Buffalo Fork Trail. Corrals are located nearby. Remember the Teton Wilderness has many miles of crisscrossing trails so you'll want to be properly prepared and equipped if you choose to navigate this wild area.

Field Notes: The trailhead and campground seem to be becoming more popular each year with both hikers and horse campers. While the Teton Range can't be seen from the campsites themselves, the high peaks can be seen by walking out to the main road.

Hatchet Campground

6,950 feet

Location/Map	East of Grand Teton National Park; Page 123
GPS Coordinates	N43° 49.47' W110° 21.29'
Sites/Spur Length	8 sites; Medium spurs—up to 30 feet
Cost	$12
Facilities/Services	Fire rings, picnic tables, water, pit toilets, trash containers, bear boxes, cellular service
Managing Agency	USDA Forest Service (Bridger-Teton National Forest)
Reservations	Not accepted—first come, first served
Season/Usage	Open June through September; Moderate use

Directions: From Moran near Grand Teton National Park, drive east on HWY 26/287 for almost 9 miles. Watch carefully on the right, as there is not a large sign like most campgrounds. The campground is just west of the Black Rock Ranger station. If traveling from Dubois, drive west on HWY 26/287 for 47 miles.

Description: Just ten minutes from Grand Teton National Park and the turnoff to Yellowstone, this campground offers the last public campsites before you reach the bustling parks themselves. It's a compact camp and some of the spurs may be tricky to maneuver into. Sites are pinched into a pine forest, offering a secluded feel, but road noise is a constant. The gorgeous peaks of the Teton Range cannot be seen from camp, but are visible from the highway.

Scenic driving: HWY 26/287 between Grand Teton National Park to a point west of Dubois, is designated as Wyoming's Centennial Scenic Byway. This 39-mile paved route crosses the Continental Divide and there is an overlook near Togwotee Pass (9,658 feet). Most of the mountain scenery north of the road belongs to the Teton and Washakie wilderness areas, and to the south, the Gros Ventre Range.

Prefer backroads to highways? From the campground, FR 30160 (Flagstaff Road) travels south through the Bridger-Teton National Forest for 6 miles to Sagebrush Flats, 7 miles to Spread Creek, and 8 miles to Lily Lake. From the lake, the road continues back to the highway, 8 miles farther. Turn left when you reach the highway and drive back to the camp to complete the 24-mile loop. Along the way, you'll find numerous secondary roads that are suitable for four-wheeling or ATV riding.

Picnicking: A developed picnic area is located several miles east of the campground on HWY 26/287.

Field Notes: Most people zip past this campground as they hurry to the Tetons and Yellowstone. However, you should consider it if you're looking to save a little money, be less crowded, or need a close-by place to stay before trying to snag a campsite in the national park.

Black bear triplets cross the highway near Hatchet Campground

NORTH - NORTHEAST
Bighorns and Black Hills

The north central and northeast region of Wyoming is a true treasure, one that is often discovered accidentally by unsuspecting motorists heading to Yellowstone. The land here is very diverse and ranges from low grassland prairie to snowy mountains. In the northeast corner, you're sure to be intrigued by Devils Tower near the Black Hills National Forest. Further west, in the Bighorn Mountains, you'll discover some of the best natural areas that the state has to offer for outdoor recreation. Whether you are going hiking, fishing, four-wheeling, or just want to spend a weekend in the mountains, the Bighorn National Forest has what you need. In fact, don't be surprised if you find this region on your next vacation itinerary rather than the more well-known areas of the state.

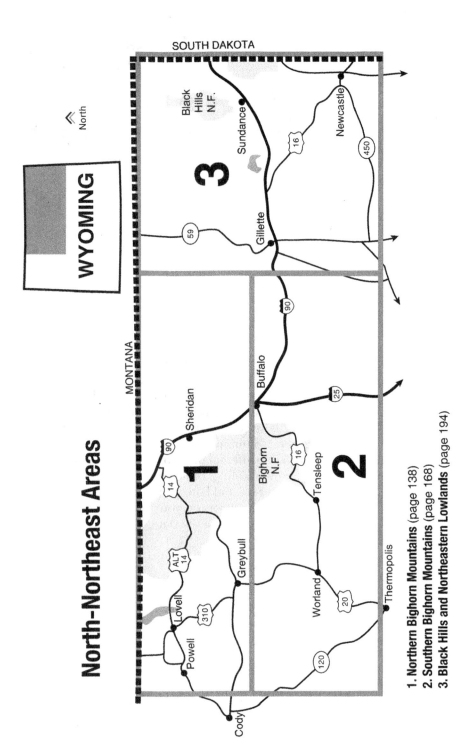

Privately-owned Campgrounds and RV Dump Stations

This section includes the general locations of privately-owned RV parks. For contact information and addresses for these businesses, look online or check out the campground directory on the Wyoming Office of Tourism website at travelwyoming.com.

Area 1: Northern Bighorn Mountains
On the east side of the Bighorn Mountains, you'll find privately-owned campgrounds in or near the towns of Sheridan and Dayton. These are easily reached from Interstate 90. On the west side of the range, RV parks can be found in Lovell (on HWY 14 ALT) or Greybull (on HWY 14). The small town of Shell, east of Greybull, also has an RV park.

Area 2: Southern Bighorn Mountains
Buffalo, on the east side of the Bighorns, has several private campgrounds. For a more remote feeling, check out the RV park at Lake DeSmet, just a few miles north of town. On the west side of the mountains, look in Tensleep and in Worland, a little further west on HWY 16.

Area 3: Black Hills and Northeastern Lowlands
Gillette, the largest town in the region, has several RV parks in or near the city limits. Closer to the Black Hills, there are campgrounds in Sundance and a pair at the entrance of Devils Tower National Monument. Keyhole State Park has private camping available in Pine Haven and also near the marina.

RV Dump Stations
The locations below include public RV dump stations. Additional dump stations can often be found at private campgrounds and large gas stations.
- Keyhole State Park
- HWY 16: Leigh Creek near Powder River Pass
- HWY 14: Burgess Junction
- Washington City Park, Basin, WY
- I-90: Sheridan Information Center, Sheridan, WY

AREA 1 NORTH - NORTHEAST
Northern Bighorn Mountains

The Bighorn Mountains stretch from the Montana border to central Wyoming. The lower elevations in this range begin at just 4,000 feet, but rise sharply to a high point of 13,167 feet at Cloud Peak, the namesake landmark for the surrounding Cloud Peak Wilderness. Encompassing the wilderness area and occupying much of the mountain range is the Bighorn National Forest, which derives its name from bighorn sheep that were once abundant in the area, but are now found in small numbers.

The Bighorn National Forest is roughly 80 miles long (from north to south) and 30 miles wide (from east to west). Add 20 to 40 miles to each of those numbers and you'll get the size of the mountain range itself.

When you visit the Bighorns, the difference in the northern half and the southern half becomes obvious. The southern area is dominated by lodgepole pine forests and rocky mountain domes. The northern region has dense forests and peaks, too, but it is the open mountain meadows where trees are confined to tiny pockets that characterize the area.

Wildlife is in abundance throughout the Bighorn Mountains, but some species have had help. Officials have focused on strengthening the small population of bighorn sheep by transporting some of these animals from Oregon to Devils Canyon. Moose were transplanted from Jackson Hole in 1948. Subsequent transplants in 1950 and 1987 have helped the herd grow to a healthy population today. While moose are distributed throughout the mountain range, you can improve your chances of viewing these massive animals by scanning willow bottoms and marshy areas. It is common to see them crossing or feeding along the roadway. Black bears are found throughout the mountains, but mostly roam the northern half of the range. Grizzly bears are not currently present here though a sighting would not necessarily be surprising as they continue to expand their range. Wolves, however, have been found in the Bighorns in recent years.

As a whole, the Bighorns are very accessible mountains. The northern region has two major highways, as well as a good network of forest roads and trails. From Sheridan, the 45-mile Bighorn Scenic Byway (US Highway 14), utilizes a number of a steep switchbacks to climb into the high country. At the top at Burgess Junction, the route heads south and crosses the crest of the range before it descends through beautiful Shell Canyon. If you find yourself on this route, be sure to stop at Shell Falls. Hydrologists estimate that the falls dump 3,588 gallons of water every second.

The second route, the Medicine Wheel Passage (US Highway 14 ALT), makes an even steeper descent from the range, but not before passing the Medicine Wheel, a rock layout of historical significance. It's easy driving to the Medicine Wheel from the east, but soon beyond, the grade exceeds 10% making the route less desirable for those with trailers and RVs.

What to Expect: Most campgrounds in the northern Bighorns are at high elevations and it's common to find snowdrifts in shady areas. Summer days bring mild, pleasant temperatures as well as fast-moving afternoon thunderstorms. Nights can be chilly, but are usually comfortable.

It's easy to find campsites throughout the Bighorns unless it's a holiday weekend—reservations are best for those weeks. If you're looking for quiet, check out the campgrounds along the highways. Camps located further back on dirt and gravel roads get heavy ATV traffic.

Shell Falls, Bighorn National Forest

Area 1: Northern Bighorn Mountains

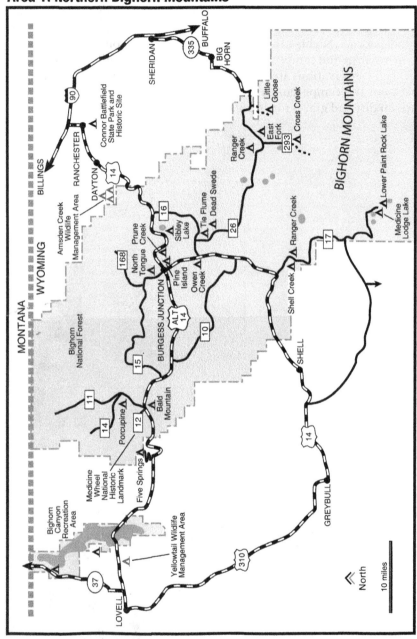

Campgrounds	Sites	Cost	Average Spur Length	Electrical Hookups	Cellular Service (varies by carrier/site)	Reservations Accepted	Page Number
Connor Battlefield State Park and Historic Site	20	$10-17	L		▂▃▅		142
Amsden Creek WHMA	3	Free	S				143
Sibley Lake Campground	25	$18-23	L	✔		✔	143
Prune Creek Campground	21	$18	L			✔	145
Pine Island Group Picnic Area and Campground	1	$75-145	L			✔	146
North Tongue Campground	12	$17	L			✔	147
Bald Mountain Campground	15	$17	L			✔	148
Porcupine Campground	16	$17	L			✔	149
Five Springs Falls Campground	19	$7	M		▂▃▅		151
Bighorn Canyon National Recreation Area	48	$15-25	L	✔	▂▃▅		152
Yellowtail WHMA	11	Free	L				154
Owen Creek Campground	8	$17	L			✔	154
Tie Flume Campground	27	$18	L			✔	155
Dead Swede Campground	21	$18	L			✔	156
Ranger Creek Campground	11	$17	M				157
East Fork Campground	12	$16	M				158
Little Goose Campground	3	Free	Tent				160
Cross Creek Campground	3	Free	Tent				161
Shell Creek Campground	15	$17	L			✔	163
Ranger Creek Campground	10	$17-145	M			✔	164
Medicine Lodge Lake Campground	8	$16	M				165
Lower Paint Rock Lake Campground	4	$16-32	M				167

Average Spur Length: S = Short (under 30 feet), M = Medium (+-30 feet), L = Long (+-40 feet)
Cellular Service: 1 bar = weak/unreliable signal, 2 bars = low usable signal, 3+ bars = reliable signal for most users

Connor Battlefield State Park & Historic Site   3,800 feet

Location/Map	Northwest of Sheridan; Page 140
GPS Coordinates	N44° 54.27' W107° 9.8'
Sites/Spur Length	20 sites; Long spurs—over 30 feet
Cost	$10 state residents, $17 nonresidents
Facilities/Services	Fire rings, grills, picnic tables, water, restrooms, pit toilets, trash containers, playground, cellular service
Managing Agency	Wyoming State Parks, Historic Sites & Trails
Reservations	Not accepted—first come, first served
Season/Usage	Open May through October; Moderate use

Directions: From Sheridan, travel north on I-90 and take Exit 9 at Ranchester. Follow HWY 14 into Ranchester and follow the signs to the campground on the south side of town.

Description: This beautiful camp is found in an oxbow of the smooth-surfaced Tongue River. The river nourishes large cottonwoods that shade the campground. Campers with large rigs are sure to love this city park-like campground because it has paved access from the Interstate and long, level parking spurs. It is often very quite during midweek, but weekends do see an increase in traffic.

So where does the battlefield reference come from? Its history dates back to 1865 when general Patrick E. Connor led a force into a battle that killed 65 Indians, destroyed their shelters and supplies, and stole over a

Connor Battlefield State Park

thousand ponies. The natives claimed the lives of eight troopers during the fight and three more in a subsequent attack two days later. It's hard to believe such a vicious event occurred in such a peaceful-looking park.

Fishing: Anglers can fly-fish for a couple species of trout (mostly cutthroat) and whitefish in the Tongue River.

Picnicking: The campground doubles as a picnic site, and a good one.

Field Notes: If the history of this area is of interest to you, be sure to visit the Fort Phil Kearny State Historic Site between Sheridan and Buffalo. Another historic site in the region (about an hour north of Sheridan on I-90) is the Little Bighorn Battlefield, the location of "Custer's Last Stand."

Amsden Creek Wildlife Habitat Management Area (Wyoming Game & Fish)

During the winter, this scenic area at the foot of the Bighorn Mountains serves as winter habitat for around 300 elk. In the summer, you'll find primitive campsites at three parking areas. There are stone fire rings and a few pit toilets in and near the parking areas. The area is closed to vehicles from November through May. No human presence is allowed between mid-November through April.

To reach the campsites from the north side of Dayton, follow CR 92 west for 2.3 miles to a fork. To reach Amsden Meadows Campground, bear right onto CR 90 and drive 1.5 miles to another fork. Stay left and drive less than a mile to reach the parking area. To reach the more scenic camps along the Tongue River, stay left on CR 92 (from the first junction) and drive less than a mile to Tongue River Campground, near the mouth of a canyon. Continue another 1.5 miles into the canyon to reach Tongue Canyon Campground, which is surrounded by towering ridges.

Sibley Lake Campground
8,000 feet

Location/Map	West of Sheridan; Page 140
GPS Coordinates	N44° 45.57' W107° 26.4'
Sites/Spur Length	25 sites; Long spurs—over 30 feet
Cost	$18 or $23 with electric hookups
Facilities/Services	Electric hookups (limited), fire rings, grills, picnic tables, water, pit toilets, trash containers, boat ramp
Managing Agency	USDA Forest Service (Bighorn National Forest); A host is often present
Reservations	Call 877-444-6777 or visit www.recreation.gov
Season/Usage	Open late May through late September; High use

Directions: From Sheridan, drive north on I-90 and take Exit 9 at Ranchester. From Ranchester, travel west on HWY 14 for 26 miles to the campground's short access road.

Description: Sibley Lake is the premier Forest Service campground in the northern half of this mountain range. The camp is divided between two loops. The larger one includes 15 campsites with electric hookups. Sites are nicely spaced and are covered by lodgepole pines. Neighboring Sibley Lake is just a short walk away. If fishing doesn't lure you to the water's edge, take a seat on the dock and let time pass by unhurriedly. There are interpretive signs and a marker near the Sibley Lake dam, which was built in 1937 by the Civilian Conservation Corps.

Scenic Driving: The Bighorn Scenic Byway (HWY 14) is a 45-mile stretch between Sheridan and Greybull. Shell Falls is worth a visit on the west side. Also of interest is Sand Turn, a turnout on the eastern side that overlooks Wyoming's plains. The steep drop from this point is a launch spot for local paragliders.

Fishing/Boating: Cutthroat and brook trout are common, but Sibley Lake mostly holds stocked rainbows. Designated parking for anglers is provided as well as a ramp for launching nonmotorized craft.

Trails: A cross-country ski trail runs from the lake to FR 16 near the Black Mountain Lookout. It's 2.5 miles and a difference of 450 feet of elevation to the road. Head on up to the mountain's summit and you can add another 2 miles and 1,500 feet of elevation to your journey.

Picnicking: There is a picnic area near the lake's inlet.

Field Notes: Reservations are strongly recommended to get a site here.

Sibley Lake

Prune Creek Campground

7,700 feet

Location/Map	West of Sheridan; Page 140
GPS Coordinates	N44° 46.19' W107° 28.15'
Sites/Spur Length	21 sites; Long spurs—over 30 feet
Cost	$18
Facilities/Services	Fire rings, grills, picnic tables, water, pit toilets, trash containers
Managing Agency	USDA Forest Service (Bighorn National Forest); A host is often present
Reservations	Call 877-444-6777 or visit www.recreation.gov
Season/Usage	Open mid-June through late September; High use

Directions: From Sheridan, drive north on I-90 and take Exit 9 at Ranchester. Travel west on HWY 14 for 28 miles.

Description: Located just off the highway, this pleasant, easily-accessed campground is located at the point where Prune Creek flows into the larger South Tongue River. The smaller creek separates two loops of grassy sites. Long and level parking spurs fit large RVs and trailers. Lodgepole pines stretch overhead and willows line the stream banks where moose forage.

ATV Trail: A 6.1-mile ATV trail can be found by driving west to the Pine Island Group Area. Start here by following FR 193 to the southeast. At 1.7 miles, the road turns into an ATV trail where it parallels the South Tongue River. The trail ends at FR 26 to the south.

Scenic Driving: The Bighorn Scenic Byway (HWY 14) is a 45-mile stretch between Sheridan and Greybull. Shell Falls is worth a visit on the west side. Also of interest is Sand Turn, a turnout on the eastern side that overlooks Wyoming's plains. The steep drop from this point is a launch spot for local paragliders.

Wildlife Viewing: Watch for moose as they feed in the willows along the Prune Creek and South Tongue River drainages.

Fishing: Rainbow and brook trout can be found in the South Tongue River next to the camp. The nearby ATV trail provides good access.

Picnicking: The Pine Island Picnic Area is located 1 mile west of the campground on HWY 14.

Field Notes: This is one of my personal favorites. On one stay at this camp, a game warden was pursuing a bull moose that had a volleyball net caught in its paddles—he invited us along. We watched as he darted the moose, removed the net, and then woke the animal up. Back at camp, we had another moose in our streamside campsite for most of the evening.

Pine Island Group Picnic Area & Campground   7,700 feet

Location/Map	West of Sheridan; Page 140
GPS Coordinates	N44° 46.74' W107° 28.62'
Sites/Spur Length	1 group site; Long spurs—over 30 feet
Cost	$75-$145
Facilities/Services	Electric outlet, picnic shelter, fire rings, grills, picnic tables, water, pit toilets, trash containers
Managing Agency	USDA Forest Service (Bighorn National Forest)
Reservations	Call 877-444-6777 or visit www.recreation.gov
Season/Usage	Open June until mid-September; Moderate use

Directions: From Sheridan, drive north on I-90 and take Exit 9 at Ranchester. Travel west on HWY 14 for 29 miles.

Description: This group area is available as a day-use picnic area or as an overnight campground for up to 150 campers. The facility is located immediately off the highway along the South Tongue River. A large parking area will hold several trailers or RVs, but tents are the better choice for large groups. Aside from the group shelter, there is a volleyball court and horseshoe pits.

ATV Trail: A 6.1-mile ATV trail can be found by driving west to the Pine Island Group Area. Start here by following FR 193 to the southeast. At 1.7 miles, the road turns into an ATV trail where it parallels the South Tongue River. The trail ends at FR 26 to the south.

Scenic Driving: The Bighorn Scenic Byway (HWY 14) is a 45-mile stretch between Sheridan and Greybull. Shell Falls is worth a visit on the west side. Also of interest is Sand Turn, a turnout on the eastern side that overlooks Wyoming's plains. The steep drop from this point is a favorite for local paragliders.

Wildlife Viewing: Watch for moose as they feed in the willows along the South Tongue River.

Fishing: Rainbow and brook trout can be found in South Tongue River next to the camp. The nearby ATV trail provides good access.

Trails: Besides the fishing paths that parallel South Tongue River, there is a short interpretive trail at Burgess Junction near the old visitor center.

Picnicking: The Pine Island Picnic Area is located 1 mile west of the campground on HWY 14.

Field Notes: The accessibility of this facility comes at a cost; it's not that private or quiet. You'll get plenty of noise from the adjacent highway as well as trucks that are parking here to unload ATVs. Even so, this is a decent place to hold a large gathering.

North Tongue Campground

7,900 feet

Location/Map	West of Sheridan; Page 140
GPS Coordinates	N44° 46.87' W107° 31.99'
Sites/Spur Length	12 sites; Long spurs—over 30 feet
Cost	$17
Facilities/Services	Fire rings, grills, picnic tables, water, pit toilets, trash containers
Managing Agency	USDA Forest Service (Bighorn National Forest); A host is often present
Reservations	Call 877-444-6777 or visit www.recreation.gov
Season/Usage	Open mid-June through late September; Moderate use

Directions: From Sheridan, drive north on I-90 and take Exit 9 to HWY 14. Travel west on HWY 14 for 32 miles, bearing right on HWY 14 ALT. Just past the junction, turn onto FR 15 and drive a mile to the camp.

Description: Tucked into the shadows of fir, spruce, and lodgepole pine, this nicely developed camp stands above the North Tongue River. The campground's central location is very convenient for making day trips around the northern Bighorns. There is a higher and lower loop, the higher feeling more quiet and separate. Longer-sized trailers and motor homes will be able to fit into the level sites and a pair of pull-throughs is also available.

Scenic Driving: The Medicine Wheel Passage (HWY 14 ALT) is a 25-mile section between Burgess Junction and Lovell; it passes the Medicine Wheel National Historic Landmark. As this road descends into Lovell, you'll encounter steep grades exceeding 10% making it a less desirable choice if you have a cumbersome trailer or RV. The steepest grade is about 10 miles long. Use a low gear and use your brakes gently. Braking just a few times with long and steady pressure on the pedal is better than braking frequently with harder pressure. The highway is closed between November and May.

The Bighorn Scenic Byway (HWY 14) is a 45-mile stretch between Sheridan and Greybull. Shell Falls is worth a visit on the west side. Also of interest is Sand Turn, a turnout on the eastern side that overlooks Wyoming's plains. The steep drop from this point is a favorite for local paragliders.

Fishing: Anglers will love fishing the various mountain streams that flow across the area including the adjacent North Tongue River. Cutthroat trout are the most dominant species, but some brook can also be caught. Most fish are under a foot in length, but there may be some surprises.

Trails: There is a short interpretive trail near the old visitor center at Burgess Junction.

4WD/ATV Routes: There are numerous 4WD roads to the west and north of this campground. Some of the longer routes include FR 178 near Little Bald Mountain and FR 149 at Dry Fork Ridge. Other options include an ascent of Skull Ridge and a loop around Freeze Out Point. Obtain a Forest map to see all your choices.

Picnicking: There is a picnic area located at Burgess Junction as well as another (also called Burgess) found a half-mile north of the campground in a scenic nook. The one north of the campground is worth a visit, even if you aren't going for a picnic.

Field Notes: You'll find this well-timbered camp to be less windy than many others in the northern Bighorns.

Bald Mountain Campground 9,100 feet

Location/Map	West of Sheridan; Page 140
GPS Coordinates	N44° 48.48' W107° 51.58'
Sites/Spur Length	15 sites; Long spurs—over 30 feet
Cost	$17
Facilities/Services	Fire rings, grills, picnic tables, water, pit toilets, trash containers
Managing Agency	USDA Forest Service (Bighorn National Forest)
Reservations	Call 877-444-6777 or visit www.recreation.gov
Season/Usage	Open mid-June through late September; Moderate use

Directions: From Sheridan, drive north on I-90 and take Exit 9 to HWY 14. Travel west on HWY 14 for 32 miles, bearing right on HWY 14 ALT. Drive 20 miles to the camp on the left. If traveling from Lovell, head east on HWY 14 ALT for 35 miles.

Description: Bald Mountain is one of the highest campgrounds in the northern Bighorns, resulting in broad views and cold temperatures. Fir trees pocket the high mountain meadows found here. The campground is tucked into the east side of one of these tiny stands to keep you sheltered from the cold breeze that often sweeps across this high country. Campsites are strung out along the campground road and, strangely, some share parking spurs. Some of the campground's namesakes include a creek that flows through the camp and the nearby summit that rises to an elevation of 10,042 feet. Hitching posts and a boarding ramp are located at the camp's entrance.

Historical Attractions/Walking: The nearby Medicine Wheel National Historic Landmark is worth a visit. To get to the site from the camp, travel west for 1 mile and turn onto FR 12, a short but narrow and steep gravel road that leads to a parking area. For more information, refer to page 150.

Scenic Driving: The Medicine Wheel Passage (HWY 14 ALT) is a 25-mile section between Burgess Junction and Lovell; it passes the Medicine Wheel National Historic Landmark. As this road descends into Lovell, you'll encounter steep grades exceeding 10% making it a less desirable choice if you have a cumbersome trailer or RV. The steepest grade is about 10 miles long. It was here where one of my brake pads broke and smoke began billowing from the wheelwell. Use a low gear and use your brakes gently. Braking just a few times with long and steady pressure on the pedal is better than braking frequently with harder pressure. The highway is closed between November and May.

Roughly 6 miles east of the campground, you'll find FR 10, a 22-mile backcountry route that crosses the crest of the Bighorns and ends at HWY 14 south of Owen Creek Campground. Highlights include good views of mountain peaks, high meadows, and summer snowdrifts. The road can be muddy and rutted, but is easily traveled in dry weather.

Field Notes: At least half of the sites in this campground are consistently found vacant. Reservations are not typically needed unless you really need to guarantee a spot.

Porcupine Campground

8,800 feet

Location/Map	West of Sheridan; Page 140
GPS Coordinates	N44° 49.83' W107° 51.54'
Sites/Spur Length	16 sites; Long spurs—over 30 feet
Cost	$17
Facilities/Services	Fire rings, grills, picnic tables, water, pit toilets, trash containers
Managing Agency	USDA Forest Service (Bighorn National Forest)
Reservations	Call 877-444-6777 or visit www.recreation.gov
Season/Usage	Open mid-June through late September; Moderate use

Directions: From Sheridan, drive north on I-90 and take Exit 9 to HWY 14. Travel west on HWY 14 for 32 miles, bearing right on HWY 14 ALT. Continue driving on HWY 14 ALT for 20.5 miles and turn onto FR 13. Drive north for 2 more miles to the camp. If traveling from Lovell, head east on HWY 14 ALT for just over 34 miles and turn north on FR 13.

Description: There's something about the name of this campground that may give you an unwelcome feeling. Don't be misled—staying in one of these handicap-accessible sites is anything but prickly. The camp is beautiful—perched atop the western slope of the Bighorn Mountains—and there are expansive views to be appreciated. Trees of spruce and pine pocket the surrounding open meadows and provide shade in the campground itself. Tent campers occupy most of the campsites and there are a number of walk-in sites for those who desire a little more privacy.

Porcupine Campground

Historical Attractions/Walking: The nearby Medicine Wheel National Historic Landmark is worth a visit. To reach it from the camp, drive 2 miles south to HWY 14 ALT, then head west for a half mile to FR 12.

Medicine Wheel National Historic Landmark

The Medicine Wheel is located at nearly 10,000 feet on a windswept hill in the northern Bighorn Mountains. This ancient Indian rock structure is the subject of wonder and mystery. The wheel is 75 feet in diameter, includes 28 spokes, and has six rock cairns around its perimeter.

To get to the site from Lovell, WY, drive east for 33 miles on HWY 14 ALT. If coming from the east, drive 22 miles west of Burgess Junction on HWY 14 ALT. Turn onto FR 12, a short but narrow and steep gravel road that leads to a parking area. Here, you'll find a small visitor center and a service road that leads to the wheel. A 1.5-mile scenic walk (3 miles round-trip) is required to reach the wheel, though some exceptions are made for those who have physical disabilities. The walk traverses an exposed ridge, so watch for afternoon thunderstorms.

Scenic Driving: The Medicine Wheel Passage (HWY 14 ALT) is a 25-mile section between Burgess Junction and Lovell; it passes the Medicine Wheel National Historic Landmark. As this road descends into Lovell, you'll encounter steep grades exceeding 10% making it a less desirable choice if you have a cumbersome trailer or RV. The steepest grade is about 10 miles long. Use a low gear and use your brakes gently. Braking just a few times with long and steady pressure on the pedal is better than braking frequently with harder pressure. The highway is closed between November and May.

Fishing: Porcupine Creek, north of the campground, holds rainbow, brook, and brown trout.

Trails: Looking out over the gently rolling mountains of the northern Bighorns, you wouldn't expect this to be waterfall country. Surprisingly, there are two impressive falls located along FR 14 north of the campground. The first, Porcupine Falls, is a stunning 200-foot cascade that spills into a scenic pool. A half-mile hike is required to view the falls. The trail is steep and some places are tricky with loose rock. Wear sturdy shoes and take a trekking pole if you have one.

A trailhead for Bucking Mule Falls and Devils Canyon can be found a couple miles farther down FR 14. It's a 2.5-mile hike to an overlook of the gorgeous 550-foot waterfall. Most people don't venture farther than the overlook as the trail gets significantly more difficult. At 3 miles, the path plummets nearly 2,000 feet to the bottom of Devils Canyon to cross Porcupine Creek. It is then a long climb out of the canyon to reach the trail's terminus at the end of Devils Canyon Road near Porcupine Campground. The trail covers about 13 miles.

Field Notes: The campground's name is fitting. I saw my first "in the wild" porcupine in this area. Black bears also occasionally saunter into camp.

Five Springs Falls Campground
6,600 feet

Location/Map	Between Sheridan and Lovell; Page 140
GPS Coordinates	N44° 48.25' W107° 58.22'
Sites/Spur Length	19 sites; Medium spurs—up to 30 feet
Cost	$7
Facilities/Services	Fire rings, picnic tables, water, pit toilets, trash containers, cellular service
Managing Agency	Bureau of Land Management (Cody Field Office); A host is sometimes present
Reservations	Not accepted—first come, first served
Season/Usage	Open May through October; Low use

Directions: From Sheridan, drive north on I-90 and take Exit 9 to HWY 14. Travel west on HWY 14 for 32 miles, bearing right on HWY 14 ALT. Continue driving on HWY 14 ALT for 30 miles.

From Lovell, travel east on HWY 14 ALT for 22 miles. Turn north onto an old paved road at the Five Springs sign. Continue up the steep grade for 2 miles. The road surface is rough in places and climbs 900 feet over some narrow hairpin turns. The road is not recommended for those towing a long trailer.

Description: You get the feeling in this campground that you are clinging to the western side of the Bighorn Mountains, trying not to fall off into the great Bighorn Basin below. There are two loops here that are flanked by tall rock walls. The lower loop includes nine tent sites tucked into a lush drainage that is shadowed by ponderosa pine and cottonwood trees. The upper loop includes ten sites, some of which have pull-through spurs for trailers and RVs. Camping is not that popular here as most visitors just pass through during the day to see the falls.

Scenic Driving: The Medicine Wheel Passage (HWY 14 ALT) is a 25-mile section between Burgess Junction and Lovell; it passes the Medicine Wheel National Historic Landmark. As this road descends into Lovell, you'll encounter steep grades exceeding 10% making it a less desirable choice if you have a cumbersome trailer or RV. The steepest grade is about 10 miles long. Use a low gear and use your brakes gently with long and steady pressure rather than frequent, hard pressure. The highway is closed between November and May.

Natural Attractions: A trail at the campground heads up the mountain a short distance to Five Springs Falls, a tumbling cascade.

Picnicking: Five Springs makes a great place for a midday picnic and no fee is charged for doing so.

Field Notes: You can burn up your brakes quickly on both the campground's access road as well as on HWY 14 ALT. I once had smoke billowing from the passenger wheel well and discovered the break pad was split in half.

Bighorn Canyon National Recreation Area 3,800 feet

Location/Map	Between Sheridan and Lovell; Page 140
GPS Coordinates	N44° 57.69' W108° 15.93'
Sites/Spur Length	48 sites; Long spurs—over 30 feet
Cost	$15 or $25 for hookups; Daily entrance fee
Facilities/Services	Electric and water hookups (limited), fire rings, grills, picnic tables, water, restrooms, trash containers, dump station, marina, boat ramp, cellular service
Managing Agency	National Park Service
Reservations	Not accepted—first come, first served
Season/Usage	Open all year; Low use

Directions: From Lovell, take HWY 14 ALT west for nearly 3 miles and turn north onto HWY 37. Drive just over 9 miles to the campground turnoff on the right. Follow this paved road for 1.5 miles to the campground.

Description: The Bighorn Canyon National Recreation Area has some fascinating attractions. Mankind created the 71-mile long Bighorn Lake by building the Yellowtail Dam in 1968, but it was nature that carved out the 1,000-foot walls of the magnificent Bighorn Canyon.

There are several campgrounds in the Bighorn Canyon Recreation Area, but Horseshoe Bend Campground is the only one south of the

Montana border. The elevation here is far below Wyoming's average, and the semi-arid badland setting makes for hot summers. The renovated campground sprawls across a flat near the lake. All sites have a full view of the sun, though a few have covered picnic tables. The improved sites are long and include wind fences, fire rings, and water and electric hookups. The remaining sites are shorter and some only have grills.

Natural Attractions: Drive north on the main park road for 5.5 miles and you'll find Devils Canyon Overlook in Montana. From the interpretive viewing platform you'll be able to peer down the sheer rock walls into the lake.

Wildlife Viewing: Bighorn sheep reside in the recreation area, especially near and north of the canyon's overlook. Also, watch for wild horses that roam the area. These animals are from the Pryor Mountain Wild Horse Range and can often be spotted from the paved road.

Fishing/Boating/Swimming: Bighorn Lake holds brown and rainbow trout, perch, sauger, and ling. Swimmers and waders will find a roped swimming area in the Horseshoe Bend area. Watersports, like water-skiing and riding jet skis, are popular. A marina near the campground offers commercial boat tours, boat rentals, and other recreational equipment.

Trails: The 1.75-mile Mouth of the Canyon Trail can be found at the north side of Loop B. This trail starts by following an old road to an overlook.

Field Notes: In drought years, you may find a dry, crumbling lake bed here instead of water. Regardless of water levels, the canyon here is remarkable and often overlooked. If you're anywhere in this area, come and see it.

Bighorn Canyon National Recreation Area

Yellowtail Wildlife Habitat Management Area (Wyoming Game & Fish)

If you're looking for primitive or free camping, check out the 20,000-acre Yellowtail Wildlife Habitat Management Area adjacent to the Bighorn Canyon National Recreation Area. This unit is known for its impressive cottonwood stands, outstanding pheasant hunting, and strong populations of deer and small game. The management area straddles the Shoshone River where you'll find numerous ponds and almost a dozen parking areas where camping is allowed. Only stone fire rings are found at most of the campsites. From Lovell, drive east on HWY 14 ALT for 8 miles and watch for the wildlife habitat management signs on both sides of the highway.

Owen Creek Campground
8,470 feet

Location/Map	West of Sheridan; Page 140
GPS Coordinates	N44° 42.37' W107° 29.87'
Sites/Spur Length	8 sites; Long spurs—over 30 feet
Cost	$17
Facilities/Services	Fire rings, grills, picnic tables, water, pit toilets, trash containers
Managing Agency	USDA Forest Service (Bighorn National Forest); A host is often present
Reservations	Call 877-444-6777 or visit www.recreation.gov
Season/Usage	Open June through late September; High use

Directions: From Sheridan, drive north on I-90 and take Exit 9 to HWY 14. Travel west on HWY 14 for 37 miles, bearing left at Burgess Junction.

Description: This small camp is tucked into the edge of an evergreen stand and faces a mountain meadow. Campsites are lined along a short lane that ends with a tiny loop where there is a lone site in the middle. Owen Creek quietly flows through the park. Due to the adjacent highway, this camp receives a lot of traffic and attention, especially when moose are present.

Scenic Driving: The Bighorn Scenic Byway (HWY 14) is a 45-mile stretch between Sheridan and Greybull. Shell Falls is worth a visit on the west side. Also of interest is Sand Turn, a turnout on the eastern side that overlooks Wyoming's plains.

Wildlife Viewing: Moose can sometimes be spotted in the willows along Owen Creek. The best viewing is often from the highway pulloff above the camp.

Fishing: Tiny Owen Creek holds small rainbow and brook trout.

4WD/ATV Routes: A primitive four-wheel drive road, FR 220 cuts through the meadow next to the campground and heads southwest. In less than 4 miles, the road intersects FR 10, a scenic and semi-improved 22-mile route that straddles the backbone of the Bighorn Mountains.

Field Notes: Easy highway access makes this camp fill quickly on weekends.

Tie Flume Campground

8,350 feet

Location/Map	West of Sheridan; Page 140
GPS Coordinates	N44° 42.91' W107° 27.04'
Sites/Spur Length	27 sites; Long spurs—over 30 feet
Cost	$18
Facilities/Services	Fire rings, grills, picnic tables, water, pit toilets, trash containers
Managing Agency	USDA Forest Service (Bighorn National Forest)
Reservations	Call 877-444-6777 or visit www.recreation.gov
Season/Usage	Open mid-June through mid-September; Moderate use

Directions: From Sheridan, drive north on I-90 and take Exit 9 to HWY 14. Travel west on HWY 14 for 37 miles, bearing left at Burgess Junction. Turn left onto FR 26 and drive 3 miles. Stay left at the junction and continue on FR 16 for a quarter mile.

Description: This two-loop campground is favored by the locals. One loop sits below a canopy of timber while the other loop is more open where it borders the beautiful South Tongue River. Tent campers are rewarded with spacious sites while trailer and RV campers can find an assortment of long parking spurs.

Natural Attractions: A blow down area can be found a short distance south of the campground on the east side of the road. Caused by a microburst on June 25, 1991, the strong winds lasted 15 minutes and blew over 1,100 acres along an 8-mile path. The storm began near HWY 14 at Granite Pass and reached a point just west of Black Mountain Lookout.

ATV Trail: A 6.1-mile ATV trail begins from FR 214211 just west of the campground. This track mostly parallels South Tongue River as it heads northward to Pine Island Group Campground.

Fishing: South Tongue River holds rainbow and brook trout.

Historical Attractions: When train tracks were being laid across Wyoming, railroad ties were cut and hewed in the forests and then flushed down the waterways to transport them out of the mountains. A tie flume is a wooden dam that aided this process by controlling a creek's water flow. You can see a very well-preserved tie flume several miles south of the campground on FR 26.

Field Notes: If you have one, bring your ATV and join the mass of riders cruising the forest roads. If traffic and road noise can ruin your weekend, you may be better off choosing a campground along the highway where there is less ATV traffic.

South Tongue River near Tie Flume Campground

Dead Swede Campground 8,400 feet

Location/Map	West of Sheridan; Page 140
GPS Coordinates	N44° 41.37' W107° 26.92'
Sites/Spur Length	21 sites; Long spurs—over 30 feet
Cost	$18
Facilities/Services	Fire rings, grills, picnic tables, water, pit toilets, trash containers
Managing Agency	USDA Forest Service (Bighorn National Forest)
Reservations	Call 877-444-6777 or visit www.recreation.gov
Season/Usage	Open mid-June through late September; Moderate use

Directions: From Sheridan, drive north on I-90 and take Exit 9 to HWY 14. Travel west on HWY 14 for 37 miles, bearing left at Burgess Junction. Turn left onto FR 26 and drive 5 miles.

Description: Dead Swede has two separate forested loops that virtually feel like two different campgrounds. The prime early-to-fill campsites are situated against the banks of the South Tongue River while the others are above and away from the river. Sites are spacious and well shaded, but don't include much privacy.

Fishing/Trails: There is a designated parking area for anglers. The placid waters of the South Tongue River hold rainbows and brook trout.

4WD/ATV Routes: There are a few miles of primitive 4x4 roads and ATV trails across the road from the campground. The roads are primarily used to access the Forest Service's Woodrock Guard Station, which is just a half-mile from FR 26.

Picnicking: There is a picnic area below the campground near the creek.

Field Notes: Look behind site #4 to find the reason behind the campground's name. Three graves, dating as far back as 1910, mark the site of those who spent time in this area long before us.

Ranger Creek Campground
7,700 feet

Location/Map	Southwest of Sheridan; Page 140
GPS Coordinates	N44° 36.03' W107° 13.1'
Sites/Spur Length	11 sites; Medium spurs—up to 30 feet
Cost	$16
Facilities/Services	Fire rings, grills, picnic tables, water, pit toilets, trash containers
Managing Agency	USDA Forest Service (Bighorn National Forest); A host is often present
Reservations	Not accepted—first come, first served
Season/Usage	Open mid-June through early September; Moderate use

Directions: This campground can be approached from the west (smoother) or from the east (rougher). For a western approach, drive north from Sheridan on I-90 and take Exit 9 to HWY 14. Travel west on HWY 14 for 37 miles, bearing left at Burgess Junction. Turn left onto FR 26 and drive 23 miles.

For a shorter, more adventurous route to the campground, head south from Sheridan on HWY 87 and turn onto HWY 335. Continue along HWY 335 (which turns into FR 26 after 10 miles) and drive just short of 21 miles to the camp. Take note that FR 26 (Red Grade Road) on the Sheridan side is steep and narrow. Trailers and RVs are not advised along this section.

Description: As the name implies, this campground is located near Ranger Creek, which flows through an adjacent meadow and past a nearby Forest Service ranger station. A single loop of roomy, somewhat-private sites are cast into the shadows by tall lodgepole pines. The forest road here is close and dust and noise can get annoying as ATV riding has become popular. Even so, this is a decent place to spend the weekend in the woods; mid-week would be even better.

Fishing: There are several fishing spots in the area. East Fork of Big Goose Creek is located near East Fork Campground. This same stream, as well as Park Reservoir, can also be accessed near Cross Creek Campground. In addition, you can travel west a few miles on FR 26 to Twin and Sawmill Lakes. These fisheries hold brook, cutthroat, and rainbow.

Trails: The closest trail in the area is the Walker Prairie Trail. From the campground, walk (or drive) to the end of FR 296, north of the ranger station. The trail starts here and works north for over 16 miles to HWY 14. The route travels through a blend of forest and grassland and crosses a few creeks (without bridges). I counted over a dozen trail and road junctions, so be sure to carry a map for this trail.

4WD/ATV Routes: Four-wheeling drivers and ATV riders can find all sorts of routes in this part of the Bighorns. One possibility, FR 312 just west of the campground, heads through the forest for a few miles toward a hiking trail. Another route, FR 299 directly south of camp, travels 4.5-miles to Weston Reservoir. A more extensive web of primitive roads can be found southeast of the campground in the Little Goose area. Refer to the Forest Service OHV map for specific routes.

Picnicking: The Twin Lakes Picnic Area is located less than 6 miles west of the campground on FR 26.

Field Notes: There is always something going on around this campground as the adjacent road receives heavy traffic. On our last visit, a pair of moose stampeded through. It always grabs your attention when you hear thumping and cracking of branches coming from the forest!

East Fork Campground
7,600 feet

Location/Map	Southwest of Sheridan; Page 140
GPS Coordinates	N44° 35.76' W107° 12.51'
Sites/Spur Length	12 sites; Medium spurs—over 30 feet
Cost	$16
Facilities/Services	Fire rings, grills, picnic tables, water, pit toilets, trash containers
Managing Agency	USDA Forest Service (Bighorn National Forest)
Reservations	Not accepted—first come, first served
Season/Usage	Open mid-June through early September; Moderate use

Directions: This campground can be approached from the west (smoother) or from the east (rougher). For a western approach, drive north from Sheridan on I-90 and take Exit 9 to HWY 14. Travel west on HWY 14 for 37 miles, bearing left at Burgess Junction. Turn left onto FR 26 and drive 23.5 miles to FR 295, a short and narrow access road.

For a shorter, more adventurous route to the campground, head south from Sheridan on HWY 87 and turn onto HWY 335. Continue along HWY 335 (which turns into FR 26 after 10 miles) and drive 21 miles to the camp's access road (FR 295). Take note that FR 26 (Red Grade Road) on the Sheridan side is steep and narrow. Trailers and RVs are not advised along this section. I've tried it while towing and can say it wasn't worth the shortcut.

Description: This quiet camp sits at the base of Big Goose Park, a mountain meadow nourished from the East Fork of Big Goose Creek. You'll find willows and shrubs among the foliage here, but evergreens dominate the camping area. Campsites are shorter than those at nearby Ranger Creek Campground, but East Fork often proves to be the more popular camp. Due to tight quarters and the single-lane access road, pulling a large trailer into this camp can get tricky.

Fishing: There are several fishing spots in the area. The East Fork of Big Goose Creek flows adjacent to the campground and attracts fly-fishing anglers. Travel west a few miles on FR 26 and you will find Twin and Sawmill Lakes. These fisheries hold brook, cutthroat, and rainbow.

Trails: The closest trail in the area is the Walker Prairie Trail. From the campground, walk (or drive) to the end of FR 296, north of the nearby ranger station. The trail starts here and works north for over 16 miles to HWY 14. The route travels through a blend of forest and grassland. A few creek fords are necessary. I counted over a dozen trail and road junctions, so be sure to carry a map for this trail.

4WD/ATV Routes: Four-wheeling enthusiasts can find many routes in this part of the Bighorns. One route, FR 299 just west of the campground, travels 4.5-miles to Weston Reservoir. More extensive roads exist south of camp, near Park Reservoir and in the Little Goose area to the east. Refer to the Forest Service OHV map for specific routes.

Picnicking: There is a picnic ground at Twin Lakes, roughly 6 miles west of the campground on FR 26.

Field Notes: East Fork is a typical campground, but this area is among my favorite places in Wyoming. There is a lot of pretty backcountry to be explored here and it's open to multi-use, so you can go by foot, ATV, truck, horse, or bike. For a little more solitude, you can head into the Cloud Peak Wilderness (foot and stock use only), where you'll experience some of Wyoming's most beautiful public lands.

Little Goose Campground

6,950 feet

Location/Map	Southwest of Sheridan; Page 140
GPS Coordinates	N44° 35.39' W107° 7.5'
Sites/Spur Length	3 sites (tents only)
Cost	Free
Facilities/Services	Fire rings, picnic tables, pit toilets
Managing Agency	USDA Forest Service (Bighorn National Forest)
Reservations	Not accepted—first come, first served
Season/Usage	Open late June through September; Low use

Directions: This campground can be approached from the west (smoother) or from the east (rougher). Either way, a four-wheel vehicle is required. For a western approach, drive north from Sheridan on I-90 and take Exit 9 to HWY 14. Travel west on HWY 14 for 37 miles, bearing left at Burgess Junction. Turn left onto FR 26 and drive 30 miles. Turn south onto a rougher road and drive southward for 2 miles. Two creeks must be forded.

For a shorter, more adventurous route to the camp, head south from Sheridan on HWY 87 and turn onto HWY 335. Continue along HWY 335 (which turns into FR 26 after 10 miles) and drive 14.5 miles to a dirt access road on the left. Follow this road southward for 2 miles, and through two creek crossings. Be advised that FR 26 (Red Grade Road) from Sheridan is steep and narrow. Trailers and RVs are not advised along this section.

Description: This is one of the least accessible campgrounds in the state, which gives it a true off-the-beaten path feel. If you're looking for a unique and remote camp, this is your place. However, the incoming road receives a fair amount of travel. The camp is tucked into a small timber stand where several creeks converge into the larger Little Goose Creek. The tent sites are walk-ins surrounded by a pole fence. Bring your water and take your trash.

Natural Attractions: Little Goose Falls can be found south of the campground off FR 314, a 4WD road. Look for a sign on the east side of the road to find two short routes to the falls; one is for ATVs and the other for foot traffic.

Fishing: Little Goose Creek flows next to the campground and holds brook, cutthroat, and rainbow trout.

4WD/ATV Routes: There is a great (and extensive) web of 4WD roads and ATV trails south of the camp. Grab a Forest Service OHV map, pick a route, and head out. Park Reservoir to the west is one worthwhile destination. Note that Little Goose Creek is not that little and must be forded to head south.

Field Notes: Use caution if you head south to ford Little Goose Creek. One camper told me the water reached the driver's side window of his pickup truck when he tried to cross it in July. Out of the handful of times I've crossed it (in July or later), it has always been above the floorboards.

Cross Creek Campground

8,300 feet

Location/Map	Southwest of Sheridan; Page 140
GPS Coordinates	N44° 32.77' W107° 12.99'
Sites/Spur Length	3 sites (tents only)
Cost	Free
Facilities/Services	Fire rings, picnic tables
Managing Agency	USDA Forest Service (Bighorn National Forest)
Reservations	Not accepted—first come, first served
Season/Usage	Open late June through September; Low use

Directions: This campground can be approached from the west (smoother) or from the east (rougher). For a western approach, drive north from Sheridan on I-90 and take Exit 9 to HWY 14. Travel west on HWY 14 for 37 miles, bearing left at Burgess Junction. Turn left onto FR 26 and drive 23 miles to FR 293. Turn south on this rough road and drive 4.5 miles. The road will go around Park Reservoir and past the west side of Spear-O-Wigwam Ranch, a private camp. A shallow ford of Cross Creek is required.

For a shorter, more adventurous route to the camp, head south from Sheridan on HWY 87 and turn onto HWY 335. Continue along HWY 335 (which turns into FR 26 after 10 miles) and drive 21 miles to FR 293. Drive south on FR 293 for 4.5 miles. A shallow ford of Cross Creek is required. Take note that FR 26 (Red Grade Road) and FR 293 are steep and narrow. Trailers and RVs are not advised along this section.

Park Reservoir

Description: This campground receives its name from tiny Cross Creek, which incidentally has to be driven through to reach the camp. There are three primitive campsites spread out in light timber; they are perfect if you are tenting and don't mind a lack of amenities in exchange for free camping. If you have a van or pickup camper, you'll be better off taking one of the dispersed sites near Park Reservoir. For either place, bring water and a shovel because there is no toilet. You'll need to pack out your trash.

Fishing: Park Reservoir holds a variety of trout including lake, rainbow, and cutthroat. Expect fish smaller than 14 inches in length. Another popular fishery is the East Fork of Big Goose Creek, which flows near the campground.

Trails: Continue south for 2.5 miles on FR 293 (4WD required) to reach Coffeen Park Trailhead at the Cloud Peak Wilderness boundary. This used to be a primitive campground, but the Forest Service decommissioned it.

The trail leaving Coffeen Park leads to numerous destinations in the northern half of the Cloud Peak Wilderness. Heading south, you'll encounter four trail junctions in just the first 1.5 miles.

If you're looking for a short trek, take the first right, to the west, which leads uphill just over a mile to Rhinehart Lakes. If you stay straight on the main trail, you'll find Geneva Lake at 3.5 miles, Geneva Pass before 6 miles, and the Solitude-Cliff Lake Trail at 8.5 miles. The first five miles of this route climb through wooded backcountry. The remaining distance beyond Geneva Lake is mostly alpine terrain.

4WD/ATV Routes: Several fun 4WD roads and ATV trails crisscross the area east of the camp. Bighorn Reservoir and Little Goose Falls are two possible destinations. Refer to a Forest Service OHV map for specific routes.

Dispersed Camping: Dispersed campsites can be found around the shores of Park Reservoir, but it can be a busy place.

Field Notes: This is one of those places where you can just disappear for a few days. For some, this is as good as it gets—a large fishing lake in the Rocky Mountains, surrounded by forests and snowy mountain peaks.

Shell Creek Campground

7,550 feet

Location/Map	Southwest of Sheridan; Page 140
GPS Coordinates	N44° 33.12' W107° 31.11'
Sites/Spur Length	15 sites; Long spurs—over 30 feet
Cost	$17
Facilities/Services	Fire rings, grills, picnic tables, water, pit toilets, trash containers
Managing Agency	USDA Forest Service (Bighorn National Forest)
Reservations	Call 877-444-6777 or visit www.recreation.gov
Season/Usage	Open mid-May through mid-September; Moderate use

Directions: From Sheridan, drive north on I-90 and take Exit 9 to HWY 14. Travel west on HWY 14 for 49 miles. If traveling from Shell, head east on HWY 14 for 16 miles and turn onto FR 17. Drive about 2 miles on FR 17.

Description: This handicap-accessible campground sits at the head of a mighty canyon with one side against Shell Creek and the other facing a sagebrush covered hill. The updated camp has piped water, level parking spurs, and solar-powered lights at the pit toilets. The facility is perfectly suited for long trailers and motor homes, and many sites have no trees to bump into when you back-in. It can get hot if you end up with one of the open sites, but take a camp chair to the shady creek and you'll be quite comfortable.

Fishing: Anglers can expect to find brown and brook trout in Shell Creek. Designated angler parking is available on the west side of the campground.

Trails/4WD/ATV Route: Hiking and off-roading routes can be found at nearby Ranger Creek Campground.

Picnicking: From the campground's entrance, there is a short 4WD road that leads to a picnic table along the creek. It takes just a few minutes to walk this route.

Field Notes: Although a breeze always seems to be blowing up through the canyon into this camp and there aren't enough trees to block it, we have stayed many a night here. On one such windy night, an out-of-state camper expressed his worry that bears and raccoons would get into his stash of food. Why on earth, he wondered aloud, would the Forest Service put hooks for hanging your food directly over the picnic table where any critter could reach it? Imagine his embarrassment when we explained that those hooks were for hanging lanterns, not food!

Ranger Creek Campground

7,650 feet

Location/Map	Southwest of Sheridan; Page 140
GPS Coordinates	N44° 32.73' W107° 29.94'
Sites/Spur Length	10 sites, 1 group site; Short to medium spurs—up to 30 feet
Cost	$17, $75-$145 for groups up to 150 people
Facilities/Services	Fire rings, picnic tables, water, pit toilets
Managing Agency	USDA Forest Service (Bighorn National Forest)
Reservations	Call 877-444-6777 or visit www.recreation.gov
Season/Usage	Open mid-May through mid-September; Moderate use

Directions: From Sheridan, drive north on I-90 and take Exit 9 to HWY 14. Travel west on HWY 14 for 49 miles. If traveling from Shell, head east on HWY 14 for 16 miles and turn onto FR 17. Drive 2.75 miles on FR 17.

Description: This campground is located in a draw where Ranger Creek flows into Shell Creek. The camp is divided on both sides of the road. The northern side includes a handful of sites near the road that are quick to fill. More sites are found in the trees on the other side of the road. Parking a small trailer is possible, albeit some leveling work would be needed. Tent campers, on the other hand, will find the camp to be very accommodating. A group site for up to 150 people can be reserved here.

Fishing: Anglers can expect to find brown and brook trout in Shell Creek.

Trails/4WD/ATV Routes: A 4WD road worth exploring is FR 277, located just a short distance west of the campground. The road travels through a beautiful valley and then climbs toward Woodchuck Pass.

Shell Reservoir and Adelaide Lake are popular destinations for ATV riders, but hikers can enjoy them too. Four-wheelers should look for the 4WD road off FR 17, roughly 9 miles from HWY 14. Two primitive roads, FR 280 and FR 271, form a 10-mile loop that tours both lakes. Hikers can reach the lakes by cutting through the Cloud Peak Wilderness. Look for a sign at Ranger Creek Trailhead (1 mile to the south) for the Adelaide Trail. It's about 5.5 miles to Adelaide Lake from the trailhead. From the lake, you can visit Shell Reservoir by following the 4WD road to the south.

Other options at the trailhead include the Bench Trail that heads west for 10 miles through Shell Canyon to the Post Creek Picnic Area. The trail descends 2,500 feet, nearly taking you out of the mountains.

Field Notes: Be aware that there are two Ranger Creek campgrounds in the northern Bighorns, one on the east side and this one on the west side.

Medicine Lodge Lake Campground

9,300 feet

Location/Map	Southwest of Sheridan; Page 140
GPS Coordinates	N44° 24.06' W107° 23.13'
Sites/Spur Length	8 sites; Medium spurs—over 30 feet
Cost	$16 ($32 for double site)
Facilities/Services	Fire rings, picnic tables, water, pit toilets, trash containers, boat ramp
Managing Agency	USDA Forest Service (Bighorn National Forest); A host is sometimes present
Reservations	Not accepted—first come, first served
Season/Usage	Open July through early September; High use

Directions: From Sheridan, drive north on I-90 and take Exit 9 to HWY 14. Travel west on HWY 14 for 49 miles to FR 17. If traveling from Shell, head east on HWY 14 for 16 miles and turn onto FR 17. Drive 24.5 miles on FR 17, which is fairly rough and can take up to an hour.

Description: This campground is found in a remote section of the Bighorn Mountains near a placid quartet of lakes. A few sites wrap along the shore of Upper Medicine Lodge Lake, where you can fish from your own campsite. Parking spurs are fairly level although tent campers have the best options. A double site is also available. Trying to maneuver a trailer or motor home down FR 17 could be frustrating at times and dangerous at others (though people do it).

Upper Medicine Lodge Lake

Fishing/Boating: Fishing the four Medicine Lodge and Paint Rock Lakes for rainbow and brook trout is a popular activity. Short hikes are required to reach Lower Medicine Lodge Lake and Upper Paint Rock Lake. There is a primitive boat ramp at the campground for small boats. We met an angler who was trying to fly-fish for the first time. He was snatching fish from the water faster than his kids could string them up.

Trails: Lower Medicine Lodge Lake can be reached by a trail from the campground or another that starts from the Paint Rock Lodge just north of the camp (both are about 1.3 miles). Another nearby trail is found at the Edelman Trailhead, 1 mile north of the lodge; this 11-mile route travels over two alpine mountain passes on its way to Coffeen Park Trailhead.

South of the camp, you can head to Paint Rock Trailhead near Lower Paint Rock Lake Campground. This trailhead has corrals and features two trails. The North High Park Trail enters the Cloud Peak Wilderness after 2 miles, intersects the Poacher Lake Trail at 5 miles, and reaches the junction with the Geneva Pass-Cliff Lake Trail at 7.5 miles. The route heading south from the trailhead is the Kinky White Trail. This connector track remains outside the wilderness as it travels to a network of other trails north of Hyatt Cow Camp. It's over 7 miles to the camp.

4WD/ATV Route: FR 344 heads south from the campground and joins Cold Springs Road near the Medicine Lodge Archaeological Site. The primitive section of the road is about 7 miles in length and travels across the high mountain meadows (spectacular views) of the western Bighorn Mountains.

Field Notes: Our first visit to this camp was a very peaceful stay that included a postcard-worthy sunset and watching a large bull moose dip its massive paddles into the lake next to our campsite. The second included overcrowding, blaring music, and lots of engine revving. The third was again quiet. Additional visits confirmed that this is usually a popular area, but if you get here just after the road becomes passable sometime in late June, or wait until late summer, you increase your chances of experiencing the area at its best. Bighorn peaks, shadowy forests, awesome sunsets, and lakes brimming with trout are a few reasons to give it a try.

Lower Paint Rock Lake Campground

9,200 feet

Location/Map	Southwest of Sheridan; Page 140
GPS Coordinates	N44° 23.68' W107° 22.97'
Sites/Spur Length	4 sites; Medium spurs—over 30 feet
Cost	$16 ($32 for double sites)
Facilities/Services	Fire rings, picnic tables, water, pit toilets, trash containers, boat ramp
Managing Agency	USDA Forest Service (Bighorn National Forest)
Reservations	Not accepted—first come, first served
Season/Usage	Open July through early September; High use

Directions: From Sheridan, drive north on I-90 and take Exit 9 to HWY 14. Travel west on HWY 14 for 49 miles to FR 17. If traveling from Shell, head east on HWY 14 for 16 miles and turn onto FR 17. Drive 25.3 miles on FR 17, which is rough in places and can take up to an hour.

Description: This small camp is located at the end of a long Forest Service road. Campsites are tucked into the edge of a timber stand and overlook Lower Paint Rock Lake. Unfortunately, the sites are directly off the road making them not so private and awkwardly sloped. So who stays here? Anglers who love to fish remote waters, hikers or horsepackers who want to explore the Cloud Peak Wilderness, and campers who don't like highways.

Fishing: Fishing the four Medicine Lodge and Paint Rock Lakes for rainbow and brook trout is a very popular activity. Short hikes are required to reach Lower Medicine Lodge Lake and Upper Paint Rock Lake. There is a primitive boat ramp near the campground for small boats.

Trails: Paint Rock Trailhead, which has corrals, is located just north of the campground and serves two trails. The North High Park Trail enters the Cloud Peak Wilderness after 2 miles, intersects the Poacher Lake Trail at 5 miles, and reaches the junction with the Geneva Pass-Cliff Lake Trail at 7.5 miles. The route heading south from the trailhead is the Kinky White Trail. This connector track remains outside the wilderness as it travels to a network of other trails north of Hyatt Cow Camp. It's over 7 miles to the camp.

4WD/ATV Route: There is a 4WD road at Medicine Lodge Lake Campground.

Field Notes: If you've driven to this campground, you've reached the end of the road and have passed all your camping options. It's a long drive back to the highway if you don't like what you see, but I think you will.

AREA 2 | NORTH - NORTHEAST
Southern Bighorn Mountains

The Bighorn Mountains of north-central Wyoming separate the grassy Powder River Basin from the arid Bighorn Basin. It is from these basins that the tall mountains can be seen for many miles. The range's high point of 13,167 feet is found at the top of Cloud Peak, a summit in a wilderness area of the same name.

If you were to see the Bighorn Mountains from the air, you would see a glacially formed land of granite domes and peaks that are surrounded by a predominately lodgepole pine forest. The outer fringes of the range are defined by canyons and rugged upland where the forests give way to grass, shrubs, sagebrush, and juniper trees.

Driving the Cloud Peak Skyway (US Highway 16) is an excellent way to experience all of the various ecosystems. The 45-mile route between Buffalo and Tensleep offers outstanding views of the peaks in and around the Cloud Peak Wilderness and Bighorn National Forest. The road travels over the crest of the range at Powder River Pass with an elevation of 9,666 feet. While the tall mountain peaks can be seen from the highway, they require a backcountry trip of at least 5 miles to reach. As the road descends to the west, it passes through Tensleep Canyon, a gorgeous gorge.

Moose are widespread across the forest and sightings are common in the Clear Creek, Crazy Woman, Piney, West Tensleep, and Rock drainages. Watch for the animals in the willows and marshy areas. Black bears are found throughout the Bighorn Mountains but mostly roam the northern half of the range. Grizzly bears are not present in the area and suggestions to reintroduce the species have been quickly defeated by opposition.

Deciding on whether to spend time in the northern half or the southern half of the Bighorn Range isn't an easy decision. Both offer incredible scenery and vast recreational opportunities. Where as the northern mountains have more extensive backroads to explore, the southern mountains provide better access to the Cloud Peak Wilderness. Anglers looking to fly-fish the rivers will do better in the north. Conversely, the southern mountains have many lakes, including Meadowlark Reservoir along HWY 16, that are popular fishing areas. Seasonal timing and conditions will also be a factor. With few exceptions, the southern camps are free of snow earlier and have easier highway access than those found in the north.

What to Expect: If you're headed to the southern Bighorns, you can expect to have a good time. This area has something for everyone: ATV trails, hiking trails, fishing lakes, grand views, and easy access to towns. Visitation is steady throughout the camping season and spikes on holiday weekends when most of the camps fill. Expect mild daytime temperatures, short afternoon thunderstorms, and cool evenings.

Area 2: Southern Bighorn Mountains

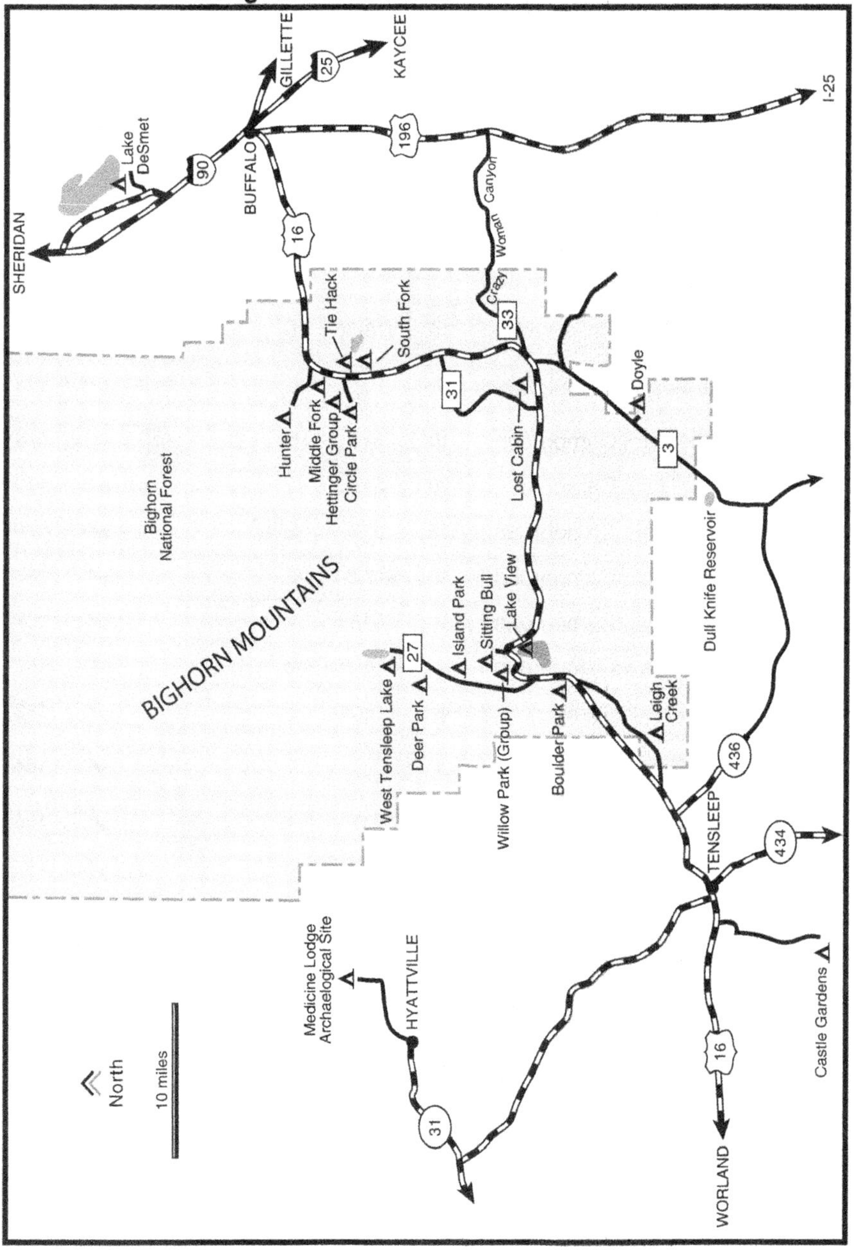

Campgrounds	Sites	Cost	Average Spur Length	Electrical Hookups	Cellular Service (varies by carrier/site)	Reservations Accepted	Page Number
Mikesell-Potts Recreation Area	60	$10-15	L	✔	▁▃▅		171
Hunter Campground	11	$10	L			✔	172
Middle Fork Campground	10	$18-36	L			✔	173
Hettinger Group Campground	1	$75-145	L			✔	174
Circle Park Campground	10	$16	S		▁▃▅	✔	175
Tie Hack Campground	20	$18	L			✔	176
South Fork Campground	15	$18	L			✔	178
Lost Cabin Campground	19	$17-34	L			✔	180
Doyle Campground	19	$16	L			✔	181
Lakeview Campground	20	$18-36	M			✔	182
Sitting Bull Campground	42	$18-36	L			✔	183
Willow Park Group Campground	1	$75-145	L			✔	184
Boulder Park Campground	32	$17	L			✔	186
Island Park Campground	10	$17	M			✔	187
Deer Park Campground	7	$17	M				187
West Tensleep Lake Campground	10	$17	M			✔	188
Leigh Creek Campground	11	$16	M			✔	190
Medicine Lodge Archaeological Site	28	$9-26	L	✔		✔	191
Castle Gardens Campground	2	Free	M		▁▃▅		193

Average Spur Length: S = Short (under 30 feet), M = Medium (+-30 feet), L = Long (+-40 feet)
Cellular Service: 1 bar = weak/unreliable signal, 2 bars = low usable signal, 3+ bars = reliable signal for most users

Mikesell-Potts Recreation Area (Lake DeSmet) 4,650 feet

Location/Map	Northeast of Buffalo; Page 169
GPS Coordinates	N44° 27.07' W106° 44.65'
Sites/Spur Length	60 sites; Long spurs—over 30 feet
Cost	$10 or $15 with electric hookups
Facilities/Services	Electric hookups, fire rings, picnic tables, restrooms, trash containers, boat ramp, cellular service
Managing Agency	Johnson County Parks; A host is often present
Reservations	Not accepted—first come, first served
Season/Usage	Open April through October; Moderate use

Directions: From Buffalo, take I-90 north for several miles to Exit 51. Follow the signs eastward to the lake and watch for two loops of campsites.

Description: Lake DeSmet is not located in the Bighorn Mountains, but rather along I-90 north of Buffalo where much of the mountain range is within view. The lake is a popular fishery and day-use area. The developed campsites—part of the Mikesell-Potts Recreation Area—includes 8 sites with electric hookups and a few dozen more along the southern shoreline. Some of these are tucked between tall shrubs, but many are out in the open with full sun. A few sites have covered picnic tables. With paved access from the Interstate, it's great for RVs. Tent campers will find grassy patches to set up. A nearby RV park at the lake has electric hookups, supplies, marina, cafe, and boat and cabin rentals.

Fishing/Boating: Crappie and rainbow trout are the primary species in the lake, and shoreline fishing is said to be productive. A popular fishing derby is held at the lake every Memorial Day weekend and registered participants are eligible for a number of prizes. Boaters will find a few ramps, but boats can be launched from the sloped shoreline when conditions are right.

Field Notes: If you're traveling along the Interstate and need an easy-to-reach public campground, look no further than this one. People love it here, though summer afternoons can be hot. There was no potable water available at the time of this writing, so bring your own just in case. On a historical note, it is said that wagon wheel ruts from the Bozeman Trail can be found on the hillside next to the lake.

Hunter Campground

8,000 feet

Location/Map	West of Buffalo; Page 169
GPS Coordinates	N44° 20.27' W106° 58.56'
Sites/Spur Length	11 sites; Long spurs—over 30 feet
Cost	$10
Facilities/Services	Fire rings, picnic tables, utility tables, water, pit toilets, trash containers, horse facilities
Managing Agency	USDA Forest Service (Bighorn National Forest); A host is sometimes present
Reservations	Call 877-444-6777 or visit www.recreation.gov
Season/Usage	Open late May through September; Moderate use

Directions: From Buffalo, head west on HWY 16 for 12 miles. Turn right onto FR 19 and drive 2.5 miles to the camp turnoff on the left. Then head west for a third of a mile.

Description: Hunter Trailhead has long served as a horse camp for backcountry horsemen who ride into the Cloud Peak Wilderness. It often looks something like a cowboy retreat here. In 2012, the Forest Service closed the old, too-small camp next to the creek and built this new one a quarter mile uphill. The modern camp is bigger and vastly improved—even the views are better. The large campsites sit in the open near an aspen stand and easily fit trucks and horse trailers. The camp is easy to drive through, has separate outfitter and trailhead parking, and offers top-notch

The southern Bighorn Mountains as seen from the Hunter Campground area

horse facilities for a public campground: corrals at each site, hitching posts, highlines, manure pit, and a mounting ramp.

Trails/4WD Routes: The Seven Brothers Lakes area is a main destination from the trailhead and a 5.5-mile hike or ride is required to reach it. Three miles of this distance can be completed with a 4WD truck or ATV, but watch for horse traffic.

Another nice 4WD drive, ride, or hike can be made just east of the campground by following FR 390 for 2.5 miles across the top of Hunter Mesa. Along the way you'll get splendid views of the Bighorn's sky-jabbing granite domes and summits.

Follow FR 396, the road that continues past the campground and you'll soon cross French Creek and reach a meadow called French Creek Swamps on the other side. The main track is 7 miles long, but there are other spurs and trails that branch off from here, some of which lead northward into the Cloud Peak Wilderness.

Field Notes: Over the last couple of decades, the Forest Service has been busy closing campgrounds and other developed recreation sites. It gets disheartening, knowing crews are pulling out picnic tables, toilets, and signs. Yet after seeing the agency commit to new recreation sites such as this one, it renews one's confidence that nice campgrounds will be around for future generations.

Middle Fork Campground

7,400 feet

Location/Map	West of Buffalo; Page 169
GPS Coordinates	N44° 18.08' W106° 18.08'
Sites/Spur Length	10 sites; Long spurs—over 30 feet
Cost	$18, $36 for group site
Facilities/Services	Fire rings, picnic tables, water, pit toilets, trash containers
Managing Agency	USDA Forest Service (Bighorn National Forest)
Reservations	Call 877-444-6777 or visit www.recreation.gov
Season/Usage	Open late May through mid-September; Moderate use

Directions: From Buffalo, head west on HWY 16 for 13 miles. The camp is on the right at the end of a short paved road.

Description: This campground is nestled in a small drainage with plenty of trees and interesting rock formations. Level sites parallel the Middle Fork of Clear Creek. There are a few good sites for trailers and motor homes and some obvious ones for tent campers. Watch for yellow-bellied marmots around the rock outcroppings. These curious critters will pop up like gophers to take a peek at you.

Scenic Driving: The 45-mile Cloud Peak Skyway traverses the Bighorns between Buffalo and Tensleep. This roadway offers astounding views of the peaks in and around the Cloud Peak Wilderness. The high point crosses Powder River Pass at 9,666 feet.

Fishing: All three forks of Clear Creek, including the one that runs through the campground, have pan-sized brook, brown, and rainbow trout. Angler parking is available at the campground entrance.

Trails: Even though there is no trail, a scramble up the steep northern hill in the campground pays off with excellent views of the Bighorns.

If you're looking for something a little more developed, check out Hunter Trailhead, just a mile north of the campground. The Seven Brothers Lakes area can be reached from this trailhead and a 5.5-mile hike is required to reach it. If you are equipped for some real four-wheeling, you can drive to a cut-off trail and lessen the hiking distance to 2.5 miles. Refer to a map to study your options.

More trails that access the Cloud Peak Wilderness can be found at nearby Circle Park Campground.

Picnicking: The North Fork Picnic Area, a mile north on FR 19, is tucked along the shady banks of the North Fork of Clear Creek.

ATV Trail: A 6-mile ATV trail runs between FR 391 to the north and Elgin Park to the south. The trail can be picked up right here near the beginning of the campground.

Field Notes: This little nook is one of my favorites. If you're a tent camper, I recommend site #3.

Hettinger Group Campground
7,650 feet

Location/Map	West of Buffalo; Page 169
GPS Coordinates	N44° 17.82' W106° 57.09'
Sites/Spur Length	1 group site; Long spurs—over 30 feet
Cost	$75-$145
Facilities/Services	Fire ring, grill, picnic tables, water, pit toilet, trash containers, playground
Managing Agency	USDA Forest Service (Bighorn National Forest)
Reservations	Call 877-444-6777 or visit www.recreation.gov
Season/Usage	Open late May through mid-September; Moderate use

Directions: From Buffalo, go west on HWY 16 for 14.5 miles. Turn right onto a gravel lane and follow it westward into the parking area.

Description: This day-use picnic area can also be reserved for overnight group camping. The gravel parking area will hold RVs and trailers while tents can be set up within the surrounding pine trees and meadows. Up to 150 campers are permitted to stay here and rates are based on group size.

Scenic Driving: The 45-mile Cloud Peak Skyway traverses the Bighorns between Buffalo and Tensleep. This roadway offers astounding views of the peaks in and around the Cloud Peak Wilderness. The high point crosses Powder River Pass at 9,666 feet.

Fishing/Boating: If you're looking for lake fishing, make the short drive to Tie Hack Reservoir (just east of Tie Hack Campground). Boating is permitted for manually-powered craft.

Trails: Hiking trails that access the Cloud Peak Wilderness can be found at nearby Circle Park Campground.

Picnicking: There is a picnic area at Tie Hack Reservoir. To get there, head south on HWY 16 for a half-mile and turn east on the gravel road. It's 2 more miles to the reservoir.

ATV Trail: A 6-mile ATV trail runs between FR 391 to the north and Elgin Park to the south. The trail passes the campground near the highway.

Field Notes: This is a great option for large family reunions, club outings, or church campouts. From the top of this hill, you'll have great views (and sunsets) over the granite domes of the Bighorns.

Circle Park Campground

8,100 feet

Location/Map	West of Buffalo; Page 169
GPS Coordinates	N44° 16.96' W106° 59.37'
Sites/Spur Length	10 sites; Short spurs—up to 20 feet
Cost	$16
Facilities/Services	Fire rings, grills, picnic tables, water, pit toilets, trash containers, limited cellular service
Managing Agency	USDA Forest Service (Bighorn National Forest)
Reservations	Call 877-444-6777 or visit www.recreation.gov
Season/Usage	Open late May through early September; Moderate use

Directions: From Buffalo, go west on HWY 16 for 14 miles. Turn right onto narrow FR 20 and drive 2 miles. A trailhead road branches off to the left just before the campground.

Description: With a bustling trailhead for the Cloud Peak Wilderness within walking distance, this is a popular campground (especially with drive-through traffic). The camp is small—some would say crammed—and sites are only conducive to tent camping and maybe pop-up trailers. Live evergreen and aspen trees crowd the campground, but a large swath of surrounding forest burned in 1988. There are a few spots on the incoming gravel road where a usable, though intermittent cellular signal can be found.

Scenic Driving: The 45-mile Cloud Peak Skyway traverses the Bighorns between Buffalo and Tensleep. This roadway offers astounding views of the peaks in and around the Cloud Peak Wilderness. The high point crosses Powder River Pass at 9,666 feet.

Wildlife Viewing: Moose frequent the willows of Circle Park Creek on FR 20.

Fishing/Boating: If you're looking for lake fishing, make the short drive to Tie Hack Reservoir (just east of Tie Hack Campground). Boating is permitted for manually-powered craft.

Trails: Circle Park Trailhead, accessible from a short road near the campground, is a popular starting point for numerous subalpine lakes in the Cloud Peak Wilderness. A fun 10-mile loop visits several of these, and a few offshoot trails travel to the most scenic gems. Families looking for a relatively easy hike can travel 1.7 miles to Sherd Lake.

Picnicking: There is a picnic area at Tie Hack Reservoir. To get there, head south on HWY 16 for a half-mile and turn east and drive 2 miles on the gravel road.

Dispersed Camping: Primitive campsites can be found along the edge of the meadows on FR 20. Dispersed camping is also popular along FR 23 (Sourdough Creek), a little over 2 miles south on HWY 16.

ATV Trail: A 6-mile ATV trail runs between FR 391 to the north and Elgin Park to the south. The trail can be picked up by using FT 187, a short connector track. Watch for this path on the north side of FR 20.

Field Notes: On a holiday weekend in the middle of the coronavirus pandemic, I found the trailhead and campground full and dozens of dispersed campers setup along the road and adjacent meadows. Only time will tell if this level of use is the new normal!

Tie Hack Campground
7,800 feet

Location/Map	West of Buffalo; Page 169
GPS Coordinates	N44° 17.03' W106° 56.68'
Sites/Spur Length	20 sites; Long spurs—over 30 feet
Cost	$18
Facilities/Services	Fire rings, picnic tables, water, pit toilets, trash containers, boat ramp
Managing Agency	USDA Forest Service (Bighorn National Forest); A host is often present
Reservations	Call 877-444-6777 or visit www.recreation.gov
Season/Usage	Open late May through mid-September; High use

Directions: From Buffalo, go west on HWY 16 for 14.5 miles. Turn left and drive a short distance to the campground entrance on the right.

Description: This campground was constructed in 2000 and replaced an older camp of the same name that was located where Tie Hack Reservoir is now. There are two loops of campsites, one being a heart-shaped loop and the other being a small cul-de-sac tucked away on its own. Campsites are long, level, and shaded by a thinned lodgepole pine forest that has little understory. If you're driving a large rig or have a long trailer, this is probably the best camping option you have on this side of the southern Bighorns. Unless it's a holiday week, you'll likely score a spot without a reservation though it is getting tougher to do that with each year.

Scenic Driving: The 45-mile Cloud Peak Skyway traverses the Bighorns between Buffalo and Tensleep. This roadway offers astounding views of the peaks in and around the Cloud Peak Wilderness. The high point crosses Powder River Pass at 9,666 feet.

Fishing/Boating: Tie Hack Reservoir, a quick drive from the campground, is relatively new as the dam was built in 1998. Anglers will find eager trout in the waters and shoreline fishing is usually productive. Boating is permitted for manually-powered craft.

Trails: Trails accessing the Cloud Peak Wilderness can be found at nearby Circle Park Campground. There is also a short trail that leads from the reservoir's boat ramp to the base of the dam.

Picnicking: There is a picnic area at Tie Hack Reservoir. To get there, follow the gravel road from the campground for less than 2 miles to the reservoir.

Tie Hack Reservoir

ATV Trail: A 6-mile ATV trail runs between FR 391 to the north and Elgin Park to the south. To find the trail, head back toward the highway and look for it on both sides of the gravel road.

Field Notes: I have spent a few nights here nearly every year since the camp opened. Though I prefer some of the other camps in the area, this is a family favorite because of its easy access and long parking spurs. Watch for deer and moose scampering through camp at dawn and dusk.

South Fork Campground
7,650 feet

Location/Map	West of Buffalo; Page 169
GPS Coordinates	N44° 16.69' W106° 57.01'
Sites/Spur Length	15 sites; Medium to long spurs—over 30 feet
Cost	$18
Facilities/Services	Fire rings, picnic tables, water, pit toilets, trash containers
Managing Agency	USDA Forest Service (Bighorn National Forest); A host is often present
Reservations	Call 877-444-6777 or visit www.recreation.gov
Season/Usage	Open late May through mid-September; High use

Directions: From Buffalo, take HWY 16 west for just over 15 miles.

Description: South Fork is a popular, compact camp nestled below rock outcroppings. The South Fork of Clear Creek sloshes through the camp and separates ten parking sites from five walk-in sites. All campsites are in a light forest and are not very private or spacious. Upgrades at the camp have made it more accommodating to modest-sized trailers and RVs, but it still has shorter spurs than most of the other campgrounds in the area.

Scenic Driving: The 45-mile Cloud Peak Skyway traverses the Bighorns between Buffalo and Tensleep. This roadway offers astounding views of the peaks in and around the Cloud Peak Wilderness. The high point crosses Powder River Pass at 9,666 feet.

Fishing/Boating: All three forks of Clear Creek, including the one that runs through the campground, have pan-sized brook, brown, and rainbow trout. If you're looking for lake fishing, make the short drive or hike to Tie Hack Reservoir near Tie Hack Campground. Boating is permitted for manually-powered craft.

Trails: Trails accessing the Cloud Peak Wilderness can be found at nearby Circle Park Campground. If you're looking to stay near camp, there is a path along the creek that leads to the edge of Tie Hack Reservoir.

Picnicking: There is a picnic area at Tie Hack Reservoir. To get there, head north on the highway for a half-mile, then turn east and follow the gravel road for 2 miles.

ATV Trail: A 6-mile ATV trail runs between FR 391 to the north and Elgin Park to the south. You'll find the trail near the campground entrance.

Field Notes: The South Fork Lodge, complete with a restaurant, cabins, store, and children's fishing pond is located across the highway.

Crazy Woman Canyon

A trip to the southern Bighorns should include a drive through Crazy Woman Canyon. From Buffalo, drive 25 miles west on HWY 16 and turn left onto FR 33. This narrow gravel road follows Crazy Woman Creek as it cuts through a beautiful canyon. The road descends steeply, losing nearly 3,000 feet over an average 8% grade. After 13.3 miles, you reach HWY 196 south of Buffalo. The road has plenty of potholes, dips, and rocks, so trailers, RVs, and low-clearance sedans are not recommended. Dispersed camping is popular along FR 33 where there are a few pullouts and primitive campsites.

It's not fully known where the name Crazy Woman was derived, but several accounts involve a woman who went crazy after an Indian attack.

Lost Cabin Campground

8,100 feet

Location/Map	Southwest of Buffalo; Page 169
GPS Coordinates	N44° 8.74' W106° 57.01'
Sites/Spur Length	19 sites; Long spurs—over 30 feet
Cost	$17, $34 for group site
Facilities/Services	Fire rings, picnic tables, water, pit toilets, trash containers
Managing Agency	USDA Forest Service (Bighorn National Forest); A host is often present
Reservations	Call 877-444-6777 or visit www.recreation.gov
Season/Usage	Open early June through early September; Moderate use

Directions: From Buffalo, take HWY 16 west for 27 miles to the short access road on the right.

Description: Lost Cabin is snuggled into a forest of skinny lodgepole pines and is a considerable distance from other campgrounds. The parking spurs (including a few pull-throughs) will accommodate most campers and RVs. The campground is slower to fill than many along the highway and you are likely to get a site without a reservation unless it's a holiday week.

Scenic Driving: The 45-mile Cloud Peak Skyway traverses the Bighorns between Buffalo and Tensleep. This roadway offers astounding views of the peaks in and around the Cloud Peak Wilderness. The high point crosses Powder River Pass at 9,666 feet.

There are a few gravel routes in the area that make nice backcountry drives. The first is FR 31, which begins 1.5 miles west of the campground on HWY 16 and rejoins the highway five miles north of FR 33 (Crazy Woman Canyon Road). There is nothing spectacular about this 10-mile route, but it does create an easy backcountry cruise.

A slightly more scenic and adventurous drive is down Crazy Woman Canyon on FR 33. See the description on the previous page for more information.

Easy drives down nearby Billy Creek Road and Hazelton Road also make pleasant trips. You'll find those about a mile back east on HWY 16.

Wildlife Viewing: Watch for moose in the camp and in the willows along the highway.

Field Notes: Even though its right along the highway, this camp has a hidden, out-of-the-way feel to it. In fact, it's easy to drive right on by and miss the turn. With a lot less ATV traffic in this area, it's also one of the area's quieter campgrounds.

Doyle Campground

8,150 feet

Location/Map	Southwest of Buffalo; Page 169
GPS Coordinates	N44° 4.39' W106° 59.31'
Sites/Spur Length	19 sites; Long spurs—over 30 feet
Cost	$16
Facilities/Services	Fire rings, grills, picnic tables, water, pit toilets, trash containers
Managing Agency	USDA Forest Service (Bighorn National Forest)
Reservations	Call 877-444-6777 or visit www.recreation.gov
Season/Usage	Open early June through mid-September; Moderate use

Directions: From Buffalo, take HWY 16 west for 26 miles. Turn south onto Hazelton Road (paved at first) and travel 6 miles to the campground entrance on the left.

Description: If you are seeking solitude or a remote setting, look no further. This is a quiet camp far from the noisy highway. Campsites are well spaced around a timbered loop and have adequate parking spurs for most trailers and motor homes. Small Doyle Creek runs in a clearing south of the campground. Although not directly visible from most sites because of the forest, a string of 10,000-foot peaks rise over the western horizon. Three of the named summits, from north to south, are Hesse Mountain, Hazelton Pyramid, and Hazelton Peak.

Scenic Driving: Head south on the Hazelton Road and you can find a number of scenic backcountry drives. One option is to take the Rome Hill Road west to the town of Tensleep. An even more impressive drive can be made by heading south on the Slip Road to reach Kaycee. It's a good hour of driving to Tensleep and a little longer to Kaycee.

Wildlife Viewing: When you drive to the campground, watch for moose in the marshy areas on the west side of the road. Across from the campground road, you'll find a beaver lodge in Doyle Creek.

Fishing: Trout can be found in Dull Knife Reservoir, located about 5 miles south on Hazelton Road. Part of the land around the reservoir is private property, but public parking is available. A short walk is required to reach the shoreline.

Dispersed Camping: There is a sole dispersed campsite at the junction of Hazelton Road and the campground road that is very popular. Other dispersed sites can be found further north on Hazelton Road near HWY 16.

ATV Trails: There are a few miles of ATV trails east of the campground. These are old roads that extend to the southern boundary of the national forest.

Field Notes: We have spent many weekends at this great getaway. But like any other campground, your stay will depend on your neighbors. The last time we stayed here an inconsiderate, unlawful group of dispersed campers stayed in the meadow across from the campground and incessantly raced ATVs through the camp until they were threatened by a camper.

Lakeview Campground

8,550 feet

Location/Map	Northeast of Tensleep; Page 169
GPS Coordinates	N44° 10.6' W107° 12.87'
Sites/Spur Length	20 sites; Short to medium spurs—up to 30 feet
Cost	$18, $36 for group sites
Facilities/Services	Fire rings, picnic tables, water, pit toilets, trash containers, boat ramp
Managing Agency	USDA Forest Service (Bighorn National Forest); A host is sometimes present
Reservations	Call 877-444-6777 or visit www.recreation.gov
Season/Usage	Open early June through mid-September; Moderate use

Directions: From Buffalo, take HWY 16 west for 42 miles to the campground entrance. If traveling from Tensleep, head east on HWY 16 for 20 miles.

Description: This campground sits on the shoreline of Meadowlark Lake, a 325-acre loch in the southern Bighorns. Some parking spurs will fit a decent-sized trailer, but this is predominantly a tenter's camp. In fact, half of the sites are designated only for tents. Shady fir trees, a high elevation, and lake-sweeping breezes make this a cool mountain getaway.

Scenic Driving: The 45-mile Cloud Peak Skyway traverses the Bighorns between Buffalo and Tensleep. This roadway offers astounding views of the peaks in and around the Cloud Peak Wilderness. The high point crosses Powder River Pass at 9,666 feet.

Fishing/Boating: Meadowlark Lake holds rainbow trout as well as some brook and cutthroat. Boat ramps are located on the north shore and at Meadowlark Lake Resort.

Trails: A short, steep, and very scenic half-mile trail leads to the James T. Saban fire lookout where you'll enjoy panoramic views of the entire mountain range. This historical structure is no longer in use. To reach it, head east on HWY 16 for a couple miles, turn south onto FR 429, and drive a short distance to a parking area near an outdoor chapel.

Picnicking: Lake Point, a picnic area, is found on the west shoreline of Meadowlark Lake. Willow Park (group campground) can also be used.

Field Notes: The only drawbacks I can think of for this camp is that you'll hear quite a bit of highway noise and the mosquitoes can be troublesome. In my last few visits, I've found the camp to be full or nearly so. Consider reservations if you want to stay in this high-altitude getaway.

Sitting Bull Campground

8,700 feet

Location/Map	Northeast of Tensleep; Page 169
GPS Coordinates	N44° 11.41' W107° 12.67'
Sites/Spur Length	42 sites; Long spurs—over 30 feet
Cost	$18, $36 for group sites
Facilities/Services	Fire rings, grills, picnic tables, water, pit toilets, trash containers, boat ramp
Managing Agency	USDA Forest Service (Bighorn National Forest); A host is often present
Reservations	Call 877-444-6777 or visit www.recreation.gov
Season/Usage	Open early June through mid-September; High use

Directions: From Buffalo, take HWY 16 west for 41.5 miles and turn north onto the access road. If traveling from Tensleep, head east on HWY 16 for 19.5 miles to the turnoff.

Description: This is one of the most attractive and popular campgrounds in the Bighorns. The first set of campsites overlook a mountain park with terrific views of the Cloud Peak Wilderness to the northeast. You'll find many of these sites (1-16) to be taken first. Almost every site comes with a generous chunk of real estate. The young forest grows thick and privacy between campers is good. Very long parking spurs appeal to the "generator-crowd"—those with larger RVs and fifth-wheel trailers. It is getting tougher to grab a site here; reservations are strongly recommended.

Scenic Driving: The 45-mile Cloud Peak Skyway traverses the Bighorns between Buffalo and Tensleep. This roadway offers astounding views of the peaks in and around the Cloud Peak Wilderness. The high point crosses Powder River Pass at 9,666 feet.

Wildlife Viewing: Moose frequent the willow-lined banks of Lake Creek along the campground's access road. Yellow-bellied marmots can also be found near the bridge at the beginning of the road.

Fishing/Boating: Meadowlark Lake holds rainbow trout as well as some brook and cutthroat. Boat ramps are located on the north shore and at Meadowlark Lake Resort.

Trails: A "Nature Trail" departs from the west side of the campground's loop road. The trail is actually a confusing interwoven network of cross-country ski paths marked only by blue diamonds on the trees (and there are a lot of them). The trail explores several marshes and ponds and is easy enough for the whole family.

4WD/ATV Routes: A 3.5-mile ATV trail starts north of the campground and travels to beautiful East Tensleep Lake. The old road gently gains a thousand feet and includes a ford of Lake Creek. For a longer route, there is a 4.9-mile

Mountain views near Sitting Bull Campground

4WD road (FR 430) that leads to the lake. The road begins from a parking area on HWY 16 just east of the campground's access road.

Picnicking: There are two picnic areas near Meadowlark Lake. Lake Point is located on the west shoreline and Willow Park, which is also a group camp, is less than a couple miles to the west.

Field Notes: This is a terrific camp! Flanking a sprawling meadow and rushing stream, and offering easy access to a fishing lake, a foot trail, and an ATV trail, it has something for everyone. People know this, of course, which is why it is so popular.

Willow Park Group Campground
8,400 feet

Location/Map	Northeast of Tensleep; Page 169
GPS Coordinates	N44° 10.91' W107° 14.27'
Sites/Spur Length	1 group site; Long spurs—over 30 feet
Cost	$75-$145
Facilities/Services	Fire rings, grills, picnic tables, water, pit toilets, trash containers, playground
Managing Agency	USDA Forest Service (Bighorn National Forest)
Reservations	Call 877-444-6777 or visit www.recreation.gov
Season/Usage	Open early June through mid-September; Moderate use

Directions: From Buffalo, take HWY 16 west for 43 miles and turn north onto the access road. If traveling from Tensleep, head east on HWY 16 for 18 miles to the turnoff.

Description: Willow Park is a day-use picnic area that can also be reserved for overnight group camping. It's an outstanding facility for a large group and it's an ideal location for such an outing. There's room here for a few trailers or RVs, but many more options exist for tents. (If you have a lot of cars to be parked, you'll quickly run out of room for trailers.) The picnic tables, grills, fire rings, and benches are all nicely scattered under the coniferous forest. Up to 150 people for day use or 60 overnight campers are permitted. Rates are based on group size.

Scenic Driving: The 45-mile Cloud Peak Skyway traverses the Bighorns between Buffalo and Tensleep. This roadway offers astounding views of the peaks in and around the Cloud Peak Wilderness. The high point crosses Powder River Pass at 9,666 feet.

Fishing/Boating: Meadowlark Lake holds rainbow trout as well as some brook and cutthroat. Boat ramps are located on the north shore and at Meadowlark Lake Resort.

Trails: This picnic area and group camp also serves as a trailhead in the winter. The network of cross-country ski paths you find here (marked by blue diamonds on the trees) total 13 miles in length. During the summer, expect some of these trails to be overgrown, though navigable by the corridor they cut through the trees.

4WD/ATV Routes: A 3.5-mile ATV trail can be found north of Sitting Bull Campground. There is also a 4.9-mile 4WD road (FR 430) that starts just east of the turnoff to Sitting Bull. Both of these routes lead to beautiful East Tensleep Lake.

Picnicking: Lake Point is a picnic area located on the west shoreline of the Meadowlark Lake.

Field Notes: When I first got into winter backpacking—showshoeing during the day and snow camping at night—I took months to carefully plan my first trip, which was going to start right here at Willow Park. The only thing I didn't plan on is what I would do if there was no snow, which is exactly what happened. I pulled in on a December morning, found not a single snowflake on the ground, and drove right back home to Casper. I've never returned in the winter since then, but in all my other summer visits, I've only seen campers here one time.

Boulder Park Campground

8,000 feet

Location/Map	Northeast of Tensleep; Page 169
GPS Coordinates	N44° 9.93' W107° 15.1'
Sites/Spur Length	32 sites; Long spurs—over 30 feet
Cost	$17
Facilities/Services	Fire rings, picnic tables, water, pit toilets, trash containers
Managing Agency	USDA Forest Service (Bighorn National Forest); A host is often present
Reservations	Call 877-444-6777 or visit www.recreation.gov
Season/Usage	Open early June through mid-September; High use

Directions: From Buffalo, take HWY 16 west for 45 miles and turn onto FR 27. If traveling from Tensleep, travel east on HWY 16 for 17 miles. Drive a short distance and watch for the campground on the left.

Description: This updated campground is favored for its easy access and is a favorite of RVers. There are two rows of sites with one strip near the banks of West Tensleep Creek. The camp is freckled with pine trees and some leftover sagebrush from Tensleep Canyon. Though this is a popular camp, a handful of sites can usually be found vacant.

Scenic Driving: The 45-mile Cloud Peak Skyway traverses the Bighorns between Buffalo and Tensleep. This roadway offers astounding views of the peaks in and around the Cloud Peak Wilderness. The high point crosses Powder River Pass at 9,666 feet.

Fishing/Boating: Meadowlark Lake holds rainbow trout as well as some brook and cutthroat. Boat ramps are located on the north shore and at Meadowlark Lake Resort.

Trails: West Tensleep Trailhead, located at the end of FR 27 near West Tensleep Lake Campground, offers access to several hiking trails in the Cloud Peak Wilderness.

Picnicking: There are a couple nearby picnic areas. Lake Point is located on the west shoreline of Meadowlark Lake and another option is Willow Park, which also serves as a group camp.

Field Notes: Upgrades to this camp were completed in 2009. Though it resulted in fewer sites, the water and sewer systems were updated and the parking spurs were realigned. If you're going to be spending time on the western side of the Bighorns, this camp is worth considering. It receives fewer ATVs and has less dusty traffic than the camps on FR 27 headed up to West Tensleep Lake.

Island Park Campground

8,550 feet

Location/Map	Northeast of Tensleep; Page 169
GPS Coordinates	N44° 12.32' W107° 14.26'
Sites/Spur Length	10 sites; Medium spurs—up to 30 feet
Cost	$17
Facilities/Services	Fire rings, picnic tables, water, pit toilets, trash containers
Managing Agency	USDA Forest Service (Bighorn National Forest)
Reservations	Call 877-444-6777 or visit www.recreation.gov
Season/Usage	Open mid-June through mid-September; Moderate use

Directions: From Buffalo, head west on HWY 16 for 45 miles and turn onto FR 27. If traveling from Tensleep, travel east on HWY 16 for 17 miles. Drive north on FR 27 for 3 miles.

Description: This campground is located in a pine forest but receives its name from an adjacent mountain meadow. There is nothing particularly exciting about the camp, but it should fit the bill if you're just looking to spend the weekend in the woods. Campsites are located along the banks of West Tensleep Creek, which separates the camp from the park. Tenting is the most common form of camping even though the sites are level and can accommodate average-sized trailers and RVs.

Fishing: West Tensleep Creek is said to be a good fishery for various trout species including rainbow, brook, brown, and cutthroat. The campground has a separate parking area for anglers.

Trails: West Tensleep Trailhead, located at the end of FR 27 near West Tensleep Lake Campground, offers access to several hiking trails. There is also a trail south of the campground that leads to East Tensleep Lake, but it is not a very popular route.

Field Notes: You'll find that this campground, along with Deer Park up the road, is popular with the locals and ATV riders. The Forest Service is planning on re-arranging some of these sites in the future.

Deer Park Campground

8,900 feet

Location/Map	Northeast of Tensleep; Page 169
GPS Coordinates	N44° 14.65' W107° 13.35'
Sites/Spur Length	7 sites; Medium spurs—up to 30 feet
Cost	$17
Facilities/Services	Fire rings, picnic tables, water, pit toilets, trash containers
Managing Agency	USDA Forest Service (Bighorn National Forest)
Reservations	Not accepted—first come, first served
Season/Usage	Open mid-June through mid-September; Moderate use

Directions: From Buffalo, head west HWY 16 for 45 miles and turn onto FR 27. If traveling from Tensleep, travel east on HWY 16 for 17 miles. Drive north on FR 27 for 6.2 miles.

Description: Deer Park is a nice campground wrapped around a small loop near West Tensleep Creek. Tent-friendly campsites are well-shaded thanks to a mixed forest of spruce and fir. The neighboring grassy park often fills with dispersed campers, especially holiday weekends and during the autumn hunting season. Reservations are not taken here.

Fishing: West Tensleep Creek is said to be a good fly-fishing stream for various trout species including rainbow, brook, brown, and cutthroat. Another stream, Middle Tensleep Creek, is a quarter mile hike to the east.

Trails: A trail located on the other side of the road leads to several destinations. Follow this route and you'll reach Middle Tensleep Creek a quarter mile to the east. Here, a separate trail travels north to Tensleep Falls; it's less than a mile to the cascade. Continuing east, you'll labor up two major climbs to reach Bear Park at 2 miles and beautiful East Tensleep Lake at 4.5 miles.

Picnicking: A picnic area is located at the West Tensleep Trailhead, just a mile up the road.

Field Notes: As of this writing, the Forest Service is planning on closing this campground and building a new one named Warner Draw closer to HWY 16. The new camp would be much larger and would easily hold long RVs and trailers.

West Tensleep Lake Campground
9,100 feet

Location/Map	Northeast of Tensleep; Page 169
GPS Coordinates	N44° 15.55' W107° 12.9'
Sites/Spur Length	10 sites; Medium spurs—up to 30 feet
Cost	$17
Facilities/Services	Fire rings, picnic tables, water, pit toilets, trash containers
Managing Agency	USDA Forest Service (Bighorn National Forest)
Reservations	Call 877-444-6777 or visit www.recreation.gov
Season/Usage	Open mid-June through mid-September; High use

Directions: From Buffalo, take HWY 16 west for 52 miles to FR 27 and head north for 7.3 miles.

Description: Well known for its beauty, this campground was developed on the east shoreline of a high mountain lake. Lightly-timbered campsites are just a few paces from the lakeshore. The picturesque waters draw anglers, photographers, and many drive-by visitors. Bald Ridge (9,870 feet) dominates the western horizon, while the rocky Bighorn peaks are seen in the north. The nearby trailhead bustles with activity as hikers and horse packers head into the Cloud Peak Wilderness.

Fishing: West Tensleep Lake, and the creek, are good trout fisheries for various species including rainbow, brook, brown, and cutthroat.

Trails: The campground is located next to West Tensleep Trailhead where three trails depart. Heading south for less than a mile is the Tensleep Falls Trail. This family-friendly path leads to a beautiful cascade. Two longer routes head north into the Cloud Peak Wilderness. The left fork heads to popular alpine gems like Lake Helen (5 miles) and Mistymoon Lake (7 miles). The more strenuous right fork heads to Mirror Lake (3 miles) and a connected duo called Lost Twin Lakes (6.5 miles). Both trails present long hauls, but their exceptional destinations are well worth the effort.

Picnicking: A picnic area is located at the trailhead.

Field Notes: The Forest Service has proposed re-locating this busy campground a half mile to the south, converting it to tent-only, and creating a foot trail to the lake. The plan may or may not happen, but it's something to be mindful of when planning a trip. Also know that the elevation here is high and the weather can be cold, even during the summer months. I've been snowed on twice at this campground in July.

West Tensleep Creek

Leigh Creek Campground

5,400 feet

Location/Map	Northeast of Tensleep; Page 169
GPS Coordinates	N44° 4.84' W107° 18.88'
Sites/Spur Length	11 sites; Short to medium spurs—up to 30 feet
Cost	$16
Facilities/Services	Fire rings, picnic tables, water, pit toilets
Managing Agency	USDA Forest Service (Bighorn National Forest)
Reservations	Call 877-444-6777 or visit www.recreation.gov
Season/Usage	Open late May through mid-September; Moderate use

Directions: From Buffalo, travel east on HWY 16 for 55 miles to a turnoff. From Tensleep, head east on HWY 16 for just over 7 miles. Drive a half-mile on old HWY 435 to the camp.

Description: This tightly packed campground sits deep inside Tensleep Canyon near a perpendicular gorge called Leigh Canyon. The geography of the carved bedrock is impressive as the limestone walls rise over a thousand feet overhead. The powerful force of Tensleep Creek and Leigh Creek fills the air with a natural rumble. This camp is at a lower elevation than most so don't expect a forest of evergreens. Instead, you'll find campsites tucked into typical canyon flora consisting of junipers, cottonwoods, pine, and aspen. The creeks nourish a thick layer of understory brush, which creates superb privacy between campers. You can fit a trailer here if you want to, but the camp is better suited for tent campers.

Scenic Driving: The 45-mile Cloud Peak Skyway traverses the Bighorns between Buffalo and Tensleep. This roadway offers astounding views of the peaks in and around the Cloud Peak Wilderness. The high point crosses Powder River Pass at 9,666 feet.

Fishing: Tensleep Creek is said to be a fair fly-fishing stream for a variety of trout species including rainbow, brook, brown, and cutthroat. You'll probably want to travel upstream to calmer waters, however.

Trails: The Salt Lick Trailhead is located on HWY 16 just a few miles downhill from the campground on BLM land. This moderate 2.5-mile trail gives you great views of Tensleep Canyon as well as distant mountain ranges.

Rock Climbing: Tensleep Canyon has a reputation for its excellent rock climbing and it's gaining more visitors every year. There are over 300 identified routes on its red and white limestone cliffs.

Dispersed Camping: Primitive camping can be found at the WigWam Fish Hatchery Access Area, 4 miles downhill on HWY 16.

Field Notes: Written across the page of my research notes was the following scribbling: "Awesome canyon walls!" A fish hatchery neighbors the campground and is worth a visit.

Medicine Lodge Archaeological Site　　4,800 feet

Location/Map	Northeast of Worland; Page 169
GPS Coordinates	N44° 17.53' W107° 32.37'
Sites/Spur Length	28 sites, 1 group area; Long spurs—over 30 feet
Cost	$9 state residents, $16 nonresidents or $19-26 for electric sites
Facilities/Services	Electric hookups, fire rings, picnic tables, water, pit toilets, trash containers, playgrounds
Managing Agency	Wyoming State Parks, Historic Sites & Trails
Reservations	Required; Call 877-996-7275 or visit wyoparks.state.wy.us
Season/Usage	Open May through October; Moderate use

Directions: From Worland, take HWY 16 north to Manderson. Turn onto HWY 31 and drive east for 21 miles to Cold Springs Road just north of Hyattville. Turn north onto this road, but turn east again after just a quarter mile. Follow this road for 4 miles, and watch for the Medicine Lodge Wildlife Habitat and Archaeological Site sign. The campground is 1.5 miles north of this sign.

Description: The Medicine Lodge Archaeological Site is one of Wyoming's unspoken treasures. Hidden in a ho-hum desert basin, the site sits in a lush draw of grass, shrubs, and trees with contrasting bright red sandstone cliffs. This unexpected micro-landscape is located in a place of transition where the rugged, dry basin sweeps up into high mountain meadows. In fact, according to Wyoming State Parks, there are five distinct vegetation zones in just a twelve-mile radius from the campground.

There are three main camping areas at Medicine Lodge: the Lower Camp, Middle Camp, and a group area. All of them feature grassy parks with plenty of shade near a scenic brook. Many of the sites will accommodate trailers of average length and tenting options are plentiful. A handful of electric sites are also available. Reservations are required for all campsites as well as the group area.

If you don't camp at Medicine Lodge, consider making it a day trip. There are several small interpretive centers, trails, and countless spots for a picturesque picnic. The main attraction is a sandstone wall carved with historical petroglyphs.

Wildlife Viewing: The archaeological site doubles as a designated wildlife habitat area. An extensive list of small mammals live here: rabbits, marmots, beavers, fox, weasels, coyotes, badgers, mink, and porcupine. Larger animals that inhabit the area include deer, bear, elk, bobcats, and mountain lions. There are also over 100 species of birds that have been noted in the area.

Fishing: Anglers can fish for brown and brook trout in Medicine Lodge Creek, which flows next to the campground. There is a sidewalk with turnouts where anglers can access the pools in the creek.

Trails: A beautiful interpretive trail, complete with designated stops, is the best way to explore the archaeological site.

4WD/ATV Routes: Departing from the north end of the archaeological site is a 12-mile 4WD/ATV route that climbs toward Black Butte in the Bighorn National Forest. The first few miles travel through a shallow, but magnificent canyon. The road ends where it intersects FR 17 near Medicine Lodge Lake Campground. There is also a short ATV trail that connects the archaeological area to Cold Springs Road to the east.

Picnicking: Medicine Lodge makes an excellent place to picnic. There are grassy lawns to spread out, or you can find a shady spot along the creek.

Field Notes: If you've never been here, you should go. It's one of Wyoming's special places.

Medicine Lodge Archaeological Site

Castle Gardens Campground

5,000 feet

Location/Map	Southwest of Tensleep; Page 169
GPS Coordinates	N43° 57.41' W107° 31.03'
Sites/Spur Length	2 sites; Medium spurs—up to 30 feet
Cost	Free
Facilities/Services	Fire rings, grills, picnic tables, pit toilets, limited cellular service
Managing Agency	Bureau of Land Management (Worland Field Office)
Reservations	Not accepted—first come, first served
Season/Usage	Open May through October; Low use

Directions: From Tensleep, take HWY 16 west for 2 miles. Make a quick jog south and turn right onto the old highway. Drive 1 mile west, make a south turn onto a dirt road and drive 5 more miles.

Description: Castle Gardens consists of a unique cirque of sandstone rock formations that are continuously eroded by wind and water. The rock shapes are quite unique; it's like stumbling upon one of God's geological experiments. There are only two sites here. One is suitable for a trailer and the other is a walk-in site. There is a cellular signal here in the greater basin, but it gets weak near the campground's rugged terrain.

Natural Attractions: There's not a lot to do here outside of having a picnic and exploring the wonder of the formations.

4WD/ATV Routes: This area has 150 miles of trails and roads as part of the Nowater OHV Trail System. These paths explore the rugged and broken basin lands west of the Bighorn Mountains. The BLM office in Worland can provide you with more information and a map (which is also available on their website).

Field Notes: I don't know if anyone actually camps here. The only other person I've seen at the site is the county sheriff. However, if you're in the area, consider checking the gardens out—they do demand a picnic visit at the least. Remember to take water if you go.

AREA 3 NORTH - NORTHEAST
Black Hills and Northeastern Lowlands

From a distance, the Black Hills—a short mountain range better described as foothills—appear as a dark dome on Wyoming's northeastern grasslands. While these mountains are synonymous with South Dakota, the portion of the range that extends into Wyoming is known as the Bear Lodge Mountains.

Much of the area surrounding the Black Hills can be considered lowlands, at least by Wyoming's standards. The countryside is mixed-grass prairie with an elevation of 4,000 feet or lower. In the Black Hills National Forest, the hillsides are covered with aspen and ponderosa pine trees. Bur oak and dense shrubbery fill in the gaps, especially in the wetter areas.

Northeast Wyoming has a strong bird population with many different species. Small mammals are also common, but it's the whitetail deer and wild turkeys that receive the most attention. While small numbers of elk are known to exist in the denser forests, sightings are rare. Black bears were thought to be absent from the area, but sightings in recent years has proven otherwise. Mountain lions and bobcats are increasing in number.

The most popular attraction in the region is found at Devils Tower National Monument where you'll see a rock column that rises over a thousand feet into the sky. The formation has become an icon for the state of Wyoming, appearing on license plates, drivers' licenses, and occasionally bumping Yellowstone and the Tetons off the cover of state tourism magazines.

Devils Tower aside, there are many other recreational opportunities in Wyoming's northeast corner. Keyhole State Park has a large reservoir that offers fishing and watersports. In the relatively tame Black Hills, you can expect mild weather while you enjoy the family-friendly hiking trails and picnic sites. This is one of the best places just to set out for a quiet walk in the forest.

What to Expect: Due to lower elevations, these campgrounds are free of snow much sooner than others in Wyoming. May and June are good times to camp in the Black Hills. Occasionally, unstable air masses in the region spawn severe thunderstorms that pound the area with lightning, wind, hail, and rain. This is especially true in neighboring South Dakota. July and August bring hotter temperatures, but fewer storms. September and October usher in milder, often perfect weather. Changing autumn colors are another incentive to visit the area before winter snows close these mountains.

Aside from holiday weekends, most of these campgrounds see light use and you'll have plenty of space to yourself. However, the annual Sturgis Motorcycle Rally in nearby Sturgis, South Dakota brings very heavy traffic to the area, especially to Devils Tower. The rally is usually held the first full week of August.

Area 3: Black Hills and Northeastern Lowlands

Campgrounds	Sites	Cost	Average Spur Length	Electrical Hookups	Cellular Service (varies by carrier/site)	Reservations Accepted	Page Number
Sand Creek Public Access Area	24+	Free	L		▂▃▄		196
Bearlodge Campground	8	$14	M				197
Cook Lake Campground	33	$24	L			✔	198
Sundance Horse Campground	10	$14	L		▂▃▄	✔	199
Reuter Campground	24	$14	M		▂▃▄	✔	200
Belle Fourche Campground Devils Tower National Monument	46	$20-30	M		▂▃▄		201
Keyhole State Park	283	$15-25	L	✔	▂▃▄	✔	203

Average Spur Length: S = Short (under 30 feet), M = Medium (+-30 feet), L = Long (+-40 feet)
Cellular Service: 1 bar = weak/unreliable signal, 2 bars = low usable signal, 3+ bars = reliable signal for most users

Sand Creek Public Access Area

3,650 feet

Location/Map	Northeast of Sundance; Page 195
GPS Coordinates	N43° 57.41' W107° 31.03'
Sites/Spur Length	24+ sites; Long spurs—over 30 feet
Cost	Free
Facilities/Services	Fire rings, pit toilets, limited cellular service
Managing Agency	Wyoming Game and Fish
Reservations	Not accepted—first come, first served
Season/Usage	Open all year; Moderate use

Directions: From Sundance, take I-90 east for 18 miles to Exit 205 at Beulah. Turn south on the gravel road and drive 2 to 3 miles to any one of the numerous turnoffs.

Description: Wyoming Game and Fish access areas often consist of nothing more than gravel lots in out-of-the-way places around the state. While Sand Creek is certainly out-of-the-way, it represents the best of public land. The mile-long camping area is found along spring-fed Sand Creek and is complemented by an arrangement of trees and canyon walls. The grassy campsites are dispersed and primitive, but many of them have stone fire rings and obvious parking spurs.

Fishing: Sand Creek is considered one of the best fishing streams in the Black Hills. It's claimed that between five and six thousand trout (brown, rainbow, and some brook) live in each mile stretch of the stream. Locals warn that rattlesnakes are thick in the area so watch your step.

Field Notes: For years I wondered where the people of northeastern Wyoming camped as they certainly don't pile into the local Forest Service campgrounds. The mystery was solved the day I rounded the bend in the road and saw Sand Creek. It can be a busy place sometimes, but it's large enough to absorb a good number of campers.

Bearlodge Campground   4,700 feet

Location/Map	North of Sundance; Page 195
GPS Coordinates	N44° 39.27' W104° 19.64'
Sites/Spur Length	8 sites; Medium spurs—up to 30 feet
Cost	$14
Facilities/Services	Fire rings, picnic tables, pit toilets, trash containers
Managing Agency	USDA Forest Service (Black Hills National Forest)
Reservations	Not accepted—first come, first served
Season/Usage	Open all year; Low use

Directions: From Alva, Wyoming, take HWY 24 east for 7 miles (it's 27 miles east of Devils Tower). You can also get to this camp from the Cook Lake Recreation Area by driving 9 miles north on FR 832 to HWY 24. Turn east and go 2 miles. The campground is located on the south side of the highway.

Description: This pleasant camp consists of a single loop in a thinned forest of ponderosa pine just off the highway. It's a campground that draws few complaints, and often just as few visitors. While most campers hurry past to Devils Tower, those looking for a shady, grassy campsite with easy access should plan a stop here. Average-sized trailers and RVs can fit in these sites, but smaller rigs or tents have the advantage.

Natural Attractions: Devils Tower National Monument, 27 miles to the west on HWY 24, offers hiking, sightseeing, and rock climbing.

Scenic Driving: The 11-mile drive on FR 830 (across the highway to the north) travels through a unique Wyoming forest. There are several revealing vantage points along this route.

Field Notes: At the time of this writing, the water system was shut off, so bring your own. Until it is restored, the campground has been charging a reduced fee.

Cook Lake Campground

4,750 feet

Location/Map	North of Sundance; Page 195
GPS Coordinates	N44° 35.35' W104° 24.22'
Sites/Spur Length	33 sites; Long spurs—over 30 feet
Cost	$24
Facilities/Services	Fire rings, picnic tables, water, pit toilets, trash containers
Managing Agency	USDA Forest Service (Black Hills National Forest); A host is often present
Reservations	Call 877-444-6777 or visit www.recreation.gov
Season/Usage	Open late-May through mid-September; High use

Directions: From Sundance, drive west on HWY 14 for 2 miles. Turn north onto FR 838 and drive 19 miles following the signs for the Cook Lake Recreation Area. The pavement ends after 8 miles and the road turns to narrow gravel. Turn west onto FR 842 and proceed 1 mile to the camp.

To get there from HWY 24, drive west from Alva for 5 miles and turn south on FR 838. Bear left at the junction and follow FR 832 for 7 miles.

Description: Devils Tower aside, Cook Lake is the premier destination in Wyoming's Black Hills. Unfortunately, instability in the slope above the lake has caused the camp to be partially (and sometimes entirely) closed since 2014. Underground monitoring stations were installed to help officials measure land movement and assess risk to the public.

Cook Lake Campground

The campground consists of an A loop (sites 1–18) and a B loop (sites 19–33) with the former being closer to the lake's shoreline. Eight sites in Loop A are walk-in sites that offer more privacy than the others. Loop B is perched in a ponderosa pine forest above the lake, with a few sites in direct view of the water. The parking spurs in Loop B are better suited for trailers and RVs.

Scenic Driving: Be sure to take a trip south through the Black Hills toward the town of Sundance. The drive is roughly 20 miles and can be completed on several different forest roads including FR 838, FR 832, and FR 841. You'll find impressive stands of aspen and the Warren Lookout Tower, which is still in use today.

Fishing/Boating: Anglers will find brown and rainbow trout in Cook Lake. Boaters are welcome, but only manually-powered craft or electric motors are permitted. There is a designated angler parking area.

Trails: A 1-mile trail loops around the lake, though it was closed as of this writing due to landslide concerns. A longer option is the 3.5-mile Cliff Swallow Trail. Open to mountain bikes, horses, and hikers, the trail explores a short ridge above the Beaver Creek drainage. Both trails are family friendly.

Picnicking: A picnic area is located along the lake.

Field Notes: As of this writing, Loop A was only open to day use. Contact the Forest Service for current conditions if you are planning a trip here.

Sundance Horse Campground

4,800 feet

Location/Map	Northeast of Sundance; Page 195
GPS Coordinates	N44° 26.57' W104° 20.84'
Sites/Spur Length	10 sites; Long spurs—over 30 feet
Cost	$14
Facilities/Services	Fire rings, picnic tables, water, pit toilets, trash containers, cellular service
Managing Agency	USDA Forest Service (Black Hills National Forest)
Reservations	Call 877-444-6777 or visit www.recreation.gov
Season/Usage	Open late-May until snow closure; Low use

Directions: From Sundance, travel east on HWY 14 for 1 mile. Turn north onto Government Valley Road and drive 2 miles to the camp.

Description: This camp is on the eastern edge of Wyoming's Bear Lodge Mountains where the pine forest transitions into the grassy plains. Right on the edge of the national forest boundary, the camp has no trees, shade, or privacy from other campers. What it does offer is a terrific view over a broad valley where whitetail deer often forage.

The ten main campsites are spaced along a single loop. The parking spurs are long, level, and wheelchair accessible. You'll have no problem putting a truck and horse trailer into one of these spots. Camping is also permitted in the main parking area for self-contained horse trailers and tow vehicles.

The camp is well equipped for pack animals and riders. There are six corrals that each hold four horses and two feed bunks that accommodate eight animals each. Hitching posts and a rider mounting ramp, for those with disabilities, also adds to the camp's accessibility features.

Trails: The camp's trailhead accesses 54 miles of trails in the Carson Draw and Sundance trail systems. The trails make excellent rides, or hikes, and are open to hoof and foot traffic, mountain biking, and cross-country skiing. Most of them gain less than a couple hundred feet in elevation. The Forest Service has a trail brochure that includes maps and route information.

Field Notes: I've never seen a camper or trail user here, with or without horses. It's a nice camp and its convenient proximity to I-90 makes it useful to campers who are just passing through to other destinations.

Reuter Campground

5,450 feet

Location/Map GPS Coordinates	Northwest of Sundance; Page 195 N44° 25.65' W104° 25.43'
Sites/Spur Length	24 sites; Medium spurs—up to 30 feet
Cost	$14
Facilities/Services	Fire rings, picnic tables, water, pit toilets, trash containers, cellular service
Managing Agency	USDA Forest Service (Black Hills National Forest); A host is often present
Reservations	Call 877-444-6777 or visit www.recreation.gov
Season/Usage	Open late-May until snow closure; Low use

Directions: From Sundance, head west 2 miles and turn north onto FR 838 (watch for the Cook Recreation Area sign). Travel 2.5 miles on the paved road to the campground.

Description: With close proximity to major highways and easy accessibility from paved roads, Reuter Campground is terrific for those who like camping in national forests without bumping along a long dusty road. The camp makes an excellent base from which you can explore the Black Hill's Bear Lodge Mountains and Devils Tower. You'll find two loops of spacious and level campsites that are shaded by a forest of ponderosa pine.

Scenic Driving: Be sure to take a trip north through the Black Hills. The drive to HWY 24 is less than 30 miles and can be completed on several different forest roads including FR 838, FR 832, and FR 841. Attractions include the Warren Lookout Tower, which is still in use today, and the Cook Lake Recreation Area where you'll find a campground, picnic area, trails, and fishing lake.

Trails: A trailhead just west of the campground accesses 54 miles of trails in the Carson Draw and Sundance trail systems. The trails make excellent rides, or hikes, and are open to hoof and foot traffic, mountain biking, and cross-country skiing. Most of them gain less than a couple hundred feet in elevation. The Forest Service has a trail brochure that includes maps and route information.

Field Notes: Surprisingly, the host is often the only occupant found at this campground during the week, but I know people who come here every year for just that reason (it's quiet!). If you're looking to just pull off the Interstate for the night, or you want a shady hideaway, this one fits the bill.

Belle Fourche Campground - Devils Tower National Monument

3,850 feet

Location/Map	Northeast of Gillette; Page 195
GPS Coordinates	N44° 34.91' W104° 42.46'
Sites/Spur Length	46 sites, 3 group tent sites; Medium spurs—up to 30 feet
Cost	$20, $30 for group sites
Facilities/Services	Grills, picnic tables, water, restrooms, trash containers, dump station, cellular service
Managing Agency	National Park Service
Reservations	Not accepted—first come, first served
Season/Usage	Open early April through October; High use

Directions: From Gillette, drive east on I-90 for 26 miles to Moorcroft. Drive north on HWY 14A for 26 miles to HWY 24. You can also take HWY 14 west from Sundance for 20 miles to this junction. Take HWY 24 north for 6 miles.

Description: This two-loop campground is next to the grassy banks of the calm Belle Fourche River (Fourche is pronounced "foosh"). Large cottonwood trees shade the campsites, providing relief on hot summer afternoons. Pull-through sites are level and will accommodate most trailers and RVs.

There are three group sites (B9-B12) for tenting groups ranging from six to twenty campers. Four vehicles are allowed at each spot.

Natural Attractions: The obvious attraction at this campground is Devils Tower. A 1,267-foot eroded volcano core, the tower stands upright from the rolling landscape of mixed grass and forest. The site is held sacred by many American Indians, who have a differing account on how the tower was created. Learn more at the visitor center.

Trails: Five trails explore the awesome Devils Tower area. The Joyner Ridge Trail is a 1.5-mile loop at the north end of the park. Conversely, the South Side-Valley View Trail forms a 1.2-mile hike near the campground to the south. The most popular trails are Tower Trail and Red Beds Trail, which form loops around the tower. The Tower Trail is the shortest route at 1.3-miles and circles the base of the rock structure. Red Beds is longer and forms a 3-mile loop that extends into the northeast corner of the park.

Rock Climbing: Climbing to the top of Devils Tower is gaining popularity. Contact the park service before planning a trip. There are annual closures to protect nesting prairie falcons. The park service also discourages climbing during June out of respect for American Indians.

Field Notes: Fall is a beautiful time to visit this area. Also, there is a private campground near the park entrance and another 3 miles to the south.

Devils Tower National Monument

THE NORTHWEST REGION

Old Faithful Geyser, Yellowstone National Park

Chief Joseph Scenic Byway

Grand Teton National Park

Lower Falls, Yellowstone National Park

THE NORTH-NORTHEAST REGION

Cloud Peak Wilderness, Bighorn National Forest

Bighorn National Forest

Sand Creek Public Access Area, Black Hills

Devils Tower National Monument

Tensleep Creek, Bighorn National Forest

Footbridge at Prune Creek Campground

Northern Bighorn Mountains

THE CENTRAL REGION

Boysen State Park

Seminoe State Park

North Platte River at Dugway Campground

Laramie Range, Medicine Bow National Forest

Sinks Canyon State Park

THE SOUTHWEST REGION

Big Sandy River, Wind River Range

Firehole Canyon, Flaming Gorge
National Recreation Area

Cottonwood Lake,
Bridger-Teton National Forest

Green River, Warren Bridge Recreation Area

THE SOUTH-SOUTHEAST REGION

Snowy Range, Medicine Bow Mountains

Vedauwoo, Medicine Bow National Forest

Aspen Alley, Sierra Madre Range

Keyhole State Park

4,100 feet

Location/Map	East of Gillette; Page 195, 203
GPS Coordinates	N44° 21.35' W104° 45.02'
Sites/Spur Length	286 sites, 3 group sites; Long spurs—over 30 feet
Cost	$15 state residents, $25 nonresidents (includes $6 or $9 day-use fee)
Facilities/Services	Hookups (Tatanka campground only), fire rings, picnic tables, water, pit toilets, trash containers, dump station, marina, boat ramps, cellular service, cabins
Managing Agency	Wyoming State Parks, Historic Sites & Trails
Reservations	Call 877-996-7275 or visit wyoparks.state.wy.us
Season/Usage	Open all year; Moderate use

Directions: From Gillette, drive east on I-90 for 38 miles and take Exit 165 for Pine Ridge Road. Turn north and drive 7 miles. You can also exit at Moorcroft (26 miles east of Gillette) and drive north on HWY 14 for 5 miles. Turn east on HWY 113, drive east 8 miles, and then head north for a short distance on Pine Ridge Road.

Description: Keyhole State Park encompasses a large reservoir in northeastern Wyoming where the rugged terrain of the Black Hills concedes to open prairie. The park consists of sagebrush flats on the west side and sparse pine forests on the eastern half. Created in 1952 and holding 14,720 acres of water, the reservoir is considered an important habitat for many species of migrating birds. The climate is known to be excellent in the spring and fall and mild during the summer. Snowmobiling is popular in the winter.

There are eight campgrounds around the reservoir's eastern bays and another two near the community of Pine Haven. Facilities vary between camps, but all of them have fire rings and pit toilets at a minimum.

Keyhole State Park

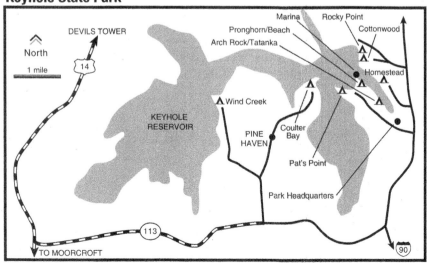

The most northern camp, Rocky Point, is near the reservoir's dam and includes 16 primitive, open sites. Nearby Cottonwood Campground is larger, and offers a pine forest, playground, and group picnic shelter.

Neighboring Pronghorn, Homestead, Arch Rock, Beach, Tatanka, and Pat's Point are mostly open camps with some stands of pine. These larger camps collectively offer more than 150 sites. Most have gravel parking spurs and a few are handicap accessible. Pat's Point has a boat ramp that can be used when water levels are high. Beach Campground has a handful of undeveloped sites that are on unlevel ground.

The premier camp, Tatanka, offers water and electric hookups, four camping cabins, a dozen tent sites, picnic sites, two group sites, and trees.

The interior campgrounds—Coulter Bay and Wind Creek—include a total of 30 undeveloped sites and are close to boat ramps. The eastern one, Coulter Bay, has mostly walk-in sites near rock cliffs and no trees. Wind Creek to the west has trees but does not have any potable water.

A marina on the east side of the reservoir provides supplies, groceries, showers, licenses, boat rentals, and ten campsites with electric hookups.

Wildlife Viewing: There are 225 species of birds in the Keyhole area. Species observed in the summer include osprey, white pelican, common yellowthroat, and savannah sparrow. Bald eagles can be spotted during the winter months. You can get a list of species at the park's headquarters.

Fishing/Boating/Swimming: Keyhole holds northern pike in addition to walleye. There are five boat ramps, a marina, and a swim beach.

Picnicking: Cottonwood, Tatanka, and Coulter Bay have group picnic shelters.

Field Notes: The nearby town of Pine Haven has a July 4th celebration that includes a fireworks show over the water as well as a boat parade.

Keyhole State Park

CENTRAL
Reservoirs, prairies, and mountains

Much of central Wyoming is rolling grassland and sagebrush prairie. Badlands and a handful of mountain ranges also lie scattered across the region, but many are tiny and lack access. Yet while droves of campers migrate to Wyoming's forested high country each summer, thousands stay in the central uplands for recreation. The reason? Water. This region holds a number of large reservoirs that are filled by the North Platte and other large rivers. Places to boat and fish in this part of the state are many.

If you are one who prefers a mountainous setting, don't overlook this region quite yet. The Laramie Mountains, Green Mountain, and the eastern front of the Wind River Mountains are all found in central Wyoming. All three ranges top 8,000 feet and have the evergreen forests that many campers seek out.

The diversity found in the central region's land is also found in its recreational opportunities. Besides boating and fishing at the reservoirs, there are hiking trails, four-wheeling routes, and natural attractions that will delight sightseers. Central Wyoming also has the lion's share of the state's best rock climbing areas.

Central Areas

1. Wind River Country (page 208)
2. Hole-in-the-Wall Hideouts (page 228)
3. Central Mountains and Reservoirs (page 236)
4. Eastern Reservoirs and Laramie Range (page 254)

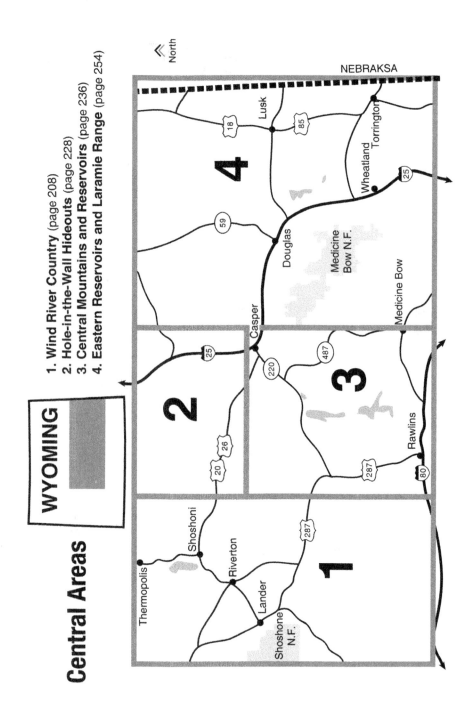

Privately-owned Campgrounds and RV Dump Stations

This section includes the general locations of privately-owned RV parks. For contact information and addresses for these businesses, look online or check out the campground directory on the Wyoming Office of Tourism website at travelwyoming.com.

Area 1: Wind River Country
Lander, Riverton, and Thermopolis all have a healthy selection of large RV parks. Some of these campgrounds are very attractive, and a few are located outside of the towns along the incoming highways.

Area 2: Hole-in-the-Wall Hideouts
The town of Kaycee, between Casper and Buffalo, has a pair of privately-owned camps.

Area 3: Central Mountains and Reservoirs
Casper, on the north end of the area, has several good RV campgrounds. Rawlins, on the south end of the area along I-80, also has a pair of private camps. The Alcova area has a small RV park.

Area 4: Eastern Reservoirs and Laramie Range
There are numerous private campgrounds along the I-25 corridor. Wheatland and Glendo have a small selection of private camps including one on the Interstate between these two towns. Douglas has a private camp on the west side of town as well as free camping at a city park along the North Platte River. Private campgrounds further east can be found in Lusk, Guernsey, and near Fort Laramie.

RV Dump Stations
The locations below include public RV dump stations. Additional dump stations can often be found at private campgrounds and large gas stations.
- Riverside City Park, Douglas, WY
- Glendo State Park
- Guernsey State Park
- Wheatland City Park, Wheatland, WY
- Boysen State Park
- Riverton Municipal Wastewater Treatment Plant, Riverton, WY
- Seminoe State Park
- Natrona County Park at Alcova Reservoir
- HWY 220: Independence Rock Rest Area
- I-25: Dwyer Rest Area north of Wheatland, WY

AREA 1 | CENTRAL
Wind River Country

The name Wind River is a broad term in Wyoming. It not only describes a major watercourse, but also an Indian reservation, a mountain range, a canyon, and the countryside surrounding the communities of Thermopolis, Lander, and Riverton.

Wind River country has an incredibly varied landscape. In some areas you'll find badlands, sprawling sagebrush flats, and rugged hills that are void of trees. But then, just a short distance away, you'll discover densely treed mountains, lush draws, and a fertile agricultural valley.

In the area's high country, deer, elk, moose, and black bears roam the forests. Grizzlies are not far away, either, and stragglers have been spotted in the mountains above Lander and also west of Thermopolis. Pronghorn antelope and coyotes thrive in the sagebrush deserts, as do sage grouse. Raptors are other birds that do well in this plant community.

There are many things to see and do in the area. A number of these destinations are not found in the high mountains, but rather in the lower, semi-arid countryside. One of the more notable natural attractions is the beautiful Wind River Canyon between Shoshoni and Thermopolis. When driving through the canyon, watch for bighorn sheep. Of course, the town of Thermopolis, with its hot springs, pools, and waterslides, is always a favorite stop for many travelers. Another worthwhile stop is South Pass City. This gold-mining community—a still occupied ghost town, if you will—is located south of Lander and has a nicely restored historical site. Those looking for a backcountry drive should check out Castle Gardens, east of Riverton. This intriguing area includes hoodoo rock formations that have distinct petroglyphs carved into them. Sinks Canyon State Park and Boysen State Park are also great places to visit, if not spend a weekend.

From almost anywhere in Wind River country, you can see the snowy peaks of the Wind River Range. The eastern front of this range stretches into central Wyoming and is a popular destination for campers. Many of the campgrounds are located near a lake and offer trout fishing and boating. This end of the Wind Rivers also has a great number of backcountry trails that lead into the beautiful wilds of the range.

What to Expect: Campgrounds in this area's lower elevations make good destinations in the early summer while the snow melts out in the higher mountains. By July, the upper trailheads and camps open for the season, which is just a few months in duration (until snow closes the roads).

If you've got a long fifth-wheel trailer or RV, the campgrounds along Louis Lake Road in the Wind River Range are not as easily accessible to you. Although the trickiest part of this road—the steep switchbacks that climb out of Sinks Canyon—is now paved, it's still a 9% grade. When the pavement ends, the road narrows, roughens, and offers few turnarounds. Most of the big rigs you spot in these mountains are dispersed camped in the parks near the southern end of Louis Lake Road, and they were driven here from the south, which has a much more gradual ascent.

Expect nearly daily thunderstorms in and around the Wind Rivers. The storms here tend to build later in the evening and you can get some impressive lightning shows a few hours after sunset.

Daytime traffic through these campgrounds is high, but many visitors head back to town for the evening. I've rarely found any of these campgrounds to be full and have always scored a terrific site.

Popo Agie Falls, Shoshone National Forest

Area 1: Wind River Country

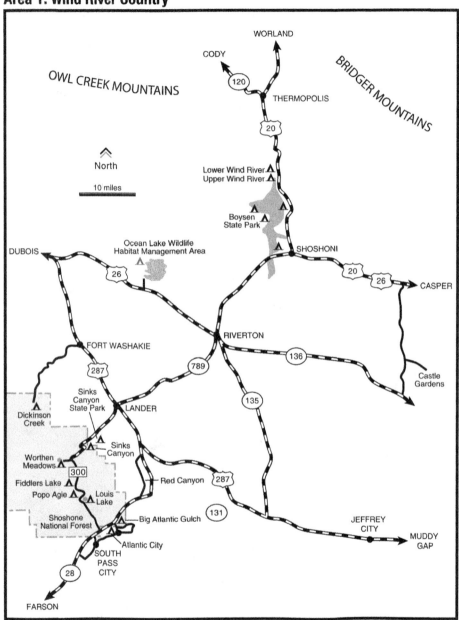

Campgrounds	Sites	Cost	Average Spur Length	Electrical Hookups	Cellular Service (varies by carrier/site)	Reservations Accepted	Page Number
Boysen State Park	286	$15-25	L		▂▄▆	✓	211
Dickinson Creek Campground	15	Free	S				215
Ocean Lake WHMA	6	Free	L		▂▄▆		216
Sinks Canyon State Park	29	$9-16	M				217
Sinks Canyon Campground	9	$15	M		▂▄▆	✓	218
Worthen Meadows Campground	28	$15	M				220
Fiddlers Lake Campground	20	$15	L				221
Little Popo Agie Campground	4	Free	S				222
Louis Lake Campground	9	$10	S				223
Big Atlantic Gulch Campground	8	$6	L				225
Atlantic City Campground	18	$6	L				226

Average Spur Length: S = Short (under 30 feet), M = Medium (+-30 feet), L = Long (+-40 feet)
Cellular Service: 1 bar = weak/unreliable signal, 2 bars = low usable signal, 3+ bars = reliable signal for most users

Boysen State Park
4,750 feet

Location/Map	Between Riverton and Thermopolis; Page 210, 212
GPS Coordinates	N43° 24.11' W108° 10.13'
Sites/Spur Length	286 sites; Long spurs—over 30 feet
Cost	$15 state residents, $25 nonresidents (includes $6 or $9 day-use fee)
Facilities/Services	Fire rings, picnic tables, water, pit toilets, trash containers, playground, dump station, marina, boat ramps, cellular service
Managing Agency	Wyoming State Parks, Historic Sites & Trails
Reservations	Call 877-996-7275 or visit wyoparks.state.wy.us
Season/Usage	Open all year; Low to moderate use

Directions: For campgrounds on the east shoreline and north of the reservoir, head north from Shoshoni on HWY 20. Turnoffs for campground access roads are located at 6 miles, 13 miles, and 15 miles. Campgrounds on the west shoreline are accessed by driving west of Shoshoni on HWY 26. Access roads are located at 1 mile and 5 miles.

Description: This state park is named after Asmus Boysen, whose vision was to build a dam for electric generation and irrigation purposes at the

Boysen State Park

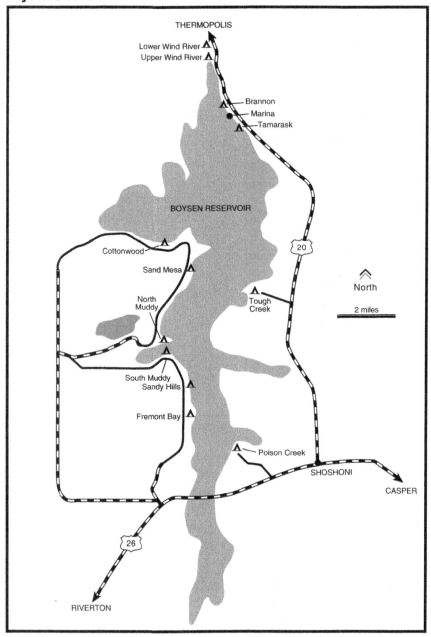

beginning of the twentieth century. A newer dam is now in use, but parts of the original structure can still be seen today.

The state park covers 40,000 acres in the high desert of central Wyoming. The surrounding area consists of sagebrush-covered terrain. The short and sparsely timbered Bridger Mountains are found to the northeast and the Owl Creek Mountains are spread out to the northwest. The higher peaks of the Wind Rivers can be seen along the southern horizon.

There are a dozen campgrounds at Boysen Sate Park. Two of these, the Lower Wind River and Upper Wind River, are located in Wind River Canyon, north of the reservoir. Combined, these very accessible camps offer 90 campsites between a beautiful river and HWY 20. You'll find shady cottonwood trees, a playground, and campground host. There is a wide variety of level parking spurs and you're likely to find one that fits just right. Occasional trains rumble through a nearby mountain tunnel.

The remaining campgrounds are situated along the reservoir's 76 miles of shoreline. Brannon campground, at the far north, has quite a few features. A changing house is provided for swimmers. A manicured grassy area serves as an inviting spot for picnickers and campers alike. Tamarask Campground is just a hop and skip from Brannon and the marina. A few shade trees dot the area and there are picnic shelters. There are 65 sites between these two camps.

Tough Creek Campground is on the reservoir's eastern shoreline. It has 65 sites, a sprinkling of shade trees, and picnic shelters. This is a popular campground that can accommodate long trailers. There is also a dock and boat ramp.

A more primitive camp, Poison Creek, is located on the southeast shore of the reservoir near the town of Shoshoni. It has no potable water and a sole picnic table. If you are looking for solitude, Poison Creek has less overnight traffic, although drive-by visitors are common during the daylight hours.

Fremont Bay is the largest camp on the reservoir's western shoreline. With just three developed sites, some campers are forced to crowd in where they can. The camp is a good option for accommodating larger gatherings if you have several vehicles in your group. It features a playground for the kids, a boat ramp, and a reservable group shelter. Make sure to bring sunscreen and plenty of water.

Further north is Sandy Hills, South Muddy and North Muddy. The first camp is essentially dispersed camping with a pit toilet. The second has just two sites amid tall shrubs. The picnic tables are covered, but if you get too warm, you can easily cool down if you are willing to take a plunge. North Muddy—trailers not advised— has a sandy beach and a pit toilet, but that's about all at this sunny campground. Sites at nearby Sand Mesa sit on a rocky bench and overlook the reservoir. The picnic tables are covered.

Surely a campground named Cottonwood would describe a cool shady oasis in a high desert like this. Well, not exactly... but there are a few trees along the beach. This campground, the furthest north on the reservoir's west side, offers covered picnic tables, a boat ramp, and a group area.

Natural Attractions: Thermopolis, just 20 minutes north of the reservoir, is home to Hot Springs State Park (which has no overnight camping). Go take a swim, soak, or scream down one of the water slides. You can also walk through the grassy parks that overlook the Bighorn River.

Scenic Driving: Following HWY 20 through Wind River Canyon makes a beautiful 12-mile drive. Wind River flows through the southern part of the canyon, but changes its name to Bighorn River at the Wedding of the Waters access area. Some of the canyon walls rise over 2,000 feet above the highway. Watch for bighorn sheep on these rocky slopes; it helps to have a sunroof!

Wildlife Viewing: The Lakeside Picnic Area, at the south end of the reservoir, doubles as a wildlife viewing point. The area is home to antelope, coyotes, golden eagles, and deer. An interpretive sign details the bird life in the marshy wetlands.

Fishing/Floating/Boating/Swimming: At least nine species of fish are found in Boysen Reservoir including trout, walleye, perch, bass, and grayling. Boaters will find several boat ramps along the shoreline, as well as a marina on the east side that offers supplies and licenses. A swimming area with a change house can be found near the marina.

The Wind River-Bighorn River to the north holds rainbow, cutthroat and brown trout—sometimes monstrous in size. An Indian reservation fishing permit is required to fish the river between Boysen Reservoir Dam and the Wedding of the Waters access area.

The Bighorn River, from the Wind River Indian Reservation to north of Thermopolis, is a popular stretch for recreation. A number of outfits in Thermopolis can get you set up on a fishing, rafting, or float trip. Be aware that there is a diversion dam south of Thermopolis that requires a portage. All put-in and take-out sites are located on the east side of the river.

Picnicking: The Lakeside Picnic Area and boat ramp are located at the southern tip of the reservoir along HWY 26. Picnic tables are covered and there is a viewing area for you photography types. Picnic sites can also be found at the campgrounds on the east side of the reservoir.

Field Notes: This state park continues to be a good destination as well as stop-over spot while traveling through the area. The staff continues to develop and improve the facilities and there are plans to create additional group sites. I've heard that Boysen has scorpions so keep this in mind if you spend time on the beaches. Remember to bring sunscreen and plenty of drinking water to this sunny patch of Wyoming.

Boysen State Park

Dickinson Creek Campground
9,400 feet

Location/Map	West of Lander; Page 210
GPS Coordinates	N42° 50.2' W109° 3.39'
Sites/Spur Length	15 sites; Short spurs—up to 20 feet
Cost	Free
Facilities/Services	Fire rings, picnic tables, pit toilets
Managing Agency	USDA Forest Service (Shoshone National Forest)
Reservations	Not accepted—first come, first served
Season/Usage	Open July until snow closure; Low use

Directions: From Lander, head northwest on HWY 287 for 15 miles to Fort Washakie. Turn onto Trout Creek/Moccasin Lake Road and drive another 19 miles to a fork. Bear left and drive 3 miles to the campground. This road traverses many steep, narrow switchbacks and only the first 5 miles of the route are paved. This is not a quick or easy drive, and you need to have a tribal fishing permit to be on the road (they use this permit as a sort of reservation access pass). The permit can be purchased at various stores in Lander and Fort Washakie.

Description: This remote campground is located at the edge of a sprawling mountain meadow in the Wind River Range. Dickinson Creek flows through the park. The looming mountain to the east is Black Mountain

(10,478 feet). Parking spurs in the campground are short, so tent and pickup campers have the best options. Besides, towing a trailer up the long, steep, and rough switchbacks is not recommended.

Trails: A couple of trails depart from a trailhead at Dickinson Creek and lead into the Popo Agie Wilderness. A popular route is the Smith Lake Trail, which heads uphill for 5.5 to 7 miles (depending on how far you go) to a cluster of five backcountry lakes. Plan on gaining roughly a thousand feet of elevation to reach these spectacular subalpine gems.

Another route that travels into the wilderness is the North Fork Trail. This course requires the fording of multiple mountain creeks, some of which may be too high to cross. The trail eventually reaches the incredible Cirque of Towers after nearly 14 miles. Another option that does not go into the wilderness is a 4.5-mile route that begins near the campground and leads to Shoshone Lake.

The Bears Ears Trailhead can be found a mile north of the campground. The trail here travels through the high alpine country of the southern Wind Rivers. Valentine and Washakie Lakes are destinations that require roughly a dozen miles of backcountry travel to reach.

Field Notes: Contact the Forest Service (or a local sporting goods store) to check on the status of the road before trying to drive to this campground. I've found this road to be closed for all sorts of reasons, a couple of which included snow and tribal litigation.

Ocean Lake Wildlife Habitat Management Area (Wyoming Game & Fish)

Located 17 miles northwest of Riverton, this vital wetland features Ocean Lake, a circular lake that is 31 feet deep. Though the management area is primarily used to support waterfowl, you'll also find pheasants, doves, deer, and a sizable list of small game mammals here. According to the Wyoming Game and Fish, the lake holds walleye, trout, bass, crappie, perch, bullhead, and ling. The agency also states that during the migration season, the area has up to 3,000 geese, 400 sandhill cranes, and 10,000 ducks.

The U.S. Bureau of Reclamation maintains half a dozen parking areas where you can camp. These sites have trash containers and pit toilets. Half of the sites also have boat ramps and picnic shelters.

To reach Ocean Lake from Riverton, head northwest on HWY 26 for at least 13 miles and watch for the signs. The lake sits 1.5 miles north of the highway and is accessed by multiple roads.

Sinks Canyon State Park

6,750 feet

Location/Map	Southwest of Lander; Page 210
GPS Coordinates	N42° 45.18' W107° 48.25'
Sites/Spur Length	29 sites; Short to medium spurs—up to 30 feet
Cost	$9 state residents, $16 nonresidents
Facilities/Services	Fire rings, picnic tables, water, pit toilets, trash and recycling containers, playground, limited cellular service, yurts
Managing Agency	Wyoming State Parks, Historic Sites & Trails
Reservations	Call 877-996-7275 or visit wyoparks.state.wy.us
Season/Usage	Open late May through early September; High use

Directions: From Lander, head southwest on HWY 131 for 6 miles to Sawmill Campground. It's another mile farther to Popo Agie Campground.

Description: Sinks Canyon State Park is simply awesome. Located in Sinks Canyon just outside of Lander, the park offers a visitor center, hiking trails, campsites, and picnic spots. The main attraction is the Middle Fork of the Popo Agie River as it rushes through the canyon and dumps itself into a mysterious cave. The water then runs an underground course for at least a quarter of a mile before reemerging through a spring-fed pool.

Sawmill Campground is the first campground you'll encounter when you enter the park. Found near the canyon's entrance, it features a fishing pier and has handicap-accessible facilities. The camp's short pull-off sites are partly shaded and border the roaring Middle Fork. With the river just a few feet away from the parking area, even tent options are limited. This campground's parking arrangement and facilities—including a playground and group picnic shelter—are better suited for day-use activities rather than overnight accommodations.

The larger Popo Agie Campground is found slightly higher upstream in the depths of the canyon. This is where most campers stay since it has better parking spurs for trailers and more room to spread out. You'll find canyon foliage throughout the camp including aspen, willows, and junipers. There are also four yurts that can be rented.

Natural Attractions: The park is centered around the Middle Fork of the Popo Agie River (pronounced po po shuh). The uniqueness of this river is that it "Sinks" into a mountainside cave. It runs underground for a short distance and then flows back into a pool called the "Rise." So where's the mystery in this? Consider these abnormalities. The volume of water that flows back to the surface is more than the river contained when it flowed into the cave. In addition, researchers have found that it takes over two hours for the water to make its short quarter-mile journey.

The Rise is full of plump trout. Although fishing is not permitted, the fish can be fed food from a vending machine located at the parking lot. Learn more about the river's natural phenomenon, and the canyon as a whole, at the visitor center.

Scenic Driving: Louis Lake Road travels 26 miles through the southeastern tip of the Wind River Range. You'll pass by several lakes, get a glimpse of high peaks, and possibly spot wildlife such as moose and loons. To start the drive from Lander, head up through Sinks Canyon. The road remains paved as it climbs into the Shoshone National Forest over several steep switchbacks. Where the route bears southward, it narrows and turns to gravel. Follow it through the pine forest until it ends at HWY 28 south of Lander.

Trails: There is a pair of short interpretive trails around the visitor center. A longer trail follows the south side of the river between the Bruce Picnic Area and the Popo Agie Campground. Other options include a 1-mile loop and a 4-mile loop that begin from a bridge at the upper end of the campground. Additional trails can be found further up the canyon.

Rock Climbing: Rock climbing is becoming quite popular in Sinks Canyon. There are numerous routes ranging between 35 to 100 feet with difficulty ratings that vary from 5.4 to 5.14a. Baldwin Creek is another popular local area for rock climbing. If this is your sport, check out the annual rock climbers' festival held at the Wild Iris area near South Pass City on the second weekend in July.

Picnicking: Look no further than the Bruce Picnic Area at high end of the canyon.

Field Notes: If you're seeking cooler temperatures and thicker forests than what Sinks Canyon State Park offers, keep driving onward into the Shoshone National Forest. If you don't camp in the park, put it down as a day trip and plan on spending at least an hour taking in the scenic river and canyon.

Sinks Canyon Campground

6,850 feet

Location/Map	Southwest of Lander; Page 210
GPS Coordinates	N42° 44.24' W108° 50.2'
Sites/Spur Length	9 sites; Medium spurs—up to 30 feet
Cost	$15
Facilities/Services	Fire rings, picnic tables, water, pit toilets, trash containers
Managing Agency	USDA Forest Service (Shoshone National Forest)
Reservations	Not accepted—first come, first served
Season/Usage	Open late May until snow closure; Moderate use

Directions: From Lander, drive nearly 9 miles on HWY 131 through Sinks Canyon State Park to the campground.

Description: You could easily assume this campground was located in Sinks Canyon State Park, but it actually resides just outside of the boundary on Forest Service land. The campground offers gorgeous views of the colorful canyon walls as well as the soothing rumble from the adjacent stream, the Middle Fork of the Popo Agie River. Sites are relatively open although a few junipers are rooted in the parched dirt. There are a few walk-in sites for tent campers.

Natural Attractions: The campground borders Sinks Canyon State Park, where plenty of outdoor activities await.

Scenic Driving: Louis Lake Road travels 26 miles through the southeastern tip of the Wind River Range. You'll pass by several lakes, get a glimpse of high peaks, and possibly spot wildlife such as moose and loons. To start the drive from Lander, head up through Sinks Canyon. The road remains paved as it climbs into the Shoshone National Forest over several steep switchbacks. Where the route bears southward, it narrows and turns to gravel. Follow it through the pine forest until it ends at HWY 28 south of Lander.

Fishing: Fishing the hurried waters of Middle Fork of the Popo Agie River for trout can be a tough business. If you don't mind a hike, calmer water can be found below the river's falls (described below).

Trails: A 1.5-mile hike from the Bruce Picnic Area will lead you to Popo Agie Falls where the river crashes over a mountainside and flows into the canyon. The trail climbs 600 feet to the falls and is suitable for families. Be sure to have a map if you are planning on hiking past the falls. There are twenty-eight different trails in this part of the Wind Rivers.

4WD/ATV Route: FR 351 is a steep and rough 4WD road that climbs out of Sinks Canyon (look for it on the north side of the road). At the top of the initial ascent, you'll find a small network of other 4WD roads around Fairfield Hill. There is also an ATV trail (FT 720) that runs westward to Shoshone Lake. It's 12 miles to reach the lake from Sinks Canyon. The ATV trail itself is extremely rugged and should only be attempted by experienced riders.

Rock Climbing: Rock climbing is becoming quite popular in Sinks Canyon. There are numerous routes ranging between 35 to 100 feet with difficulty ratings that vary from 5.4 to 5.14a. Baldwin Creek is another popular local area for rock climbing. If this is your sport, check out the annual rock climbers' festival held at the Wild Iris area near South Pass City on the second weekend in July.

Picnicking: The Bruce Picnic Area, just a short distance to the west in the canyon, is the easiest place to have a picnic.

Field Notes: Just as the higher Forest Service campgrounds are closing for the season, this campground is at its best. Late September and early October are especially nice times to visit because the temperatures are mild and the autumn foliage is at its peak.

Worthen Meadows Campground

8,850 feet

Location/Map	Southwest of Lander; Page 210
GPS Coordinates	N42° 41.85' W108° 55.75'
Sites/Spur Length	28 sites; Medium spurs—up to 30 feet
Cost	$15
Facilities/Services	Fire rings, picnic tables, water, pit toilets, trash containers, bear boxes, boat ramp
Managing Agency	USDA Forest Service (Shoshone National Forest)
Reservations	Not accepted—first come, first served
Season/Usage	Open July until snow closure; Moderate use

Directions: From Lander, take HWY 131 through Sinks Canyon State Park and continue up FR 300 (Louis Lake Road) for 17 miles to the camp turnoff. From the turnoff, continue 2.5 miles along a narrow and bumpy access road. The road is paved to the turnoff, but includes steep grades and tight curves on multiple switchbacks.

Description: Worthen Meadows is just one of several campgrounds along Louis Lake Road. The nicely maintained campground is divided into two sections around the shoreline of Worthen Meadows Reservoir. One group of campsites is tucked into conifers while the other sites are more open but closer to the water. Although the Forest Service reports that parking spurs are just 28 feet long, configurations almost twice that size exist near the reservoir. However, it is questionable whether you will want to haul a large rig into this part of the woods.

Scenic Driving: Louis Lake Road travels 26 miles through the southeastern tip of the Wind River Range. You'll pass by several lakes, get a glimpse of high peaks, and possibly spot wildlife such as moose and loons. To start the drive from Lander, head up through Sinks Canyon. The road remains paved as it climbs into the Shoshone National Forest over several steep switchbacks. Where the route bears southward, it narrows and turns to gravel. Follow it through the pine forest until it ends at HWY 28 south of Lander.

Fishing/Boating: Small brook and rainbow trout are found in the reservoir and there is a launch ramp for boaters. Frye Lake, a mile northeast of the Worthen Meadows turnoff, can also be fished.

Trails: Two trails leave from separate trailheads near the campground. The Sheep Bridge Trail leads to a historic creek crossing at 2.1 miles. A left turn at a nearby junction takes you to Twin Lakes, 2 miles from Sheep Bridge.

The Stough Creek Lakes Trail, the other route that leaves the campground, heads southwest for 6.5 miles to a large cluster of alpine lakes (I counted fifteen of them). The lakes are in a basin surrounded by mountains that rise over 11,000 feet.

Picnicking: A picnic area is located near the boat ramp.

Field Notes: The only drawback we noted here was the continuous noise made by hikers coming out of the nearby trailhead, well past midnight. Perhaps the intense cracking and rumbling of the night's thunderstorm was driving them from their backcountry sites.

Fiddlers Lake Campground — 9,400 feet

Location/Map	Southwest of Lander; Page 210
GPS Coordinates	N42° 38.12' W108° 52.51'
Sites/Spur Length	20 sites; Long spurs—over 30 feet
Cost	$15
Facilities/Services	Fire rings, grills, picnic tables, water, pit toilets, trash containers, bear boxes, boat ramp
Managing Agency	USDA Forest Service (Shoshone National Forest); A host is often present
Reservations	Not accepted—first come, first served
Season/Usage	Open July until snow closure; Moderate use

Directions: From Lander, take HWY 131 through Sinks Canyon State Park and continue up FR 300 (Louis Lake Road) for 23 miles. The road is paved to the turnoff for Worthen Meadows, but includes steep grades and tight curves on multiple switchbacks. Those with trailers or RVs might consider accessing Louis Lake Road from the south by taking HWY 28 south of Lander for 30 miles.

Fiddlers Lake Campground

Description: Level parking spurs, upgraded facilities, snow-covered peaks on the horizon, and inspirational sunrises on the shoreline of a mountain lake are just a few reasons to consider this camp. Sites are wide and some include enough cover for a relatively private setting. Others, with less privacy, are pull-offs that are located right along the campground road. Tent campers will find several nice walk-in sites along a small brook near the camp's entrance. The best trailer sites are found at the end of the campground road in a short loop.

Scenic Driving: Louis Lake Road travels 26 miles through the southeastern tip of the Wind River Range. You'll pass by several lakes, get a glimpse of high peaks, and possibly spot wildlife such as moose and loons. To start the drive from Lander, head up through Sinks Canyon. The road remains paved as it climbs into the Shoshone National Forest over several steep switchbacks. Where the route bears southward, it narrows and turns to gravel. Follow it through the pine forest until it ends at HWY 28 south of Lander.

Fishing/Boating: Fiddlers Lake holds small brook trout and pan-sized rainbows. A boat ramp and large parking area are located near the entrance.

Trails: A trailhead is found a half-mile south of the campground on Louis Lake Road. The main route heads 4.3 miles to Christina Lake, which is said to have some of the best fishing in the region. A separate, shorter route heads west toward Silas Canyon and Upper Silas Lake in the Popo Agie Wilderness.

Another option is to hike to the Blue Ridge Lookout. To reach this scenic overlook, find the signed 4WD road just north of the campground and then follow it up about a mile.

Field Notes: This campground is considerably higher than others near Lander. Remember to bring warm clothes and bedding for chilly nights.

Little Popo Agie Campground

8,800 feet

Location/Map	Southwest of Lander; Page 210
GPS Coordinates	N42° 36.5' W108° 51.29'
Sites/Spur Length	4 sites; Short spurs—up to 20 feet
Cost	Free
Facilities/Services	Fire rings, picnic tables, pit toilets
Managing Agency	USDA Forest Service (Shoshone National Forest)
Reservations	Not accepted—first come, first served
Season/Usage	Open July until snow closure; Low use

Directions: From Lander, take HWY 131 through Sinks Canyon State Park and continue up FR 300 (Louis Lake Road) for 26 miles. The road is paved to the turnoff for Worthen Meadows, but includes steep grades and tight curves on multiple switchbacks.

Description: Little Popo Agie may be better described as an overnight parking lot rather than a campground. There is no water or trash containers, but a few fire rings are available, as well as a pit toilet. This campground is surrounded by pines and is found along the banks of the Little Popo Agie River. It's convenient if the other camps get too busy or if you're looking for fishing access near the road. The parking spurs are short and are best suited for tents, pickup campers, or camper vans.

Scenic Driving: Louis Lake Road travels 26 miles through the southeastern tip of the Wind River Range. You'll pass by several lakes, get a glimpse of high peaks, and possibly spot wildlife such as moose and loons. To start the drive from Lander, head up through Sinks Canyon. The road remains paved as it climbs into the Shoshone National Forest over several steep switchbacks. Where the route bears southward, it narrows and turns to gravel. Follow it through the pine forest until it ends at HWY 28 south of Lander.

Fishing: The camp is near a bridge where the Little Popo Agie River flows below Louis Lake Road. The watercourse is reported to hold some of the best fishing for brook and rainbow trout in this area.

Picnicking: A picnic area is on the north shoreline of nearby Louis Lake.

Field Notes: There are two things I remember most about this campground. The first is the tranquil stretch of river near the campground's entrance, which is quite photogenic. The second is the narrow, curvy road where I repeatedly had to swerve out of the way of oncoming vehicles—be careful.

Louis Lake Campground   8,550 feet

Location/Map	Southwest of Lander; Page 210
GPS Coordinates	N42° 35.51' W108° 50.61'
Sites/Spur Length	9 sites; Short spurs—up to 25 feet
Cost	$10
Facilities/Services	Fire rings, picnic tables, pit toilets, trash containers, boat ramp
Managing Agency	USDA Forest Service (Shoshone National Forest)
Reservations	Not accepted—first come, first served
Season/Usage	Open July until snow closure; High use

Directions: From Lander, take HWY 131 through Sinks Canyon State Park and continue up FR 300 (Louis Lake Road) for 28 miles to the access road on the left. Drive 1 mile to the campground (this access road is often rough and muddy). Louis Lake Road is paved to the turnoff for Worthen Meadows, but includes steep grades and tight curves on multiple switchbacks. Those with trailers or RVs might consider accessing Louis Lake Road from the south by taking HWY 28 south of Lander for 30 miles.

Description: When people think of the mountains outside of Lander, they think of Louis Lake and its rugged backdrop. Half of the lake is guarded by rock-laden slopes while the other half is crowded by hills of pine. It gets quite busy around here during the day, but many visitors are long gone by nightfall. The campground is a compact loop that is littered with big boulders. These campsites fill quickly, much sooner than the sites in the other nearby camps. Tents are best here. Trailers over 20 feet long are not suitable although some locals squeeze them in.

Scenic Driving: Louis Lake Road travels 26 miles through the southeastern tip of the Wind River Range. You'll pass by several lakes, get a glimpse of high peaks, and possibly spot wildlife such as moose and loons. To start the drive from Lander, head up through Sinks Canyon. The road remains paved as it climbs into the Shoshone National Forest over several steep switchbacks. Where the route bears southward, it narrows and turns to gravel. Follow it through the pine forest until it ends at HWY 28 south of Lander.

Fishing/Boating/Swimming: Louis Lake holds brook, rainbow, and lake trout. There is a boat ramp as well as a pair of beaches for swimmers.

Trails/4WD Route: A foot trail starts near the Louis Lake Resort (on the west side of the lake) and travels 4.5 miles to Christina Lake. It's an uphill hike through an alternating mix of timber and meadows that gains 1,400 feet of elevation. A 9-mile 4WD road (FR 355) also leads to the lake, but starts on Louis Lake Road about 3 miles south of the campground. The first half of the road can be tackled by most 4x4s, but the last half is very rough. Without an ATV, most drivers usually end up parking somewhere and hiking the remaining distance.

Picnicking: A picnic area is located on the north shoreline of Louis Lake. It is a great place to spend a lazy summer afternoon.

Field Notes: Your experience at this small campground will depend upon your neighbors (any obnoxious noises here will fill the camp). If you don't like what you see, check out the campgrounds further north on Louis Lake Road or choose a dispersed site.

Red Canyon
Wyoming's Red Canyon is an impressive natural feature. Located 20 miles south of Lander on HWY 287/28, the canyon features a narrow valley flanked by a 500-foot band of crimson colored cliffs. The land is managed by several agencies and organizations, including the BLM, The Nature Conservancy, and Wyoming Game & Fish. A 10-mile dirt road runs through the bottom of the canyon and can be driven from mid-May through November. Dispersed camping is allowed in some areas, but there are no facilities or services.

Big Atlantic Gulch Campground

7,850 feet

Location/Map	South of Lander; Page 214
GPS Coordinates	N42° 31.15' W108° 42.86'
Sites/Spur Length	8 sites; Long spurs—up to 30 feet
Cost	$6
Facilities/Services	Fire rings, picnic tables, water, pit toilets, trash containers
Managing Agency	Bureau of Land Management (Lander Field Office)
Reservations	Not accepted—first come, first served
Season/Usage	Open May through October; Moderate use

Directions: From Lander, head south on HWY 28 for 27 miles to Atlantic City Road. Drive this road for a half mile and then turn onto BLM Road 2324 (Fort Stambaugh Loop Road). Drive a half-mile east to the campground.

Description: This BLM campground is hidden in an aspen stand along Little Atlantic Gulch (Big Atlantic Gulch itself is a short distance to the east). While there are quite a few trees here, the individual campsites don't receive much shade. Parking spurs, including a couple of pull-throughs, are long enough to hold big trailers or RVs.

Historical Attractions: South Pass City is a Wyoming historic site that is fun to visit. See the description on page 227 for more information.

Trails: The Continental Divide Trail passes through South Pass City, and the local post office sometimes holds re-supply packages for long-distance hikers who will be passing through. This is certainly not the most spectacular stretch of the CDT, but it's always fun to hike along America's backbone. You will find the trail near the historic site.

Rock Climbing: The city of Lander has a growing reputation for great rock climbing and an annual rock climbers' festival is held on the second weekend in July. Some of this sport takes place at Sinks Canyon State Park, but the hot spot is an area named Wild Iris, on Limestone Mountain. You can find the climbing walls by heading back out to HWY 28 and driving north for nearly 4 miles to FR 326 on the left. Drive 1.3 miles on this dirt lane and take a right on the next road. There are numerous climbing areas; the most popular wall requires a 20-minute hike to the north.

ATV/4WD Routes: The BLM lands in this area are crisscrossed with backroads that make fun trips on an ATV or 4x4. The nearby Shoshone National Forest also has miles of trails and roads.

Field Notes: Expect hot days and pleasantly cool nights at this campground. Afternoon and evening thunderstorms can also be expected.

Atlantic City Campground

7,950 feet

Location/Map	South of Lander; Page 210
GPS Coordinates	N42° 30.95' W108° 43.34'
Sites/Spur Length	18 sites; Long spurs—over 30 feet
Cost	$6
Facilities/Services	Fire rings, picnic tables, water, pit toilets, trash containers
Managing Agency	Bureau of Land Management (Lander Field Office); A host is often present
Reservations	Not accepted—first come, first served
Season/Usage	Open May through October; Moderate use

Directions: From Lander, head south on HWY 28 for 27 miles to the Atlantic City Road, then continue south for 2 mostly paved miles.

Description: This is a semi-arid and treeless area, so it may come as a surprise that this camp is tucked into an inviting forest of aspen and evergreens (some of which have been killed by pine beetles). Looking around the surrounding countryside, this doesn't look like terrain that sits 8,000 feet above sea level, though July snowdrifts help drive home the point.

Sites are situated around a single loop and have good privacy. This campground receives more visitation than nearby Big Atlantic Gulch Campground and sometimes fills on mid-summer weekends. If you're in the area, do consider spending a night here. It's a nice camp and affordable.

Historical Attractions: South Pass City is a Wyoming historic site that is fun to visit. See the description on page 227 for more information.

Trails: The Continental Divide Trail passes through South Pass City, and the local post office sometimes holds re-supply packages for long-distance hikers who will be passing through. This is certainly not the most spectacular stretch of the CDT, but it's always fun to hike along America's backbone. You will find the trail near the historic site.

Rock Climbing: The city of Lander has a growing reputation for great rock climbing and an annual rock climbers' festival is held on the second weekend in July. Some of this sport takes place at Sinks Canyon State Park, but the hot spot is an area named Wild Iris, on Limestone Mountain. You can find the climbing walls by heading back out to HWY 28 and driving north for nearly 4 miles to FR 326 on the left. Drive 1.3 miles on this dirt lane and take a right on the next road. There are numerous climbing areas; the most popular wall requires a 20-minute hike to the north.

ATV/4WD Routes: The BLM lands in this area are crisscrossed with backroads that make fun trips on an ATV or 4x4. One of these routes starts here in camp. Find the gate near a shed on the upper half of the loop. From here, the road climbs out of the timber and reaches an awesome overlook of the Wind River Range. The trail splits into multiple paths at this point.

Field Notes: I stayed at this camp for several days while researching this book. Here's what I discovered. Summer days get very hot, but the mild nighttime temperatures are perfect, especially compared to the cold nights you get in the higher Wind River Range campgrounds. There is considerable ATV traffic in the area, but riders tend to be respectful and quiet around camp.

South Pass City Historic Site

When gold was discovered in the Wind River Range in 1867, South Pass City became a thriving mining town. During its best days, the community had more than 1,000 residents and over 300 structures. The excitement was short lived. Just five years later, most people had moved on to better climates, easier work, or to another promising gold prospect.

Today the town survives with a population of around thirty. However, the original part of South Pass City is a Wyoming historic site that features a partially restored gold-mining boom town complete with historians who work in the stores. There may be no better place than this to experience what an authentic western town was like in the 1800s. You can take a stroll down the dusty main street, stop and talk to the blacksmith, or buy some candy from the general store. On a hot day, head over to the saloon and grab a bottle of root beer.

Gold Rush Days is an annual celebration held here during the middle of July. The event includes a vintage baseball tournament, food, games, interpretive programs, music, and mining competitions.

AREA 2 | CENTRAL
Hole-in-the-Wall Hideouts

Much of the area between Casper and the Bighorn Mountains is known as Hole-in-the-Wall Country. The name derives from a hideaway used by Butch Cassidy and the Sundance Kid, famous robbers who operated in many of the Rocky Mountain States. The Wild Bunch, as their group was called, would hang out in this remote area where they could not only hide themselves, but also their loot (commonly cash, horses, and cattle).

A drive through the area will reveal that not much has changed in the region since the days of the Wild Bunch. Aside from some oil fields and cattle ranches, the open range remains largely undeveloped. The only human presence some of this rugged country sees is from roaming sheepherders.

The uplands in this part of the state are actually southern remnants of the Bighorn Mountains. The landscape is unusual and beautiful with bright red hogbacks and buttes that create a broken horizon. Sagebrush and mixed grass carpet the ground, providing habitat for pronghorn antelope. In the higher elevations, pockets of evergreens and mountain mahogany fill the topographical seams.

On a map, this part of Wyoming appears as a wide swath of emptiness, an area either forgotten or unfit for human occupation. But immerse yourself into these parts and you'll recognize a truly special area of the West. It represents what many consider the best of Wyoming: vast open spaces, endless horizons, and an enveloping sky.

What to Expect: This area includes the state's most remote and isolated campgrounds that are located dozens of miles from the most basic services, such as a gas station. If you're bothered by the thought of changing a flat tire or running into some rough road conditions, this isn't the place for you. If you're reasonably self-reliant (or at least tell someone where you're going and when you'll be back), then you certainly shouldn't let the isolation dissuade you from visiting this fascinating area. After all, you will (probably) encounter other adventurous travelers on these roads, or at least a periodic logging truck or local rancher.

The camping season starts a few weeks after the cold weather leaves these hinterlands (mid-June or later allows any lingering snowdrifts to melt away). In the camps, you can expect light traffic during the days, dead-quiet nights, and the best stargazing you can imagine.

A view from the Wild Bunch's Hole-in-the-Wall

Area 2: Hole-in-the-Wall Hideouts

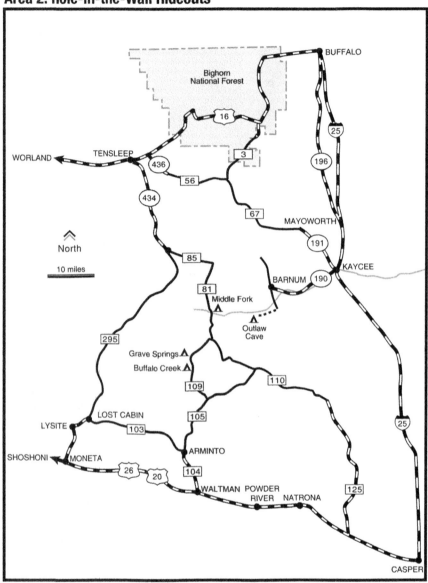

Campgrounds	Sites	Cost	Average Spur Length	Electrical Hookups	Cellular Service (varies by carrier/site)	Reservations Accepted	Page Number
Outlaw Cave Campground	7	Free	S				231
Middle Fork Campground	5	Free	S				233
Grave Springs Campground	6	Free	M				234
Buffalo Creek Campground	6	Free	M				234

Average Spur Length: S = Short (under 30 feet), M = Medium (+-30 feet), L = Long (+-40 feet)
Cellular Service: 1 bar = weak/unreliable signal, 2 bars = low usable signal, 3+ bars = reliable signal for most users

Outlaw Cave Campground

6,050 feet

Location/Map	Southwest of Kaycee; Page 230
GPS Coordinates	N43° 35.34' W106° 56.84'
Sites/Spur Length	7 sites; Short spurs—up to 20 feet
Cost	Free
Facilities/Services	Fire rings, picnic tables, pit toilets, trash containers
Managing Agency	Bureau of Land Management (Buffalo Field Office)
Reservations	Not accepted—first come, first served
Season/Usage	Open mid-April through mid-November; Low use

Directions: From Kaycee (between Casper and Buffalo), go west on HWY 191 for a mile and turn south onto HWY 190. Drive 16 miles to the end of the pavement. Turn left at the BLM sign and travel another 8.5 miles on the Outlaw Cave access road. Most of this scenic drive passes over smooth road surfaces, but the last 3 miles is best driven with a four-wheel drive or a high clearance vehicle.

Description: There is a lot of history in these parts. Butch Cassidy and the Sundance Kid used this awesome terrain as a fugitive hangout. With a fairly long drive, you can hang out here, too, but hopefully under better circumstances than the outlaws did! The semi-primitive campground is perched on the exposed rim of a magnificent canyon where the Middle Fork of the Powder River rumbles several hundred feet below your feet. Due to access, tents and pickup campers, work best. Trees are scarce and a fire burned many of the ones that used to be here along the canyon rim.

Natural Attractions: This part of Wyoming is fantastic. The red sandstone escarpments near the campground are stunningly beautiful. Even more impressive is the deep canyon that the river has carved below the camp.

Fishing: The Middle Fork of the Powder River is a wild trout fishery for brown and rainbows. The river is usually too high to cross during the early season, but late season visits permit wading.

Trails: There are three separate trails that descend into the canyon from Outlaw Cave Road. All three are rugged, steep, and potentially hazardous. The trail nearest to the campground drops the most elevation but promises to be the best route to the river. Numerous switchbacks take you from 300 to 600 feet below the canyon's rim depending on the trail you choose. Take trekking poles if you have them.

4WD Route: A rugged and rocky path continues west from the campground. This is big country out here and it comes with mixed ownership so you may encounter locked gates and private property depending on where you go. The BLM offers a good map of the area that shows land ownership and roads. There are prehistoric sites that you may find along the way that include petroglyphs, cairns, and stone circles. Please respect these features and leave them intact.

Field Notes: To prevent any confusion, this road leads to Outlaw Cave Campground, not the actual cave itself, which is purported to be somewhere in the canyon. The road also does not lead to the Hole-in-the-Wall, which is only 5 miles south of here but requires a 60-mile drive (and 4-mile hike) to reach because of private property.

Outlaw Cave Campground views

Middle Fork Campground

7,300 feet

Location/Map	Northwest of Casper; Page 230
GPS Coordinates	N43° 34.6' W107° 8.56'
Sites/Spur Length	5 sites; Short spurs—up to 20 feet
Cost	Free
Facilities/Services	Fire rings, water, pit toilets, trash containers
Managing Agency	Bureau of Land Management (Worland Field Office)
Reservations	Not accepted—first come, first served
Season/Usage	Open May through September; Moderate use

Directions: From Waltman (between Casper and Shoshoni on HWY 20/26), take CR 105 north for 23 miles. Turn left onto CR 109 (Bighorn Mountain Road) and drive 17 miles to CR 81 (Hazelton Road). Take CR 81 north for 6 miles. The county roads in the area are somewhat rocky, rough, and have a couple of creek crossings. A high clearance vehicle is recommended.

If traveling from the north, take HWY 434 south from Tensleep. Travel 20 miles and turn east onto CR 85 (Big Trails Stock Drive Road). Drive 11 miles and then turn south onto CR 81 (Hazelton Road). Proceed another 13 miles to the campground.

Description: Even though this campground is found in a remote area of central Wyoming, it receives steady visitation due to its great trout fishing. However, few of the people who pass through here during the day actually stay to camp.

The campground is tucked into the forested drainage of the Middle Fork of the Powder River where the Bighorn Mountains begin their rise. The surrounding hills give this site a "closed in" feel as if you're tucked into a small topographical hole. The camp itself is very simple—a narrow lane with a few short spurs near the babbling creek.

Fishing: The Middle Fork of the Powder River is a blue-ribbon fishery for brown and rainbow trout.

4WD Routes: This area consists of a vast tract of BLM and state land with dozens of secondary roads and trails. Be sure to obtain maps before heading out to help navigate the maze of possible routes.

Field Notes: Don't plan on visiting this campground (or any in Hole-in-the-Wall Country for that matter) if the weather has been wet. Several stretches on the incoming roads can be tricky to drive when wet. Caution is also warranted during easier, dry conditions. After leaving this campground and driving north on Hazelton Road, I hit a rut hard enough that it broke loose my exhaust manifold.

Grave Springs Campground

8,300 feet

Location/Map	Northwest of Casper; Page 230
GPS Coordinates	N43° 27.67' W107° 13.64'
Sites/Spur Length	6 sites; Medium spurs—up to 30 feet
Cost	Free
Facilities/Services	Fire rings, pit toilets, trash containers
Managing Agency	Bureau of Land Management (Casper Field Office)
Reservations	Not accepted—first come, first served
Season/Usage	Open June through October; Low use

Directions: From Waltman (between Casper and Shoshoni on HWY 20/26), take CR 105 north for 23 miles. Turn left onto CR 109 (Bighorn Mountain Road) and drive 11 miles to the entrance of the camp. The county roads in the area are somewhat rocky, rough, and have a couple creek crossings. A high clearance vehicle is recommended.

Description: If you're fed up with fighting for a spot at other campgrounds, this is your place. Of course, you'll forfeit quick and easy access since this campground is roughly an hour or more from the nearest paved road. The high foothills found here do not have a lot of trees although the camp itself is tucked into a stand of conifers. Campsites are similar to those found at Buffalo Creek Campground. They can accommodate trailers, but few people want to tow them here.

4WD Routes: This area consists of a vast tract of BLM and state land with dozens of secondary roads and trails. Be sure to obtain maps before heading out to help navigate the maze of possible routes.

Field Notes: The camp's eerie name describes the nearby graves of deceased sheepherders. A local rancher told me about the graves and you can find them with a little exploration.

Buffalo Creek Campground

8,300 feet

Location/Map	Northwest of Casper; Page 230
GPS Coordinates	N43° 26.26' W107° 13.4'
Sites/Spur Length	6 sites; Medium spurs—up to 30 feet
Cost	Free
Facilities/Services	Fire rings, pit toilets, trash containers
Managing Agency	Bureau of Land Management (Casper Field Office)
Reservations	Not accepted—first come, first served
Season/Usage	Open June through October; Low use

Buffalo Creek near Buffalo Creek Campground

Directions: From Waltman (between Casper and Shoshoni on HWY 20/26), take CR 105 north for 23 miles. Turn left onto CR 109 (Bighorn Mountain Road) and drive 9 miles to the entrance of the camp. The county roads in the area are somewhat rocky, rough, and have a couple of creek crossings. A high clearance vehicle is recommended.

Description: This camp, along with Grave Springs to the north, offers plenty of solitude. Although most of this area consists of barren foothills and rocky plateaus, the camp itself resides in a forest of conifers near Buffalo Creek. This isn't the easiest place to get a large camper, or any camper for that matter, but I have found long fifth-wheel trailers in these sites.

4WD Routes: This area consists of a vast tract of BLM and state land with dozens of secondary roads and trails. Be sure to obtain maps before heading out to help navigate the maze of possible routes.

Field Notes: Remote! Driving this far from a paved road or town may make some people uncomfortable, but many will love it. It's one of the places in Wyoming where you can look out and not see a trace of mankind. Also worth mentioning: I've never seen a greater concentration of butterflies anywhere than along Buffalo Creek.

AREA 3 CENTRAL
Central Mountains and Reservoirs

Central Wyoming has a scattering of high desert mountain ranges. The Seminoe, Ferris, Pedro, Granite, and Shirley Mountains are rarely mentioned, but appreciated, as they add islands of interest in a sea of tedious sage and mixed-grass prairie.

It's not these mountains that draw campers, but the water between them. After gathering its headwaters in Colorado, the North Platte River runs through the hills, filling a trio of large reservoirs (Seminoe, Pathfinder, and Alcova) along the way. Fishing the reservoirs is common, and a portion of the river itself is nationally known for its blue-ribbon "Miracle Mile." Boating and riding personal watercraft are perhaps even more popular. Rock climbing is also a favored activity. Fremont Canyon near Pathfinder Reservoir has hundreds of routes that overhang the North Platte.

Not all mountains in central Wyoming are of the short, barren variety. With elevation—trees and roads, too— comes recognition. Casper Mountain, Muddy Mountain, and Green Mountain are not only well known, but also well visited. These mountains feature mostly pine forests where campgrounds, hiking trails, and cooler temperatures await.

Deer, mountain lions, and black bears live on Casper Mountain and Muddy Mountain. Antelope and wild horses roam the open expanses below Green Mountain, but it is elk, and some large ones, that live in the mountain's dark timber and aspen stands.

What to Expect: When camping in this part of Wyoming, know that the busiest places are those closest to Casper: Alcova Reservoir and Casper Mountain. The farther you travel from Wyoming's second-largest city, the thinner the crowds become.

During the summer, the campgrounds in this area are largely weekend destinations. Stop by one of these during the middle of the week and you'll likely get the spot of your choice. This trend changes once cool weather settles in and the fall hunting seasons begin. When that time comes, activity shifts from the reservoirs to the mountain camps as people pursue deer, antelope, elk, and small game such as grouse.

Regardless of the season, you can expect wind here. Wind speeds are often tolerable during the summer months, but all bets are off if you are here during the other seasons. The gales that blast this part of Wyoming often topple semi-trucks and have even blown trains off their tracks.

Be sure to fill your fuel tank before you leave. It's possible to log a couple hundred miles across these expanses before you'll find another gas station. One last note—summer temperatures can swell in this sun-baked country so bring plenty of water and sunscreen.

Fremont Canyon near Pathfinder Reservoir

Area 3: Central Mountains and Reservoirs

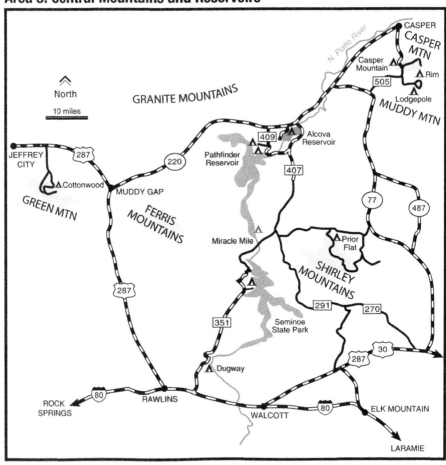

Campgrounds	Sites	Cost	Average Spur Length	Electrical Hookups	Cellular Service (varies by carrier/site)	Reservations Accepted	Page Number
Casper Mountain Campgrounds	100	$10	M		2 bars		239
Lodgepole Campground	15	$7	M		2 bars		241
Rim Campground	8	$7	L		2 bars		242
Alcova Reservoir	150	$10-35	L	✔	2 bars	✔	243
Pathfinder Reservoir	80	$10	L		2 bars		246
Cottonwood Campground	18	$6	M				249
Prior Flat Campground	15	Free	M				250
Seminoe State Park	94	$15-25	L		2 bars	✔	251
Dugway Campground	6	Free	M				253

Average Spur Length: S = Short (under 30 feet), M = Medium (+-30 feet), L = Long (+-40 feet)
Cellular Service: 1 bar = weak/unreliable signal, 2 bars = low usable signal, 3+ bars = reliable signal for most users

Casper Mountain Campgrounds

8,000 feet

Location/Map	South of Casper; Page 238, 240
GPS Coordinates	N42° 44.08' W106° 18.86'
Sites/Spur Length	100 sites; Short to medium spurs—up to 30 feet
Cost	$10
Facilities/Services	Fire rings, picnic tables, water, pit toilets, trash containers, playground, cellular service
Managing Agency	Natrona County Parks
Reservations	Not accepted—first come, first served
Season/Usage	Open late May through mid-October; High use

Directions: From Casper, take HWY 251 (Casper Mountain Road) south for approximately 6 miles to the top of Casper Mountain. Stay left on CR 505 for another mile. The campgrounds are located on both sides of the road.

Description: There are five campgrounds on Casper Mountain. The most popular of these is Beartrap Meadows, which has the most level sites and includes the area's only trash containers and potable water. The camp also includes a playground and large group picnic shelters. The other four campgrounds are located east of the road and include Skunk Hollow Park, Deer Haven Park, Elkhorn Springs Park, and Tower Hill Park. Most sites in these primitive campgrounds have short, uneven parking spurs.

Casper Mountain and Muddy Mountain

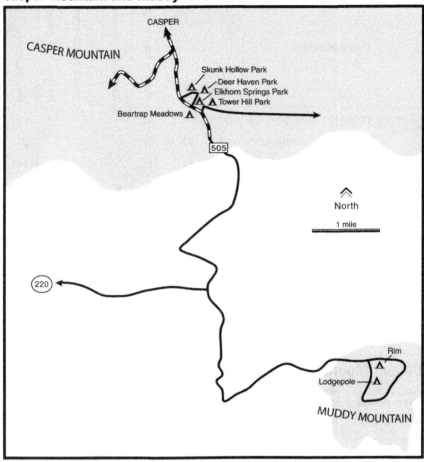

Camping on Casper Mountain is best left for those with tents or short, self-contained campers. Of all the campsites, only a pair at Beartrap will reasonably accommodate trailers and most campers don't bother towing a unit up the mountain's steep, curvy grade.

Much of the coniferous forest in the campground area has been thinned, reducing privacy between sites. Don't expect much solitude either. The locals flock to this area on the weekends and the campgrounds bustle with heavy day use and moderate overnight use.

Natural Attractions/Picnicking: Garden Creek Waterfall is a cascade found at the northern base of Casper Mountain near the junction of HWY 252 (Garden Creek Road) and HWY 251 (Casper Mountain Road). A short hike is required to reach the waterfall.

Trails: Mountain bikers can take advantage of a vast network of winter ski trails that traverse the top of Casper Mountain. Most of these are signed and blue diamonds mark the routes.

Hikers will find two excellent loops in the area. The first is the Lee McCune Braille Trail in Skunk Hollow Campground, on Strube Loop. It makes a short, but very nice trek. The longer route is the excellent 4.5-mile Bridle Trail near Garden Creek Waterfall. The trail gains nearly 2,000 feet as it travels through dense forest on the north slope of Casper Mountain.

Field Notes: This is a nice place, especially for daytime activities. However, the last time we stayed in Beartrap Meadows, kids with paintball guns ran rampant through occupied sites barraging trees with blue paint. That visit was only slightly worse than the one before it. If you are looking for a more serene escape, check out one of the lesser-visited camps on Casper Mountain or Muddy Mountain to the south.

Lodgepole Campground

8,100 feet

Location/Map	South of Casper; Page 238, 240
GPS Coordinates	N42° 40.64' W106° 15.81'
Sites/Spur Length	15 sites; Medium spurs—up to 30 feet
Cost	$7
Facilities/Services	Fire rings, picnic tables, water, pit toilets, trash containers, cellular service
Managing Agency	Bureau of Land Management (Casper Field Office); A host is often present
Reservations	Not accepted—first come, first served
Season/Usage	Open mid-June through late November; Moderate use

Directions: From Casper, take HWY 251 (Casper Mountain Road) south for approximately 6 miles to the top of Casper Mountain. Stay left on CR 505 and continue down the south side of the mountain into a narrow valley. Bear left at the fork and follow the signs to the top of Muddy Mountain, a few miles up the road. At the top you'll find another junction near an information kiosk. Turn right and drive south for a quarter of a mile.

Description: This camp is found burrowed into a mature lodgepole pine forest on the top of Muddy Mountain. Though close to Wyoming's second largest city, the mountain emanates a feeling of seclusion and usually makes a quiet place to spend the night. Sites are level and long enough for most trailers or RVs, and a few pull-throughs are also available.

Trails: Muddy Mountain has an interpretive trail system that consists of 2 miles of easy walking paths (pedestrian-use only). An overview map is located at the information kiosk, which is easily found on the way to the campground. Need a longer stroll? Consider walking the 2.25-mile road that loops around the top of Muddy Mountain.

Field Notes: Though Muddy Mountain can feel quite tame, it does possess "big mountain" characteristics, black bears and mountain lions included.

Rim Campground

8,100 feet

Location/Map	South of Casper; Page 238, 240
GPS Coordinates	N42° 40.84' W106° 15.51'
Sites/Spur Length	8 sites; Long spurs—over 30 feet
Cost	$7
Facilities/Services	Fire rings, picnic tables, water, pit toilets, trash containers, cellular service
Managing Agency	Bureau of Land Management (Casper Field Office)
Reservations	Not accepted—first come, first served
Season/Usage	Open mid-June through late November; Low use

Directions: From Casper, take HWY 251 (Casper Mountain Road) south for approximately 6 miles to the top of Casper Mountain. Stay left on CR 505 and continue down the south side of the mountain into the shallow divide. Bear left at the fork and follow the signs to the top of Muddy Mountain, a few miles up the road. At the top you'll find another junction near an information kiosk. Keep left at the junction and watch for the campground on the left.

If you're towing a trailer, consider reaching this camp by heading south out of Casper on HWY 220 to HWY 487. Then take CR 505 eastward to the turnoff for Muddy Mountain. This eliminates pulling over Casper Mountain's steep grades.

Description: This is a nicely-maintained campground that comes with views. The lightly timbered sites are configured along the north rim of Muddy Mountain and offer excellent vantage points of Casper Mountain.

While most sites are back-ins, a few pull-through sites are available. Muddy Mountain receives far less use than Casper Mountain, but still sees moderate traffic during the day. Evenings are quiet, barring a lightning storm. If you do get a storm here, you'll be in for quite a light show.

Natural Attractions: There is a viewing platform at the campground that overlooks the scenic valley that separates Casper Mountain from Muddy Mountain. Both mountains rise 1,300 feet from the grassy valley floor.

Trails: Muddy Mountain has an interpretive trail system that consists of 2 miles of easy walking paths (pedestrian-use only). Large signs with maps and descriptions are located near the campground. Need a longer stroll? Consider walking the 2.25-mile road that loops around the top of Muddy Mountain.

Field Notes: There are several places on this mountain where you can look south and spot Elk Mountain and the Medicine Bow Mountains. Though those summits are 80 miles away as the crow flies, it's no problem seeing them across the clear Wyoming sky.

Rim Campground on Muddy Mountain

Alcova Reservoir
5,500 feet

Location/Map	Southwest of Casper; Page 238, 244
GPS Coordinates	N42° 31.8' W106° 46.69'
Sites/Spur Length	150+ sites; Long spurs—over 30 feet
Cost	$10 or $35 with full hookups
Facilities/Services	Full hookups (limited), fire rings, picnic tables, pit toilets, trash containers, playground, dump station, boat ramps, marina, cellular service
Managing Agency	Natrona County Parks
Reservations	Call 307-235-9311 for RV sites, group picnic shelters, or boat docks
Season/Usage	Open all year; High use

Directions: To access campgrounds on the reservoir's west side, head southwest from Casper on HWY 220 to Alcova (about 31 miles). Continue past Alcova for a mile and turn south onto CR 406, marked with a large swinging map sign. Meander along this paved road for up to 5 miles.

To access campgrounds on the reservoir's east side, turn south on CR 407 at the town of Alcova. Drive 3 miles to the Black Beach access road or 5 miles to the Cottonwood Beach access road.

Description: Alcova Reservoir is Casper's summertime playground and a scenic one at that. The blue waters contrast sharply with the surrounding

Alcova Reservoir

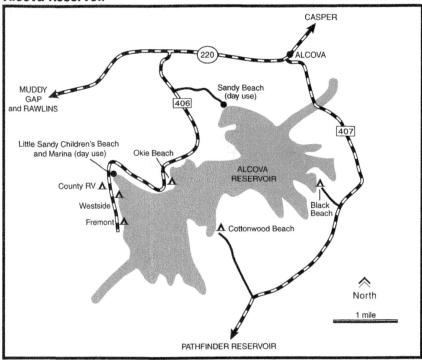

red bluffs that encompass the reservoir. There is a sprinkling of cedar trees in the campgrounds, but they are inadequate to provide any shade. A large dam and powerplant are located on the reservoir's northeast side. All of the campgrounds have fire rings, at least one handicap-accessible site, and picnic tables that may or may not be covered. However, not all sites have a picnic table and there is no water at any of the camps (except the RV camp, which has hookups).

Okie Beach, Westside, and Fremont Campgrounds are strung together on the reservoir's sandy west shoreline. Sites are not exactly defined here; it's more of a park-near-a-fire-ring style of camping. There is not much shade, but cool waters provide refreshment. The county offers a small RV campground (across the road from the marina) with full hookups. This side of the reservoir also includes multiple boat ramps and two beaches.

Black Beach Campground has a couple dozen sites on the reservoir's east shoreline. Most of these have covered picnic tables. Out of all Alcova campgrounds (the RV camp excluded), Black Beach is best suited for trailers or RVs; it has the most level sites and is the least cramped.

The last camp is Cottonwood Beach, also on the east side. Nearly three dozen sites are scattered here around rocky terrain. Unlevel roads and tracks wind disorderly between, over, under, and around a slope of fire rings. A few picnic tables are covered. It's a confusing arrangement, but it looks like a fun place to pull up for a day or weekend.

Fishing: Anglers can try for walleye, brown, and rainbow trout in Alcova. You can also fish the North Platte River between Alcova and Casper. There are nearly a dozen established public access points along the highway.

Boating/Swimming: Watersports are very popular on the reservoir, and you'll see a lot of personal watercraft and skiers gliding across the lake during the summer. The reservoir's marina is located on the reservoir's west side and includes a restaurant as well as boat and dock rentals. Boaters will find eight boat ramps along the shoreline. There are also two beaches on the west side of the reservoir that are open to day use—Sandy Beach and Little Sandy Children's Beach, which has a playground.

Trails: The Cottonwood Creek Dinosaur Trail is an interpretive route that begins just east of Cottonwood Campground. This trail steeply climbs the side of a mountain where signs describe the geology and ancient beasts that once roamed the area. Climb high enough and you'll have a great overlook of the reservoir.

Rock Climbing: Fremont Canyon is found south of the reservoir near Pathfinder Reservoir. The gorge's walls are as deep as 500 feet in places, offering rock climbers hundreds of routes that rate up to 5.12 in difficulty.

Picnicking: Westside Campground, Black Beach Campground, and Cottonwood Campground all have a covered group picnic shelter that can be reserved. Picnic tables are also available at the reservoir's two beaches.

A scenic picnic area can also be found at Fremont Canyon, south of the reservoir near the intersection of CR 407 and CR 408. There is an awesome overlook here where you can peer into the deep canyon.

Camping at Alcova Reservoir

Field Notes: Watch out for the weekends—that's when the town of Casper overruns the area for watersports and partying. A sign in Alcova says it all: "Population: 100, Summer: 35,000. It's a dam site."

Pathfinder Reservoir   5,850 feet

Location/Map	Southwest of Casper; Page 238, 247
GPS Coordinates	N42° 28.26' W106° 51.08'
Sites/Spur Length	80+ sites; Long spurs—over 30 feet
Cost	$10
Facilities/Services	Fire rings, grills, picnic tables, pit toilets, trash containers, dump station, boat ramps, marina, cellular service
Managing Agency	Natrona County Parks
Reservations	Call 307-235-9311 for group picnic shelters
Season/Usage	Open all year; Moderate use

Directions: From Casper, head southwest on HWY 220 for 31 miles to Alcova. Turn south on CR 407 and drive south 7 miles to CR 408 that crosses Fremont Canyon. Take this meandering road for 7 miles to the reservoir.

For a direct route to the campgrounds, continue west from Alcova on HWY 220 for 6 miles. Turn south on CR 409. To reach Bishop Point, drive south for 3.6 miles, then turn west and drive 4 miles. For all other campgrounds, continue south on CR 409 for another 3 miles.

Campsite at Pathfinder Reservoir

Pathfinder Reservoir

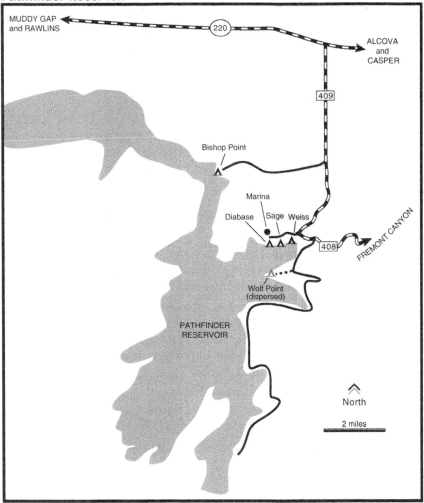

Description: Pathfinder Reservoir is the middle link in a four-reservoir chain in central Wyoming (Seminoe Reservoir is located to the south and Alcova Reservoir and the smaller Gray Reef to the north). The reservoir's dam, 214 feet in height, was built in 1909. It received a taller, modified spillway in 2012 to better accommodate years of high water, such as the levels experienced in 2010 and 2011. In those years, the reservoir spilled over the dam and created a remarkable, thunderous waterfall that attracted thousands of people.

The reservoir area itself is a year-round recreational destination that receives more use during the winter than you might expect. Bring windproof clothing if you visit during the colder months. If you visit during the summer, be sure to bring sunscreen and insect repellent.

Four developed campgrounds can be found at Pathfinder. All of them are situated in a high and dry landscape with very few trees. There are three campgrounds with about 40 combined campsites on the northeast shoreline of Pathfinder. These include Weiss, Sage, and Diabase. Some sites are developed and have covered picnic tables. A few are handicap accessible. More primitive sites are also mixed into the arrangement and these don't have tables. The Diabase camp is next to the marina where there is a small, private RV lot with hookups.

Bishop Point, located several miles to the northwest, is a lonely campground with over a dozen sites, covered tables, and a group picnic shelter. There are two boat ramps here for both high and low water levels.

Another camping option is the Wolf Point Primitive Camping Area. This is a dispersed camping area that only offers pit toilets. It is accessed from a rough, steep 4WD road on the east side of the reservoir, south of CR 408 and the Cardwell Public Access Area.

Scenic Driving: The 67-mile Seminoe-Alcova Backcountry Byway travels from Alcova to Sinclair. The road is mostly paved, but also has a steep gravel stretch that is not suitable for larger camping units. Highlights of the drive include sand dunes and the Pedro and Seminoe Mountains.

Fishing: Anglers will find walleye, brown, and rainbow trout in Pathfinder. Ice fishing is popular on the reservoir during the winter season. Delighting local anglers, the Cardwell Public Access Area was completed in 2002. The project restored year-round river flows between the reservoir and Fremont Canyon for the first time in nearly a century.

Boating: Watersports are common on the reservoir, and you'll see plenty of jet skis and boats out on the water. With three boat ramps and 117 miles of shoreline, you're sure to claim a portion of the lake to yourself.

Trails: A 1.7-mile interpretive trail can be found near the reservoir's dam. This is a fun route that descends to a bridge at the river, then climbs back up to end at an overlook parking area.

Rock Climbing: The North Platte River, between Pathfinder and Alcova, flows through Fremont Canyon. The gorge's walls are as deep as 500 feet in places, offering rock climbers hundreds of routes that can rate up to 5.12 in difficulty.

Picnicking: A scenic picnic area can be found at Fremont Canyon, northeast of the reservoir near the intersection of CR 407 and CR 408. There is an awesome overlook here where you can peer into the chasm.

Field Notes: This entire area—Seminoe, Pathfinder, and Alcova—has interesting terrain and views. If you're not coming to camp, consider coming this way for a day trip. The footbridge below the dam, Fremont Canyon, and the dam overlook are a few features that are worth a stop.

Cottonwood Campground (Green Mountain)   8,100 feet

Location/Map	Between Lander and Casper; Page 238
GPS Coordinates	N42° 21.88' W107° 41.01'
Sites/Spur Length	18 sites; Medium spurs—up to 30 feet
Cost	$6
Facilities/Services	Fire rings, picnic tables, water, pit toilets, trash containers
Managing Agency	Bureau of Land Management (Lander Field Office)
Reservations	Not accepted—first come, first served
Season/Usage	Open early June through November; Moderate use

Directions: From Jeffrey City (between Lander and Muddy Gap), take HWY 287 east for 6 miles to BLM Road 2411 (Green Mountain Road). Follow this washboarded road southward for over 6 miles, then bear left at the fork and drive 3 more miles. The campground has two entrances.

Description: Green Mountain is a refreshing forested island surrounded by hundreds of square miles of high desert flats. After traveling across the sage prairie, you'll feel like you're in the Washington Cascades by the time you get here. Simply put, Green Mountain is a gem and its growing popularity in recent years attests to that. Most campsites are located in an aspen and pine forest. Many spurs will accommodate long trailers while a handful of sites are walk-ins, accessible by footbridges that span a small creek. The spurs are well spaced along the roadway, which improves privacy.

Rockhounding: Jade and agate can be found in the Green Mountain area.

Scenic Driving/Wildlife Viewing: Continue up the mountain road and you'll come to a large warning sign where the road turns rough (rockier and rutted). If you have a high clearance vehicle, or are a skilled backcountry driver, continue up the steep 14% grade if conditions permit. The 15-mile road climbs to the top of Green Mountain (8,951 feet) where long views of central Wyoming await. A sign at the top points the way to the Wild Horse Point Overlook and Picnic Area, 3 miles farther. From the viewing area, you can look out across Wyoming's Great Divide Basin and, if you're lucky, the wild horses that live there. There are elk on Green Mountain so keep an eye out for those as well. From the flat summit, the road returns to the mountain's north side.

Fishing: The East Fork of Cottonwood Creek flows next to the campground. It's a tiny creek but is said to hold brook trout.

Picnicking/Other Camping: There is a picnic area at the top of Green Mountain. A more accessible option is Green Mountain Park, a small grassy picnic area maintained by Fremont County. It sits on the north flank of Green Mountain along the West Fork of Middle Cottonwood Creek. To get there, follow the directions to Cottonwood Campground, except bear right at the main fork and drive 2.5 miles. Elevation at the park is 7,950 feet.

Field Notes: In recent years, the pine beetle has destroyed some of the forest in this area, but the mountain still remains a terrific place to visit. Stay here during the middle of the week (except during the hunting season) and you'll enjoy plenty of solitude.

Prior Flat Campground   7,800 feet

Location/Map	Southwest of Casper; Page 238
GPS Coordinates	N42° 14.49' W106° 35.06'
Sites/Spur Length	15 sites; Medium spurs—up to 30 feet
Cost	Free
Facilities/Services	Fire rings, picnic tables, pit toilets, and trash containers
Managing Agency	Bureau of Land Management (Rawlins Field Office)
Reservations	Not accepted—first come, first served
Season/Usage	Open June through mid-November; Low use

Directions: From Casper, head southwest on HWY 220 for 16 miles and turn south on HWY 487. Drive 27 miles and bear right on HWY 77. Take the highway south about 12 miles to a signed turnoff for CR 102. Drive west on the county road for 9 miles and then turn south onto BLM Road 3511. The camp is located in the trees at the base of the mountain.

Description: This remote campground is situated at the northern base of the Shirley Mountains—an isolated mini-range that rises above the Shirley Basin in central Wyoming. A BLM road divides a handful of sites in an aspen stand from a full loop of sites that are hidden in a mixed forest of aspen and pine. While the Shirley Basin itself is void of much vegetation, the underbrush at the campground is thick, making this one of the most private camps in the region. Sites are level and large enough to satisfy tent and trailer campers alike. Traffic during the summer is light (often none), but that changes in September when nearly every site holds an antelope or grouse-hunting party.

Scenic Driving: The Shirley Mountain Loop Road (BLM Road 3511) makes a nice drive on and around this isolated mountain. The loop, starting from HWY 77, is 34 miles long. Four-wheel drive is recommended due to the rocky, rutted roadway.

Fishing: World-class fishing for walleye, brown, and rainbow trout can be found at Miracle Mile, 19 miles to the west. The famous stretch is located between Seminoe Reservoir and Pathfinder Reservoir and is known as a trophy-sized trout fishery.

Field Notes: If this stunted mountain was located in the Midwest, it would be a state park. But this is central Wyoming and the small mountain ranges that adorn this region go largely ignored.

Miracle Mile: Blue Ribbon Trout Fishing
The Miracle Mile is a 7-mile segment of the North Platte River between Seminoe State Park and Pathfinder Reservoir. The river here offers world-class fishing for brown and rainbow trout—thousands of them per mile. There are primitive campsites here on both sides of the river. The Miracle Mile is located along the Seminoe-Alcova Backcountry Byway, some 40 miles north of Sinclair, Wyoming and 60 miles southwest of Casper.

Seminoe State Park
6,400 feet

Location/Map	Northeast of Rawlins; Page 238, 252
GPS Coordinates	N42° 8.19' W106° 54.39'
Sites/Spur Length	94 sites; Long spurs—over 30 feet
Cost	$15 state residents, $25 nonresidents (includes $9 or $9 day-use fee)
Facilities/Services	Fire rings, picnic tables, water, pit toilets, trash containers, playground, dump station, boat ramps, private boat club, cellular service
Managing Agency	Wyoming State Parks, Historic Sites & Trails
Reservations	Call 877-996-7275 or visit wyoparks.state.wy.us
Season/Usage	Open all year; Moderate use

Directions: From Casper, head southwest on HWY 220 for 31 miles to Alcova. Turn south on CR 407/351 and drive 40 miles (there are some steep gravel sections). If coming from I-80, exit at Sinclair (5 miles east of Rawlins). Take CR 351 north for 30 miles. This approach is all paved.

Description: With 180 miles of shoreline, Seminoe is the largest reservoir in the Wyoming State Parks' system. The massive concrete dam was completed in 1939 and is 295 feet high, 85 feet wide at the base, and 530 feet in length. The reservoir is located in the rugged Seminoe Mountains, offering fine outdoor recreation in a remote setting.

Seminoe has three campgrounds on the reservoir's west shoreline: North Red Hills, South Red Hills, and Sunshine Beach. The Red Hills camps have a number of pull-through sites that accommodate large trailers or motor homes. Both camps are in the open with only a scattering of trees. They both include playgrounds, some covered picnic tables, boat ramps, and a few handicap-accessible sites. Each also has a group site that must be reserved during the peak season of mid-May through mid-September. There is a dump station at North Red Hills.

Sunshine Beach Campground is found at the bottom of a hill and has seven sites with short spurs. Three of these have covered picnic tables. The road to Sunshine Beach is steep and can be difficult in bad conditions; a 4x4 vehicle is recommended and large trailers and RVs are not allowed.

Scenic Driving: The 67-mile Seminoe-Alcova Backcountry Byway travels from Alcova to Sinclair. The road is mostly paved, but also has a steep gravel stretch that is not suitable for larger camping units. Highlights of the drive include sand dunes and the Pedro and Seminoe Mountains.

Seminoe State Park

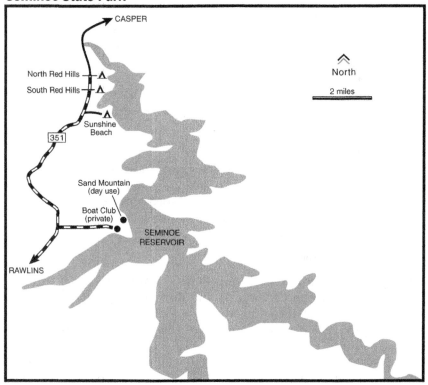

Fishing: Seminoe Reservoir holds walleye, brown, and rainbow trout.

Boating: Use of personal watercraft and boats on the reservoir is very popular. Boat ramps are located at the North Red Hills and South Red Hills campgrounds. A privately-owned boat club is located south of the campgrounds near Coal Creek Bay. The club has a fee-based boat ramp, food, fuel, and a private campground.

Picnicking: The Sand Mountain day use area can be found south of the campgrounds near the boat club. In addition, you can find covered group picnic areas at the campgrounds themselves.

ATV Routes: The state has prohibited ATV use along the beaches and shoreline, which used to be very popular. However, there are still many nearby sandy tracks and dunes that are open to off-road vehicle use.

Field Notes: Despite not having shade, people love Seminoe and it draws a lot of visitors from neighboring states without ever feeling very busy. The sandy beaches, the spacious campgrounds, and the rugged scenery make this a weekend favorite for many campers.

Seminoe State Park

Dugway Campground

6,400 feet

Location/Map	Northeast of Rawlins; Page 238
GPS Coordinates	N41° 51.83' W107° 3.6'
Sites/Spur Length	6 sites; Medium spurs—up to 30 feet
Cost	Free
Facilities/Services	Fire rings, picnic tables, pit toilets, trash containers
Managing Agency	Bureau of Land Management (Rawlins Field Office)
Reservations	Not accepted—first come, first served
Season/Usage	Open all year; Low use

Directions: From Rawlins, travel east 5 miles on I-80 and exit at Sinclair. Take CR 351 north for 8 miles.

Description: Dugway is a small camp located on the grassy banks of the North Platte River. It's characterized by an interesting rock wall that rises on the other side of the river. The well-spaced campsites occupy a parcel of treeless land. It gets plenty hot in this part of Wyoming on summer days, but a perpetual breeze helps.

Fishing: The North Platte River holds walleye, brown, and rainbow trout.

Floating: The North Platte is an excellent river for float trips. There is a primitive launch ramp and a sign near the ramp shows estimated float times to various destinations.

Field Notes: This camp sometimes gets flooded by the river during the spring runoff. Also, keep in mind that there are rattlesnakes here.

AREA 4 CENTRAL
Eastern Reservoirs and Laramie Range

Much of east-central Wyoming is rolling mixed-grass prairie. Around the towns of Wheatland, Torrington, and Lusk, the land is used for agriculture or remains as native grassland. It's a gentle landscape, and for emigrants following the North Platte River in the mid-1800s, this flatland was part of the easiest route west. At Oregon Trail Ruts State Historic Site near Guernsey, the trails that were traveled by covered wagon can still be seen.

Today, the North Platte River still plays an important role in the area. Glendo and Guernsey Reservoirs are two of five major reservoirs in Wyoming that are filled by this large river. The recreation that takes place on and around these two reservoirs is astonishing. On summer weekends, Interstate 25 is busy with travelers toting trailers, boats, and other watercraft. You don't have to be into watersports to enjoy Glendo or Guernsey. The two state parks are found in uniquely rugged country—a mix of prairie and mountain land. The scenery at Guernsey is particularly beautiful with dramatic sandstone cliffs and canyons.

From almost anywhere in the east-central region, Laramie Peak (10,272 feet) can be seen looming on the horizon. The peak is the ceiling of the Laramie Range. These jagged but short mountains are carpeted in grass, sagebrush, and pine forests. There is excellent hiking, four-wheeling, and camping in this northern unit of the Medicine Bow National Forest, but typically its only the locals who take advantage of the area.

The recreation areas on the eastern plains and in the Laramie Range are rarely mentioned. That's just fine with the people that come here. But when people head out to "just a windy place in Wyoming" several times each summer, you know they are onto something.

What to Expect: The reservoirs in this area offer terrific camping in the spring and fall and a trip during these times will not disappoint you. When summer comes, so do the crowds. Thousands of campers go to Glendo and Guernsey State Parks on Memorial Day weekend and the 4th of July. If you're looking for a good time, and you like company, these are the places for you.

The national forest campgrounds in the Laramie Range tend to be underutilized, but they also are terrific places to escape for a weekend. Make your visit during the week and you'll have the mountain range to yourself. Most of these camps are lower in elevation and open earlier than those in the Snowy Range or Bighorn Mountains.

One thing to keep in mind here during the summer is the possibility of severe weather. When cool mountain air mixes with the warmer, moist air from the plains, you get big storms. Impressive lightning storms and hail are common in the late afternoon and evening hours.

When driving the roads through the Laramie Range, a detailed state atlas or national forest map is a good thing to have. These are long roads and sometimes confusing. They are also prone to getting muddy and snowdrifted, so finding an alternative route is sometimes necessary.

Medicine Bow National Forest in the Laramie Range

Area 4: Eastern Reservoirs and Laramie Range

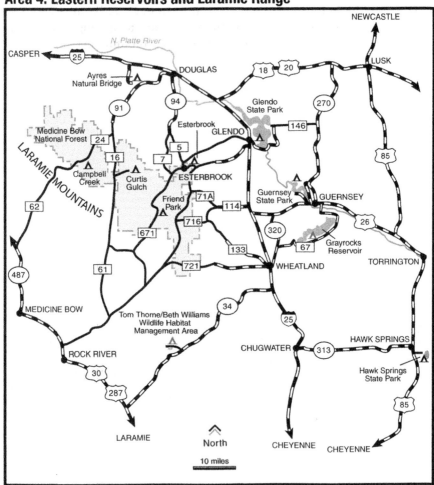

Campgrounds	Sites	Cost	Average Spur Length	Electrical Hookups	Cellular Service (varies by carrier/site)	Reservations Accepted	Page Number
Hawk Springs State Park	24	$15-25	L		▫▫▫		257
Grayrocks Reservoir WHMA	13+	Free	L		▫▫▫		258
Guernsey State Park	240	$15-25	L	✔	▫▫▫	✔	258
Glendo State Park	568	$15-25	L		▫▫▫	✔	262
Ayres Natural Bridge Campground	8	Free	M				265
Esterbrook Campground	12	$10	M		▫▫▫		266
Friend Park Campground	11	$10	S				267
Curtis Gulch Campground	6	$10	S				268
Campbell Creek Campground	6	$10	S				269
Tom Thorne/Beth Williams WHMA	3	Free	M				270

Average Spur Length: S = Short (under 30 feet), M = Medium (+-30 feet), L = Long (+-40 feet)
Cellular Service: 1 bar = weak/unreliable signal, 2 bars = low usable signal, 3+ bars = reliable signal for most users

Hawk Springs State Park

4,500 feet

Location/Map	Northeast of Cheyenne; Page 256
GPS Coordinates	N41° 42.75' W104° 11.81'
Sites/Spur Length	24 sites; Long spurs—over 30 feet
Cost	$15 state residents, $25 nonresidents (includes $6 or $9 day-use fee)
Facilities/Services	Fire rings, picnic tables, water, pit toilets, trash containers, boat ramp, cellular service
Managing Agency	Wyoming State Parks, Historic Sites & Trails
Reservations	Not accepted—first come, first served
Season/Usage	Open all year; High use

Directions: From Cheyenne, head north on I-25 and take Exit 17. Drive east on HWY 85 for 51 miles to CR 225/K4 (the access road) and travel 3.5 miles along this gravel road. If traveling from Torrington, drive south on HWY 85 for 26 miles to the access road on the left.

Description: Hawk Springs State Park was established in the late 1980s. Since then, the recreation area has become a local favorite for Cheyenne residents. Campers will find twelve roadside sites against the shoreline of Hawk Springs Reservoir. The water's edge is shaded by large cottonwoods and is right along the road. The other dozen sites are arranged along a small loop at the end of the row. The loop is mostly open and not nearly as attractive as the shady shoreline. Nearly all trailers and RVs can fit into the loop sites, but tent camping is common.

Wildlife Viewing: Blue heron can be observed, especially by boat at the south end of the reservoir. Geese, mallards, and other birds may also be seen.

Fishing/Boating: Fish in Hawk Springs Reservoir include walleye, bass, perch, crappie, and catfish. There is a boat ramp on the west side. Ice fishing during the winter is said to be excellent.

Field Notes: I've seen some pretty rowdy parties at this park, but park rangers have since cracked down on it. This area can also get severe thunderstorms in the early summer so watch the forecast.

Grayrocks Reservoir Wildlife Habitat Management Area (Wyoming Game & Fish)

Grayrocks Reservoir is located along the Laramie River and has 7.5 miles of shoreline. The reservoir holds walleye. The area provides habitat for waterfowl, small game, deer, and antelope. Camping is allowed in the parking areas on the southern shoreline of the reservoir and boaters can camp along the northern shore. There is also a trail that leads to an archeological site in Cottonwood Draw. To reach the reservoir from the north end of Wheatland, take HWY 320 north for 2.3 miles and then bear right and follow CR 67 (Grayrocks Road) east for 12.5 miles. To reach the reservoir from Guernsey, take CR 109S (South Guernsey Road) south for 12 miles to Grayrocks Road and then west for a few miles to the reservoir.

Guernsey State Park

4,350 feet

Location/Map	Southeast of Douglas; Page 256, 259
GPS Coordinates	N42° 16.89' W104° 46.13'
Sites/Spur Length	245 sites; Long spurs—over 30 feet
Cost	$15 state residents, $25 nonresidents (includes $6 or $9 day-use fee)
Facilities/Services	Full hookups (limited), fire rings, picnic tables, water, pit toilets, trash containers, boat ramps, dump station, cellular service, yurts
Managing Agency	Wyoming State Parks, Historic Sites & Trails
Reservations	Call 877-996-7275 or visit wyoparks.state.wy.us
Season/Usage	Open all year; High use

Directions: Exit I-25 at Guernsey (Exit 92) and drive 15 miles on HWY 26 to the park's entrance. From the entrance, keep left for campgrounds that are best suited for trailers and motor homes. For all others, bear right, cross the dam, and follow the tight road along the reservoir.

Description: The Bureau of Reclamation completed a 105-foot dam in 1927 to create Guernsey Reservoir. The water is used for irrigation, power

Guernsey State Park

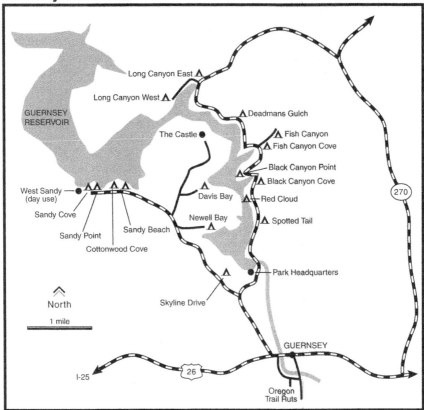

generation, and recreation. The state park was created later by the Civilian Conservation Corps (CCC). Fine examples of the work they performed in the 1930s are visible today throughout the park. One such example is the Guernsey Museum, located on a hill overlooking the reservoir. Other examples include rock steps and picnic shelters.

There are 16 campgrounds at Guernsey State Park, and there are great differences between them. The first campground past the southern entrance booth is Skyline Drive. It has water and pit toilets, but is not near the water's edge. Don't expect any shade unless you are bringing it with you. Farther north along the road, just past a canyon where there is a railroad (trains do rumble through here), is a dirt road that provides access to Newell Bay Campground. The camp doesn't have water, but it does sit at the edge of a bay with the same name. There are only a couple of camping options in this camp and neither are trailer or RV friendly. Another access road leads to Davis Bay where a handful of level tent sites can be found. The camp is treed, offers access to trails, has a pit toilet, but has no potable water.

If you have a longer trailer or RV, stay on the main paved road to reach the most accessible campgrounds. The first of these is Sandy Beach Campground, which has a few dozen sites including 15 with water and electric hookups. This is the best camp in the park for large trailers and motor homes. You'll find level parking spurs and decent tree coverage at the shoreline sites (not the ones with hookups). The next three camps—Cottonwood Cove, Sandy Point, and Sandy Cove—are clustered next door along the southern shoreline of the reservoir. Again, sites that are on the shoreline are shaded by sizable cottonwood trees. Some of the sites that don't have trees have covered picnic tables. You'll find a good mix of long and level camping spurs at these camps.

Guernsey Reservoir's scraggly east shoreline is peppered with a handful of yurts and several campgrounds. Most of these camps are best suited for tent and pickup truck campers because they have shorter, unlevel parking spurs, and a narrow access road. If you choose to camp on this side of the park, you'll be rewarded with views of the reservoir's dramatic canyon walls.

The first campground past the dam is Spotted Tail. It features pit toilets, water, and a group picnic shelter with a mix of treed and open sites. The compact sites at nearby Red Cloud are nearly identical to those at Spotted Tail, but they also have a group picnic shelter. The next two campgrounds, Black Canyon Cove and Black Canyon Point, offer just a handful of sites between them. The first is the most primitive and begs the use of the other's facilities. Black Canyon Point is more open and has the best views.

Three other campgrounds along this winding road are Fish Canyon Cove, Fish Canyon (the largest with pull-through sites), and Deadman's Gulch. Both Fish Canyon camps have pit toilets and water. Deadman's Gulch lacks those simple necessities but does have two picnic tables. Although sparse, a number of cedars adorn the campgrounds.

Finally, near the north tip of the reservoir, you'll find the Long Canyon East and Long Canyon West campgrounds. These camps are aligned in a single row on the Long Canyon access road, nuzzled up against the shore. There are pit toilets on both ends and potable water at the east campground.

Historical Attractions: Within the park, be sure to check out The Castle and the Guernsey State Park Museum—both are excellent displays of the work completed by the CCC. Outside the park, there are two historic sites south of Guernsey where you can see signs of the Oregon Trail—deep wagon wheel ruts and a register cliff. There is an interpretive trail at the wagon ruts.

Fort Laramie, another interesting historical site, is located east of Guernsey State Park. From Exit 92 at I-25, drive east for 28 miles, and then drive south for 3 miles on HWY 160.

Guernsey State Park

Trails: The state park has numerous trails near Davis Bay and several others scattered about the park. The trails, 14 miles in all, are excellent for mountain biking and family hiking. You can obtain a free trail map at one of the entrance booths.

Boating/Swimming: Guernsey Reservoir is popular for boating and waterskiing. The tall cliffs enclose a portion of the reservoir, making this a truly unique area. There are four boat ramps with the main one located near the dam. Fishing at this reservoir is considered poor because of fluctuating water levels and it's not even mentioned in most Wyoming fishing books. There is a swim beach at the West Sandy day use area.

Guernsey Reservoir is drained each year around the 4th of July. Water levels usually return to normal by the beginning of August, but other drawdowns also occur so contact the park before your trip if you are planning on water sports.

Picnicking: There are numerous picnic areas in the state park, including one below the dam. A few group picnic shelters can be found on the east side. Perhaps the best is The Castle at the end of the interior road.

Field Notes: Nearby Glendo State Park offers more trails, arguably better campsites, a bigger reservoir, and more to do. It also has more traffic. Guernsey offers a quieter recreation area (at least when I've been here) and it feels more remote and rugged. Either way you go, they are both very worthwhile places to spend some time.

Glendo State Park

4,700 feet

Location/Map	Southeast of Douglas; Page 256, 264
GPS Coordinates	N42° 28.93' W105° 0.45'
Sites/Spur Length	568 sites; Long spurs—over 30 feet
Cost	$15 state residents, $25 nonresidents (includes $6 or $9 day-use fee)
Facilities/Services	Electric hookups (limited), fire rings, picnic tables, water, pit toilets, trash containers, boat ramps, dump station, cellular service, yurts
Managing Agency	Wyoming State Parks, Historic Sites & Trails
Reservations	Call 877-996-7275 or visit wyoparks.state.wy.us
Season/Usage	Open all year; High use

Directions: Exit I-25 at Glendo (Exit 111) and follow the signs to the park, taking note of the north and south entrances. Head north for the Elk Horn, Bennett Hill, Waters Point, and Red Hills campgrounds. Head south for all of the others.

The isolated Sandy Beach camping area requires a longer drive to the other side of the reservoir. From the fee booth just south of Glendo, take the road 13 miles around the southern edge of the reservoir, over the dam, and briefly eastward out of the park. The road soon bends back toward the reservoir. Turn left at the campground sign and head for the grove.

Description: Glendo State Park has evidence of Indian and Spanish artifacts that suggest the area was important in the day-to-day life of our

Glendo State Park

predecessors. Today, consisting of 10,000 acres of land and 12,000 acres of water, the park is known for its recreation value as it draws staggering numbers of people from across the region.

The reservoir is just one of many fed by the North Platte River in Wyoming. Construction on the 167-foot high dam was completed in 1957 and the nearby powerplant a year later.

There are nearly twenty campgrounds scattered around Glendo Reservoir. Not all campgrounds have pit toilets or drinking water, so keep that in mind if you are not camping in a self-contained RV or trailer. In addition to individual campsites, you can also reserve picnic shelters, yurts, and group sites.

Elk Horn, Bennett Hill, Red Hills, Reno Cove, Soldier Rock, Custer Cove, Colter Bay, and Mule Hill are found on the eastern side of the park. Of these, Bennett Hill, Custer Cove, Reno Cove, or Red Hills have pit toilets. You can find water at Reno Cove, Red Hills, and Bennett Hills. Red Hills and Bennett Hills also have some sites with electrical hookups. Don't plan on having shade in these camps unless you pull your awning.

The Whiskey Gulch, Sagebrush, and Shelter Point Campgrounds are found along the reservoir's southern offshoot. Some of these sites are shaded under tall cottonwood trees, but most are not. You'll find pit toilets at Whiskey Gulch and Shelter Point. You'll find water at Whiskey Gulch and Sagebrush.

Two Moon Campground is Glendo's largest campground, and park staff will tell you that it is the best. It's also the most developed and includes water, pit toilets, a playground, and 14 of its sites have electric hookups. There is also a nearby dump station. The nicely timbered camp looks out of place on Wyoming's treeless plains. Short cedars and plenty of ponderosa pines provide great shade. Sites are also spacious and some feel as if you have your own acre. There are pull-throughs and back-in spurs along several paved, winding roads. One shortcoming, for those who care, is the lack of a beach or shoreline. The edge of the campground drops down a steep slope to the reservoir where lake access is impractical.

The east side of the park features the more remote Sandy Beach area. The beach isn't as sandy as you'd hope, but choices are limited in this region and so it's good enough to attract swimmers and sunbathers from several neighboring states. There are several campgrounds here. The larger two—the Sandy Beach Dune and Sandy Beach Willow—have pit toilets and potable water. Dune also has 27 sites with electric hookups, a group picnic area, and several group sites.

The remaining campgrounds, Broken Arrow, Indian Point, and Cottonwood have pit toilets and campsites near the beautiful cottonwood-lined sandy shoreline. Even if you don't camp on this side of the state park, it's worth spending some time in this area.

Glendo State Park

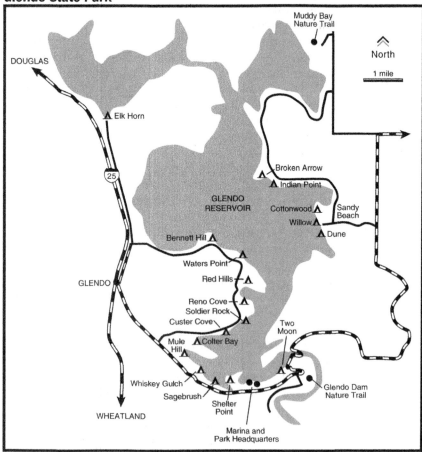

Natural Attractions: A scenic overlook can be found at the northeast edge of Two Moon Campground. An even more impressive overlook is found above the dam. Look to the west to find Laramie Peak (10,272 feet).

Trails: There are a few hiking trails in the state park. A .75-mile trail leads through the forested shoreline between Two Moon Campground and the Glendo Marina.

An even better route is the 4-mile (round trip) trail east of the powerplant near the reservoir's spillway. An access road near Two Moon Campground descends to a parking area with a pit toilet. From there, the wide trail has a couple of docks where you can sit and relax, picnic, or watch wildlife along the beautiful riparian area. Other trails branch off this route to reach routes on the adjacent timbered ridge.

The Muddy Bay Wetland Interpretive Trail, a 1.5-mile loop, is located at the far northeast corner of the park. It makes a worthwhile walk under large deciduous trees.

Over the last decade, nearly 50 miles of hiking and mountain biking trails were constructed in the park. These are mostly located above the reservoir's dam and the area between the dam and Sandy Beach. Trail maps are available online.

Fishing/Boating/Swimming: Obviously, watersports are the highlight of any reservoir this size. Glendo doesn't disappoint. The reservoir has six boat ramps. Those closest to the marina receive the heaviest use. Walleye and catfish are the two primary species found in the reservoir and are best fished by boat. There is also a swim beach on the park's east side.

Picnicking: There are seven group picnic shelters in the park for larger gatherings and activities.

Field Notes: Recreation use at Glendo is heavy throughout the summer but is at its highest during the 4th of July holiday. Early spring is a terrific time to visit if you want to experience this great park without the crowds. Also note that the park has changed how it operates over the years. No longer can you just pull up anywhere you want for the night. Make a reservation and only plan on having one camping unit per designated campsite.

Ayres Natural Bridge Campground

5,300 feet

Location/Map	Between Casper and Douglas; Page 256
GPS Coordinates	N42° 44.04' W105° 36.83'
Sites/Spur Length	10 sites; Medium spurs—up to 30 feet
Cost	Free
Facilities/Services	Fire rings, grills, water, pit toilets, trash containers
Managing Agency	Converse County
Reservations	Call 307-358-3532
Season/Usage	Open April through October; Moderate use

Directions: Take I-25 west from Douglas or east from Casper to Exit 151. Drive south on paved CR 13 for 5 miles.

Description: Unsuspecting Interstate travelers probably have no idea that there is a small patch of paradise hidden among the miles of open expanse in central Wyoming. You can find this oasis where Ayres Natural Bridge straddles LaPrele Creek as it flows through a sink of beautiful red sandstone walls. Cottonwoods and other trees shade the lush landscaping that seems out-of-place.

Camping, which is restricted to a single grassy area, is limited to 3 days and you'll need to obtain permission from the caretaker to do so. Half of the sites are for tents and the other half are for shorter RVs or trailers. Expect heavy traffic on the weekends. Gates are locked from 8 p.m. to 8 a.m., so you'll likely have a quiet night.

Natural Attractions: Standing 30 feet high and spanning 90 feet across a trout stream, the natural bridge is one of the few remaining in Wyoming that still has water flowing under it. It's a great family destination—kids love wading and splashing in the cool water.

Picnicking/Outdoor Activities: The small park is mostly used as a day-use picnic area. Group picnics, wading, and yard games such as croquet and horseshoes are common. Large picnic shelters are available as well as a playground and volleyball court. Keep an eye out for fairy gardens.

Field Notes: Visiting this little nook is like getting a brief taste of the vivid-colored rock country in Utah or Arizona. Unlike those states, though, it's a great place to go when summer temperatures swell.

Esterbrook Campground
6,300 feet

Location/Map	South of Douglas; Page 256
GPS Coordinates	N42° 25.33' W105° 19.29'
Sites/Spur Length	12 sites; Medium spurs—up to 30 feet
Cost	$10
Facilities/Services	Fire rings, grills, picnic tables, water, pit toilets, trash containers, cellular service
Managing Agency	USDA Forest Service (Medicine Bow National Forest)
Reservations	Not accepted—first come, first served
Season/Usage	Open June through October; Moderate use

Directions: From Douglas, head south on HWY 94 and CR 5 for 28 miles. Turn east onto FR 633 and drive 3 miles. If driving from Glendo, take I-25 south to Exit 115 (Horseshoe Creek Road) and continue west on the well-maintained gravel road for 16.5 miles. Turn north onto FR 633 and drive 2 miles to the camp.

Description: This camp is on the eastern fringe of the Laramie Range and used to be a sleepy place to camp. However, it has become more popular in recent years and weekends now see moderate traffic. The combination of elevation and shade from the light ponderosa pine forest is just enough to take the edge off the hot summer temperatures that bake the plains a few miles to the east. If you are looking to park a motor home or trailer, this is probably the best campground for it in the Laramie Range. Sites are spacious with room to spread out.

Trail/ATV Route: An ATV trailhead for the Sunset Ridge Trail is located a half mile west of the campground. (Hikers can also find unmarked paths that connect to the trail at both ends of the campground.) The short 1.6-mile loop gently climbs to the top of Sunset Hill to the north. It's less than 400 feet of elevation to gain the rocky platform. From the top, you can look across the Laramie Mountains to the southwest and Glendo Reservoir to the east.

Field Notes: I love this campground for a number of reasons, but the prevailing one is simply that it's a nice facility and a good area to do a little cross-country exploration. Afternoon thunderstorms are common here and throughout this mountain range.

Friend Park Campground

7,500 feet

Location/Map	Southwest of Douglas; Page 256
GPS Coordinates	N42° 15.34' W105° 29.14'
Sites/Spur Length	11 sites; Short spurs—up to 20 feet
Cost	$10
Facilities/Services	Fire rings, grills, picnic tables, water, pit toilets, trash containers
Managing Agency	USDA Forest Service (Medicine Bow National Forest)
Reservations	Not accepted—first come, first served
Season/Usage	Open June through October; High use

Directions: From Douglas, head south on HWY 94 for 45 miles as it turns into CR 5, travels through Esterbrook, and turns into FR 653. Turn onto FR 671 and drive 3 miles. Then, turn onto FR 661 and proceed 1 final mile to the camp. A state atlas or national forest map is a good resource to have, especially if you're traveling from Wheatland or Laramie.

Description: Eleven jam-packed sites in close range loop around this little camp in thinned pine. There isn't much privacy or solitude, but nobody really camps here looking for peace and quiet anyway. A good number of the people that come through here are doing so to hike, drive, or ride up Laramie Peak. What better way to conquer the summit than to camp at the mountain's base? Between boulders in the camp, you'll find short sites that could fit a pop-up trailer although it's not much fun (or common) to tow something to this remote setting. There are three walk-in sites if you are tenting and want to put a little space between you and everybody else.

Trails/ATV Routes: The strenuous route leading to the summit of Laramie Peak is a favorite in this part of Wyoming. The trail is open to horses, ATVs, motorcycles, mountain bikers, and hikers. You can expect to see all of these on the 5.25-mile trail. The first mile is gentle as it travels to an excellent picnic spot at Friend Creek. It's a great destination for families or those looking for a short stroll. Past the creek the climbing gets serious as the trail gains 2,700 feet of elevation. Note that upper portions of the trail are often snow-covered well into June. The trailhead is located just north of the campground. You can also use a connector trail from the camp.

If you want a quieter hike, look for the Friend Park Trail that begins near the pit toilet in the campground. The 3-mile route climbs 1,700 feet through an area that burned in June, 2012. Even so, the views and prolific wildflowers along this route continue to impress.

Friend Park Campground

Field Notes: This campground competes with Curtis Gulch as the most well-known recreation area in the Laramie Range. Weekends are always busy, but the campground is considerably quieter during the workweek. Of course, this is a lightly visited area of the state and "busy" can be defined as 25 people or so around the campground and trailhead.

Curtis Gulch Campground 6,650 feet

Location/Map	Southwest of Douglas; Page 256
GPS Coordinates	N42° 24.44' W105° 37.42'
Sites/Spur Length	6 sites; Short spurs—up to 20 feet
Cost	$10
Facilities/Services	Fire rings, grills, picnic tables, water, pit toilets, trash containers
Managing Agency	USDA Forest Service (Medicine Bow National Forest)
Reservations	Not accepted—first come, first served
Season/Usage	Open May through October; Moderate use

Directions: From Douglas, take HWY 91 south for 23 miles, then CR 24 for 3 miles. Turn onto CR 16 (Fetterman Road) and drive 13 miles. Turn east onto FR 658 and proceed 4 miles to the camp.

Description: Curtis Gulch is a scenic and popular area of the Laramie Range. Towering canyon walls make for interesting terrain and the area teems with wildlife and recreational opportunities. Campsites are positioned along a compact loop and have adequate spurs for short pop-up trailers, but are best suited for tent campers. A light pine forest embraces the campground along adjacent La Bonte Creek, but you'll get plenty of sun at most of the sites. Daytime traffic (especially ATVs) is high.

Fishing: La Bonte Creek carries rainbow trout as it flows from west to east.

Trails: The Curtis Gulch Trail travels through a scenic gulch of the same name. This 2-mile trail makes a nice family trek past rock outcrops that overhang a small valley. The trail ends at private property.

4WD Routes: A popular ATV trail is the 2.9-mile route up La Bonte Canyon. While motorized travel is permitted, hiking is also great way to experience this gorgeous drainage. This is a wildlife-rich area of the Medicine Bow National Forest. I've seen wild turkeys, deer, grouse, and considerable bear sign. The canyon is frequented by anglers and photographers.

Just west of the campground, you'll find an ATV trail that crosses the creek and heads south. The first 4 miles ascend Big Bear Canyon. At the junction, turn east and climb over Devils Pass, 3 miles farther.

Dispersed Camping: There are numerous dispersed campsites along the creek on the incoming access road. Respect private property where warranted, but don't be fooled by landowners who post signs on public land.

Field Notes: When this campground was being renovated during the first writing of this book, we had to laugh at a sign that read: "Campground closed due to lack of funding. It will have new, upgraded facilities when it reopens." How can the federal government improve something it can't afford to keep open? Years have passed since then and the campground is indeed improved.

Campbell Creek Campground
7,950 feet

Location/Map	Southwest of Douglas; Page 256
GPS Coordinates	N42° 27.32' W105° 50.16'
Sites/Spur Length	6 sites; Short spurs—up to 25 feet
Cost	$10
Facilities/Services	Fire rings, picnic tables, water, pit toilets
Managing Agency	USDA Forest Service (Medicine Bow National Forest)
Reservations	Not accepted—first come, first served
Season/Usage	Open mid-June through October; Low use

Directions: From Douglas, take HWY 91 south for 26 miles (this road turns into CR 24). Bear right at the fork and continue along CR 24 for 11 miles.

Description: Half the pleasure of staying at this secluded camp is getting there. Magnificently stacked boulders adorn the grassy countryside allowing you to capture some interesting photos along the way. Campbell Creek is a cramped campground that is hidden in a pretty stand of mixed conifers beside a creek of the same name (a second stream, LePrele Creek, parallels the access road). Although trailers are sometimes found parked on the spurs, there is not much room to maneuver them and it takes a confident person to try. Strong afternoon and evening thunderstorms routinely pound this region during the summer months.

Trail/ATV Route: The Twin Peaks Trail can be found 2 miles to the north on CR 24. It's a 2.7-mile route that climbs to a small saddle between two "peaks," which are really just rock outcroppings. The route gains 2,500 feet, but the views are worth the effort.

Field Notes: This campground is an awesome getaway in the middle of nowhere. However, if you want a little more comfort, check out the cabin at LePrele Guard Station (just north of the campground). It holds up to 10 people and can be rented on a daily or weekly basis. Call 877-444-6777 or visit www.recreation.gov for reservation information.

Tom Thorne/Beth Williams Wildlife Habitat Management Area (Game & Fish)

Aside from Pole Mountain between Laramie and Cheyenne, there are few public recreation areas on the southern end of the Laramie Range. However, this small wildlife management area along HWY 34 in Sybille Canyon offers free camping and other activities, such as deer hunting and trout fishing in tiny Johnson Creek Reservoir. On the south side of the highway, you'll find a wildlife research center where you can view elk, deer, bighorn sheep, and birds from roadside pullouts. To reach this area from Wheatland, drive south 6 miles on I-25 and take Exit 73. Drive west on HWY 34 for 28 miles.

SOUTHWEST
Mountain ranges around the high desert

You'll find two extremes in southwest Wyoming: dry, sun-baked deserts and frozen, snow-covered mountain peaks. No other part of the state has such a visible contrast. You can stand on the cracked soil of a sagebrush flat and admire the glacially-carved peaks of the Wind River Range.

The desert lands, namely the state's Red Desert, receive very little precipitation and some areas are best described as rock and dirt. But even the deserts are painted with beautiful colors. When the grasses and sagebrush are green and the yellow buttes and mesas rise into a bright blue sky, the landscape is stunning. Admittedly, there is not a lot to do in the desert, aside from cross-country exploration, but the large reservoirs found in the southwestern region will appeal to boaters, anglers, and sun junkies.

Mountain lovers will find some of the most spectacular high country in the Lower 48. The Wind River Range is celebrated for its rugged beauty and wild character. The range includes Gannett Peak (13,804 feet), Wyoming's tallest. It also holds over 150 glaciers, including seven of the top ten largest in the continental United States. Even though the Wind Rivers monopolize the area, they shouldn't. The Wyoming Range and Salt River Range, gorgeous mountains that parallel the Wyoming-Idaho border, can boast of their own magnificence.

Southwest Areas

WYOMING

1. **Snake River Range** (page 274)
2. **Western Ranges** (page 281)
3. **Wind River Range** (page 297)
4. **Southwestern Desert and Mountains** (page 320)

Privately-owned Campgrounds and RV Dump Stations

This section includes the general locations of privately-owned RV parks. For contact information and addresses for these businesses, look online or check out the campground directory on the Wyoming Office of Tourism website at travelwyoming.com.

Area 1: Snake River Range
The area's closest private campgrounds are located south of Jackson near Hoback Junction. A pair of RV parks are located north of this junction, and more options are found in Jackson itself.

Area 2: Western Ranges
A handful of RV parks are located in Wyoming's Star Valley on HWY 89, mostly around Alpine and Thayne. Some of these are quite nice.

Area 3: Wind River Range
A number of privately-owned RV parks can be found in towns south of the Wind River Range, such as Marbleton and Boulder.

Area 4: Southwestern Desert and Mountains
Several private campgrounds are spread out along the I-80 corridor. There is at least one RV park in each of the following towns: Evanston, Lyman, Green River, and Rock Springs. The largest and cheapest (though the open lots are certainly not for everyone) is the Sweetwater Events Complex in Rock Springs with 1,200 sites that include cell service, showers, full hookups for $30, or dry camping for $10. One other option in the area is an RV park located next to Buckboard Campground at the Flaming Gorge National Recreation Area.

RV Dump Stations
The locations below include public RV dump stations. Additional dump stations can often be found at private campgrounds and large gas stations.
- Bear River State Park
- Fontenelle Creek Campground
- Warren Bridge Campground
- Allred Flat Campground
- Afton City Park, 180 Washington St., Afton, WY
- Pinedale RV Dump Station, 957 West Pine, Pinedale, WY

AREA 1 SOUTHWEST
Snake River Range

The Snake River Range is a small mountain cluster that stretches from Idaho toward Jackson, Wyoming. The lower slopes of these mountains are robed in dense forests, but the trees thin with elevation and wildflower-chocked meadows are found in the higher areas. The tallest point is Mt. Baird (10,025 feet), but you don't have to climb that high to be rewarded with panoramic views of the surrounding mountain ranges. It's gorgeous country that is simply overshadowed by the Teton Range and Grand Teton National Park.

Deer, elk, and moose are all found in the mountain's Bridger-Teton National Forest as well as black bears and an occasional grizzly. You may also encounter raptors and other large birds, such as blue herons.

The southern edge of the mountain range is defined by what is called the Grand Canyon of the Snake River. With steep forested slopes, it's not your typical rock-walled canyon. The corridor is prized for its bald eagles and natural state, although development in the canyon (a golf course and luxury homes) threatens to turn the area into a mini-Jackson.

Rafting along the canyon's Snake River is big business. When water levels are high, during late spring and early summer, buses of floaters are shuttled between put-in and take-out points. You can go it alone, of course, but the rafting companies in Jackson are full-service and make it easy to have a thrilling day on the water.

Outside of rafting, hiking and camping are the area's main attractions. Backcountry travelers who venture into the Snake River Range will find rugged, little-traveled trails that lead to destinations that consist mostly of high overlooks. The highway that mimics the Snake River's course has a handful of terrific campgrounds. If you plan on touring Grand Teton National Park but want to stay outside of the park, give one of these campgrounds serious consideration.

What to Expect: Day use and highway traffic along this stretch of the Snake River is very high, but most travelers are just hurrying past leaving the campgrounds mostly empty until late afternoon or evening. On weekends, you'll likely share camp with groups of river runners. The town of Alpine, to the west, is a charming place to grab a bite to eat or restock your supplies.

Area 1: Snake River Range

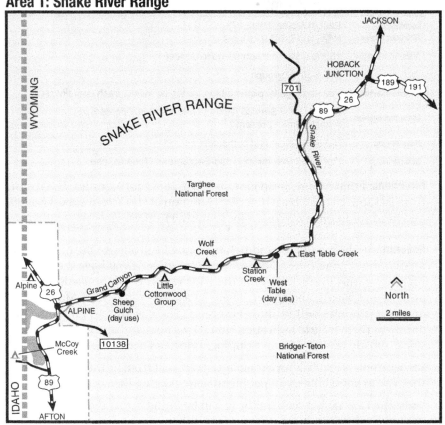

Campgrounds	Sites	Cost	Average Spur Length	Electrical Hookups	Cellular Service (varies by carrier/site)	Reservations Accepted	Page Number
East Table Creek Campground	18	$15-30	M				276
Station Creek Campground	16	$15-70	M			✔	277
Wolf Creek Campground	26	$15	M				278
Little Cottonwood Group Campground	1	$60	S			✔	279
Alpine Campground	15	$12-50	L		▁▃▅	✔	280
McCoy Creek Campground (ID)	18	$10	S		▁▃▅		280

Average Spur Length: S = Short (under 30 feet), M = Medium (+-30 feet), L = Long (+-40 feet)
Cellular Service: 1 bar = weak/unreliable signal, 2 bars = low usable signal, 3+ bars = reliable signal for most users

East Table Creek Campground

5,820 feet

Location/Map	East of Alpine; Page 275
GPS Coordinates	N43° 12.77' W110° 48.46'
Sites/Spur Length	18 sites; Medium spurs—up to 30 feet
Cost	$15, $30 for groups
Facilities/Services	Fire rings, grills, picnic tables, water, pit toilets, trash containers
Managing Agency	USDA Forest Service (Bridger-Teton National Forest); A host is often present
Reservations	Not accepted—first come, first served
Season/Usage	Open late May through mid-September; Moderate use

Directions: From Alpine, head east on HWY 26/89 for 12 miles. If traveling from Jackson, go to Hoback Junction (junction of HWY 26/89 and 191/189) and head south on HWY 26/89 for roughly 11 miles.

Description: The camp is found below forested hillsides of burnt spruce in an unburned, spared stand of conifers. On one side you have the drone of highway traffic; on the other are the wide waters of the Snake River. Sites are spacious, shady, and spaced nicely on a grassy forest floor. Most trailers and motor homes will fit into these sites. There is also an amphitheater, although there is little indication that it ever sees any use. Overflow camp space, mostly used for group camping, is located across the highway.

Fishing: Anglers can fish for brown and cutthroat trout in the Snake River if they can avoid the flurry of people that are floating the water.

Trails: The East Table Creek trailhead can be found across the highway from the campground. A foot trail runs uphill here for 5 miles to intersect the Station Creek Trail. It's less than 2 miles farther to the Cabin Creek-Wolf Mountain trail. This is a mostly forested route that becomes indistinct in places. If you make it to the intersection, you can hike another 4 miles toward Cabin Creek Campground. There is also an optional 2.5-mile route that tops Wolf Mountain (9,483 feet).

Rafting/Kayaking: This stretch, called the Grand Canyon of the Snake River, attracts crowds of river-runners during the summer months. Rafting and kayaking companies based in nearby Jackson can arrange a complete trip that includes equipment, lunch, a guide, and shuttle services. Both the East and West Table Creek boat launch points are located west of the camp.

Picnicking: For a fee, the campground is open to picnicking.

Rock Climbing: A limestone crag known as the Rodeo Wall can be found 2 miles south of Hoback Junction on HWY 26/89. This wall offers about a dozen single-pitch routes that range from 5.8 to 5.11 in difficulty.

Field Notes: This camp is my personal favorite in the area. Station Creek, just down the road, is a strong competitor but is not as close to the river.

Station Creek Campground

5,800 feet

Location/Map	East of Alpine; Page 275
GPS Coordinates	N43° 12.3' W110° 50.07'
Sites/Spur Length	16 sites, 2 group sites; Medium spurs—up to 30 feet
Cost	$15, $61-$70 group site
Facilities/Services	Fire rings, grills, picnic tables, water, pit toilets, trash containers, bear boxes
Managing Agency	USDA Forest Service (Bridger-Teton National Forest); A host is often present
Reservations	Group sites only, call 877-444-6777 or visit www.recreation.gov
Season/Usage	Open late May through mid-September; High use

Directions: From Alpine, head north on HWY 26/89 for 11 miles. If traveling from Jackson, go to Hoback Junction (junction of HWY 26/89 and 191/189) and head south on HWY 26/89 for 12.5 miles.

Description: Station Creek is one of the nicest camps along this stretch of highway. Sites are spacious, private, and come with thick tree cover to provide a shady canopy for your hammock. Sites also have tent platforms. Two reservable group sites are available across the road and hold 40 people each. Although the Snake River flows adjacent to the camp, a steep, fenced-off slope hinders direct access to its banks.

Fishing: Anglers can fish for brown and cutthroat trout in the Snake River if they can avoid the flurry of people that are floating the water.

Trails: Look for the Wolf Creek Trailhead less than 3 miles west of the campground on the north side of the road. The trailhead sign shows it's 1.5 miles to a trail that leads up Dry Fork of Wolf Creek and 8 miles to Red Pass. The mileages appear to be exaggerated. Maps show the distances to be 1.1 miles to the Dry Fork Trail and 6 miles to Red Pass, which is just below Wolf Mountain (9,483 feet). The trail splits into three separate routes at Red Pass.

Rafting/Kayaking: This stretch, called the Grand Canyon of the Snake River, attracts crowds of river-runners during the summer months. Rafting and kayaking companies based in nearby Jackson can arrange a complete trip that includes equipment, lunch, a guide, and shuttle services. There is a boat ramp at nearby East Table Creek.

Picnicking: For a fee, the campground is open to picnicking.

Rock Climbing: A limestone crag known as the Rodeo Wall can be found 2 miles south of Hoback Junction on HWY 26/89. This wall offers about a dozen single-pitch routes that range from 5.8 to 5.11 in difficulty.

Field Notes: My daughter saw a clover patch here and started looking for a four-leaf clover. To my surprise, it took her less than a minute to find one.

Wolf Creek Campground

5,800 feet

Location/Map	East of Alpine; Page 275
GPS Coordinates	N43° 11.91' W110° 54.19'
Sites/Spur Length	26 sites; Medium spurs—up to 30 feet
Cost	$15
Facilities/Services	Fire rings, picnic tables, water, pit toilets, trash containers, bear boxes
Managing Agency	USDA Forest Service (Bridger-Teton National Forest); A host is often present
Reservations	Not accepted—first come, first served
Season/Usage	Open late May through mid-September; Moderate use

Directions: From Alpine, head east on HWY 26/89 for 7 miles. If traveling from Jackson, go to Hoback Junction (junction of HWY 26/89 and 191/189) and head south on HWY 26/89 for 16 miles.

Description: The original Wolf Creek Campground, which was located on the river side of the highway, was decommissioned in 1995. A decade later, the Forest Service opened this newer one on the opposite side of the highway. There are three loops of sites and many of them are pull-throughs so it's easy to park a trailer. Most parking spurs are located in the open where they get plenty of sun. Without trees to get in the way, there is a good view of the Snake River Range.

Fishing: Anglers can fish for brown and cutthroat trout in the Snake River if they can avoid the flurry of people that are floating the water.

Rafters on the Snake River

Trails: Look for the Wolf Creek Trailhead east of the campground. The trailhead sign shows a distance of 1.5 miles to Dry Fork of Wolf Creek and 8 miles to Red Pass. The mileages appear to be exaggerated. Maps show the distances to be 1.1 miles to the Dry Fork trail and 6 miles to Red Pass, which is just below Wolf Mountain (9,483 feet). The trail splits into three separate routes at Red Pass.

Rafting/Kayaking: This stretch, called the Grand Canyon of the Snake River, attracts crowds of river-runners during the summer months. Rafting and kayaking companies based in nearby Jackson can arrange a complete trip that includes equipment, lunch, a guide, and shuttle services. There is a boat ramp at nearby East Table Creek.

Field Notes: This roadside camp gets a lot of traffic noise, but it has interesting views and it's an easy in and out if you're on your way to somewhere else.

Little Cottonwood Group Campground 5,900 feet

Location/Map	East of Alpine; Page 275
GPS Coordinates	N43° 11.52' W110° 56.24'
Sites/Spur Length	1 group site; Short spurs—up to 20 feet
Cost	$60 for up to 30 people, $1 per additional person
Facilities/Services	Fire rings, picnic tables, water, pit toilets, trash containers, bear boxes
Managing Agency	USDA Forest Service (Bridger-Teton National Forest)
Reservations	Call 877-444-6777 or visit www.recreation.gov
Season/Usage	Open late May through mid-September; Moderate use

Directions: From Alpine, head north on HWY 26/89 for 5 miles. If traveling from Jackson, go to Hoback Junction (junction of HWY 26/89 and 191/189) and head south on HWY 26/89 for roughly 18 miles.

Description: A group campground, Little Cottonwood can hold between 30 and 40 people and roughly 10 vehicles. The camp is tucked into thick evergreens and understory along the banks of the Snake River. Reservations are required here as this is a popular place for river-running groups.

Fishing: Anglers can fish for brown and cutthroat trout in the Snake River if they can avoid the flurry of people that are floating the water.

Rafting/Kayaking: This stretch, called the Grand Canyon of the Snake River, attracts crowds of river-runners during the summer months. Rafting and kayaking companies based in nearby Jackson can arrange a complete trip that includes equipment, lunch, a guide, and shuttle services. A boat ramp and restroom/changing room can be found at Sheep Gulch, just 1.5 miles west of the campground.

Field Notes: It is common to see a few vans and trailers crowded in here with rafts lashed to them. This is definitely the spot for river runners.

Alpine Campground

5,700 feet

Location/Map	Northwest of Alpine; Page 275
GPS Coordinates	N43° 11.82' W111° 2.46'
Sites/Spur Length	15 sites, 3 group sites; Long spurs—over 30 feet
Cost	$12, $50 group site
Facilities/Services	Fire rings, picnic tables, water, pit toilets, trash containers, limited cellular service
Managing Agency	USDA Forest Service (Caribou-Targhee National Forest); A host is often present
Reservations	Call 877-444-6777 or visit www.recreation.gov (The campground is listed as Alpine North Loop in Idaho)
Season/Usage	Open late May through early September; Moderate use

Directions: From Alpine, head north on HWY 26 for just over 2 miles.

Description: This camp is easily accessed from the scenic town of Alpine. You'll find private and roomy sites with tent platforms. Lots of understory, complemented by an attractive aspen and evergreen forest, helps isolate campers from one another. Palisades Reservoir can be seen from camp when the water level is high enough.

Fishing: The lion's share of Palisades Reservoir resides in neighboring Idaho, so be sure to obtain an Idaho fishing license if you cast a line on the other side of the border. Cutthroat and brown trout are the predominant species of fish, though mackinaw and kokanee are also present. Water levels during the summer months can make fishing access a bit tricky. Ice fishing in the winter is said to be the best time to fish these waters, with many people electing to fish the nearby rivers during the summer months.

Boating: Built in 1957, Palisades Reservoir is used for irrigation, power generation, flood control, and, of course, recreation. It is open to boats and personal watercraft and has seven boat ramps along its shoreline.

Field Notes: Even though we have yet to spend the night here, it is one of our favorites in western Wyoming. The campground host has always been friendly and welcoming—he certainly has a lot of ownership in this well-maintained camp.

McCoy Creek Campground (Caribou-Targhee National Forest, Idaho)

McCoy Creek Campground is located on the southwestern end of Palisades Reservoir in neighboring Idaho. The camp includes 18 sites that are hidden in thick brush and trees along the shoreline. Parking spurs are short and best suited for tent campers. Small craft can be launched from a primitive boat ramp. Sites cost $10 a night and a host is often present. To reach the camp from Alpine, take HWY 89 south for 3.2 miles to CR 87 (Salt River-McCoy Road). Drive west on this gravel road for about 6 miles.

SOUTHWEST AREA 2
Western Ranges

Located along the Wyoming-Idaho border, the Salt River Range and Wyoming Range are north-south running mountains separated by the Greys River. Both ranges are part of the Overthrust Belt, a geologic fold that stretches from Canada to Utah. One of the most visible differences in these mountains is their color. While many of Wyoming's mountains have a granitic, metamorphic, or volcanic core, the Salt River and Wyoming Range are formed from limestone. The result is a unique grayish-tan color streaked with black and red.

The two mountain ranges are rugged and steep. The high point on the Salt River Range is 10,907 feet, while the Wyoming Range reaches 11,378 feet. You'll find alpine plant communities in the high country, especially in the Wyoming Range. Grass, shrubs, and dark timber adorn the lower elevations.

Wildlife is thick on this side of Wyoming, and the Bridger-Teton National Forest provides critical habitat to large animals. Mule deer and moose are common inhabitants of the mountains. Elk are also plentiful and several winter feeding grounds are in the area. Wolves and grizzly bears are not normally found in these ranges, but the existence of both has been confirmed. The riparian areas support large birds such as white pelicans, sandhill cranes, trumpeter swans, eagles, blue herons, and osprey.

Recreation activities in the western mountains are many. While rock climbing and four-wheeling may be better in other parts of Wyoming, the Salt River and Wyoming ranges are excellent locations to camp, hike, fish, kayak, and hunt. The mountains are among the best for wildlife viewing, scenic driving, and photography. Since the ranges are eclipsed by the Teton Range, you'll find campgrounds that are greatly under-utilized and trails that see little summertime traffic. Outside of locals from the Star Valley, visitation is limited to those "in the know" from nearby Utah and Idaho. If the mountains were located anywhere else, you can bet they would be overrun favorites.

What to Expect: In these parts, dispersed camping trumps staying in the developed campgrounds. You'll find many of the locals pulled into the roadside meadows. This practice frees up the Forest Service campgrounds for those who prefer the facilities and services of a developed site. Whichever you prefer, you won't be caught without a place to camp.

Area 2: Western Ranges

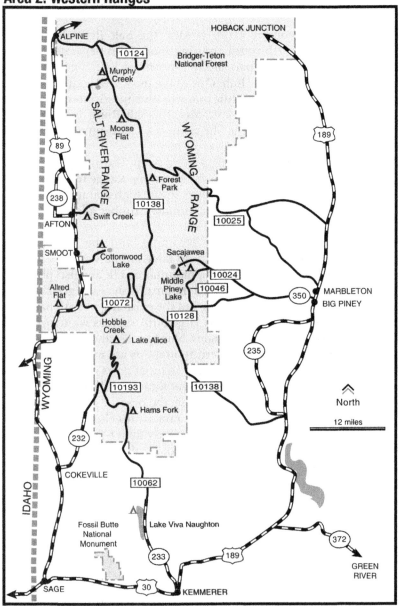

Campgrounds	Sites	Cost	Average Spur Length	Electrical Hookups	Cellular Service (varies by carrier/site)	Reservations Accepted	Page Number
Sacajawea Campground	24	$7	M				283
Middle Piney Lake Campground	5	Free	S				284
Murphy Creek Campground	10	$10	M				286
Moose Flat Campground	10	$10	M				287
Forest Park Campground	13	$10	M				289
Hobble Creek Campground	14	$10	M				290
Hams Fork Campground	13	$7	M				292
Lake Viva Naughton	24	Free	L				293
Swift Creek Campground	13	$10	S				293
Cottonwood Lake Campground	18	$10-35	M			✔	295
Allred Flat Campground	32	$10	M				296

Average Spur Length: S = Short (under 30 feet), M = Medium (+-30 feet), L = Long (+-40 feet)
Cellular Service: 1 bar = weak/unreliable signal, 2 bars = low usable signal, 3+ bars = reliable signal for most users

Sacajawea Campground
8,400 feet

Location/Map	West of Big Piney; Page 282
GPS Coordinates	N42° 37.1' W110° 31.86'
Sites/Spur Length	24 sites; Medium spurs—up to 30 feet
Cost	$7
Facilities/Services	Fire rings, picnic tables, water, pit toilets, trash containers
Managing Agency	USDA Forest Service (Bridger-Teton National Forest)
Reservations	Not accepted—first come, first served
Season/Usage	Open late June through late September; Low use

Directions: From Big Piney, head west on HWY 350 for almost 10 miles. Continue straight on FR 10046 (Middle Piney Road) for another 12 miles. Bear left on FR 10024 for a final 1.5 miles.

Description: With roomy sites fanned out along a single loop, this little-known campground packs plenty of satisfaction. The camp is located along Middle Piney Creek in a thinned pine, spruce, and fir forest at the base of a hill. It's a great location for hikers and anglers who want to set up base camp and then head further into the Wyoming Range.

The name Sacajawea comes from a Shoshone girl who helped guide and ensure the success of the Lewis and Clark Expedition between 1804-1806. She died at Fort Washakie near Lander at 96 years of age.

Natural Attractions: The Red Castles rock formations are found north of the campground on FR 10046.

Fishing: Middle Piney Lake, just 2.3 miles farther up the road, offers trout fishing. The access road is not suitable for trailers or RVs.

Trails: The Long Hollow Creek Trailhead is located roughly 1 mile before the campground on FR 10054. From the trailhead, a path travels 4 miles to reach North Piney Lake. Less than a mile in, a separate route heads west, passes Lewis Falls at 3 miles, and joins the Wyoming Range National Recreation Trail at 4.3 miles. More hiking trails are located at Middle Piney Lake Campground.

A few miles to the north, there is a 4.5-mile ATV trail that also leads to North Piney Lake; it's a gorgeous route that travels up the North Piney Creek drainage with options to end at the lake or travel higher into the Wyoming Range.

Dispersed camping: Dispersed camping is found a half-mile to the east.

Field Notes: At the time of this writing, the camp was closed for improvements. As always, be sure to check the status with the Forest Service.

Middle Piney Lake Campground

8,900 feet

Location/Map	West of Big Piney; Page 282
GPS Coordinates	N42° 36.18' W110° 33.94'
Sites/Spur Length	5 sites; Short spurs—up to 20 feet
Cost	Free
Facilities/Services	Fire rings, picnic tables, pit toilets, boat ramp
Managing Agency	USDA Forest Service (Bridger-Teton National Forest)
Reservations	Not accepted—first come, first served
Season/Usage	Open early July through late September; High use

Directions: From Big Piney, head west on HWY 350 for almost 10 miles. Continue straight on FR Road 10046 (Middle Piney Road) for another 12 miles. Bear left on FR 10024, pass Sacajawea Campground, and continue 2.3 miles along a narrow and somewhat rough road to the campground. Trailers are not permitted and RVs and other cumbersome vehicles are discouraged. The upper portion of this road does not usually open until early July.

Description: Nestled in the mountains on a short rise above Middle Piney Lake, this recreation area has the potential of becoming one of your favorites. Sites are lined along the edge of an evergreen stand and are not

Peaks of the Wyoming Range cap Middle Piney Lake

very private, but that's just fine with many of the locals who favor this scenic camp. Due to compact quarters and road conditions, trailers are not recommended. This clears the way for tents, vans, and pickup campers.

Visit during midweek if you want to experience this high mountain lake at its finest. The difference in visitation between a Wednesday and a Saturday is dramatic.

Fishing/Boating: Anglers will find trout in Middle Piney Lake. A small boat launch is available for small watercraft that have electric motors or are manually powered.

Trails: The Middle Piney Trail can be found behind Site 1. The trail heads west from the campground to Upper and Lower Wohelo Falls (2.5 miles) before joining the Wyoming Range National Recreation Trail at 4 miles.

Field Notes: At the time of this writing, this campground was closed due to reconstruction of the Middle Piney Lake dam. It is expected to re-open for the 2022 season.

Murphy Creek Campground

6,200 feet

Location/Map	Southeast of Alpine; Page 282
GPS Coordinates	N43° 4.41' W110° 50.16'
Sites/Spur Length	10 sites; Medium spurs—up to 30 feet
Cost	$10
Facilities/Services	Fire rings, grills, picnic tables, water, pit toilets, trash containers
Managing Agency	USDA Forest Service (Bridger-Teton National Forest)
Reservations	Not accepted—first come, first served
Season/Usage	Open June through October; Moderate use

Directions: From Alpine, drive south on FR 10138 (Greys River Road) for 14 miles.

Description: A stand of pines shade a number of nice sites in this campground along the Greys River. The parking spurs are spaced apart from each other for good privacy. You'll find a double-site as well as a few pull-throughs (including one very long one) within the mix.

Scenic Driving: One of the most scenic drives in the state can be found on FR 10138 (Greys River Road). Approximately 60 miles long, this drive follows the Greys River as it flows between the Salt River Range and the Wyoming Range. The road starts in the town of Alpine and heads south to Tri-Basin Divide where you can return to Alpine or follow another scenic road to reach Afton, LaBarge, or Big Piney.

Wildlife Viewing: This is a great place to visit if you love looking for wildlife. The Greys River drainage is one of the best wildlife habitats in the state. A sizable elk herd calls this home and is supported by a Wildlife Habitat Management Area during the winter. Deer and moose are also common and can be found near the river and on neighboring slopes. You may also spot Canada geese, bald eagles, great blue herons, osprey, and white pelicans. Reports of grizzly bears and wolves are rare but may increase as these animals migrate south from the national parks.

Fishing/Kayaking: Nearby Murphy Lakes makes an attractive fishing destination. To get there from the campground, drive south for a half-mile, then turn west on the road and drive 2 miles. The Greys River is also a favorite for anglers looking to catch cutthroat trout. The largest, unstocked fish can be found upstream from this campground. Kayaking is also possible on the river when conditions are favorable.

Trails: The Middle Ridge Trail is a long 18-mile route that traverses the high ridges of the Salt River Range. The trail begins on FR 10138 (Greys River Road) roughly 8 miles south of Alpine, just beyond the intersection of FR 10124 (Little Greys River Road). It travels southward to Deadman Creek near FR 10005. A pair of shorter, unmarked connector trails can be found near Murphy Creek Campground—one to the north of the camp and the other south of the camp. Be advised that the trail receives little traffic and has several unofficial secondary trails that branch off the main route.

Field Notes: While I'd rate this campground as average, the area itself is top notch; you'll enjoy abundant wildlife, prolific wildflowers, and unforgettable scenery. However, road traffic does kick up dust.

Moose Flat Campground

6,400 feet

Location/Map	Southeast of Alpine; Page 282
GPS Coordinates	N42° 58.29' W110° 46.13'
Sites/Spur Length	10 sites; Medium spurs—up to 30 feet
Cost	$10
Facilities/Services	Fire rings, grills, picnic tables, water, pit toilets, trash containers
Managing Agency	USDA Forest Service (Bridger-Teton National Forest); A host is often present
Reservations	Not accepted—first come, first served
Season/Usage	Open June through October; Moderate use

Directions: From Alpine, drive south on FR 10138 (Greys River Road) for 22 miles.

Description: This campground is located amid a truly beautiful landscape with the Wyoming Range to the east and Salt River Range to the west.

Salt River Range

While not astonishingly high or jagged, the peaks of these ranges present a unique beauty found nowhere else in the state. If you plan on staying anywhere along Greys River Road, give Moose Flat a look. Level parking spurs in a diverse and relatively dense forest provide an excellent place to settle in for a few days. The next campground to the south is 13 miles away and is also friendly to trailers and RVs.

Scenic Driving: One of the most scenic drives in the state can be found on FR 10138 (Greys River Road). Approximately 60 miles long, this drive follows the Greys River as it flows between the Salt River Range and the Wyoming Range. The road starts in the town of Alpine and heads south to Tri-Basin Divide where you can return to Alpine or follow another scenic road to reach Afton, LaBarge, or Big Piney.

Wildlife Viewing: This is a great place to visit if you love looking for wildlife. The Greys River drainage is one of the best wildlife habitats in the state. A sizable elk herd calls this home and is supported by a Wildlife Habitat Management Area during the winter. Deer and moose are also common and can be found near the river and on neighboring slopes. You may also spot Canada geese, bald eagles, great blue herons, osprey, and white pelicans. Reports of grizzly bears and wolves are rare but may increase as these animals migrate south from the national parks.

Fishing/Kayaking: The largest cutthroat trout in the Greys River are said to be south of this campground. Kayaking is also possible when conditions are favorable.

Trails: There are two trails south of camp: Pearson Creek and Middle Ridge. The Pearson Creek Trail starts with a river ford across the road from the campground and travels uphill toward Visser Peak (named after a fallen state trooper) and its southeastern neighbor, Virginia Peak. Both peaks stand around 10,000 feet.

The Middle Ridge Trail is a long 18-mile route that traverses the high ridges of the Salt River Range. The trail begins on FR 10138 (Greys River Road) roughly 8 miles south of Alpine, just beyond the intersection of FR 10124 (Little Greys River Road). It travels southward to Deadman Creek near FR 10005. A pair of shorter, unsigned connector trails can be found near Murphy Creek Campground—one to the north of the camp and the other south of the camp. Be advised that the trail receives little traffic and has some unofficial secondary trails that branch off of the main route.

Picnicking: A sole roadside picnic table is located south of the campground.

Field Notes: Easy gravel road access, appealing sites, and views of the river and surrounding mountains make this campground one of my favorites in western Wyoming.

Forest Park Campground

7,000 feet

Location/Map	Southeast of Alpine; Page 282
GPS Coordinates	N42° 49.86' W110° 41.49'
Sites/Spur Length	13 sites; Medium spurs—up to 30 feet
Cost	$10
Facilities/Services	Fire rings, grills, picnic tables, water, pit toilets, trash containers
Managing Agency	USDA Forest Service (Bridger-Teton National Forest)
Reservations	Not accepted—first come, first served
Season/Usage	Open June through October; Low use

Directions: From Alpine, drive south on the FR 10138 (Greys River Road) for 35 miles to the camp on the left.

Description: If you want a remote setting with smooth road access, this is your camp. Sites are found in a stand of conifers a third of a mile east of the Greys River. Roomy and level parking spurs make it easier to park a trailer. This is the last developed campground along Greys River Road. Further south the road becomes rougher and much narrower. If you're driving or towing a larger unit, this would be a good place to turn around.

Scenic Driving: One of the most scenic drives in the state can be found on FR 10138 (Greys River Road). Approximately 60 miles long, this drive follows the Greys River as it flows between the Salt River Range and the Wyoming Range. The road starts in the town of Alpine and heads south to Tri-Basin Divide, where you can return to Alpine, or follow another scenic road to reach Afton, LaBarge, or Big Piney.

Wildlife Viewing: This is a great place to visit if you love looking for wildlife. The Greys River drainage is one of the best wildlife habitats in the state. A sizable elk herd calls this home and is supported by a Wildlife Habitat Management Area during the winter. Deer and moose are also common and can be found near the river and on neighboring slopes. You may also spot Canada geese, bald eagles, great blue herons, osprey, and white pelicans. Reports of grizzly bears and wolves are rare but may increase as these animals migrate south from the national parks.

Fishing/Kayaking: The largest cutthroat trout in the Greys River are said to be near (and to the south of) this campground. Kayaking is also possible when conditions are favorable.

Trails: This area has several trails to choose from, but here are just two descriptions. The Marten Creek Trail follows the north side of a small stream and passes by Marten Creek Falls before joining the Wyoming Range Trail at 4 miles. The trailhead is located 6 miles south of Forest Park Campground.

The Crow Creek Trail is located 7.5 miles south of Forest Park Campground. The trail can be tricky to find initially—some wading is required—but look for tree blazes on the north side of Crow Creek. This trail follows and crosses the creek before intersecting the Way Trail just shy of 4 miles. A right turn leads to Crow Creek Lake (less than 2 miles to the northwest) and Lake Barstow (5 miles to the north). A southern turn puts you on a trail that runs south over a dozen miles to join a trail network near Corral Creek.

Field Notes: If you don't find this campground empty, it'll likely be close to it. Any camping south of this location will be dispersed.

Hobble Creek Campground 7,350 feet

Location/Map	Northwest of Kemmerer; Page 282
GPS Coordinates	N42° 23.87' W110° 47.03'
Sites/Spur Length	14 sites; Medium spurs—up to 30 feet
Cost	$10
Facilities/Services	Fire rings, picnic tables, water, pit toilets, trash containers
Managing Agency	USDA Forest Service (Bridger-Teton National Forest)
Reservations	Not accepted—first come, first served
Season/Usage	Open July through late October; Moderate use

Directions: It's a long way to this camp and it's not an easy drive. If you are near Hams Fork Campground, you can get to Hobble Creek by continuing past Hams Fork and following the signs to the campground, which is still over an hour's drive away.

Another approach begins from Cokeville. Start by taking HWY 232 out of town for 13 miles until the pavement ends. Bear right and follow FR 10062 for about 9 miles. Then turn left at the junction, head north, and drive 5 miles to another junction. Bear left and drive the remaining 9 miles to the camp. In these last 9 miles, you will negotiate a few tight switchbacks that drop a thousand feet in elevation into the drainage below. There is an unbridged stream crossing right before the campground that can cause some anxiety depending on the previous winter's snowpack. Don't hesitate to turn back if it's too deep, but a spread of underwater concrete blocks usually makes this an easy ford.

Description: This could be Wyoming's most difficult campground to access. Yet, after all the effort of getting here, you may be surprised to see a number of long fifth-wheel trailers occupying some of the camp's southern sites. Wyoming folks apparently have nerves of steel. The campground occupies rough terrain consisting of small humps and rocks that may prevent tent campers from finding a good stake spot unless it is on the parking spur itself. Many of the sites are overgrown with knee-high vegetation. While the campground itself is under-utilized, the trailhead for Lake Alice gets plenty of use and is the area's main attraction. Many campers pack in to the lake.

Natural Attractions: Lake Alice (7,750 feet) was formed when a natural landslide dammed Poker Creek. The result is a scenic three-mile lake nestled below 9,000-foot mountains. The lake offers backcountry camping, fishing, and picnicking. The shoreline is a 1.5-mile hike from the campground (see below).

Wildlife Viewing: Moose and deer can often be found around Hobble and Spring Lake Creek. At Lake Alice watch for bald eagles, ospreys, and waterfowl.

Fishing: Bonneville cutthroat trout can be found in Lake Alice. This is the only kind in the fishery because the lake's outlet seeps through a natural dam, preventing other species from entering the lake.

Trails: An uphill 1.5-mile trail links Hobble Creek Campground with Lake Alice. The trail is open to foot-traffic, pack animals, and mountain bikes. The route continues around the south side of the lake and continues another 10 miles along Poker Creek to FR 10138. Other trails intersect this route, creating some long backpacking options. The trailhead is located at the northeast corner of the campground.

Picnicking: A picturesque picnic area overlooks Lake Alice at the southwest end of the lake.

Field Notes: Surprisingly, I found more people backpacking at Lake Alice (12) than car camping at Hobble Creek Campground (6).

Lake Alice
This scenic loch is hidden in the southern hinterlands of the Bridger-Teton National Forest. The lake was naturally formed when a landslide dammed Poker Creek. The resulting flood created a three-mile lake at 7,745 feet that is surrounded by 9,000-foot mountains. Fishing, picnicking, and camping are common here, and there are nine primitive backcountry campsites on the southern shore that are sometimes referred to as the Lake Alice Campground. To reach Lake Alice, drive to Hobble Creek Campground where you'll find a trailhead. Then follow the 1.5-mile trail (open to foot, horse, and non-motorized bike traffic).

Hams Fork Campground

8,000 feet

Location/Map	Northwest of Kemmerer; Page 282
GPS Coordinates	N42° 15.09' W110° 43.82'
Sites/Spur Length	13 sites; Medium spurs—up to 30 feet
Cost	$7
Facilities/Services	Fire rings, picnic tables, water, pit toilets, trash containers
Managing Agency	USDA Forest Service (Bridger-Teton National Forest)
Reservations	Not accepted—first come, first served
Season/Usage	Open late May through late October; High use

Directions: From Kemmerer, drive north on HWY 189 and bear left onto HWY 233. Drive north for nearly 38 miles (the first 18 miles are paved). The road then changes to a well-maintained county road and then into bumpy FR 10062 for the last 7 miles.

Description: Have an ATV and like to fish? You'll fit right in. This is a buzzing campground with roomy and fairly private sites under a canopy of lodgepole pine. It fills easily on weekends (and even on weekdays) with anglers who use four-wheelers to access fishing points along the nearby river. It's a pretty spot to spend the weekend.

Wildlife Viewing: One of Wyoming's largest concentrations of moose can be found along the Hams Fork River drainage. Watch for these massive ungulates in the riverside willows. Elk can also be spotted in meadows during the early morning and evening. The forested area around the campground is noted for its wide variety of birds, and the upper portions of nearby Lake Viva Naughton are known to harbor Sandhill cranes and geese.

Fishing/Boating: There are multiple public access points for the Hams Fork River along the road leading to the camp. Lake Viva Naughton and Kemmerer Reservoir, 15 miles north of Kemmerer, also offer fishing. These waters contain numerous species of trout including rainbow, brown, cutthroat, and brook.

Trails: An extensive network of pack and foot trails, including the Elk Trail, are accessible from trailheads located north of the campground. The closest trailhead has a corral and is located less than a mile from the camp.

Dispersed Camping: There are dispersed campsites to the north and south of the campground along the forest roads. Some of these have picnic tables and stone fire rings.

Field Notes: We arrived at this busy camp on a Tuesday afternoon and found it to be full. Even if a site opened up, it looked like there were plenty of other people in line to take it. ATV use is steady, so you'll want to go elsewhere if you're looking for a quiet spot.

Lake Viva Naughton (Wyoming Game and Fish)

Lake Viva Naughton is a popular recreation area for bird watching, fishing, hunting, and boating. Camping is also permitted and you'll find roughly two dozen primitive sites around this reservoir's shoreline. There are a pair of boat ramps. To reach the lake from Kemmerer, drive north on HWY 189 and bear left onto HWY 233. Continue north for 15 miles.

Swift Creek Campground
6,300 feet

Location/Map	East of Afton; Page 282
GPS Coordinates	N42° 43.5' W110° 54.39'
Sites/Spur Length	13 sites; Short spurs—up to 20 feet
Cost	$10
Facilities/Services	Fire rings, grills, picnic tables, pit toilets, trash containers
Managing Agency	USDA Forest Service (Bridger-Teton National Forest)
Reservations	Not accepted—first come, first served
Season/Usage	Open late May through late September; Low use

Directions: From Afton, drive east on Swift Creek Canyon Road for 1.5 miles.

Description: Tucked in between steep hillsides, this shady campground is found under a thick canopy of evergreens. Thick brush creates a barrier between sites. The sites vary in size; some are compact while others are massive. The camp is arranged in a tight area and is best suited for tent camping, not for large trailers and motor homes.

Fishing: Swift Creek flows through the forested canyon next to the campground, but its banks are tough to fish due to thick brush. A better option is to use one of the Salt River public access areas along HWY 89.

Trails: The Swift Creek Trailhead is 3 miles past the campground at the end of the road. Hiking to Intermittent Spring (also called the Periodic Spring) is the most popular hike in this area. From the trailhead, it's an easy .75 mile trek to reach the peculiar spring that gushes roughly every 18 minutes. There is a picnic table and an interpretive sign at the site.

If you choose to hike farther, you'll find the junction to the Elk Creek Trail at 3 miles; it's a side trail that takes a northeast bearing through a small roadless area to eventually reach FR 10138 (Greys River Road) nearly a dozen miles to the west.

At 8 miles, you'll reach Coral Creek Lake. This high mountain lake is southeast of the trailhead and sits encompassed in a bowl. The trail continues past the lake to reach the Greys River, 8 miles to the west.

Field Notes: No trip to Afton would be complete without seeing the Intermittent Spring (see next page). If you are going to be passing through the area, be sure to set aside about two hours to go to it.

Intermittent Spring

West of Afton, Wyoming, you'll find a natural oddity known as the Intermittent Spring (also called the Periodic Spring). This peculiar cold water geyser gushes out of a rocky ravine roughly every 12 to 18 minutes, effectively turning the creek here on and off. This cycle is most consistent, and best viewed, between August and May (not during June and July). The spring is the largest of only three fluctuating springs that have been discovered in the world. To reach the spring, drive east of Afton on Swift Creek Canyon Road for 4.5 miles to a trailhead. From the parking area, it's an easy .75-mile trek to the site, which includes picnic tables and an interpretive sign.

Cottonwood Lake Campground

7,550 feet

Location/Map	Southeast of Afton; Page 282
GPS Coordinates	N42° 38.32' W110° 49.09'
Sites/Spur Length	18 sites, 1 group site; Medium spurs—up to 30 feet
Cost	$10, $35 group site
Facilities/Services	Fire rings, picnic tables, water, pit toilets, trash containers, boat ramp
Managing Agency	USDA Forest Service (Bridger-Teton National Forest)
Reservations	Group site only, call 877-444-6777 or visit www.recreation.gov
Season/Usage	Open mid-May through late September; Moderate use

Directions: From Smoot, travel east on CR 153/FR 10208 for just over 6 miles. The final stretch is narrow, but easily passable.

Description: With a nearby lake, a creek, trailheads, and a picnic area, this campground has a little bit of something for everyone. The camp has two loops. The first loop includes wooded sites and is suitable for tent camping or for those with horses (hitching posts and a corral are provided). The second loop, not as heavily timbered, has some pull-throughs and a few walk-in tent sites. Because of the camp's narrow access road, large camping units are not recommended.

The camp also has one reservable group site that can hold up to 25 people. However, only two vehicles can be parked at the site itself. Another six vehicles can be parked at the lake's day use area.

Fishing/Boating: Small but scenic, Cottonwood Lake sits in a forested depression and offers fishing for trout. Motorized boats are prohibited, but you are welcome to use boats or crafts that are manually powered. There is a primitive boat ramp.

Trails/ATV Routes: The North Fork Trailhead is a great access point for a number of backcountry trails including a 6-mile ATV trail that heads north toward FR 10079. At 3 miles, you'll intersect with the Dry Creek Trail. At 4.5 miles, you'll encounter the Sheep Pass Trail, a longer south-bearing foot route that traverses the crest of the Salt River Range at elevations over 10,000 feet.

The Slide Lake Trailhead, located at Cottonwood Lake, offers hikers a shorter trip. The trail is an old 4WD road that heads 1.5 miles to Slide Lake. You can continue past the lake to connect with other area trails, as well.

Picnicking: A reservable group picnic area (day use only) is on the west side of the lake.

Field Notes: The Cottonwood Lake Campground and Cottonwood Group site present some of the best camping Wyoming has to offer. The mountain scenery is beautiful, especially in late spring and early summer when snow still covers the mountaintops.

Allred Flat Campground

6,750 feet

Location/Map	South of Afton; Page 282
GPS Coordinates	N42° 29.11' W110° 57.69'
Sites/Spur Length	32 sites; Long spurs—over 30 feet
Cost	$10
Facilities/Services	Fire rings, picnic tables, water, pit toilets, trash containers, dump station
Managing Agency	USDA Forest Service (Bridger-Teton National Forest); A host is often present
Reservations	Not accepted—first come, first served
Season/Usage	Open late May through late October; Moderate use

Directions: From Afton, travel south on HWY 89 for 20 miles.

Description: This quiet campground sits at the bottom of Salt River Pass (7,630 feet). Aspen trees stretch across much of the area although the camp itself has some lodgepole pines mixed into it. Well-spaced parking spurs and thick shrubs create excellent privacy between sites. Little White Creek can be found along the east side of the campground, though beavers impede much of its downhill flow.

Scenic Driving: One of the most scenic drives in the state can be found on Greys River Road (FR 10138). Approximately 60 miles long, this drive follows the Greys River as it flows between the Salt River Range and the Wyoming Range. There are several ways to access the road, but the most direct route from the campground is via FR 10072 (Smiths Fork Road), which is 6.5 miles to the north on HWY 89. Take Smiths Fork Road for 22 miles to reach Greys River Road. From the junction, turn onto Greys River Road and follow it north for 60 miles to the town of Alpine.

Fishing: Anglers can pursue trout in Salt Creek, which flows near the campground. There are also numerous public access points for the Salt River along HWY 89 in the Star Valley.

Trails: Horse packers and backpackers will find a network of long trails, namely the Spring Creek Trail, starting from a trailhead about a mile south of the campground. The trails travel through foothills while skirting the Wyoming-Idaho border. A shuttle trip is made possible by utilizing a second trailhead located a few miles southwest of the town of Fairview.

Day hikers can hike the North Trail, which begins behind a tiny sign at the far end of the campground and follows the creek upstream.

Picnicking: A group picnic area is available at the campground.

Field Notes: This is a very nice campground and I only have one complaint about it: the mosquitoes! Some sites are unlevel and overgrown, but you can typically find one that is suitable.

SOUTHWEST AREA 3
Wind River Range

The Wind River Range in western Wyoming is spectacular. Stretching continuously for over 100 miles from Lander to Togwotee Pass northwest of Dubois, these rugged mountains consist of jagged peaks and spires that shape the Wyoming skyline. The range includes Gannett Peak (13,804 feet), the state's tallest, as well as 53 other summits that exceed 13,000 feet. Over 150 glaciers still pocket the glacially-carved high country, and over 1,600 lakes are said to be in the greater Wind River region.

Much of the mountain range is protected as designated wilderness. The Bridger, Popo Agie, and Fitzpatrick Wilderness areas encompass 728,685 acres. Only the outer fringes of the range are unprotected, but even that land is largely roadless and undeveloped. The Bridger-Teton National Forest covers most of the western mountains while the eastern side is managed by the Shoshone National Forest.

Nearly every Wyoming-native animal that comes to mind can be found in, or along the base, of the Wind River Range. Pronghorn antelope, sage grouse, rabbits, waterfowl, raptors, and songbirds are found in the dry, sagebrush environs at the edge of the mountains. In the wooded high country, deer, elk, and moose can be found, as can smaller animals like coyotes, badgers, and beavers. Black bears have a major presence throughout the range and encounters (including sightings) are somewhat common. Grizzlies also inhabit parts of the range and are expanding their habitat by an estimated 4% to 11% a year. The big bear isn't welcome so much and local communities have been at odds with federal and state authorities as the grizzly continues to migrate into popular areas.

Recreationally speaking, the Wind River Range is first-rate. The rock climbing and mountaineering opportunities in these mountains are nationally recognized. Many consider the range to be the best, if not the most scenic, hiking and backpacking country in the continental United States. The glacially formed lakes along the southern base of the range are popular fisheries and boating is common. Camping is also a major pastime, though you might be surprised to find some campgrounds in the Wind Rivers to be quiet and lightly visited. The exceptions are the campgrounds found around Pinedale as well as those located on the far eastern end of the range, which are described in the Central (Wind River Country) chapter of this book.

What to Expect: Forest Service campgrounds nearest Pinedale are busy ones—arrive early to grab a site. The BLM camps here used to be sleepy, but have seen an uptick in use in recent years. Weekdays are still slow, but it's not uncommon for these camps to fill on weekends.

Regardless of where you stay, you are likely to love it. However, there are a few things you should know. First, know that the Wind River Range spawns impressive thunderstorms during the summer months. Many of these roll off the mountains during the evening to create exciting weather for the surrounding flats. Second, expect cold nights. With camp elevations ranging from 7,300 feet to 9,380 feet, you'll find that the temperature plummets when the sun sets. Last, be prepared to combat an endless population of mosquitoes. I've only found them to be worse in Alaska.

Green River Lake

Area 3: Wind River Range

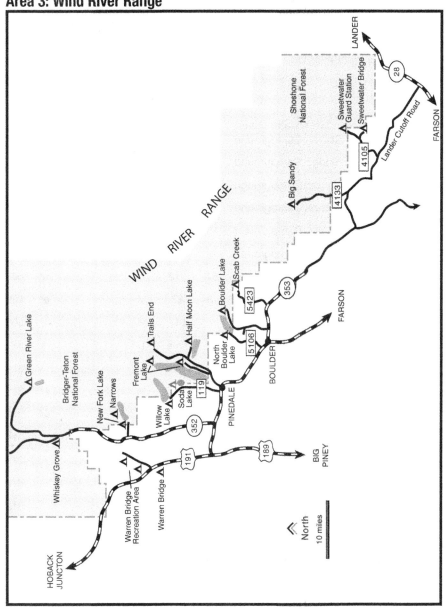

Southwest 299

Campgrounds	Sites	Cost	Average Spur Length	Electrical Hookups	Cellular Service (varies by carrier/site)	Reservations Accepted	Page Number
Sweetwater Guard Station Campground	10	Free	L				300
Sweetwater Bridge Campground	8	Free	M				301
Big Sandy Wilderness Campground	12	$7	S				302
Scab Creek Campground	12	Free	L				304
Boulder Lake Campground	15	$7	M				305
North Boulder Lake Campground	5	Free	M				306
Fremont Lake Campground	54	$12	L		▁▃▅	✔	307
Half Moon Lake Campground	18	$7	M			✔	308
Trails End Campground	8	$12	M		▁▃▅		309
Willow Lake Campground	6	Free	L				310
Soda Lake WHMA	12	Free	L		▁▃▅		311
New Fork Lake Campground	15	$7	M			✔	311
Narrows Campground	19	$12	M			✔	312
Whiskey Grove Campground	9	$12	M				314
Green River Lake Campground	39	$12	L				315
Warren Bridge Recreation Area	25	Free	L		▁▃▅		317
Warren Bridge Campground	16	$5	L		▁▃▅		319

Average Spur Length: S = Short (under 30 feet), M = Medium (+-30 feet), L = Long (+-40 feet)
Cellular Service: 1 bar = weak/unreliable signal, 2 bars = low usable signal, 3+ bars = reliable signal for most users

Sweetwater Guard Station Campground 8,250 feet

Location/Map	Between Lander and Pinedale; Page 299
GPS Coordinates	N42° 33.77' W109° 3.93'
Sites/Spur Length	10 sites; Long spurs—over 30 feet
Cost	Free
Facilities/Services	Fire rings, picnic tables, pit toilets
Managing Agency	Bureau of Land Management (Rock Springs Field Office)
Reservations	Not accepted—first come, first served
Season/Usage	Open all year; Moderate use

Directions: From HWY 28 between Farson and Lander, turn west off the highway onto Lander Cutoff Road. This road is approximately 43 miles southwest of Lander and 33 miles northeast of Farson. Drive 15 miles on the gravel road and then turn north onto BLM Road 4105 (Sweetwater Gap Road). Follow the signs for 8 miles to the campground.

Description: This campground offers roomy campsites on two loops. The first few sites are at the edge of a sparse pine forest, but these are mostly sunny and open. The real gems are tucked between the trees along the river, including a walk-in site (the most private). Getting a site isn't a problem, but you might not be able to claim one of the prime ones as they are among the first picked and are suitable for trailers. The Wind River Range stands mightily to the north and makes a scenic backdrop.

Fishing: Sweetwater River flows along the east side of camp and holds brown and brook trout.

Trails: Contrary to the bustling Big Sandy Recreation Area to the west, Sweetwater Gap is one of lesser-used trailheads in the Wind Rivers. To reach the trailhead from the Guard Station, find the rough road north of the camp and travel 2 miles to its end. The trailhead offers access to two separate routes. The Little Sandy Trail travels through an area burned in 1988 to reach Little Sandy Lake at 4 miles. The trail continues past the lake and travels into the Bridger Wilderness to intersect additional trails. The other route, the Sweetwater Gap Trail, leads north and crosses Sweetwater Gap, a mountain pass at the edge of the Popo Agie Wilderness, at 6 miles.

Dispersed/Other Camping: The Blucher Creek area, several miles to the west on BLM Road 4110, offers dispersed camping as well as a recently improved camping area with picnic tables, fire rings, and pit toilets.

Field Notes: A caution: The BLM reports that this campground, and nearby Sweetwater Bridge, are open all year, but snow can block access as late as May. Also know that many of the pine trees here have died in recent years, but there are still many healthy ones.

Sweetwater Bridge Campground   7,900 feet

Location/Map	Between Lander and Pinedale; Page 299
GPS Coordinates	N42° 31.17' W109° 2.99'
Sites/Spur Length	8 sites; Medium spurs—up to 30 feet
Cost	Free
Facilities/Services	Fire rings, picnic tables, pit toilets
Managing Agency	Bureau of Land Management (Rock Springs Field Office)
Reservations	Not accepted—first come, first served
Season/Usage	Open all year; Moderate use

Directions: From HWY 28 between Farson and Lander, turn west off the highway onto the Lander Cutoff Road. This road is approximately 43 miles southwest of Lander and 33 miles northeast of Farson. Drive 15 miles on the gravel road, and then turn north onto BLM Road 4105 (Sweetwater Gap Road). Drive 6 miles, bear right at the fork, and continue 2 more miles.

Description: It's a long drive to this campground, as well as to nearby Sweetwater Guard Station Campground, but that only adds to the appeal. Sweetwater River cuts a course through the campground, feeding tall willows along its banks. Rock outcroppings poke up between a peppering of evergreen trees, but there is no shade to speak of. Average-sized trailers and motor homes fit best on the spurs. There is also a walk-in site along the riverbank.

Fishing: Sweetwater River contains brown and brook trout. There are two theories on how the river was named. One version tells of a bag of sugar that fell off a pack animal, resulting in the sweetening of the water. The other holds that in 1823, General Ashley referred to the river as sweet in comparison to the bitter alkali water that he and some fellow trappers had been drinking.

Trails: A trailhead is located near Sweetwater Guard Station Campground.

Dispersed/Other Camping: The Blucher Creek area, several miles to the west on BLM Road 4110, offers dispersed camping as well as an improved camping area where picnic tables, fire rings, and pit toilets were installed in 2011.

Field Notes: As with nearby Sweetwater Guard Station Campground, many of the pines surrounding this camp have died. That hasn't deterred campers, though. When I last visited this camp, it was completely full. Riding ATVs and dirt bikes is popular here on the BLM roads.

Big Sandy Wilderness Campground   9,100 feet

Location/Map	Southeast of Pinedale; Page 299
GPS Coordinates	N42° 41.22' W109° 16.29'
Sites/Spur Length	12 tent sites; Short spurs—up to 20 feet
Cost	$7
Facilities/Services	Fire rings, picnic tables, pit toilets
Managing Agency	USDA Forest Service (Bridger-Teton National Forest)
Reservations	Not accepted—first come, first served
Season/Usage	Open mid-June through mid-September (snow dependent); High use

Directions: From Pinedale, head south on HWY 191 for 12 miles to HWY 353 and then drive east on this highway for 19 miles to a gravel road. Turn east on the gravel road and continue 9 miles. Turn east again on the gravel Lander Cutoff Road and drive 7 miles before turning north on BLM 4113 toward the Big Sandy Recreation Area. It's a 10-mile drive along a winding, narrow road to the campground and trailhead.

If you're traveling from the east on HWY 28, turn west off the highway onto Lander Cutoff Road. This road is approximately 43 miles southwest of Lander and 33 miles northeast of Farson. Drive 25 miles on the gravel road, and then turn north on BLM 4113 toward the Big Sandy Recreation Area. It's 10 miles further along the rough and narrow road. Large RVs and trailers are not recommended.

Description: Big Sandy is one of three major entry points to the Wind River backcountry. Though it's a remote trailhead, it receives very heavy use during the summer. The trailhead and campground are located at the end of a forest road where Big Sandy Creek flows through gorgeous mountain parks. Within the camp, most sites are shaded by a forest of large evergreens. Some sites are practically incorporated into the trailhead parking lot, but a handful of them are separated by a short rocky rise that keeps them slightly out of traffic's way. The best sites include a few spacious ones that flank the river. Mosquitoes and hikers are everywhere— trailers, RVs, and ATVs are not. Surprisingly, it's common to find a couple of open sites as most visitors are backpacking.

Although some Forest Service information shows Big Sandy as a tent-only campground, there is nothing at the camp itself that proves that requirement. However, due to the condition of the incoming road, high traffic, and tight conditions within the recreation area, most people would not want to bring a trailer or RV here.

Big Sandy Campground

Fishing: The Big Sandy River holds several species of trout, kokanee salmon, and mountain whitefish.

Trails/Rock Climbing/Mountaineering: The Big Sandy Trailhead is the second most popular starting point in the Wind Rivers. Thousands of hikers, backpackers, rock climbers, and mountaineers come from afar to take advantage of this starting point, which offers the shortest distance to the Cirque of Towers, a spectacular semi-circle of 12,000-foot peaks and alpine lakes. From the campground's trailhead, it is 5 to 6 miles to Big Sandy Lake (depending on the route you choose) and just over 8 miles to the Cirque of Towers. The distance to Big Sandy Lake is easily covered; the remaining distance is not. Be sure to carry a map of the area.

Dispersed Camping: There are dozens of dispersed campsites along the meadows on both sides of the incoming access road. With views of Wind River peaks and a clear mountain stream, some of these sites are extremely scenic. Bring ample amounts of insect repellent if you camp here—the mosquitoes along the creek are terrible.

Field Notes: On my quietest visits to this campground (including one when it was closed and the road was washed out), there were still nearly two dozen vehicles at the trailhead. On a visit a few years earlier, we saw over two hundred cars crammed into the campground, trailhead parking lot, and everywhere in between. Dozens of backpackers blocked the way—loading, unloading, playing with equipment, talking, or standing around in the road. You may not be able to predict how many people you'll encounter here, but it's safe to bet that you won't be alone.

Scab Creek Campground
8,200 feet

Location/Map	Southeast of Pinedale; Page 299
GPS Coordinates	N42° 49.25' W109° 33.16'
Sites/Spur Length	12 sites, 1 group site; Long spurs—over 30 feet
Cost	Free
Facilities/Services	Fire rings, picnic tables, water, pit toilets, trash containers
Managing Agency	Bureau of Land Management (Pinedale Field Office)
Reservations	Not accepted—first come, first served
Season/Usage	Open May through mid-November; Low use

Directions: From Pinedale, head south on HWY 191 for 12 miles to HWY 353. Head east on the highway for 6.5 miles. Turn onto CR 23-122/BLM 5423 (Scab Creek Road) and drive another 1.5 miles. Bear left at the Scab Creek sign and proceed a final 7 miles.

Description: The Scab Creek Recreation Site has newer facilities and services. The improvements made over the years include better access, new individual campsites, a group site, water, and three separate parking lots for backpackers, horse trailers, and overflow parking.

The primary sites are spaced along a single loop that is surrounded by tall hills. Parking spurs are long and level. Unfortunately, most of the forest that once cast this camp into dark shadows is now gone due to the western bark beetle outbreak. What remains are a few spindly pines and some aspen trees. Until the forest regenerates, you'll get plenty of sun here. The group site includes four picnic tables and a large parking spur. Although the nearby trailhead receives moderate use, the campground itself remains relatively quiet leaving you with plenty of solitude and excellent stargazing.

Trails: The nearby trailhead provides access to the Bridger Wilderness. The Scab Creek Trail heads uphill for 2 miles to enter the wilderness near Boundary Line Lake. The route reaches Toboggan Lake at 4 miles, Divide Lake at 6 miles, Dream Lake at 10 miles, and the Fremont Trail soon after. There are numerous trails around Dream Lake so be sure to consult a map.

Field Notes: I love the changes that were made to this trailhead camp, but it doesn't appear to be drawing the crowds. I've only seen one car in the campground each time I have visited on summer weekends.

Boulder Lake Campground
7,300 feet

Location/Map	East of Pinedale; Page 299
GPS Coordinates	N42° 51.4' W109° 37.03'
Sites/Spur Length	15 sites; Medium spurs—up to 30 feet
Cost	$7
Facilities/Services	Fire rings, grills, picnic tables, pit toilets, boat ramp
Managing Agency	USDA Forest Service (Bridger-Teton National Forest)
Reservations	Not accepted—first come, first served
Season/Usage	Open early June through mid-October; Low use

Directions: From Pinedale, head south on HWY 191 for 12 miles to HWY 353. Turn east on the highway for 2.4 miles and turn left onto CR 125 (Boulder Lake Road). Continue along this gravel lane for 10 miles.

Description: This campground is located along Boulder Creek where it rushes into Boulder Lake at the base of the Wind River Range. The lake is just one of ten that pool in the large glacial basins here at the foot of these mountains. The water is not visible from the campground, but is within easy walking distance.

While most of the area consists of sage-covered slopes, the camp itself has level sites that are concealed by thick foliage consisting of lodgepole pine, aspen, and tall grass. You'll find most campsites to be overgrown, making them quite private. If you're looking to camp in the Pinedale area without the crowds, give this campground a shot.

Fishing/Boating: Anglers can fish for rainbow trout and mackinaw in Boulder Lake. There is a boat ramp on the southwest shoreline. It's here where I met a teenager carrying a stringer full of plump trout back to camp. His assessment: "This place is better than anything in Colorado!"

Trails: Trail users will find horse corrals and a "backpacker assembly area" for the Boulder Canyon Trail just outside the campground. The rocky trail follows Boulder Creek uphill through a canyon and fire area from a 1988 burn. There is also a vast network of trails north of the lake that leads into the Bridger Wilderness. The wilderness has over 600 miles of trails, so be sure to obtain a trail map if you are serious about traveling these routes.

Dispersed Camping: There are a considerable number of dispersed camping spots around the lake including some BLM sites that have picnic tables and pit toilets. Most of these are on the west side of the lake near the dam. Stokes Crossing, found on a road that branches westward off Boulder Lake Road, includes two developed sites with tables and a pit toilet.

Field Notes: Over the years, this camp has changed from a coniferous one to a predominately deciduous one. The aspen stand here is getting thicker.

North Boulder Lake Campground

7,300 feet

Location/Map	East of Pinedale; Page 299
GPS Coordinates	N42° 50.50' W109° 42.1'
Sites/Spur Length	5 sites; Medium spurs—up to 30 feet
Cost	Free
Facilities/Services	Fire rings, grills, picnic tables, pit toilets
Managing Agency	Bureau of Land Management (Pinedale Field Office)
Reservations	Not accepted—first come, first served
Season/Usage	Open mid-June through September; Moderate use

Directions: From Pinedale, head south on HWY 191 for 11 miles to BLM 5106 (Burnt Lake Road). Drive north on this gravel road for 7.2 miles. Bear right on Boulder Lake Dam Road and drive a half mile. Turn left and follow the rough track for nearly another half mile to the stand of trees.

Description: This small, primitive camp is located on the western side of Boulder Lake. All of the sites share a common parking area without much separation. Five indistinct sites are nestled up against an isolated stand of aspen and conifers. The boggy shoreline is just a skip away.

Fishing/Boating: Anglers can fish for rainbow trout and mackinaw in Boulder Lake. There is a boat ramp on the other side of the dam, accessed from Boulder Lake Road.

Field Notes: There is not much to this camp and yet it stays fairly busy.

Fremont Lake Campground

7,600 feet

Location/Map	Northeast of Pinedale; Page 299
GPS Coordinates	N42° 56.42' W109° 47.81'
Sites/Spur Length	54 sites; Long spurs—over 30 feet
Cost	$12, $24 double site, $35 group site
Facilities/Services	Fire rings, picnic tables, water, pit toilets, trash containers, boat ramp, cellular service
Managing Agency	USDA Forest Service (Bridger-Teton National Forest)
Reservations	Call 877-444-6777 or visit www.recreation.gov
Season/Usage	Open late May through mid-September; High use

Directions: From Pinedale, travel north on Fremont Lake Road for 4 miles, then turn onto the paved access road and follow the signs for 4 more miles.

Description: Occupying nearly 7,500 acres and stretching almost 12 miles long, Fremont Lake is Wyoming's second largest natural lake (Yellowstone Lake is larger). Spanning across both high desert and forested foothills, the lake is glacier-fed and serves as Pinedale's water source. The not-so-distant peaks of the Wind River Range can be seen along the horizon.

Fremont Campground has two paved loops with roomy, private sites that can accommodate large camping rigs. Although much of the area consists of dry, treeless terrain, the sites at the campground are hidden in a thick forest consisting of evergreens, aspen, and shrubs. The sites fill quickly on weekends, so arrive early or make a reservation.

A remote campground called Upper Fremont is located in the conifers at the north end of the lake. The camp has five sites (but only one table and fire ring) and is accessible only by boat or a foot trail from the Bridger Wilderness. There is a small boat dock at the shoreline, but it may be inaccessible if the water level is too low.

Fishing/Boating/Swimming: Most facilities are located at the southern end of the lake. These include a marina, lodge, and a designated beach area that is used for wading and swimming. Boaters can launch from two boat ramps: one at the south end of the lake and one on the east side at the main campground. Anglers will find kokanee, mackinaw, and brown and rainbow trout in Fremont's waters.

Trails: There are biking and walking paths at CCC Ponds—a wildlife habitat interpretive area located at the south end of Fremont Lake. A short dirt road leads to the parking lot. This is a great place for families to get out.

Picnicking: A few group picnic areas are available for day use along the lake's southern shoreline.

Field Notes: With its quick access to Pinedale, this is a campground that lends itself well to extended stays of a week or more. Easy access, beautiful scenery, and nice sites won't leave you disappointed.

Fremont Lake

Half Moon Lake Campground 7,600 feet

Location/Map	Northeast of Pinedale; Page 299
GPS Coordinates	N42° 56.24' W109° 45.67'
Sites/Spur Length	18 sites; Medium spurs—up to 30 feet
Cost	$7
Facilities/Services	Fire rings, picnic tables, pit toilets, trash containers, boat ramp
Managing Agency	USDA Forest Service (Bridger-Teton National Forest); A host is often present
Reservations	Call 877-444-6777 or visit www.recreation.gov
Season/Usage	Open June through mid-September; High use

Directions: From Pinedale, travel north on Fremont Lake Road and drive 7 miles. Watch for the Half Moon Lake sign and turn east onto FR 743. Drive another 1.2 miles and then turn right on FR 114 to access the campground.

Description: This interesting camp nestled in the Wind River's forested foothills is incredibly dense with aspen trees, willows, and shrubs. By late summer the vegetation grows into a jungle so thick that the road transforms into a sort of tunnel. Some sites have direct access to the lakeshore while others are tucked further back on the sandy beach. The camp best accommodates tents, vans or small trailers and motor homes.

Putting a larger rig here will require a skilled and persistent driver to squeeze into a spot.

Resort: A resort located near the campground offers horseback trips into the backcountry as well as guided fishing tours and other outdoor activities.

Fishing/Boating/Swimming: Boaters and anglers can toss hooks to catch mackinaw and rainbow trout. There is a boat ramp and trailer parking on the north side of the lake. Swimming and water-skiing are permitted, and there is a sandy beach along a portion of the shoreline.

Trails: Day hikers can find the Half Moon Trail just past the marina. The trail meanders along the north side of the lake and explores the area around Little Half Moon Lake and Fayette Lake.

Field Notes: The lush, tall brush makes this campground very unique. You will not find another one like it in Wyoming. The last time I visited, the camp was completely full on a Thursday of a non-holiday week. You'll want to arrive early to secure a site or play it safe and make a reservation.

Trails End Campground
9,380 feet

Location/Map	Northeast of Pinedale; Page 299
GPS Coordinates	N43° 0.37' W109° 45.13'
Sites/Spur Length	8 sites; Medium spurs—up to 30 feet
Cost	$12
Facilities/Services	Fire rings, picnic tables, water, pit toilets, trash containers, limited cellular service
Managing Agency	USDA Forest Service (Bridger-Teton National Forest)
Reservations	Not accepted—first come, first served
Season/Usage	Open late June through mid-September; High use

Directions: From HWY 191 in east Pinedale, turn onto the paved Fremont Lake Road and head north for 14 miles.

Description: Bordering Elkhart Park Trailhead and just around the bend from a scenic overlook, Trails End is a popular campground with a lot of daytime drive-through traffic. It's also the highest campground in the Pinedale area, resulting in a shorter operating season and cooler temperatures. The camp consists of two loops near the edge of a steep hillside. The upper loop has more shade and is better suited for truck campers, vans, or tents. The lower loop will hold short trailers or RVs. There are only a handful of sites for this busy area, so you'll need to arrive early to get one.

Natural Attractions/Scenic Driving: Skyline Drive, the name of the incoming road, is a fun climb from the high flats to the forested high country of the Wind Rivers. If you want to see the wilderness without traveling far from camp, you are in luck. There is a lofty vantage point less than a mile from the campground. From the scenic overlook, you can see Fremont Lake and a good sampling of high peaks in the Bridger Wilderness. A sign shows the names and elevations of the peaks.

Trails/Rock Climbing/Mountaineering: Elkhart Park Trailhead is the most popular starting point for backpackers and climbers in the Wind River Range. Its two huge parking lots are often jam packed with cars. The west parking lot provides access to the Pine Creek Canyon Trail. Destinations along this trail include Long Lake (2 miles), Fremont Lake (4 miles), Trapper Lake (10 miles), Summit Lake (15 miles), and even Green River Lake Campground, nearly 30 miles to the north.

The east (and busier) parking lot provides ingress on the Pole Creek Trail, which is used to reach other major routes such as the Highline Trail and Seneca Lake Trail. Popular destinations, such as Seneca Lake and Titcomb Basin, are deep inside the Bridger Wilderness and often require roundtrips varying between 20 and 40 miles.

Field Notes: Expect afternoon thunderstorms and cool temperatures here. This is the second highest campground in western Wyoming.

Willow Lake Campground

7,720 feet

Location/Map	Northwest of Pinedale; Page 299
GPS Coordinates	N42° 59.36' W109° 53.97'
Sites/Spur Length	6 sites; Long spurs—over 30 feet
Cost	Free
Facilities/Services	Fire rings, picnic tables, pit toilets, boat ramp
Managing Agency	USDA Forest Service (Bridger-Teton National Forest)
Reservations	Not accepted—first come, first served
Season/Usage	Open June through mid-September; Low use

Directions: From Jackson Street on the west side of Pinedale, travel north on CR 119 (Willow Lake Road) for 11 miles past Soda Lake, across the National Forest line, and to the camp. The final stretch is rough, steep, and narrow.

Description: This camp is located on Forest Service land, though there really is no forest. That doesn't keep folks from settling here and at nearby Soda Lake, many with patio grills blazing next to their large fifth-wheel campers. They come to fish and they come to grill the catch. Sites are lined along the sandy southwestern shore of Willow Lake. The Wind River Range drapes across the northern horizon, and sage countryside encompasses the other 270 degrees.

Fishing/Boating: Willow Lake offers fishing for landlocked salmon, mackinaw, and rainbow trout as well as opportunities to swim and boat. There is a boat launch with trailer parking.

Trails: A lightly used trailhead can be found at Spring Creek Park. To get there, turn onto the access road between Soda Lake and Willow Lake and follow it for 2 rough miles (4WD suggested) to the trailhead. Some maps show two separate routes here that essentially parallel each other and eventually merge into the better-known Pine Creek Canyon Trail.

The most common route, the Glimpse Lake-Trapper Lake Trail, traverses the crest of a ridge and reaches Glimpse Lake at about 5 miles. Trapper Lake can be found 3 miles to the north from this point. You'll also find a trail to Summit Lake and other routes that run deep into the Bridger Wilderness. Keep in mind that this is grizzly and black bear country.

Field Notes: This camp used to cost a few dollars, but the fee board has been removed and it is now free of charge. Remember to bring your own water.

Soda Lake Wildlife Habitat Management Area (Wyoming Game & Fish)

This nearly 4,000-acre habitat area includes Soda Lake, which holds brook and brown trout. The north side of the lake has an area for viewing waterfowl. There are a dozen primitive camping areas around the lake that have pit toilets and there are two boat ramps. To get there from Jackson Street in Pinedale, drive north on CR 119 (Willow Lake Road) for 7 miles.

New Fork Lake Campground
7,825 feet

Location/Map	Northwest of Pinedale; Page 299
GPS Coordinates	N43° 4.94' W109° 57.96'
Sites/Spur Length	15 sites, 1 group site; Medium spurs—up to 30 feet
Cost	$7, $35 group site
Facilities/Services	Fire rings, grills (group site), picnic tables, pit toilets, trash containers, boat ramp
Managing Agency	USDA Forest Service (Bridger-Teton National Forest)
Reservations	Single sites: Not accepted—first come, first served Group sites: Call 877-444-6777 or visit www.recreation.gov
Season/Usage	Open late May through mid-September; Moderate use

Directions: From Pinedale, travel west on HWY 191 for 5 miles. Turn north onto HWY 352 and drive nearly 15 miles. Turn onto New Fork Lake Road and proceed 3.5 miles to a junction. The group sites are straight ahead on the left. For the single sites, turn right at the junction and watch for the camp entrance on the left. The camp road is sandy and can get a bit rough.

Description: New Fork Lake consists of a regular campground of single sites and a completely separate area with group sites.

Campsites are nestled in a stand of quaking aspen trees and dense shrubs on the western side of a deep glacial lake in the lower foothills of the Wind River Range. Many spurs are best suited for tent camping and a few have a view of the water. Other spurs are longer and will nicely fit an average-sized trailer or RV. The sun can be scorching during the days of summer. Fortunately, it cools off quickly in the evenings.

The group area is a third of a mile away from the main camp—also away from the lake—and offers group-sized picnic tables, grills, and a campfire area. You will have to provide your own drinking water. The site here holds up to 150 people, 30 cars, and will fit trailers of any length. The site is an open area surrounded by lodgepole pines. It's available by reservation.

Fishing/Boating: Trolling for kokanee and a variety of trout is popular on New Fork Lake. There is a primitive boat ramp at the camp, but a better one is found on the road leading to Narrows Campground to the north.

Trails: A trailhead with trailer parking and a corral is at Narrows Campground.

Field Notes: Of the two campgrounds at New Fork Lake, this one is not as popular and offers fewer amenities than nearby Narrows Campground. While the lake itself is nearby, it takes a short walk to get there. Bring plenty of sunscreen and water if you camp here.

Narrows Campground

7,850 feet

Location/Map	Northwest of Pinedale; Page 299
GPS Coordinates	N43° 6.23' W109° 56.5'
Sites/Spur Length	19 sites, Medium spurs—up to 30 feet
Cost	$12
Facilities/Services	Fire rings, picnic tables, water, pit toilets, trash containers, boat ramp
Managing Agency	USDA Forest Service (Bridger-Teton National Forest); A host is often present
Reservations	Call 877-444-6777 or visit www.recreation.gov
Season/Usage	Open late May through mid-September; High use

Directions: From Pinedale, travel west on HWY 191 for 5 miles. Turn north onto HWY 352 and drive nearly 15 miles. Turn onto New Fork Lake Road and continue 6 miles to the camp.

Description: The Narrows is a scenic camp with two loops in an aspen and shrub forest above New Fork Lake. Sites have limited privacy, but most overlook the lake or have views of New Fork Canyon and the surrounding Wind River Range. Tent camping is common in the loop that has short parking spurs. The longer spurs are found in a loop that is accessed by a steep lane that has tight curves and is prone to big dips. Even so, folks still squeeze in some long trailers and RVs into these sites.

Narrows Campground

Wildlife Viewing: Moose can be found in the willows that grow along the New Fork River drainage. Watch for these massive animals on the northeast side of the lake.

Fishing/Boating: Trolling for kokanee and a variety of trout is popular on New Fork Lake. A boat ramp is located 1 mile west of the campground.

Trails: The New Fork Canyon Trail travels into a tall and spectacular canyon within the Bridger Wilderness. The trail crosses the river several times before reaching New Fork Park at 6.5 miles. Be aware that the river water may be very high and unwise to ford. Past the park, the trail continues deeper into the wilderness to access other backcountry routes. The trailhead is located at the campground and has a corral and trailer parking.

Field Notes: The term "Narrows" refers to a tiny channel that connects the two New Fork Lakes. In a drought year, the lakes were low enough that you could actually get to the other side of them by hopping over the gap. Beetles have killed many of the pine trees on the adjacent slopes. Take note that the campground sits on a brushy hill above the lake and there is no access to the shoreline; you'll need to head back to the west to reach it.

Whiskey Grove Campground

7,700 feet

Location/Map	Northwest of Pinedale; Page 299
GPS Coordinates	N43° 15.34' W110° 1.54'
Sites/Spur Length	9 sites, Medium spurs—up to 30 feet
Cost	$12
Facilities/Services	Fire rings, picnic tables, water, pit toilets
Managing Agency	USDA Forest Service (Bridger-Teton National Forest)
Reservations	Not accepted—first come, first served
Season/Usage	Open mid-June through mid-September; Moderate use

Directions: From Pinedale, travel west on HWY 191 for 6 miles. Turn onto HWY 352 and drive 28 miles to a half-mile access road. Turn west onto the road and follow it to the campground. Most of the route is paved.

Description: This campground is isolated in a small pocket of pines in a bend of the Green River. Because it sits in a small depression, it is hidden discretely beneath rounded hillsides and can't be seen from the main road. Sites are fairly roomy and have decent understory; privacy ought not be a concern. A few appealing sites butt right up against the riverbanks. There are no trash containers in camp, but there are at nearby Kendall Guard Station. Expect about half of the sites to be occupied on a weekend.

Natural Attractions: Be sure to explore the Kendall Warm Springs just 2 miles north of the campground. This is the only place in the world known to harbor Kendall dace, a tiny minnow fish that grows to a whopping full-grown length of two inches. The warm water is around 85° F, but wading is prohibited.

Scenic Driving/4WD Routes: The beautiful 42-mile drive over Union Pass (9,500+ feet) is well worth the long ride. The gravel road creeps upwards to reach the Continental Divide, providing awesome views of the Absaroka and Wind River mountains. There is a short interpretive foot-trail at the top of the pass. The road begins at a bridge about a half-mile north of the campground and ends on HWY 26/287 near Dubois. A number of secondary 4WD roads and ATV trails are also found in this area of the Winds. Obtain a OHV map from the Forest Service for route information.

Fishing: Green River washes through the sagebrush valley around the campground. Anglers can work around the willows to find a variety of trout and mountain whitefish.

Field Notes: This campground would make an ideal location for a base camp. Since most of the incoming road is paved, it's easy to pull a trailer here, unhook, and then make day trips to Green River Lake and Union Pass.

Green River Lake Campground

8,000 feet

Location/Map	North of Pinedale; Page 299
GPS Coordinates	N43° 18.93' W109° 51.78'
Sites/Spur Length	39 sites, 3 group sites; Long spurs—over 30 feet
Cost	$12, $35 group sites
Facilities/Services	Fire rings, picnic tables, water, pit toilets, trash containers, bear boxes
Managing Agency	USDA Forest Service (Bridger-Teton National Forest); A host is often present
Reservations	Group site only, call 877-444-6776 or visit www.recreation.gov
Season/Usage	Open mid-June through mid-September; Moderate use

Directions: From Pinedale, travel west on HWY 191 for 6 miles. Turn onto HWY 352 and drive 45 miles. The first 25 miles are paved but give way to a bumpy washboarded gravel road for the remaining distance.

Description: It's a long and jarring drive to this camp, but certainly worth the trip. Panoramic views of lofty peaks will surely summon the camera from your pocket. A short walk or drive will place you along the shores of scenic Green River Lake—one of the most commonly photographed areas in the state—with inimitable Squaretop Mountain towering in the southeast.

The camp has a loop for hard-sided campers, a tent loop, and a group area with three large sites. Level parking spurs are positioned in a mature forest that has become increasingly thin over the years as trees are felled and removed. This makes shade and privacy inconsistent between sites; good at some, nonexistent at others. Adding to the campground's appeal are the pit toilet housings, which resemble miniature log cabins.

There are often plenty of sites here that remain available. However, if you find the campground to be full, you can find primitive dispersed sites along the incoming road. Just be careful around the beetle-killed trees.

The group sites have extra picnic tables and larger parking areas. Two of the campsites can accommodate up to 35 people each. The third campsite can accommodate a gathering of 50 people.

Natural Attractions: The prominent uplift to the southeast is called White Rock. Squaretop Mountain (11,695 feet), one of the most recognized peaks in Wyoming, is centered over the lake. Get up early in the morning, walk to the lake, and see if you're fortunate enough to watch the river fog sweep across the lake. It's an awesome and mystical sight to see.

Scenic Driving: The beautiful 42-mile drive over Union Pass (9,500+ feet) is well worth the long ride. The gravel road creeps upward to reach the Continental Divide, providing awesome views of the Absaroka and Wind River mountains. There is a short interpretive foot-trail at the top of the pass. The road begins at a bridge near Whiskey Grove Campground (16 miles from Green River Lake) and ends on HWY 26/287 near Dubois.

Fishing/Limited Boating: Lower Green River Lake, and the river itself, hold rainbow trout. There is a primitive access ramp for non-motorized boats.

Trails: The camp's Green River Lakes Trailhead provides access to several serious backpacking trails. If you plan on hiking in the area, be sure to obtain a trail map. Corrals are provided for horse packers.

The Highline Trail, one of the main routes through the Wind Rivers, travels dozens of miles through the backcountry. The popular destinations, such as mountain parks or alpine lakes, are found between 10 and 20 miles from the trailhead.

The Lakeside-Porcupine Trail, which begins between the lake and campground, is better suited for day hikers. The trail skirts the edge of Lower Green River Lake and travels to Porcupine Creek Falls, 3 miles total distance. The trail continues over a high pass and intersects the New Fork Trail after 11 miles.

Field Notes: This is a terrific place to spend a few days and you'll never tire of the awesome scenery. Drawbacks include unrelenting mosquitoes (especially down by the lake) and a shortage of trash containers and bear boxes. Keep in mind that grizzly bears are active in this area. In the past, the Forest Service restricted this camp to only hard-sided trailers when a bear was causing trouble.

Green River Lake Campground

Warren Bridge Recreation Area

7,600 feet

Location/Map	Northwest of Pinedale; Page 299
GPS Coordinates	N43° 1.28' W110° 7.25'
Sites/Spur Length	25 sites, 3 group sites; Long spurs—over 30 feet
Cost	Free
Facilities/Services	Fire rings, picnic tables, pit toilets, limited cellular service
Managing Agency	Bureau of Land Management (Pinedale Field Office)
Reservations	Not accepted—first come, first served
Season/Usage	Open all year; Moderate use

Directions: From Pinedale, travel west on HWY 191/189 for a little over 20 miles and turn right after you cross the Green River. Drive north on BLM 5201 (Warren Bridge Road) for up to 8.2 miles to the camping area of your choice.

Description: This unique recreation area stretches along the Green River in the Upper Green River Valley. From the highway, a well-maintained gravel road leads northward across rolling sagebrush-covered hills. Short access roads branch off to the east and lead to the riverbanks. Some of these roads are easy to drive, others are steep and may require four wheel drive depending on road conditions (there are signs that show which areas may require high clearance).

You'll find more than a dozen designated "River Access Areas" that consist of flat grassy landings along the river. Most have pit toilets, fire rings, and tables. Though there are few trees and virtually no shade, some sites do have willows and a spotting of conifers. Cottonwood trees have recently been replanted along this river after they were cut down and used for railroad ties several generations ago.

If you're using a tent or a camper under 30 feet, you'll fit into any of the access areas. If your rig is longer than 30 feet, you'll want to head for areas 3, 4, 7, 10, or 12a. Areas 1, 2, 8, and 9 are limited to one trailer or RV per site. Group camping is allowed in areas 4, 7, and 12. Confusing? All of this information is available on the BLM website and the signs at the recreation site are excellent. This is a well-managed area.

Fishing/Boating/Floating: The trout fishing here must be excellent. I found dozens of fishing skiffs on the river in late July. There are thirteen river access points where you can launch your craft. The BLM recommends only non-motorized crafts be used.

Trails: There is a sign for the Warren Bridge Hiking Trail near HWY 191/189 and another at the north end of the recreation area near a dilapidated bridge. One could deduce that these are the endpoints of a 10-mile foot trail, but this wasn't confirmed.

Warren Bridge Recreation Area

Field Notes: I learned that there are more than 20,000 visits to this recreation area each year. Really? In the sage-strewn country below the mighty Wind River Range that only sees a few decent months of good weather every year? My most recent visit doused my suspicions as I found a couple hundred people here in mid-summer either fishing, camping, or just enjoying this chunk of public land. Summertime temperatures remain milder than you'd think. Watch for grouse and antelope. Even bears and moose wander down this drainage, though a sighting would be lucky.

Warren Bridge Campground

7,500 feet

Location/Map	Northwest of Pinedale; Page 299
GPS Coordinates	N43° 1.08' W110° 7.1'
Sites/Spur Length	16 sites; Long spurs—over 30 feet
Cost	$10
Facilities/Services	Fire rings, grills, picnic tables, pit toilets, trash containers, dump station (fee charged), cellular service
Managing Agency	Bureau of Land Management (Pinedale Field Office); A host is often present
Reservations	Not accepted—first come, first served
Season/Usage	Open all year; Low use

Directions: From Pinedale, travel west on HWY 191/189 for 20 miles.

Description: Spread out on a sagebrush bench above the Green River, this campground does not have shade but does have unobstructed views of the surrounding mountain ranges. Look north to see the Wind Rivers and look west and southwest to spot the Wyoming Range. With long, level pull-throughs, this is a great camp for those lumbering RVs and jumbo fifth-wheel trailers. From here, you could make day trips along the Green River, into the Wind Rivers, or even into Grand Teton National Park.

Fishing/Boating/Floating/Other Camping: The Green River Recreation Area across the highway offers excellent trout fishing, hiking, camping, and river access for boating or floating. Read the description on the previous two pages for more information.

Picnicking: A picnic area at the campground makes a convenient stop for those traveling along the highway.

Field Notes: A friendly host often greets visitors at this roadside camp along a busy route. It's not much of a destination, but it's a very convenient place to pull into after dark on your way to or from Yellowstone or Grand Teton National Park. You could also use it as a rest stop; it is an excellent place to make lunch and eat it along the banks of the river with a view of the Wind River Range.

AREA 4 | SOUTHWEST
Southwestern Desert and Mountains

Southwestern Wyoming is characterized by its dry deserts and vast expanses. Although you can see across dozens of miles of sagebrush-carpeted terrain, the landscape is punctuated with escarpments and mesas and at least one mountain range is usually visible.

Sage grouse, mule deer, desert elk, and antelope inhabit the deserts, but these aren't the only animals that have lived in the area. It may be hard to believe, but this region was once subtropical with a coastal-like environment that supported plants, such as palm trees, and animals like turtles and crocodiles. Proof of this exists at Fossil Butte National Monument, 15 miles west of Kemmerer.

The Red Desert that surrounds Rock Springs holds the Killpecker Sand Dunes, the largest active dune field in North America. West of the dunes, you'll find White Mountain and Pilot Butte where there are petroglyphs, herds of wild horses, and a proposed wind energy farm (turbines). Boar's Tusk, a volcanic plug similar to Devils Tower, is also found in the area. As intriguing as these attractions are, there are no developed public campgrounds in the vicinity. Dispersed camping, however, is widely available.

Wherever you find water, you will find campgrounds. This corner of Wyoming has three major reservoirs, all filled by the Green River. The largest reservoir is in the Flaming Gorge National Recreation Area. The geology around the gorge is fascinating, and the name is fitting for the red-orange walls that are found near the Wyoming-Utah border.

South of I-80 near Evanston, a tiny portion of Utah's mighty Uinta Mountains extend across the Wyoming border. These mountains hold virtually the only forests you'll find in the region and they offer excellent camping, hiking, four-wheeling, fishing, and boating without the high desert heat.

What to Expect: If you'll be traveling through southwest Wyoming (particularly on the backroads), try to be self-sufficient. The roads here are long and towns and fueling stations often have dozens of miles between them. Even though I-80, a transcontinental highway, bisects this part of Wyoming, it is a remote and undeveloped stretch that offers few services.

The campgrounds in this corner of the state are among the least visited, offering visitors heavy doses of solitude. For this reason, many of them don't offer the basics such as water and trash collection.

Though the majority of these campgrounds are not in the mountains, they are still found at elevations above 6,100 feet. The best months to visit are June through September. Late September is especially nice and you'll avoid muddy road conditions that occur in late spring. Expect warm to hot days and cool evenings.

Area 4: Southwestern Desert and Mountains

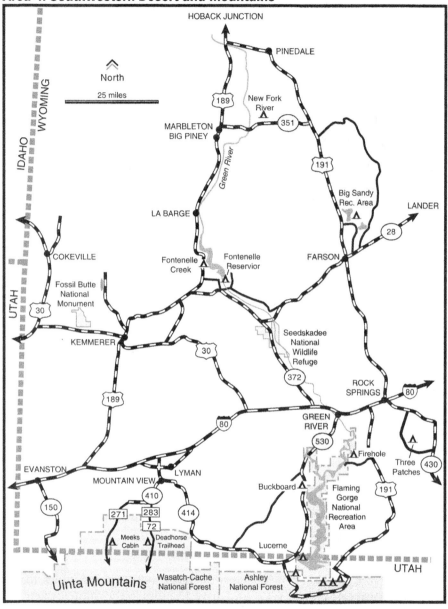

Campgrounds	Sites	Cost	Average Spur Length	Electrical Hookups	Cellular Service (varies by carrier/site)	Reservations Accepted	Page Number
New Fork River Campground	4	Free	M				322
Big Sandy Recreation Area	18+	Free	L		2 bars		323
Fontenelle Creek Campground	55	$7	L		2 bars		324
Fontenelle Reservoir Campgrounds	32+	Free	L		2 bars		325
Three Patches Campground	5	Free	M				328
Buckboard Crossing Campground - Flaming Gorge NRA	68	$22-31	L	✔	2 bars	✔	329
Firehole Campground - Flaming Gorge NRA	40	$22-44	L			✔	331
Flaming Gorge NRA (UT)	320+	$12-50	L	✔		✔	333
Deadhorse Trailhead Campground	4	$14	M				334
Meeks Cabin Campground	24	$18	M				336

Average Spur Length: S = Short (under 30 feet), M = Medium (+-30 feet), L = Long (+-40 feet)
Cellular Service: 1 bar = weak/unreliable signal, 2 bars = low usable signal, 3+ bars = reliable signal for most users

New Fork River Campground

6,850 feet

Location/Map	East of Big Piney and Marbleton; Page 321
GPS Coordinates	N42° 36.34' W109° 51.39'
Sites/Spur Length	4 sites; Medium spurs—up to 30 feet
Cost	Free
Facilities/Services	Picnic tables, pit toilets, boat ramp
Managing Agency	Bureau of Land Management (Pinedale Field Office)
Reservations	Not accepted—first come, first served
Season/Usage	Open early June through late September; Low use

Directions: From Big Piney, head north on HWY 189 for a few miles to HWY 351. Turn east on HWY 351 and drive 13 miles to the camp located near a bridge. If approaching from Pinedale, head south on HWY 191 to HWY 351 and turn west. Drive 12 miles to New Fork River.

Description: This primitive campground—really a dirt lot with a few picnic tables—is found along the banks of New Fork River, a sizable tributary of the Green that originates from New Fork Lakes near Pinedale. The camp sits in the open; all the shade trees are on the opposite side of the river. The

Wind River Range can be seen on the northern horizon. The campground has little to offer, but it work if you are looking for river access or need a place to park for the night.

Fishing/Floating: Both the New Fork River and Green River (5 miles to the west) offer fishing for plump trout. Floaters will find a small boat launch near the highway.

Field Notes: I can't imagine anyone camping at this exposed roadside stop, but I used the camp for a picnic on my way to the mountains.

Big Sandy Recreation Area
6,800 feet

Location/Map	North of Farson; Page 321
GPS Coordinates	N42° 14.53' W109° 26.53'
Sites/Spur Length	18+ sites; Long spurs—over 30 feet
Cost	Free
Facilities/Services	Fire rings, picnic tables, pit toilets, trash containers, boat ramp, cellular service
Managing Agency	Bureau of Reclamation
Reservations	Not accepted—first come, first served
Season/Usage	Open all year; Low use

Directions: From Farson, head north on HWY 191 for 9.5 miles to the sign. Turn right and drive over a mile to the camps near the shoreline.

Description: This is sagebrush country with only a dotting of trees, but the distant views of the Wind River Range to the north are widespread. This is your place if you are looking for reservoir-style camping, which consists mostly of parking a camper along a shoreline and firing up a barbecue grill. There is not a developed campground at Big Sandy Reservoir, but there are four sites along the south shore and seven slightly more developed sites with overflow camping on the west shore. On the east side, you'll find a handful of sites including one near the spillway. Some of these have covered picnic tables. Don't forget your sunscreen and a fishing pole.

Rockhounding: The area around the reservoir, as well as Eden Reservoir to the south, are noted for rockhounding. Perhaps more appealing to the masses are the millions of small flat stones that blanket the reservoir's shoreline when water levels are low. If ever there were a National Rock Skipping Competition, this would be the place to hold it. I got a sore arm from trying to best my wife's record of 9 discernible skips.

Fishing/Boating: Rainbow, cutthroat and brown trout, as well as catfish are the common species found in Big Sandy Reservoir. A boat ramp is located on the west shoreline.

Big Sandy Reservoir

Picnicking: A group picnic shelter is available on the west side of the reservoir.

Field Notes: Most people would scoff at the idea of spending time in this barren region. I certainly did until I actually turned off the truck's ignition and spent some time here. I've since developed an admiration for the area. You might too.

Fontenelle Creek Campground　　　　　　　　6,600 feet

Location/Map	Between LaBarge and Green River; Page 321, 326
GPS Coordinates	N42° 4.4' W110° 9.15'
Sites/Spur Length	55 sites; Long spurs—over 30 feet
Cost	$7
Facilities/Services	Fire rings, grills, covered picnic tables, water, restrooms, trash containers, boat ramp, playground, pay phones, dump station, cellular service
Managing Agency	Bureau of Land Management (Kemmerer Field Office)
Reservations	Not accepted—first come, first served
Season/Usage	Open late May through early September; Low use

Directions: Take HWY 189 northeast out of Kemmerer for 32 miles or south out of Big Piney for 36 miles and watch for the Fontenelle Reservoir signs. The campground is about a mile east of the highway.

Description: Despite its name, it's Fontenelle Reservoir, not the adjacent creek of the same name, that will capture your attention. The campground is located on the west shore of the reservoir and includes level parking spurs, paved roads, and developed facilities that are comparable to those found in national parks. There are no trees, but who needs them? There are sun and wind shades over the picnic tables. Less developed campgrounds are located to the south near the reservoir's dam.

Wildlife Viewing: The sagebrush-covered country surrounding the reservoir is home to the largest population of sage grouse known to exist. The birds aren't alone. Tens of thousands of antelope from the Sublette herd migrate to the area in the fall.

Seedskadee Wildlife Refuge, located southeast of Fontenelle Reservoir along HWY 372, is home to all sorts of wildlife. Great blue herons live among the cottonwoods and feed off fish from the Green River. Larger animals that live at the refuge include antelope, deer, and even moose. The viewing center, near the intersection of HWY 28, is a great place to view the area's waterfowl.

Fishing/Boating: Anglers can fish for trout in Fontenelle Reservoir. A boat ramp is located near the campground.

Field Notes: This is such a big, fancy campground, but it has so few campers. In fact, I've only seen one camper here over several visits. I spent a couple of hours here flying a kite, skipping rocks, and watching pelicans with my daughter. She loved it. We'll go back.

Fontenelle Reservoir Campgrounds
6,600 feet

Location/Map	Between LaBarge and Green River; Page 321, 326
GPS Coordinates	N41° 58.81' W110° 3.67'
Sites/Spur Length	32+ sites; Long spurs—over 30 feet
Cost	Free
Facilities/Services	Fire rings, grills, picnic tables, pit toilets, trash containers, cellular service
Managing Agency	Bureau of Land Management (Kemmerer Field Office)
Reservations	Not accepted—first come, first served
Season/Usage	Open all year; Moderate to high use

Directions: Take HWY 189 northeast out of Kemmerer for 24 miles, or south from La Barge for 24 miles to reach HWY 372. Drive east on the highway for 8.2 miles to where the highway turns south at a four-way junction. To reach Weeping Rock Campground, turn north here and drive 3 miles on CR 316 to the camp's access road. To reach Slate Creek Campground from the junction, stay east (leaving the highway) and drive .8 mile to the camp. Tail Race Campground is found on the east end of the dam. To reach it from

Slate Creek, continue east to cross a bridge and then follow CR 52 to the north for 3.7 miles to a turnoff. Turn left, drive a third of a mile and then turn left again onto the camp's rocky access road. These roads in and around the dam can only be described as obfuscated. Once when I visited, the county road signs were mistakenly (or perhaps as a prank) posted on the wrong roads.

Fontenelle Reservoir

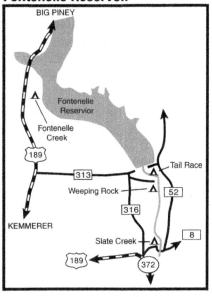

Description: Three fairly primitive campgrounds exist along the Green River, immediately south of Fontenelle Reservoir. Found in the high Wyoming desert, these campgrounds have quite an oasis feel to them. Some campsites have fire rings, some have grills, and others have picnic tables. The best sites have all three.

Weeping Rock Campground is tucked along the west banks of the river and has roomy sites in a stand of cottonwoods. This camp is closest to the reservoir's boat ramp.

Slate Creek Campground, the southern-most campground, is also on the west side of the river and offers a grassy area with large cottonwood trees and willows. Depending on where you drive in from, these may be the first trees you'll have seen for 100 miles! The camp is crisscrossed with connecting dirt tracks that lead to at least 20 spacious campsites. The camp remains surprisingly busy, even during the middle of the week. Many campers park their large RVs and fifth-wheel trailers here.

Tail Race Campground is found on the eastern side of the river near the dam and is the least suitable for large trailers. Stone fire rings are scattered among cottonwood trees.

Overlook Point: There is a reservoir overlook on the west side of the dam where you can look out over the water. An interpretive sign explains the reservoir's history. In short, the dam and nearby powerplant were completed in 1964 for the initial purpose of storing irrigation water and generating electric power. Today, the reservoir is used to hold water for municipalities, industry, and wildlife. The reservoir covers nearly 13 square miles and is 20 miles long when completely full.

Wildlife Viewing: The sagebrush-covered country surrounding the reservoir is home to the largest population of sage grouse known to exist. The birds

Slate Creek Campground at Fontenelle Reservoir

aren't alone. Tens of thousands of antelope from the Sublette herd migrate to the area in the fall.

You may spot trumpeter swans around the campgrounds. These are impressive birds to watch. While not protected by the Federal Endangered Species Act, they are at risk and have faced the possibility of extinction. As North America's largest waterfowl, they weigh more than 22 pounds and have a wingspan of nearly 8 feet.

Seedskadee Wildlife Refuge, located southeast of Fontenelle Reservoir along HWY 372, is home to all sorts of wildlife. Great blue herons live among the cottonwoods and feed off fish from the Green River. Larger animals that live at the refuge include antelope, deer, and even moose. The viewing center, near HWY 28, is a great place to view the area's waterfowl.

Fishing/Boating: Anglers can fish for trout in Green River as well as in Fontenelle Reservoir. A boat ramp is located on the west side of the reservoir. In addition, river floaters will find primitive launch ramps at the campgrounds.

Field Notes: The bugs can get thick around the river and reservoir so be sure to bring insect repellent. Days get sunny and hot here so toss in some sunscreen also. I needed both when I had a tire blowout on the rocks near Tail Race Campground.

Three Patches Campground

8,400 feet

Location/Map	Southeast of Rock Springs; Page 321
GPS Coordinates	N41° 25.33' W109° 7.49'
Sites/Spur Length	5 sites; Medium spurs—up to 30 feet
Cost	Free
Facilities/Services	Fire rings, picnic tables, pit toilets, trash containers
Managing Agency	Bureau of Land Management (Rock Springs Field Office)
Reservations	Not accepted—first come, first served
Season/Usage	Open May through late October; Low use

Directions: From the southern edge of Rock Springs, take HWY 430 south for 3 miles to CR 27 (Aspen Mountain Road). Turn onto CR 27 and follow the road signs for 13 miles past several junctions. Bear left at the recreation site sign and drive a final mile to the campground. The latter part of this road is steep as it climbs to the top of Quaking Aspen Mountain.

Description: This recreation site takes full advantage of a very rare commodity in this part of the state—trees. As the campground's name implies, there are three distinct aspen stands on the side of Quaking Aspen Mountain (8,667 feet). Walk-in sites are positioned on the inside of a circular loop road, but paved parking spurs make it easy to level out a van or pickup camper. Expect solitude during the week and traffic on the weekends.

Scenic Driving: The drive to the campground is fantastic. The road climbs high to gain sweeping views of southwestern Wyoming's dry, but beautiful desert landscape. To make an extended loop, consider driving south from the campground for 13 miles to South Baxter Road or 25 miles to Titsworth Gap. Roads at both of these junctions head east to return to HWY 430.

Picnicking: Three Patches is not only a campground, but a picnic area.

Field Notes: Rock Springs certainly isn't known for being in the most scenic part of the state, but a visit to this high perch helps give a whole new appreciation for Wyoming's beautiful southwestern desert.

Buckboard Crossing Campground

6,100 feet

Location/Map	West side of Flaming Gorge National Recreation Area; Page 321
GPS Coordinates	N41° 14.85' W109° 36.14'
Sites/Spur Length	68 sites; Long spurs—over 30 feet
Cost	$22 or $31 with electric hookups
Facilities/Services	Electric hookups (limited), fire rings, grills, covered picnic tables, water, restrooms, showers, dump station, boat ramp, supply store/marina, cellular service
Managing Agency	USDA Forest Service (Ashley National Forest); A host is often present
Reservations	Call 877-444-6777 or visit www.recreation.gov
Season/Usage	Open May through mid-September; Moderate use

Directions: From Green River, head south on HWY 530 for 23 miles, then turn east at the Buckboard sign and drive 1.5 miles on a paved access road.

Description: Buckboard Crossing is one of two campgrounds found on the Wyoming side of Flaming Gorge Reservoir. This is a relatively open two-loop camp with a lot of sagebrush and scattered Russian olive trees. Most sites will gain more shade from the provided sun shelters than from the trees. Parking spurs are flat and include a few pull-throughs. The campground comes fully loaded with facilities and services: electric hookups (at 9 sites), restrooms, showers, marina, and a store.

Scenic Driving: From the town of Green River, a scenic 150-mile loop can be made around the Flaming Gorge National Recreation Area. Traveling down the west side of the reservoir, the road winds southward through the high sagebrush-grassland desert. The scenery changes quickly as the road crosses into Utah and travels upwards into the forested mountains of the Ashley National Forest. The Red Canyon Visitor Center is located along this stretch as are numerous picnic areas and overlooks. Be sure to stop at the dam to learn more about the history of this area. Heading back north, the road departs far to the east of the reservoir and travels through scenic badlands and high desert plains to a high point of 8,000 feet. Be sure to make the side trip to Firehole Campground to see the rock structures.

Wildlife Viewing: Simply traveling along the reservoir's perimeter road is one way to begin your wildlife pursuit. In the northern portion of the area, watch for small mammals like coyotes, prairie dogs, and rabbits. Antelope and badgers also reside in this open country. In the forested region in Utah, skilled observers may find moose, elk, deer, black bear, and bighorn sheep. The east side of the recreation area is home to wild horses. The wetlands here also provide habitat for osprey, geese, eagles, and pelicans. Bald eagles are often seen during the winter months. Mountain lions prowl the entire area.

Flaming Gorge National Recreation Area as seen from Utah

Fishing: World record-sized fish have been pulled from these waters including lake trout in excess of 50 pounds and 25-pound rainbow trout. Other common species include mackinaw, kokanee salmon, and smallmouth bass. A fishing license from either Utah or Wyoming is required. You can buy a special-use stamp to fish in both states.

Trails: On the Utah side of the Flaming Gorge, near the spillway, there are multi-use trails that are suitable for hiking, mountain biking, and horseback riding (except on the Little Hole Trail). Distances range from 3 to 7 miles in length. Be sure to pick up a map or trail brochure.

Boating: There is a boat ramp and marina near the camp. Overall, the reservoir has three marinas and ten boat ramps.

Remote Camping/Dispersed Camping: In all, there are over 600 campsites in the Flaming Gorge National Recreation Area, many of which are dispersed or considered primitive. In addition, there are a number of developed campgrounds that are accessible only by boat. One of these is Hideout Campground. It is located 20 miles north of the dam near the Sheep Creek Bay boat ramp. Boaters also have access to several floating camps located 4 miles south of Buckboard Crossing and 3 miles south of the Squaw Hollow boat ramp.

Field Notes: This windy camp is probably one of the least scenic of the area, but it does have its perks. There is also a private RV park with full hookups across the road.

Firehole Campground

6,100 feet

Location/Map	East side of the Flaming Gorge National Recreation Area; Page 321
GPS Coordinates	N41° 20.98' W109° 26.76'
Sites/Spur Length	40 sites, 1 group site with shelter; Long spurs—over 30 feet
Cost	$22, $44 group site
Facilities/Services	Fire rings, covered picnic tables, water, restrooms, showers, boat ramp, dump station
Managing Agency	USDA Forest Service (Ashley National Forest); A host is often present
Reservations	Call 877-444-6777 or visit www.recreation.gov
Season/Usage	Open May through mid-September; Moderate use

Directions: From Green River or Rock Springs, take I-80 to Exit 99. Drive south on HWY 191 for about 14 miles to the Firehole Canyon area. Turn onto CR 33 and drive 10 miles. This paved road has a steep grade of 9%.

Description: This is a unique campground with interesting rock formations spread across the horizon. It's a scenic backdrop in an otherwise open area with sagebrush ground cover and a few Russian olive trees. Most campsites are grouped in pairs; they share a parking pad and the enclosed picnic tables are together under a cabana... it's quite different. While it might be too close if you don't know your neighbor, chances are you'll get a site to yourself unless it's a busy holiday. Families who are camping together will find the "double sites" to be convenient. A group site and shelter south of the camp can hold up to 10 campers and two vehicles.

Scenic Driving: From the town of Green River, a scenic 150-mile loop can be made around the Flaming Gorge National Recreation Area. Traveling down the west side of the reservoir, the road winds southward through the high sagebrush-grassland desert. The scenery changes quickly as the road crosses into Utah and travels upwards into the forested mountains of the Ashley National Forest. The Red Canyon Visitor Center is located along this stretch as are numerous picnic areas and overlooks. Be sure to stop at the dam to learn more about the history of this area. Heading back north, the road departs far to the east of the reservoir and travels through scenic badlands and high desert plains to a high point of 8,000 feet.

Wildlife Viewing: Simply traveling along the reservoir's perimeter road is one way to begin your wildlife pursuit. In the northern portion of the area, watch for small mammals like coyotes, prairie dogs, and rabbits. Antelope and badgers also reside in this open country. In the forested region in Utah, skilled observers may find moose, elk, deer, black bear, and bighorn sheep. The east side of the recreation area is home to wild horses. The wetlands here also provide habitat for osprey, geese, eagles, and pelicans. Bald eagles are often viewed during the winter months. Mountain lions prowl the entire area.

Fishing: World record-sized fish have been pulled from these waters including lake trout in excess of 50 pounds and 25-pound rainbow trout. Other common species include mackinaw, kokanee salmon, and smallmouth bass. A fishing license from either Utah or Wyoming is required. You can also buy a special-use stamp to fish in both states.

Trails: On the Utah side of the Flaming Gorge, near the spillway, there are multi-use trails that are suitable for hiking, mountain biking, and horseback riding (except on the Little Hole Trail). Distances range from 3 to 7 miles in length. Be sure to pick up a map or trail brochure for more information. Closer to this camp, to the south, there are many ATV tracks.

Boating/Swimming: There is a boat ramp next to the campground as well as a beach that is ideal for wading and swimming. Overall, the reservoir has three marinas and ten boat ramps. Obtain a lake map to identify hazards.

Remote Camping/Dispersed Camping: In all, there are over 600 campsites in the Flaming Gorge National Recreation Area, many of which are dispersed or considered primitive. In addition, there are a number of developed campgrounds that are accessible only by boat. One of these is Hideout Campground, located 20 miles north of the dam near the Sheep Creek Bay boat ramp. Boaters also have access to several floating camps located 4 miles south of Buckboard Crossing and 3 miles south of the Squaw Hollow boat ramp.

Picnicking: There is a picnic area at the campground where you can munch while appreciating the rock scenery of Firehole Canyon. The tall columns to the northeast are named North and South Chimney Rock.

Firehole Campground

Field Notes: If you are passing through on I-80, but want to see a bit of the Flaming Gorge National Recreation Area, this camp fits the bill. You'll get a glimpse of the reservoir and will see Firehole Canyon.

Utah Campgrounds at the Flaming Gorge NRA (Ashley National Forest)

Although much of the Flaming Gorge National Recreation Area is in Wyoming, most of the developed campgrounds are in Utah. The fantastic facilities and scenery you find here are worth the drive across state lines.

The largest camp here is Lucerne, accessed from Wyoming on the reservoir's west side, but located just south of the Utah border. This camp has it all: 135 paved sites, electric hookups, showers, a store and more.

From Manila, Utah, you can use HWY 44 to head further south. Camps in this area, such as Carmel, Willow, and Mann, are nudged up against colorful rock cliffs. You can tour the area's rock formations from the Sheep Creek Geologic Loop road.

Climbing higher into the Uinta Mountains, HWY 44 bears east as it wraps around the southern end of Flaming Gorge Reservoir. Here, you'll find Canyon Rim Campground and sites that are edged on the rim of Red Canyon, a 1,700-foot gorge of spectacular beauty. A light ponderosa pine forest shades these sites, as well as those in nearby Green Lakes and Skull Creek campgrounds. Be sure to stop at the Red Canyon Visitor Center.

Using HWY 191 to head north into Wyoming, you'll pass many more campgrounds such as Greendale, Firefighters Memorial, Deer Run, Cedar Springs, Arch Dam, Dipping Springs, Mustang Ridge, and Antelope Flat. As you drive north and lose elevation, the forests at these camps transition from ponderosa pine to juniper and pinion pine, and then finally to just sagebrush. A handful of these camps are along the Green River and have boat ramps. Many also offer double and group campsites.

Deadhorse Trailhead Campground

8,700 feet

Location/Map	Southeast of Evanston; Page 321
GPS Coordinates	N41° 2.02' W110° 21.96'
Sites/Spur Length	4 sites; Medium spurs—up to 30 feet
Cost	$12
Facilities/Services	Fire rings, picnic tables, pit toilets
Managing Agency	USDA Forest Service (Uinta-Wasatch-Cache National Forest)
Reservations	Not accepted—first come, first served
Season/Usage	Open June through late October; Low use

Directions: From Mountain View, head south on paved CR 410 for 6 miles. Take wide CR 283 for 8 miles as it turns into FR 72. Follow this road, which becomes rough, for 3 miles and watch for the Deadhorse Trailhead sign.

Description: This is a little-known trailhead campground that is rarely shown on maps and recreational literature. The camp consists of a large parking area with spacious sites tucked into a light pine forest. The beautiful Uinta Mountains in Utah can be seen from the road, but not from the campground.

Fishing/Boating: Stateline Reservoir is located 4 miles to the south in Utah and is accessible from the rough forest road. This reservoir holds rainbow, brook, and cutthroat trout. Stream fishing can also be found below the reservoir on the East Fork of the Smith Fork River. Remember that you'll need a Utah fishing license if you choose to fish these waters.

Trails/ATV Routes: The multi-use trails that begin from the campground lead through the area's lodgepole pine forest. The trails are used by hikers in the summer and cross-country skiers in the winter. This is also the starting point for the Deadhorse ATV trail network, which is comprised of about 20 miles of winding loops and tracks. There is a good trail map on a sign at the campground, but you can also stop by the Forest Service office in Mountain View to obtain a trail brochure.

Other Camping: Continue south another 5-10 miles to find several attractive campgrounds in Utah. Stateline, East and West Marsh Lake, Bridger Lake, and China Meadows are just a few that are nearby and easy to reach. There are also dispersed campsites near China Meadows.

Field Notes: I've been here on a couple of summer weekends and have never seen another vehicle. Though I wouldn't expect anyone to stay the night at this camp, I'm surprised I haven't seen more trail use.

An overlook of the Uinta Mountains

Meeks Cabin Campground

8,900 feet

Location/Map	Southeast of Evanston; Page 321
GPS Coordinates	N41° 0.32' W110° 35.0'
Sites/Spur Length	24 sites; Medium spurs—up to 30 feet
Cost	$18
Facilities/Services	Fire rings, grills, picnic tables, water, pit toilets, boat ramp
Managing Agency	USDA Forest Service (Uinta-Wasatch-Cache National Forest)
Reservations	Not accepted—first come, first served
Season/Usage	Open June through late October; Moderate use

Directions: From Mountain View (just south of I-80 near Lyman), head south on paved CR 410 for 13 miles. Turn left onto CR 271 (Meeks Cabin Access Road) and drive 15 miles. Turn left at the campground sign and drive less than 1 mile to the east. The wide roads are well-maintained and easily traveled.

Description: This campground in the Uinta Mountains makes for a great escape from the extensive high desert landscape that characterizes so much of southwestern Wyoming. You'll find fairly private sites arranged in a forest of aspen and lodgepole pine. Some parking spurs face east to catch the morning sun and overlook the reservoir. Most pads are level and a few are paved.

Fishing/Boating: Meeks Cabin Reservoir offers fishing for cutthroat trout. Boating is permitted on the reservoir. In addition, several public access points for the Blacks Fork River are available along CR 271.

Outdoor Recreation: If you are looking for more recreational activities, head south into Utah. There are numerous campgrounds, fishing holes, and trails to be found. The summit of Kings Peak, the highest point in Utah at over 13,000 feet, is a popular destination for strong hikers.

Field Notes: Most of the Uinta-Wasatch-Cache National Forest resides in Utah, so you won't find much information about it in Wyoming. However, there is a Forest Service district office in Mountain View that can be helpful.

SOUTH - SOUTHEAST
Southern mountain ranges

Wyoming is a land of diverse landscapes: deserts, grasslands, canyons, dense forests, and high mountain peaks. All of these variations are found in the south-southeastern region of the state. Cheyenne, the capital city tucked away in the corner, is found amid high grasslands that extend to each end of the horizon. A little further west, the gentle landscape is broken by rock outcrops where the southern tip of the stunted Laramie Mountains begins protruding through the earth's surface. Interstate 80, America's transcontinental highway, travels over an 8,000-foot summit here, offering many Interstate drivers their only taste of mountain driving as they pass through the state. From the summit the roadway bends northward, following the path of least resistance, and leaves the beautiful mountains of southeastern Wyoming to those who actually want to explore their wilds.

Two mountain ranges dominate this part of the state, the Medicine Bow and the Sierra Madre. The Medicine Bow is a land of alpine beauty where a dramatic row of peaks called the Snowy Range stands high above dozens of clear trout-filled tarns. The Sierra Madre is a gentler, but wilder, range that straddles the Continental Divide. West of these ranges, the land turns arid where miles of sagebrush fill the expanse known as Wyoming's Red Desert.

South-Southeast Areas

WYOMING

1. Sierra Madre Range (page 340)
2. Medicine Bow Mountains (page 350)
3. Vedauwoo and Vicinity (page 379)

338 The Wyoming Camping Guide

Privately-owned Campgrounds and RV Dump Stations

This section includes the general locations of privately-owned RV parks. For contact information and addresses for these businesses, look online or check out the campground directory on the Wyoming Office of Tourism website at travelwyoming.com.

Area 1: Sierra Madre Range
An attractive RV park is located in Riverside-Encampment along the banks of the Encampment River. Further north, you'll find another camp in Saratoga.

Area 2: Medicine Bow Mountains
On the west side of the area, there are RV parks in Riverside-Encampment, Ryan Park, and Saratoga. On the east side, look no further than in Laramie. The small settlement of Woods Landing, near the Colorado border, also has an RV park.

Area 3: Vedauwoo and Vicinity
Laramie has a pair of RV parks. Further east, along I-80 and I-25, check in Cheyenne. There are nearly ten privately-owned campgrounds in this area, many of which fill to capacity during Cheyenne Frontier Days (rodeo and concerts in July).

RV Dump Stations
The locations below include public RV dump stations. Additional dump stations can often be found at private campgrounds and large gas stations.
- Curt Gowdy State Park
- I-25: Rest Area/Information Visitor Center south of Cheyenne, WY
- I-80: Wyoming Territorial Prison in Laramie, WY
- Encampment City Park, Encampment, WY
- Burns Public RV Dump Station, Burns, WY

AREA 1 SOUTH – SOUTHEAST
Sierra Madre Range

Despite their natural beauty and rich history, the Sierra Madre remains one of Wyoming's best-kept secrets. Rising between two valleys in south-central Wyoming, these mountains demonstrate a peaceful demeanor, even when visitation is highest during the hunting season.

While much of the Sierra Madre is robed in dense lodgepole pine, the western slope of the range is timbered extensively with quaking aspen. Perhaps the most popular area in the range is known as Aspen Alley, where a forest road travels briefly through one of these mature deciduous stands. The higher regions of the range consist of subalpine-alpine meadows of grass and wildflowers between stands of spruce and fir.

You'll find powerful rivers, lush meadows, and an abundance of wildlife. Mule deer and elk are found in respectable numbers. Bighorn sheep and moose are present but comprise a much smaller population. River otters, raptors, and blue grouse may also be spotted.

The Sierra Madre Mountains have two designated wilderness areas—the Encampment River Wilderness, near the eastern edge, and the Huston Park Wilderness, located at the crest of the range. Both places have excellent hiking trails where solitude awaits.

Drivers looking for a scenic trip will appreciate Wyoming Highway 70—a paved route that crosses the Continental Divide at 10,000-foot Battle Pass. The best part of this roadway is found on the range's west side where views across Wyoming and into Colorado are grand.

Perhaps one of the best ways to begin an excursion in the Sierra Madre is to visit the Grand Encampment Museum in the town of Encampment. You'll learn about local battles that were fought, the fate of the mining industry, and why the United States Air Force operated seismic equipment here under a veil of secrecy. The museum also has a collection of interesting historical buildings including a tie hack's cabin, a two-story outhouse, and a retired fire-lookout tower that gives a bird's perspective of the range.

What to Expect: The campgrounds in this range tend to have slow and steady traffic from July through October. The fall hunting seasons bring more use to the area. Most visitors are local Wyoming residents or Coloradoans from the Steamboat Springs area, which is directly to the south. Occasionally, you'll get a curious interstate straggler that comes through looking for a more scenic drive than I-80 offers. Overall, the people you'll encounter here are those who keep coming back year after year—folks that like it here and have no reason to go elsewhere.

If you join them, don't arrive too early in the season. Secondary roads throughout the range (everything but the main gravel trunk roads) are often found muddy through late spring. At higher elevations, you can encounter snowdrifts into early July. Once summer reaches these parts, you can expect glorious days coupled with cool and quiet evenings.

A view across the Sierra Madre Range

Area 1: Sierra Madre Range

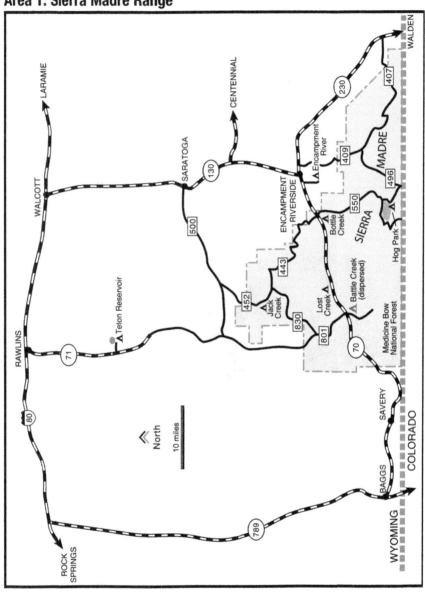

Campgrounds	Sites	Cost	Average Spur Length	Electrical Hookups	Cellular Service (varies by carrier/site)	Reservations Accepted	Page Number
Encampment River Campground	8	$10	M				343
Bottle Creek Campground	16	$10	L				344
Hog Park Campground	50	$10	L			✔	345
Lost Creek Campground	14	$10	L				347
Jack Creek Campground	16	$10	M				348
Teton Reservoir Recreation Site	5	Free	L		▫▫▫		349

Average Spur Length: S = Short (under 30 feet), M = Medium (+-30 feet), L = Long (+-40 feet)
Cellular Service: 1 bar = weak/unreliable signal, 2 bars = low usable signal, 3+ bars = reliable signal for most users

Encampment River Campground

7,300 feet

Location/Map	Southeast of Rawlins; Page 342
GPS Coordinates	N41° 11.01' W106° 47.8'
Sites/Spur Length	8 sites; Medium spurs—up to 30 feet
Cost	$10
Facilities/Services	Fire rings, picnic tables, water, pit toilets
Managing Agency	Bureau of Land Management (Rawlins Field Office)
Reservations	Not accepted—first come, first served
Season/Usage	Open June through mid-November; Moderate use

Directions: From Encampment, drive west on HWY 70 for a half-mile and turn south onto CR 353, which turns into BLM Road 405. Follow the gravel road for 1.7 miles to the campground.

Description: This nicely placed BLM campground is located along the timbered banks of the Encampment River. While the surrounding area consists of sagebrush-dotted foothills, the campground itself is shady due to leafy cottonwood trees that line the river. The area receives heavy use from anglers and other day-use visitors but quiets soon after dusk. The long and level parking spurs can accommodate most trailers, but the BLM suggests that only those 25 feet or shorter are used because of the tight quarters and lack of a good turnaround. Vans, tents, and pickup campers are best.

Fishing: The Encampment River is an excellent fishery for large brown trout. Cutthroat and rainbow trout can be expected, although they are usually much smaller.

Trails: A trailhead for the Encampment River Trail is located at the end of the campground where a bridge crosses the river. The 16-mile route leaves the dusty hills and travels into the thickly forested mountains of the Encampment River Wilderness. The trail ascends 1,100 feet as it traverses varying ecosystems. The upper stretch passes through a scenic rocky canyon. Visitors can expect low to moderate traffic on the trail. Hikers are common in the higher canyon while anglers frequent the lower elevations.

A much shorter trail in the area is a .5-mile route that leads to Indian Bathtubs. These tubs are actually deep impressions in granite outcrops that fill with water. Indians used the pools to bathe and play. To get to the trailhead, drive 1 mile east of Encampment-Riverside and turn south on CR 211 (Blackhall Road). The trail starts 1 mile south of this intersection.

Kayaking/Floating: When water levels are high, the Encampment River attracts kayakers to its rapid torrents. The calmer stretches (from the campground northward to Saratoga) are popular with floaters.

Field Notes: This is a camp that seems to be gaining popularity and for good reason. If you don't stay here, consider stopping by for a picnic.

Bottle Creek Campground   8,700 feet

Location/Map	South of Rawlins; Page 342
GPS Coordinates	N41° 10.49' W106° 53.9'
Sites/Spur Length	16 sites; 1 group picnic site (day use only), Long spurs—over 30 feet
Cost	$10, $50 for reservable picnic site
Facilities/Services	Fire rings, grills, picnic tables, pit toilets, trash containers
Managing Agency	USDA Forest Service (Medicine Bow National Forest); A host is often present
Reservations	Group picnic site only, call 877-444-6777 or visit www.recreation.gov
Season/Usage	Open June through October; Moderate use

Directions: From Encampment, drive west on HWY 70 for 6 miles and turn left on FR 550. Then turn right onto the campground's short access road.

Description: Bottle Creek is a tiny, hidden brook that trickles through this sunny camp; you're not likely to see it. The camp was completely logged in 2009 due to beetle-killed trees. Over a decade later, short conifers and aspen are starting to fill in the space between the stumps. More than half of the sites are lined along the top of a small rise that overlooks the rolling mountainous terrain to the south. Many parking spurs are long enough to accommodate long trailers or RVs. A group picnic site can be reserved and can accommodate 200 people, though it needed some maintenance as of my last visit.

Scenic Driving: The Forest Service has designated an interpretive 50-mile driving tour that begins from the highway and follows FR 550 south toward Hog Park Reservoir. From the reservoir, the route utilizes FR 496 near the Colorado border and then FR 409 to return to Riverside-Encampment. You'll see historical ruins, forested mountainsides, and areas of timber harvesting along the drive. The Forest Service office in Saratoga sometimes has a brochure that covers the highlights of this drive. There is also a brochure box near the beginning of the road, but it is often found empty.

Trails: The photogenic Green Mountain Falls are worth the effort needed to get to them. From the campground, drive 2 miles south on FR 550 to a trailhead on FR 5502H. From the parking area, follow the rough four-wheel drive road west for 2 miles to a small meadow where a foot trail continues west. Follow the foot trail for 1.2 miles as it gently ascends to the beautiful tumbling cascade.

The Bottle Creek cross-country ski trails can be found just west, and north, of the campground along HWY 70. There are 10 miles of loops that explore a small section of the Sierra Madre's eastern slope. The trails are marked with signs, but many are overgrown with vegetation during the summer.

Field Notes: Though it's nothing compared to its prior glory, young trees are renewing the beauty of this campground. However, it needs some work. As of this writing, the water pumps were disabled, the trash containers were locked shut, and several of the sites were overgrown. You can also expect a lot of wind. But, I easily got the site of my choice on Labor Day weekend.

Hog Park Campground

8,450 feet

Location/Map	South of Rawlins; Page 342
GPS Coordinates	N41° 1.43' W106° 51.98'
Sites/Spur Length	50 sites, Long spurs—over 30 feet
Cost	$10
Facilities/Services	Fire rings, picnic tables, water, pit toilets, trash containers, boat ramp
Managing Agency	USDA Forest Service (Medicine Bow National Forest); A host is often present
Reservations	Call 877-444-6777 or visit www.recreation.gov
Season/Usage	Open mid-June through October; Moderate use

Directions: From Encampment, drive west on HWY 70 for 6 miles and turn left on FR 550. Drive south for 16 miles and then 2 miles on FR 496. Turn right onto the reservoir's short access road and follow it to the campground.

Hog Park Campground

Description: Hog Park is a large campground on the edge of Hog Park Reservoir near the Wyoming-Colorado border. The camp features a few dozen back-in spurs and pull-throughs, some near the water. This camp was clearcut over a decade ago to remove beetle-killed trees, but there is now a young and healthy forest of pine and spruce. The return of trees has also brought back the campers. This is the only campground in the range that accepts reservations and you'd be smart to make one before making the long drive to this remote area.

Scenic Driving: The Forest Service has designated an interpretive 50-mile driving tour that begins from HWY 70 and follows FR 550 south toward Hog Park Reservoir. From the reservoir, the route utilizes FR 496 near the Colorado border and then FR 409 to return to Riverside-Encampment. You'll see historical ruins, forested mountainsides, and areas of timber harvesting along the drive. The Forest Service office in Saratoga sometimes has a brochure that covers the highlights of this drive. There is also a brochure box near the beginning of the road, but it is often found empty.

Fishing/Boating: Hog Park Reservoir is the Sierra Madre's primary fishing destination. Anglers will find cutthroat, rainbow, and brook trout. Boaters will find a ramp on the south shoreline near the campground and another at a picnic area on the other side of the reservoir.

Trails: The Encampment River Trail is a 16-mile route that descends from the thickly forested mountains near Hog Park to the sagebrush hills near Encampment. The upper stretch passes through a scenic, rocky canyon. The trailhead can be found at Commissary Park east of the camp on FR 496.

Picnicking: A picnic area and angler parking are on the lake's northwest side.

Field Notes: A few trends that I've seen here over the years is an increase in trailers (instead of tents), more ATV use, and motorized boats giving way to non-motorized use of the lake (canoes, sailboats, and paddle boards).

Lost Creek Campground — 8,800 feet

Location/Map	South of Rawlins; Page 342
GPS Coordinates	N41° 8.46' W107° 4.76'
Sites/Spur Length	14 sites, Long spurs—over 30 feet
Cost	$10
Facilities/Services	Fire rings, picnic tables, water, pit toilets, trash containers
Managing Agency	USDA Forest Service (Medicine Bow National Forest)
Reservations	Not accepted—first come, first served
Season/Usage	Open mid-June through October; Moderate use

Directions: From Encampment, drive west on HWY 70 for 19 miles.

Description: This pleasant camp offers a mix of camping options along a semi-open loop. While some sites receive decent shade from mature evergreens and aspens, other sites get little to none. Lost Creek flows nearby and creates a nice babble, but not enough to drown out highway noise. Most parking spurs are large and will fit long trailers and RVs. The camp receives light use—it is quite underutilized really—until bow season starts in September.

Scenic Driving: The 46-mile drive between Encampment and Savery makes a scenic tour. You'll travel up the east slope of the Sierra Madre to the crest of the Continental Divide. The west slope of the mountain range has some great views of the Sierra Madre Range as well as the jagged Colorado peaks. The west side also includes the largest stand of aspen trees in Wyoming including "Aspen Alley," which is a mile north of the highway on FR 801.

Trails: Cross the highway to find the Baby Lake Trail. The first half-mile of this fairly strenuous trail descends steeply on an old road to the Huston Park Wilderness boundary at Battle Creek. From here the trail climbs over 1,000 feet to join the Continental Divide Trail, a little over 4 miles away.

4WD Route: FR 811 is a 9-mile primitive track that skirts the edge of the Huston Park Wilderness. The road starts at the trailhead on the other side of the highway.

Dispersed Camping: Three primitive sites can be found at the former Battle Creek Campground, 5 miles to the west on FR 807 (a steep, winding road).

Field Notes: This is a nice campground with easy access and mature trees. It serves as a good base camp from which you can explore the Sierra Madre.

Lost Creek Campground

Jack Creek Campground

8,400 feet

Location/Map	South of Rawlins; Page 342
GPS Coordinates	N41° 17.16' W107° 7.28'
Sites/Spur Length	16 sites, Medium spurs—up to 30 feet
Cost	$10
Facilities/Services	Fire rings, picnic tables, water, pit toilets, trash containers
Managing Agency	USDA Forest Service (Medicine Bow National Forest)
Reservations	Not accepted—first come, first served
Season/Usage	Open mid-June through mid-November; Moderate use

Directions: From Saratoga, head west on CR 500 for 19 miles. Bear left onto FR 452 for a final 8 miles. Another approach may be made from Encampment. From town, drive west for nearly 23 miles on HWY 70 to FR 801. Follow the signs along FR 801, FR 830, and FR 452 for 24 miles to the camp.

Description: Jack Creek is a popular camp with the locals in the northern edge of the Sierra Madre. Open campsites are spaced along a loop in a thinned evergreen forest. Most campers use tents, but small trailers and truck campers fit nicely as well. A few pull-throughs will fit larger trailers or RVs. The mellow waters of Jack Creek flow through a meadow outside of the camp's entrance and entice anglers throughout the day.

Fishing: Although I couldn't verify which species of fish are found in Jack Creek, most Sierra Madre streams hold pan-sized trout.

Trails: Ambitious hikers can find a trailhead for the Continental Divide Trail at McLain Park, roughly 2 miles north of the campground on FR 452. Trail navigation can be tricky in this area; obtain a forest and topo map to help find your way.

Field Notes: This is a camp that feels as remote as it is. Maybe that's why the locals like to escape to this nook and stay here awhile. You won't want to come here if you mind the sound of ATVs as folks use them to sputter around on the forest roads.

Teton Reservoir Recreation Site
7,050 feet

Location/Map	South of Rawlins; Page 342
GPS Coordinates	N41° 36.18' W107° 15.33'
Sites/Spur Length	5 sites, Long spurs—over 30 feet
Cost	Free
Facilities/Services	Fire rings, grills, picnic tables, pit toilets, boat ramp, limited cellular service
Managing Agency	Bureau of Land Management (Rawlins Field Office)
Reservations	Not accepted—first come, first served
Season/Usage	Open all year; Low use

Directions: From Rawlins, travel south on HWY 71 for 15 miles and turn east on BLM Road 3418. Travel less than a mile to reach the campground.

Description: Don't be misled by the name of this barren recreation area. The majestic peaks of the Tetons are located 250 miles to the northwest, obviously out of view from this windswept dirt patch. What you will find here is a broad sagebrush upland disrupted by the occasional ridge or knob.

Campsites are found atop an open rise above Teton Reservoir. The sun can get hot and the wind can be fierce and cold, but free camping a reasonable distance from I-80 lures campers to this recreation area. Just remember that this isn't the Tetons and you won't have to wait in line to get a spot.

Fishing/Boating: Teton Reservoir holds rainbow and brown trout. The reservoir also has a boat ramp on the north shore, though boating is limited on such a small body of water. Manually powered crafts and float tubes are the best choice.

Picnicking: A few picnic tables overlook the reservoir and are intended for day use.

Field Notes: Social media and camping websites have helped turn this once obscure spot into a favorite for those traveling across the southern part of the state. It's not for everyone, but if you enjoy open spaces, stargazing, and decent fishing with few people around, give it a shot.

AREA 2 SOUTH - SOUTHEAST
Medicine Bow Mountains

The Medicine Bow Mountains do not compose an overly large range, but what is lost in size is made up in beauty. The main attraction in these mountains is the Snowy Range, a 5-mile strip of high peaks adorned with alpine lakes that radiate with postcard scenery. This mountain grandeur is easily accessible by way of the Snowy Range Scenic Byway (Wyoming Highway 130). This scenic 29-mile stretch is usually open from Memorial Day Weekend through mid-October.

The Medicine Bows reach a high point of 12,013 feet at the top of Medicine Bow Peak. Due to this elevation, much of the Snowy Range is covered in alpine tundra, scrubby spruce, and hardy wildflowers. The lower elevations have forests of aspen, spruce, subalpine fir, and lodgepole pine. Many of the pines and spruce across the range, however, have been killed by a bark beetle outbreak. As a result, many of the campgrounds are now void of trees, though young conifers, shrubs, and aspen are taking root. Replacing a mature forest takes many decades, but some locals claim these mountains already look better than they did just a few years ago.

Smaller animals that call the Medicine Bow National Forest home are beavers, badgers, pikas, and marmots. Elk, deer, mountain lions, and bears can be found throughout the forest, though the area's two wilderness areas—Platte River and Savage Run—are a proven habitat for these larger animals. The moose population has grown steadily and these ungulates are now spotted on a regular basis. Watch overhead for a variety of birds, including raptors like prairie falcons and eagles, particularly along the forest's western boundary near the North Platte River.

Of all the recreational opportunities in the Medicine Bow National Forest, and there are many, hikers and anglers have it best. The Snowy Range is a trove of trout-filled alpine lakes. Two reservoirs and the North Platte River add to an angler's choices. Hikers, on the other hand, can spend more time trekking across alpine meadows and less time climbing into the high country because many of the trails begin above 9,000 feet. The many miles of forest roads are very popular for ATV riding.

What to Expect: When heading to the Medicine Bow, you should expect the unexpected. No other national forest in Wyoming has left me as surprised as this one. Campgrounds that were supposed to be open were closed. Roads have been found snowdrifted shut in August. Fallen trees have blocked the way many times. Flash floods have washed out forest roads and even a state highway. More recently, the huge Mullen Fire in late 2020 burned nearly 200,000 acres, further casting doubt on the status and future of recreation sites in the southern part of the range.

With that disclaimer aside, these are still astonishingly beautiful mountains that don't disappoint. Just pack a little flexibility in your plans and be prepared to change course.

Area 2: Medicine Bow Mountains

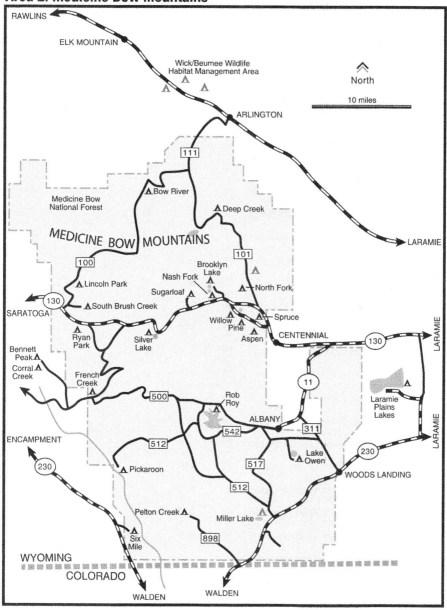

Campgrounds	Sites	Cost	Average Spur Length	Electrical Hookups	Cellular Service (varies by carrier/site)	Reservations Accepted	Page Number
Laramie Plains Lakes	24+	Free	L		▂▃▅		353
Wick/Beumee WHMA	10	Free	L		▂▃▅		354
Bow River Campground	13	$10	M				354
Deep Creek Campground	11	$10	M				355
Aspen Campground	8	$10	M				356
Pine Campground	6	$10	M				357
Willow Campground	16	$10	M				358
Spruce Campground	7	$10	M				359
North Fork Campground	60	$10	L				360
Nash Fork Campground	27	$10	L				361
Brooklyn Lake Campground	19	$10	L			✔	362
Sugarloaf Campground	16	$10	M				364
Silver Lake Campground	17	$10	M				365
Ryan Park Campground	48	$10-100	M			✔	367
South Brush Creek Campground	20	$10	L				368
Lincoln Park Campground	12	$10	L				369
Lake Owen Campground	35	$10	L				370
Rob Roy Campground	65	$10	L				372
French Creek Campground	11	$10	S				373
Corral Creek Campground	8	Free	L				374
Bennett Peak Campground	11	$10	L				375
Pickaroon Campgrounds	14	Free	M				376
Miller Lake Dispersed Camping Area	7	$10	L				377
Pelton Creek Campground	9	$10	M				377
Six Mile Campground	9	$10	M				378

Average Spur Length: S = Short (under 30 feet), M = Medium (+-30 feet), L = Long (+-40 feet)
Cellular Service: 1 bar = weak/unreliable signal, 2 bars = low usable signal, 3+ bars = reliable signal for most users

Laramie Plains Lakes

7,250 feet

Location/Map	Southwest of Laramie; Page 351
GPS Coordinates	N41° 13.53' W105° 53.41'
Sites/Spur Length	Dozens of sites, Long spurs—over 30 feet
Cost	Free
Facilities/Services	Stone fire rings, grills, picnic tables, pit toilets, boat ramp, cellular service
Managing Agency	Wyoming Game and Fish
Reservations	Not accepted—first come, first served
Season/Usage	Open mid-June through October; Moderate use

Directions: From Laramie, take HWY 230 southwest for 16 miles and turn north onto CR 44 at Harmony. Drive north on CR 44 for 5 miles to the lake of your choice. The lakes can also be accessed taking HWY 130 west from Laramie for 13 miles. Turn south onto Big Hollow Road and drive 5 miles to the lakes.

Description: Outstanding fishing, inviting beaches, and free camping make part of this grassy basin a popular place to spend a weekend. Camping around the lakes is considered to be dispersed, though the largest, Lake Hattie, offers the most common campground amenities. There are few trees, and you will need to be prepared for windy conditions, except during the summer when the wind seems to slow to catch its breath. Many Laramie and Cheyenne residents come here, as do Coloradoans, but there is plenty of room.

Fishing/Boating: Laramie Plains Lakes consists of several fishing holes including Meeboer Lake, Gelatt Lake, Twin Buttes Lake, Phillips Lake, and the largest, Lake Hattie. Fishing at the lakes is said to be excellent for large lake, brown, and rainbow trout. Most fish are over a foot in length, and some that have been caught have exceeded two feet. Lake Hattie has a launch ramp for boaters.

Field Notes: In 2001, the Denver Post had this to say about Laramie Plains Lakes: "Wyoming's most important trout fishery comes without soaring mountain views or, for that matter, a single significant river. Sorry about that, Jackson. Maybe later, Pinedale. That distinction goes instead to a flat, barren expanse that contains a series of nondescript reservoirs collectively known as the Laramie Plains Lakes. None gets high marks for beauty. The last time anyone saw terrain such as this, a lunar landing module flashed across the screen. The only difference is, the moon doesn't grow antelope. The fishing is quite another matter. Ah, the fishing… a fingerling rainbow stocked in Lake Hattie today will grow to be a real string-stretcher in a couple years." A couple decades later, folks are still bragging about the fishing.

Wick/Beumee Wildlife Habitat Management Area (Wyoming Game and Fish)

This nearly 20,000-acre area straddles I-80 north of the Medicine Bow Mountains. It provides important habitat for elk, deer, antelope, and a long list of other animals. Trout fishing in the streams and ponds is also possible. Primitive camping is allowed here and there are several parking areas that have pit toilets. The area is closed from mid-November through May. To reach it from Laramie, drive west on I-80 for 40 miles to Exit 272 at Arlington. A gravel road here accesses some of the southern portions of the management area. Other access roads can be reached at Exit 267.

Bow River Campground   8,600 feet

Location/Map	West of Laramie; Page 351
GPS Coordinates	N41° 30.85' W106° 22.29'
Sites/Spur Length	13 sites, Medium spurs—up to 30 feet
Cost	$10
Facilities/Services	Fire rings, grills, picnic tables, water, pit toilets, trash containers
Managing Agency	USDA Forest Service (Medicine Bow National Forest)
Reservations	Not accepted—first come, first served
Season/Usage	Open late May through October; Low use

Directions: From Laramie, drive west on I-80 for 40 miles to Exit 272 (Arlington). Turn onto FR 111 and drive 8 miles to FR 120. Take FR 120 for 4 miles and turn onto FR 105. Proceed 2 miles and turn south onto FR 100. The campground is on the left. If traveling from HWY 130, take FR 100 (Brush Creek Road) north for 20 miles.

Description: You won't have to fight for a spot at this isolated, distant campground along the narrow-but-mighty Medicine Bow River. Average-sized campsites are situated around a single loop in a thinned forest of aspen and conifers. Many campgrounds in the Medicine Bow lost all their trees due to the pine beetle outbreak or fire, but the forest here still provides a nice backdrop of surrounding greenery.

Fishing: Anglers can fly-fish for trout in the nearby Medicine Bow River. Lake fishing for brook trout can be found 6 miles to the south at Turpin Reservoir.

Trails: Long Lake, just a mile south of the campground, is a riparian area with dozens of ponds. A web of crude paths cross the area around the ponds.

Field Notes: Early in the season, you'll find the Medicine Bow River to be a white-water rumbler, but it is often low and quiet by late summer. The camp's elevation is much higher than it looks, so be prepared for cool, even cold, temperatures.

Deep Creek Campground

10,100 feet

Location/Map	West of Laramie; Page 351
GPS Coordinates	N41° 27.47' W106° 16.41'
Sites/Spur Length	11 sites, Medium spurs—up to 30 feet
Cost	$10
Facilities/Services	Fire rings, picnic tables, water, pit toilets, trash containers
Managing Agency	USDA Forest Service (Medicine Bow National Forest)
Reservations	Not accepted—first come, first served
Season/Usage	Open July through mid-September; Low use

Directions: From Laramie, drive west 40 miles on I-80 to Exit 272 (Arlington). Turn onto FR 111 and drive south for 13 miles to FR 101. Take FR 101 just short of 2 miles to the camp. Another approach can be made from HWY 130 near Centennial. Turn north onto FR 101 (Sand Lake Road) and drive north 17 miles.

Description: Sick of bustling, loud campgrounds near highways? Here's one solution. This attractive campground will put some space between you and civilization although the nearby trailheads do receive a modest flow of traffic. Sites are timbered by a thinned spruce forest and the spurs are a bit longer than the 22 feet reported by the Forest Service. Lush meadows and pretty Deep Creek are found outside of the campground. Take note that this camp is over 10,000 feet above sea level; you can expect chilly evenings and crisp mornings.

Fishing: Sand Lake is just a half-mile southwest from the campground and holds splake, brook and rainbow trout. The same species can be found in Deep Creek near the campground.

Trails: There are three great hiking routes in the immediate area. The Deep Creek-Rock Creek Trail leaves the campground and heads 11 miles downhill to a trailhead near Arlington. The trail presents an awesome trek through a progression of ecological communities as you walk from alpine meadows to the edge of semi-arid prairies.

If you'd prefer to stay in the high country, head across the road to the Sand Lake Trailhead. The route here leads to several alpine lakes near the Snowy Range.

The family-friendly Crater Lake Trail can be found about 2 miles north on FR 113. The first mile is an easy walk through the woods that ends at a beautiful overlook of Crater Lake. The trail continues to the lake, but it's a very steep and narrow descent.

Field Notes: This campground seems to be gaining in popularity; expect a handful of occupied sites on a typical weekend.

Aspen Campground

8,600 feet

Location/Map	West of Laramie; Page 351
GPS Coordinates	N41° 19.114' W106° 9.65'
Sites/Spur Length	8 sites, Medium spurs—up to 30 feet
Cost	$10
Facilities/Services	Fire rings, picnic tables, water, pit toilets, trash containers
Managing Agency	USDA Forest Service (Medicine Bow National Forest)
Reservations	Not accepted—first come, first served
Season/Usage	Open June through mid-October; Low use

Directions: From Centennial, drive west on HWY 130 for 2 miles, and turn left onto FR 351 (paved Barber Lake Road), then into the campground on the right.

Description: The first campground along Libby Creek, Aspen offers a unique arrangement. A tight circular clearing in the forest provides a communal parking area. There is no privacy between vehicles or camping units. Fire rings and picnic tables are tucked into thinned pines behind each parking space. Those with the most shade will be tent campers who pitch their tents in the timber.

Scenic Driving: The Snowy Range Scenic Byway (HWY 130) runs 29 miles over the Medicine Bow Mountains and reveals some of Wyoming's most beautiful and accessible alpine country. At the crest of the range, drivers will find clear fishing lakes, meadows of alpine wildflowers, and sheer rock cliffs.

Fishing: Fly-fishing Libby Creek for small rainbow and brook trout is possible, though not very popular. Most anglers prefer the high mountain lakes in the Snowy Range or even tiny Barber Lake, just up the road.

Trails: The Corner Mountain network is composed of 7 miles of meandering trails. The cross-country ski trails are wide, have gentle grades, and are easy to follow through the pine and aspen forest. The trail can be started from the main trailhead, located 2.5 miles west of Centennial on HWY 130. There is also short connector trail at the campground and another along the road near Barber Lake.

Picnicking: There are two picnic grounds in the area that have tables near Libby Creek. The Fir Picnic Area neighbors the campground. The other option is Barber Lake, which is located less than a mile up the road from the campground.

Field Notes: This isn't exactly an introvert's idea of camping, but it is a great place for groups.

Pine Campground

8,600 feet

Location/Map	West of Laramie; Page 351
GPS Coordinates	N41° 19.22' W106° 10.0'
Sites/Spur Length	6 sites, Medium spurs—up to 30 feet
Cost	$10
Facilities/Services	Fire rings, grills, picnic tables, water, pit toilets, trash containers
Managing Agency	USDA Forest Service (Medicine Bow National Forest)
Reservations	Not accepted—first come, first served
Season/Usage	Open June through mid-October; Moderate use

Directions: From Centennial, drive west on HWY 130 for 2 miles and turn left onto FR 351 (paved Barber Lake Road). Drive a quarter mile to the campground on the right.

Description: This is a tiny camp along Libby Creek, which includes several sites that are strung along a one-way lane. The parking pads are angled to help ease trailer parking, but only shorter units will easily fit. The trees have all been removed (due to a beetle outbreak), but Libby Creek flows along the north side of the campground. A few sites at nearby Willow Campground can be seen on the other side of the stream. The camp often holds a few campers, but rarely reaches capacity.

Scenic Driving: The Snowy Range Scenic Byway (HWY 130) runs 29 miles over the Medicine Bow Mountains and reveals some of Wyoming's most beautiful and accessible alpine country. At the crest of the range, drivers find clear fishing lakes, meadows of alpine wildflowers, and sheer rock cliffs.

Fishing: Fly-fishing Libby Creek for small rainbow and brook trout is possible, though not very popular. Most anglers prefer the high mountain lakes in the Snowy Range or even tiny Barber Lake, just up the road.

Trails: The Corner Mountain network is composed of 7 miles of meandering paths. The cross-country ski trails are wide, have gentle grades, and are easy to follow through the pine and aspen forest. The trail can be started from the main trailhead, located 2.5 miles west of Centennial on HWY 130. There are also short connector trails at Aspen and Willow Campgrounds as well as one on the road near Barber Lake.

Picnicking: There are two picnic grounds in the area that feature tables near Libby Creek. The Barber Lake Picnic Area is less than a mile up the road from the camp. The other option is the Fir Picnic Area, located to the east.

Field Notes: When trees are cut down, campers are usually slow to return, but this camp seems to be bucking the trend. I have seen more people enjoying this campground since it was cleared than when it was timbered.

Willow Campground

8,600 feet

Location/Map	West of Laramie; Page 351
GPS Coordinates	N41° 19.26' W106° 10.19'
Sites/Spur Length	16 sites, Medium spurs—up to 30 feet
Cost	$10
Facilities/Services	Fire rings, grills, picnic tables, water, pit toilets, trash containers
Managing Agency	USDA Forest Service (Medicine Bow National Forest)
Reservations	Not accepted—first come, first served
Season/Usage	Open June through mid-October; Moderate use

Directions: From Centennial, drive west on HWY 130 for 2 miles and turn left onto FR 351 (paved Barber Lake Road). Drive less than a mile to the campground on the right.

Description: Willow is the largest campground along Barber Lake Road and is nothing like its downhill neighbors. There are two separated camping areas. The first row of sites includes some prizes along the banks of Libby Creek. The other sites are isolated in a cramped cul-de-sac at the end of the road. There is one pull-through, although it's too tight to be of much use to those who would benefit from one. Both camping areas are far enough away from the main road that passing traffic is not much of a bother. Despite a widespread beetle outbreak in these mountains, this camp has retained much of its forest—a profusion of aspens, pines, and willows.

Scenic Driving: The Snowy Range Scenic Byway (HWY 130) runs 29 miles over the Medicine Bow Mountains and reveals some of Wyoming's most beautiful and accessible alpine country. At the crest of the range, drivers find clear fishing lakes, meadows of alpine wildflowers, and sheer rock cliffs.

Fishing: Small Barber Lake, just up the road, is the site of an annual children's fishing derby in June. Fly-fishing Libby Creek for small rainbow and brook trout is possible, though not very popular. Most anglers prefer the high mountain lakes in the Snowy Range.

Trails: The Corner Mountain network is composed of 7 miles of meandering paths. The cross-country ski trails are wide, have gentle grades, and are easy to follow through the pine and aspen forest. The trail can be started from the main trailhead, located 2.5 miles west of Centennial on HWY 130. There are also short connector trails at Aspen and Willow Campgrounds as well as one on the road near Barber Lake.

Picnicking: The Barber Lake Picnic Area is just a quarter mile up the road from the campground. There are numerous tables in the pine forest next to Libby Creek.

Field Notes: This camp has a tucked-in "retreat" feel to it.

Libby Creek during the spring runoff

Spruce Campground
8,550 feet

Location/Map	West of Laramie; Page 351
GPS Coordinates	N41° 19.17' W106° 9.45'
Sites/Spur Length	7 sites, Medium spurs—up to 30 feet
Cost	$10
Facilities/Services	Fire rings, grills, picnic tables, water, pit toilets, trash containers
Managing Agency	USDA Forest Service (Medicine Bow National Forest)
Reservations	Not accepted—first come, first served
Season/Usage	Open June through mid-October; Moderate use

Directions: From Centennial, drive west on HWY 130 for a little over 2 miles. The campground is on the left, just past the turnoff for Barber Lake Road.

Description: This campground neighbors Libby Creek in a mixed forest of aspen, pine, and spruce. Most sites are short pull-throughs. Although most trailers won't be able to fit here, there is a sole parking spur nearly fifty feet long directly below the highway. Speaking of the highway, it generates a lot of noise, but campers also appreciate the accessibility it offers.

Scenic Driving: The Snowy Range Scenic Byway (HWY 130) runs 29 miles over the Medicine Bow Mountains and reveals some of Wyoming's most beautiful and accessible alpine country. At the crest of the range, drivers find clear fishing lakes, meadows of alpine wildflowers, and sheer rock cliffs.

Trails: The Corner Mountain network is composed of 7 miles of meandering paths. The cross-country ski trails are wide, have gentle grades, and are easy to follow through the pine and aspen forest. The trail can be started from the main trailhead that is located about a half mile west of the campground on HWY 130. There are also short connector trails at Aspen and Willow Campgrounds as well as one on the road near Barber Lake.

Field Notes: At the time of this writing, this once-busy campground was closed due to beetle-killed trees. It may re-open in the future, as others here have, but that process can take years.

North Fork Campground
9,200 feet

Location/Map	West of Laramie; Page 351
GPS Coordinates	N41° 21.59' W106° 10.22'
Sites/Spur Length	60 sites, Long spurs—over 30 feet
Cost	$10
Facilities/Services	Fire rings, picnic tables, water, pit toilets, trash containers
Managing Agency	USDA Forest Service (Medicine Bow National Forest); A host is often present
Reservations	Not accepted—first come, first served
Season/Usage	Open June through October; High use

Directions: From Centennial, drive west on HWY 130 for 4 miles and turn north onto FR 101 (Sand Lake Road). Drive 1.5 miles to the campground entrance.

Description: This is one of the largest campgrounds in the Medicine Bow Mountains and one of the best for longer trailers or motor homes. The parking spurs are mostly level and easy to get into. The pine forest has been drastically thinned in recent years. Even so, the sites are so spacious that you'll still have decent privacy and plenty of room to spread out.

From the campground's entrance, you can take your pick from two separate camping areas. The northern section includes a loop of campsites as well as a few along the North Fork of the Little Laramie River. The southern section consists of a straight one-way lane with sites on both sides; half of these are along the creek.

Fishing: Fly-fishing the North Fork is popular with anglers looking to catch brook and rainbow trout. The best fishing spots are found upstream near some foot bridges along the North Fork Trail. From the trailhead at the campground (see below), hike uphill a short distance to reach the bridges.

Trails: The North Fork Trail departs from the camp's north loop and heads uphill for 4.5 miles to FR 317 near Brooklyn Lake Campground. A separate trailhead is located a half-mile north of the campground on FR 101.

The Little Laramie cross-country ski network consists of nearly 10 miles of easy trails for summertime hiking or biking. The main trailhead is found near the intersection of HWY 130 and FR 101, but you can also access the trails from FR 101, just south of the campground at a large parking area.

Dispersed Camping: Dispersed campsites can be found along the incoming road (FR 101), immediately south of the campground's exit on FR 330, and along FR 329, directly east above the campground on a ridge.

Field Notes: The elevation at this camp is very deceiving—it's much higher than it looks and is among the highest campgrounds in Wyoming. Be prepared for cold nights and snow, especially in early June, September, and October. It's not uncommon for summer lows to dip below freezing.

Nash Fork Campground
10,200 feet

Location/Map	West of Laramie; Page 351
GPS Coordinates	N41° 21.52' W106° 14.0'
Sites/Spur Length	27 sites, Long spurs—over 30 feet
Cost	$10
Facilities/Services	Fire rings, picnic tables, water, pit toilets, trash containers
Managing Agency	USDA Forest Service (Medicine Bow National Forest); A host is often present
Reservations	Not accepted—first come, first served
Season/Usage	Open July through mid-September; High use

Directions: From Centennial, drive west on HWY 130 for 8 miles to FR 317 (Brooklyn Lake Road). Turn north on this road and watch for the campground entrance on the left.

Description: Nash Fork was once one of the most appealing campgrounds in southern Wyoming before a bark beetle outbreak killed the mature spruce that towered over the campsites. After a decade of no activity, crews have begun removing the dead trees. As of this writing, the campground is still closed, but hopefully this camp will re-open in the future like others have.

Parking spurs are a mix of pull-throughs and back-ins, short and long, level and sloped—something for everyone. Nash Fork, a crystal clear mountain stream, runs between the campsites and the incoming road. A few sites are along the creek. Wildflowers are abundant in mid-summer.

Scenic Driving: The Snowy Range Scenic Byway (HWY 130) runs 29 miles over the Medicine Bow Mountains and reveals some of Wyoming's most beautiful and accessible alpine country. At the crest of the range, drivers find clear fishing lakes, meadows of alpine wildflowers, and sheer rock cliffs.

Fishing: The campground is located south of two scenic high lakes that have brook and cutthroat trout. Follow FR 317 north for 1 mile to Little Brooklyn Lake or 2 miles to the larger Brooklyn Lake.

Trails: The North Fork Trail is a 4.5-mile route that descends 1,300 feet from FR 317 to North Fork Campground. You'll pass through high forest, lush meadows, and a tight ravine while following the North Fork of the Little Laramie River. The trail starts from the east side of FR 317, just 1 mile north of the campground.

Additional hiking trails can be found near Brooklyn Lake Campground.

Field Notes: Trees or not, when this campground re-opens, I expect that it'll be as loved as ever due to its great location and subalpine beauty.

Brooklyn Lake Campground

10,500 feet

Location/Map	West of Laramie; Page 351
GPS Coordinates	N41° 22.43' W106° 14.83'
Sites/Spur Length	19 sites, Medium spurs—up to 30 feet
Cost	$10
Facilities/Services	Fire rings, picnic tables, water, pit toilets, trash containers
Managing Agency	USDA Forest Service (Medicine Bow National Forest); A host is often present
Reservations	Call 877-444-6777 or visit www.recreation.gov
Season/Usage	Open July through mid-September; High use

Directions: From Centennial, drive west on HWY 130 for 8 miles to FR 317 (Brooklyn Lake Road). Turn north and drive 2 miles to the camp. The forest road is usually free of snowdrifts by mid-July.

Description: This scenic and heavily-used campground is found at the base of the Snowy Range in a mostly-cleared stand of spruce. The high alpine setting makes for cool days and cold nights, but that doesn't dampen the mood. Some campers are able to squeeze large trailers into the parking spurs, but small and average-sized units are better. Picturesque Brooklyn Lake sits in a basin just down slope from the camp.

Brooklyn Lake

Scenic Driving: The Snowy Range Scenic Byway (HWY 130) runs 29 miles over the Medicine Bow Mountains and reveals some of Wyoming's most beautiful and accessible alpine country. At the crest of the range, drivers will find clear fishing lakes, meadows of alpine wildflowers, and sheer rock cliffs.

Fishing: The campground is above the shoreline of Brooklyn Lake. Little Brooklyn Lake is just a mile south on FR 317. This pair hold brook and cutthroat trout. There are no boat ramps at these lakes.

Trails: The Lost Lake Trail leaves the campground and heads west for 3.5 miles to a trailhead near Sugarloaf Campground. You'll traverse alpine terrain and see tiny glaciers, clear lakes, and meadows of wildflowers. It's a great trail for families with mild elevation gains and declines.

Another trailhead is found just south of the campground. The route here travels through the open high country and has numerous destinations including North Twin Lakes (1.5 miles), Sheep Lake (3.5 miles), and Sand Lake (8 miles). The trail ends at 8.2 miles near Deep Creek Campground. You can also split off at Sheep Lake and wrap around the northern front of the Snowy Range.

Field Notes: There are two structures that are sure to grab your attention on the way to this campground. One is a small chapel that is used, in part, for summertime weddings. The other is a Forest Service cabin that can be rented by the public. By the way, don't try to reach this campground until the road is officially open—we pulled a Jeep out of a small snowdrift here in July. Had the driver been successful in getting through it, he would have found much larger ones further uphill.

Sugarloaf Campground

10,800 feet

Location/Map	West of Laramie; Page 351
GPS Coordinates	N41° 21.28' W106° 17.64'
Sites/Spur Length	16 sites, Medium spurs—up to 30 feet
Cost	$10
Facilities/Services	Fire rings, picnic tables, water, pit toilets, trash containers
Managing Agency	USDA Forest Service (Medicine Bow National Forest)
Reservations	Not accepted—first come, first served
Season/Usage	Open mid-July through mid-September; High use

Directions: From Centennial, drive west on HWY 130 for 11 miles to the Sugarloaf Recreation Area turnoff. Follow the road for a mile to the camp.

Description: This top-of-the-world campground is sure to freeze out all but the most prepared campers, even in July. If you can bear the climate of this high alpine country, you'll be able to brag about camping at Wyoming's highest campground. You'll also be rewarded with unsurpassed views of the Snowy Range. Nearby Sugarloaf Mountain rises to 11,398 feet—only 600 feet higher than the campground itself. Beside the campground is Libby Lake and Lewis Lake. The camp is open less than two months out of the year and is filled on many nights during that time. Trees are shorter at these elevations, sometimes scrubby, so don't expect to find much privacy. Tents and small trailers are the best choices for this campground. Don't forget your warm hat and gloves.

Scenic Driving: The Snowy Range Scenic Byway runs 29 miles over the Medicine Bow Mountains and reveals some of Wyoming's most beautiful and accessible alpine country. At the crest of the range, drivers find clear fishing lakes, meadows of alpine wildflowers, and sheer rock cliffs.

Fishing: Two scenic lakes, Libby and Lewis, are located a short walk from the campground. Both alpine lakes have splake, brook, and cutthroat trout.

Trails: Two incredible trails depart from the nearby trailhead. The Medicine Bow Peak-Lakes Trail travels 1 mile to a three-way junction. Turn left and you'll follow the family-friendly Lakes Trail for 1.7 miles to the Mirror Lake Picnic Area. Turn right and you'll huff-and-puff your way up to the top of Medicine Bow Peak (12,013 feet). It's not much over a half mile to the top, but it's a steep climb that feels longer. The trail is usually free of snow by late July.

The other route at the trailhead heads northeast for a short distance to a junction. The trail to the left travels a couple of miles to South and North Gap Lakes before leading to Sheep Lake. Stay right and you'll follow the Lost Lakes Trail. Lost Lake is less than 2 miles farther, but there are some gorgeous lakes before it. The trail ends at Brooklyn Lake Campground, a little over 3 miles from the junction.

Picnicking: A beautiful picnic area is located at Libby Lake near the campground.

Field Notes: This campground is too high and exposed for some, but everyone I have talked to who has stayed here has loved it, especially if it snowed on them in July or August. The view is unbeatable.

Silver Lake Campground

10,400 feet

Location/Map	West of Laramie; Page 351
GPS Coordinates	N41° 18.89' W106° 21.56'
Sites/Spur Length	17 sites, Medium spurs—up to 30 feet
Cost	$10
Facilities/Services	Fire rings, picnic tables, water, pit toilets, trash containers
Managing Agency	USDA Forest Service (Medicine Bow National Forest)
Reservations	Not accepted—first come, first served
Season/Usage	Open July through mid-September; Moderate use

Directions: From Centennial, head west on HWY 130 for 17 miles to the camp turnoff on the left. From Saratoga head south, then east on HWY 130 for 32 miles to the camp.

Description: This campground is located atop a hill above Silver Lake on the southwest side of the Snowy Range. The camp was closed for years after bark beetles killed the spruce trees, but it has since re-opened. Though it looks much different now, it's still a fantastic place to spend a few days.

Due to the camp's elevation, it has a short operating season, and snow sometimes blocks its entrance well into July and—at least once—even in August. True to its name, the lake is nearby, just down the hill and just out of sight from the campsites. Spurs are best suited for tents and short campers, though a couple of sites will accommodate long trailers or motor homes. There are also a few walk-in sites.

Scenic Driving: The Snowy Range Scenic Byway (HWY 130) runs 29 miles over the Medicine Bow Mountains and reveals some of Wyoming's most beautiful and accessible alpine country. At the crest of the range, drivers find clear fishing lakes, meadows of alpine wildflowers, and sheer rock cliffs.

Snowy Range

The Snowy Range, often called "the Snowies," is the rocky crest of Wyoming's Medicine Bow Mountains. Spectacular scenery consisting of towering vertical cliffs, alpine wildflowers, and dozens of lakes will keep you reaching for your camera. You can drive to the most popular lakes—Lake Marie, Mirror Lake, Libby Lake, Lewis Lake, Little Brooklyn Lake, and Brooklyn Lake. The other tarns are reached by backcountry foot trails.

The Snowy Range has its name for a reason; you can expect to find huge snowdrifts here throughout the summer. Side roads open late, so July and August are the best months to visit. To get here from Centennial, drive west on HWY 130 for 14 miles. From Saratoga, follow HWY 130 to the south and then east for 35 miles.

Fishing: Silver Lake is under ice until July, but once thawed, it's one of the most fun fishing lakes in the Snowy Range. The lake, which holds naïve brook trout, sits in a basin below the campground and requires a brief, steep hike to reach it. The last time I fished here, the fish were practically jumping into our nets. During a feeding frenzy that lasted 15 minutes, we could barely get our lines cast before they were tugging on the other end.

Trails: The Meadow Falls Trail leaves from the campground's entrance and returns near the lake. The 2.7-mile loop travels through spruce forests and subalpine meadows with a small cascade at the halfway point. It has gentle grades and makes a great trail for families who don't mind fording a small creek. There is also a trail that follows the perimeter of the lake.

4WD/ATV Routes: There are a number of nearby backcountry roads and ATV trails that lead to high mountain lakes. To locate the roads, look for a large parking area at the beginning of FR 103 a little over a mile north of the campground. Obtain an OHV map from the Forest Service for specific route information and restrictions.

Field Notes: This was always one of my favorite campgrounds and after being closed for ten years, I was quick to return when the gates swung back open.

Ryan Park Campground 8,450 feet

Location/Map	West of Laramie; Page 351
GPS Coordinates	N41° 19.6' W106° 29.59'
Sites/Spur Length	48 sites, 1 group site, Long spurs—over 30 feet
Cost	$10, $100 group site
Facilities/Services	Fire rings, grills, picnic tables, water, pit toilets, trash containers
Managing Agency	USDA Forest Service (Medicine Bow National Forest); A host is often present
Reservations	Call 877-444-6777 or visit www.recreation.gov
Season/Usage	Open late May through mid-November; Moderate use

Directions: From Saratoga head south, then east on HWY 130 for nearly 23 miles to the camp on the right.

Description: If you climb higher toward the Snowy Range, you'll discover a slew of scenic subalpine campgrounds. But not everyone wants to spend a cold night at 10,000 feet. Ryan Park isn't as popular as other campgrounds in this range (some sites are overgrown), but it still attracts a solid number of campers as it is easy to get to and the sites can be reserved.

There are three loop roads including one loop that is a reservable group site for up to 140 campers. Most of the beetle-killed pine trees were removed, but some sites are tucked into an aspen stand. If you don't get one of those, you'll be camping in a sunny clearing. There is plenty of room to park a large trailer or RV.

Ryan Park is rich in history. The campground area has served as a P.O.W. camp as well as an encampment for CCC workers. Interpretive signs at the camp's entrance give a more thorough glimpse into the area's past.

Scenic Driving: The Snowy Range Scenic Byway (HWY 130) runs 29 miles over the Medicine Bow Mountains and reveals some of Wyoming's most beautiful and accessible alpine country. At the crest of the range, drivers find clear fishing lakes, meadows of alpine wildflowers, and sheer rock cliffs.

Trails: The short, primitive Moose Trail loops around the campground and along the creek. Elsewhere, there is an extensive network of trails found east of the nearby Brush Creek Visitor Center along HWY 130. There are 8.5 miles of gentle cross-country ski trails that wind through the pine and aspen forest. Look for the trailhead behind the visitor center.

Field Notes: Everyone goes for the timbered sites on the east side, but getting a whole loop to yourself under a big blanket of stars is pretty great.

South Brush Creek Campground
8,350 feet

Location/Map	West of Laramie; Page 351
GPS Coordinates	N41° 20.68' W106° 30.26'
Sites/Spur Length	20 sites, Long spurs—over 30 feet
Cost	$10
Facilities/Services	Fire rings, grills, picnic tables, water, pit toilets, trash containers
Managing Agency	USDA Forest Service (Medicine Bow National Forest)
Reservations	Not accepted—first come, first served
Season/Usage	Open late May through early November; Moderate use

Directions: From Saratoga head south, then east on HWY 130 for 20 miles to FR 100 (Brush Creek Road). Turn north and drive a half-mile before turning right onto narrow FR 200 for another 1.5 miles.

Description: South Brush Creek Campground was once hidden under a enchanting forest of huge mixed evergreens along a raging creek of the same name. That was before the trees were killed by beetles and cleared in 2010. Today, the camp is much more sunny and young conifers and aspens are growing well. Even without the shadowy forest, it's still great to camp on the banks of a swift and beautiful mountain creek.

There are two loops and each has its own entrance. Longer trailers are often found in the pull-throughs of the eastern loop although similar sites also exist in the western loop. Level parking spurs are varied in length and welcome tent and trailer campers alike.

Fishing: South Brush Creek flows behind the campground and is filled with brook, brown, and rainbow trout. There is an angler parking area between the campground's two entrances. Lake fishing for brook trout can be found 12 miles to the north at Turpin Reservoir.

Trails: A trailhead can be found at the end of FR 200, just east of the campground. There are 8.5 miles of gentle cross-country ski trails that wind through the pine and aspen forest.

4WD Route: Continue east from the campground on FR 200 and you'll soon be on a rough and rocky track that parallels the willow-lined banks of South Brush Creek. Follow this road for several miles to join FR 200.2A, which will then lead you to Phantom Lake as well as other roads and ATV trails. It's 7 miles to the lake.

Picnicking: A group fire ring with benches is found on the forest road just outside the campground.

Field Notes: This is a camp I stay in every year. It's always quiet. Although I miss the mature old-growth forest, the young trees are coming back nicely.

Lincoln Park Campground
8,100 feet

Location/Map GPS Coordinates	West of Laramie; Page 351 N41° 22.44' W106° 30.86'
Sites/Spur Length	12 sites, Long spurs—over 30 feet
Cost	$10
Facilities/Services	Fire rings, grills, picnic tables, water, pit toilets, trash containers
Managing Agency	USDA Forest Service (Medicine Bow National Forest); A host is often present
Reservations	Not accepted—first come, first served
Season/Usage	Open late May through early November; Moderate use

Directions: From Saratoga head south, then east on HWY 130 for 20 miles to FR 100 (Brush Creek Road). Drive north for 2.7 miles to the camp.

Description: This busy camp is found at the confluence of Lincoln Creek and North Brush Creek. There are two loops here—an obvious loop near the road and another that is concealed on the other side of the stream. Thick willows along the creek completely separate the loops. While over half of the sites sit exposed without shade, the rest are found along the edge of a timber stand. Parking spurs are long and level.

Scenic Driving: If you're not afraid of high mountain roads, make the fun backcountry drive to the top of Kennaday Peak. There is a fire lookout tower at the top of the 10,810-foot summit. The 6-mile gravel route can be found on FR 100, just over 3 miles north of the campground.

Wildlife Viewing: Moose are commonly spotted in this area and can sometimes be spotted along FR 100, as well as along North and South Brush Creek.

Fishing: Anglers can try for brook, brown, and rainbow trout. South Brush Creek, 2.5 miles to the south, affords the same opportunity. Lake fishing for brook trout can be found 10 miles to the north at Turpin Reservoir.

ATV Routes: The Stump Hollow Trail, located across the road from the campground, is a short 1.5-mile ATV route that climbs to a forested saddle. From here, you can tie into the North and Middle Cedar ATV trails. Another ATV trail can be found by heading east on the forest road next to the campground to the Mullison Trail on the left. The trail is unsigned so a Forest Service OHV map is helpful to distinguish it.

Trails: An extensive trail network (for foot and bicycle traffic only) is found near the highway east of the Brush Creek Visitor Center. There are 8.5 miles of gentle cross-country ski trails that wind through the forest.

Dispersed Camping: Dispersed sites can be found on the road east of camp.

Field Notes: Weekend visitation here is erratic. Some weekends see just a few quiet campers. On others, you'll find a nearly full camp with ATVs running up and down the adjacent roads.

Lake Owen Campground

9,000 feet

Location/Map	West of Laramie; Page 351
GPS Coordinates	N41° 8.66' W106° 6.0'
Sites/Spur Length	35 sites, Long spurs—over 30 feet
Cost	$10
Facilities/Services	Fire rings, grills, picnic tables, water, pit toilets, trash containers, boat ramp
Managing Agency	USDA Forest Service (Medicine Bow National Forest)
Reservations	Not accepted—first come, first served
Season/Usage	Open June through mid-October; High use

Directions: From Albany, drive east on FR 500 for 2.5 miles and turn south onto FR 513. Drive 2.5 miles and turn left onto FR 517. Drive 1.5 miles and turn south onto FR 540. Follow this road 3 miles to the campground.

Description: This is an open lakeside camp with distant views of the Snowy Range on the northern horizon. There are two loops of roomy sites. The most popular ones are close to the shore, leaving the inland sites open for the taking. Parking spurs will accommodate most camping units.

The mountain lake is anything but a secret, and with a train caboose on one side and heavy ATV use, the area has lost some of its backcountry feel. However, it's still an excellent lake in which to take out a canoe or other manual watercraft.

Lake Owen

Fishing/Boating: Like most fishing holes in the Medicine Bows, anglers can expect good fishing for rainbow, cutthroat, and brook trout in Lake Owen. Boat ramps and angler parking areas are available on the south and west sides of the lake.

Trails: A wide 1.7-mile track forms an easy loop around the lake. You'll also find a trailhead on the west side of Lake Owen at a caboose. This is a trailhead for the Medicine Bow Rail Trail, a 23-mile track that utilizes an old railroad bed. The trail is open to foot, horse, and bike use, but not motorized vehicles. You can head north or south on the trail from this point—either direction will take you to a different trailhead on FR 517.

Dispersed Camping: If you like dispersed camping, you're in luck. There are many dispersed campsites along FR 540 near the reservoir and also to the north in Dry Park. The drawback, if you are looking for solitude, is that ATV traffic is heavy in this area.

Field Notes: At the time of this writing, the campground was closed and its status and future were uncertain due to the Mullen Fire, a nearly 200,000-acre blaze that covered this area in the fall of 2020.

Rob Roy Campground

9,550 feet

Location/Map	West of Laramie; Page 351
GPS Coordinates	N41° 12.95' W106° 15.01'
Sites/Spur Length	65 sites, Long spurs—over 30 feet
Cost	$10
Facilities/Services	Fire rings, picnic tables, water, pit toilets, trash containers, boat ramp
Managing Agency	USDA Forest Service (Medicine Bow National Forest); A host is often present
Reservations	Not accepted—first come, first served
Season/Usage	Open June through September; High use

Directions: From Albany, drive west on FR 500 for 8 miles and turn south on the access road.

Description: Rob Roy Reservoir is a well-known destination in the timbered mountains between the Snowy Range and the Colorado border. The campground is perched on a rise near the north end of the reservoir. People come to fish, boat, camp, and ride ATVs on the many miles of surrounding backroads.

The camp features four loops that offer a variety of looks. Some sites face the water while others are tucked further back. The distance between campsites is generous, and some sites offer just enough extra space to park a boat trailer or a pair of ATVs. The forest has mostly been cleared here so there is plenty of sunshine at most of the sites.

Fishing/Boating: Rob Roy Reservoir holds brook, rainbow, and cutthroat trout. There is a boat ramp near the campground's entrance.

Trails: Three hiking trails can be found several miles to the west in the Savage Run Wilderness, but be aware that the Mullen Fire in 2020 may have destroyed these paths. The primary route is the 8-mile Savage Run Trail that traverses the wilderness area. Two short connector trails, Cottonwood and Extension, are located at the southern edge of the wilderness.

To reach the main trailhead from the campground, head west on FR 500 for 5.5 miles to the well-marked turnoff. The trailhead is at the end of a 1.2-mile road that requires high clearance. The more accessible southern trailheads can be reached by driving west to FR 511 and turning south. Drive 3 miles, then turn west on FR 512, and drive to the Cottonwood and Extension Trailheads, 5 and 8 miles respectively.

Field Notes: This camp lost a lot of its luster when the pine trees died and were removed. Ironically, the younger trees growing up here may be the greenest you'll now find in the area. As of this writing, the Mullen Fire had reached the shores of the reservoir, and much of the surrounding forest, but had spared the campground itself.

French Creek Campground

7,800 feet

Location/Map	West of Laramie; Page 351
GPS Coordinates	N41° 13.54' W106° 28.85'
Sites/Spur Length	11 sites, Short spurs—up to 25 feet
Cost	$10
Facilities/Services	Fire rings, picnic tables, water, pit toilets, trash containers
Managing Agency	USDA Forest Service (Medicine Bow National Forest)
Reservations	Not accepted—first come, first served
Season/Usage	Open mid-June through October; Low use

Directions: From Riverside-Encampment, head east on HWY 230 for 4 miles and turn north onto CR 201 (French Creek Road). Drive approximately a quarter mile to CR 660 and take this road for 14 miles. Turn onto FR 206 at the fork and drive to the camp.

From Saratoga, head south, then east on HWY 130 for 23 miles to FR 225. Follow this road south for several miles to the junction with FR 227. Continue south along FR 225 for 6 miles to the intersection with FR 206. Take FR 206 for 4 miles to the campground.

Description: This slightly overgrown campground is found in a stand of aspen and thick brush at the western edge of the Medicine Bow National Forest. Tents are best here, though a couple of sites will fit a trailer. A swift mountain creek flows along one side and is mostly hidden behind vegetation. The camp sees moderate visitation on weekends but remains quiet during the week.

Fishing: The campground is located near the confluence of North French Creek and South French Creek. Common species in these creeks include rainbow, brook, and cutthroat trout.

Trails: The Tie Hack Trail makes a nice day hike or mountain bike ride through a lightly visited portion of the Medicine Bow. The 4-mile route travels through a dense draw with intermittent sagebrush meadows. You can find the trailhead just a short distance east of the campground on FR 500.

Field Notes: Black bears have been troublesome here in the past and mountain lions also live in the area. Although the posted warnings about these critters have been removed, it's still a good idea to be careful. Also, the Forest Service warns that this can be a very wet camp when river conditions are high.

Corral Creek Campground

7,300 feet

Location/Map	West of Laramie; Page 351
GPS Coordinates	N41° 15.8' W106° 34.36'
Sites/Spur Length	8 sites, Long spurs—over 30 feet
Cost	Free
Facilities/Services	Fire rings, grills, picnic tables, water, pit toilets, trash containers
Managing Agency	Bureau of Land Management (Rawlins Field Office)
Reservations	Not accepted—first come, first served
Season/Usage	Open June through mid-November; Low use

Directions: From Riverside-Encampment, head east on HWY 230 for 4 miles to CR 201 (French Creek Road). Drive a quarter mile and then take CR 660 for another 12 miles. Turn onto rougher BLM Road 3404 and drive north for 5.5 miles to the camp's short access road.

Description: This camp is situated above the banks of the North Platte River. Small junipers pop up where they can, and there are some cottonwoods, but this is a dry slope and there is no decent shade. Parking spurs are varied and can accommodate a variety of camping units, but nearby Bennett Peak Campground is better for most trailers. If you stay here, you are likely to have a night of solitude under a blanketing starlit sky.

Fishing: Large numbers of rainbow and brown trout can be found in the North Platte River.

Corral Creek Campground

Trails: There are two foot trails that start at the campground and explore the area around the North Platte River. At .75 mile in length, Willow Trail is a short route that follows the brushy riverbank. Boulder Gap Trail, a longer 2-mile route, climbs a ridge to reach a scenic vantage point before descending to the river.

Floating: The North Platte River invites floaters and waders to its waters. This is also a take-out point for multi-day raft trips along the river.

Field Notes: If you're a hiker and find yourself in the area, be sure to do the Boulder Gap Trail, even if it's just the first mile. From the trail's highpoint, you'll get a good view of the North Platte River, the nearby mountain ranges, and a perfectly balanced boulder.

Bennett Peak Campground

7,200 feet

Location/Map	West of Laramie; Page 351
GPS Coordinates	N41° 16.22' W106° 35.35'
Sites/Spur Length	11 sites, Long spurs—over 30 feet
Cost	$10
Facilities/Services	Fire rings, picnic tables, water, pit toilets, trash containers
Managing Agency	Bureau of Land Management (Rawlins Field Office)
Reservations	Not accepted—first come, first served
Season/Usage	Open June through mid-November; Low use

Directions: From Riverside-Encampment, head east on HWY 230 for 4 miles to CR 201 (French Creek Road). Drive a quarter mile and turn onto CR 660 for another 12 miles. Turn onto rougher BLM Road 3404 and drive north for 7 miles.

Description: This BLM camp offers outstanding access to the North Platte River and several sites are right against the water. Rock outcrops and Bennett Peak itself (8,314 feet) provide interesting scenery within a mostly sagebrush-filled landscape dotted with juniper and evergreen trees. Parking spurs are long, level, and somewhat sandy—some have tent pads. If you can drive it here, you can park it here.

Fishing: Large numbers of rainbow and brown trout can be found in the North Platte River.

Floating: The North Platte River invites floaters and waders to its waters. This is also a take-out point for rafters who have embarked on multi-day trips along the river. A small launch ramp is located along the shoreline.

Field Notes: I spent a morning exploring Bennett Peak after being told there was a registry box on its summit. I never found the registry, but the views from the top were well worth the effort.

Pickaroon Campground

7,800 feet

Location/Map	West of Laramie; Page 351
GPS Coordinates	N41° 8.61' W106° 26.89'
Sites/Spur Length	14 sites, Medium spurs—up to 30 feet
Cost	Free
Facilities/Services	Fire rings, picnic tables, pit toilets
Managing Agency	USDA Forest Service (Medicine Bow National Forest)
Reservations	Not accepted—first come, first served
Season/Usage	Open mid-June through mid-October; Moderate use

Directions: From Albany, head west on FR 500 for 2.5 miles, then left onto FR 542 for 5.6 miles. Continue straight on FR 511 for 3 miles, and then take FR 512 for just over 10 miles, passing between the Savage Run and Platte River wilderness areas. The last section has tight, sandy switchbacks and can be muddy. Longer trailers are towed here, but it's not advised.

You can also get to the camps from HWY 230 to the south. From Woods Landing, drive southwest on HWY 230 for 8.5 miles and turn north on FR 512 toward Fox Park. Follow FR 512 to the camps.

Description: Reaching this camp (and the former Pike Pole Campground next to it) takes some effort. Surprisingly, it can get crowded. Sites are strung out over a half mile along the North Platte River and are partially covered by large cottonwoods. Overgrown parking spurs are short, level, and best suited for tents, vans or truck campers. Those with longer trailers often disperse camp in the nearby meadows.

Fishing/Rafting/Floating: The North Platte River is a blue-ribbon fishery for foot-long brown and rainbow trout. The river is also a favored waterway for kayaking and floating in May and June. While kayakers negotiate class III-IV rapids in the upper canyon (south of Six Mile Gap Campground), floaters will appreciate the smoother waters found here at the campground.

Trails: All trails from these campgrounds lead into the Platte River Wilderness, but be aware that the Mullen Fire in 2020 may have destroyed these paths. A trailhead at the end of the road accesses the Douglas Creek Trail, a 9.3-mile route that descends 800 feet to Pelton Creek Campground. The trail parallels the creek and is used by hunters and backpackers.

A trailhead near the camp gives entry to the west side of the wilderness where the North Platte River flows. The trail begins by fording Douglas Creek. From the ford, the sometimes-indistinct path skirts the east side of the river for 3.5 miles before requiring a ford to join the trail on the other side. The ford can only be done in late summer when water levels are lower.

Field Notes: The Forest Service is no longer maintaining this campground. The pit toilets are still there, but consider this area to be similar to dispersed camping; take your own toilet paper and carry home your trash.

Miller Lake Dispersed Camping Area

This former campground was closed, clearcut, abandoned, and then reopened as a semi-primitive camping area. It still has 7 medium-length parking spurs around a small loop, but the other amenities are gone. (A small pit toilet also remains, but don't count on it being usable.) Miller Lake—a small and peaceful lake not directly visible from the campsites—draws a steady flow of angler traffic. ATV drive-by traffic is also common.

The camp has easy access. To reach it from Woods Landing, drive southwest on HWY 230 for 8.5 miles and turn north on FR 512 toward Fox Park. Drive less than a mile to the turnoff on the left.

Pelton Creek Campground 8,250 feet

Location/Map	Southwest of Laramie; Page 351
GPS Coordinates	N41° 4.35' W106° 18.19'
Sites/Spur Length	9 sites, Medium spurs—up to 30 feet
Cost	$10
Facilities/Services	Fire rings, grills, picnic tables, water, pit toilets, trash containers
Managing Agency	USDA Forest Service (Medicine Bow National Forest)
Reservations	Not accepted—first come, first served
Season/Usage	Open mid-June through mid-October; Moderate use

Directions: From Woods Landing, drive southwest on HWY 230 for 15 miles just past the Colorado border and then turn northward onto FR 898. Proceed another 9 miles on the gravel road.

Description: This campground is a good distance from the busiest attractions in this national forest and it's also a local favorite. They know the campground has it all: few tourists, roomy sites, mountain streams, and a trailhead. You can usually find solitude here during the week, but weekends and the hunting season bring heavier visitation. A few pull-through sites are available, but tents or pop-up campers work best here.

Wildlife Viewing: The Pelton Creek area is rich with wildlife. The streams outside of the camp are great places to view beaver lodges. Moose can be spotted in the streambeds, while deer and elk can sometimes be seen on the slopes of the surrounding mountains. Elk numbers rise in autumn as the animals migrate down from the high country. Bighorn sheep can be found in the Devils Gate area of the Platte River Wilderness.

Fishing: Small Pelton Creek and larger Douglas Creek offer fly-fishing for rainbow, brook, and cutthroat trout.

Trails: A foot trail begins from the campground and heads into the Platte River Wilderness. A connector trail for horses is just outside the camp entrance. The path runs above Douglas Creek a short distance to a fork. Turn right and you'll ford Douglas Creek and follow the stream uphill for

9 miles to Pickeroon Campground. A left turn at the fork puts you on the Platte Ridge Trail. This route makes an 8-mile arc through the wilderness and eventually intersects Douglas Creek Trail. Be aware that these trails may have been obliterated by the Mullen Fire.

Field Notes: At the time of this writing, the campground was closed and its status and future were uncertain due to the Mullen Fire, a nearly 200,000-acre blaze that covered this area in the fall of 2020.

Six Mile Campground   7,800 feet

Location/Map	West of Laramie/Southeast of Saratoga; Page 351
GPS Coordinates	N41° 2.65' W106° 24.06'
Sites/Spur Length	9 sites, Medium spurs—up to 30 feet
Cost	$10
Facilities/Services	Fire rings, picnic tables, water, pit toilets, trash containers
Managing Agency	USDA Forest Service (Medicine Bow National Forest)
Reservations	Not accepted—first come, first served
Season/Usage	Open mid-May through October; Moderate use

Directions: From Riverside-Encampment (south of Saratoga), drive south on HWY 230 for 23 miles. Turn east onto FR 492 and drive 2 more miles.

Description: Six Mile receives heavy daytime use and moderate overnight use. Most campers who stay here are looking to fish the North Platte River or are planning (or returning from) a trip on the water.

The campground sits well above the river and a quarter-mile trek with a 170-foot elevation drop is required to reach the riverbank. Some of the sites are tucked into a short aspen forest with steps leading up from the parking spur. The best sites for trailers and RVs are pull-throughs along the side of the campground's sunny loop road.

Fishing: Large numbers of rainbow and brown trout can be found in the North Platte River.

Trails: The Platte River Trail is a popular route that parallels the North Platte as it flows north. The most traveled portion is 5.5 miles long. From that point, you'll have to ford the river, if possible, to find the indistinct trail on the other side that continues downstream toward Pickaroon Campground. Ticks can be a problem early in the season.

Floating: The North Platte River is inviting to floaters. The area is a take-out point for rafters who have embarked on multi-day trips along the river.

Field Notes: Due to mud and slop, it can be difficult to make the uphill drive out of the campground during the shoulder seasons. We've seen several stuck and abandoned vehicles here.

SOUTH – SOUTHEAST AREA 3
Vedauwoo and Vicinity

Just west of Cheyenne, a band of rocky spikes breaks the grassy horizon. These spikes are part of the Sherman Mountains, a stunted range formed from weathered Sherman granite. This southern extension of the Laramie Range includes Curt Gowdy State Park as well as the popular Pole Mountain and Vedauwoo recreation areas.

The forests around Pole Mountain—consisting mostly of ponderosa, limber, and lodgepole pines—are treasured for their recreational value. Boasting a complex maze of cross-country ski trails, this area provides winter recreation for skiers and summertime routes for hikers, joggers, and mountain bikers.

The Vedauwoo (pronounced vee-da-voo) area, which is an American Indian term meaning "Earth-born," is a rock-climber's paradise with routes ranging from 5.0 to 5.14 in difficulty. On any given summer day, dozens of climbers can be found scaling the vertical faces. It's also a preferred destination for many walkers, photographers, and picnickers.

What to Expect: Welcome to southeastern Wyoming's outdoor playground! Since this area is located between two of the state's largest towns—Cheyenne and Laramie—it gets steady visitation throughout the year. (Keep in mind that this is Wyoming and "steady visitation" can mean that you'll see a couple dozen cars on a given day.) Interstate 80 cuts across Pole Mountain and brings a fair number of highway visitors with it. Sometimes in camp, you'll be able to hear truck traffic from the Interstate.

Void of big mountain peaks and surrounded by grassy plains, Pole Mountain doesn't look that high and the elevation may surprise you. Most campgrounds are above 8,000 feet. You can expect warm (if not hot) days during the summer and comfortably cool evenings. Days are bright and sunny, but afternoon thunderstorms are common. Wind is also common, especially during the winter months when relentless gales blast the I-80 corridor in southeastern Wyoming.

Area 3: Vedauwoo and Vicinity

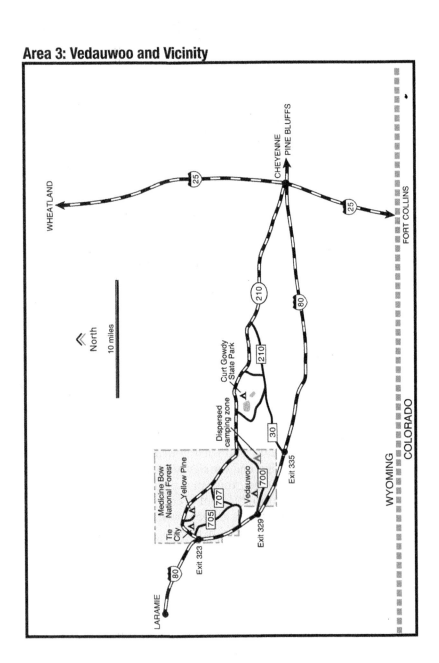

Campgrounds	Sites	Cost	Average Spur Length	Electrical Hookups	Cellular Service (varies by carrier/site)	Reservations Accepted	Page Number
Curt Gowdy State Park	159	$15-25	L	✔	2 bars	✔	381
Vedauwoo Campground	28	$10	L		2 bars		384
Vedauwoo Designated Dispersed Camping Zone	85+	Free	L		2 bars		385
Yellow Pine Campground	19	$10	M		2 bars		386
Tie City Campground	18	$10	M		2 bars		387

Average Spur Length: S = Short (under 30 feet), M = Medium (+-30 feet), L = Long (+-40 feet)
Cellular Service: 1 bar = weak/unreliable signal, 2 bars = low usable signal, 3+ bars = reliable signal for most users

Curt Gowdy State Park
7,300 feet

Location/Map	West of Cheyenne; Page 380, 382
GPS Coordinates	N41° 11.42' W105° 14.52'
Sites/Spur Length	159 sites, 8 group sites; Long spurs—over 30 feet
Cost	$10 state residents, $17 nonresidents (includes $6 or $9 day-use fee)
Facilities/Services	Hookups (limited), fire rings, picnic tables, water, pit toilets, trash containers, dump station, playground, boat ramp, camp store, cabins, cellular signal
Managing Agency	Wyoming State Parks, Historic Sites & Trails
Reservations	Call 877-996-7275 or visit wyoparks.state.wy.us
Season/Usage	Open all year; High use

Directions: From I-25 in Cheyenne, take Exit 10B (Happy Jack Road – HWY 210) and drive west for 24 miles. If traveling from Laramie, take I-80 east to Exit 323 (Summit Rest Area). Then follow HWY 210 east for 15 miles.

You can reach the park's southern entrance from Exit 335 (Buford) on I-80. From this point, take gravel CR 30-210 northeast for 7 miles.

Description: This popular state park is located on the eastern flank of the Sherman Mountains between Cheyenne and Laramie. Here, the flat grassy plains to the east give way to lightly-timbered hills, peaceful brooks, and photogenic granite formations. Elevations vary from 6,450 to 7,500 feet.

Curt Gowdy State Park was established in 1971 and inherited its name from a famous University of Wyoming athlete and professional broadcaster. Historically, the region was used as camping grounds for the Comanche, Pawnee, Crow, and Shoshone Indians while they pursued bison.

Curt Gowdy State Park

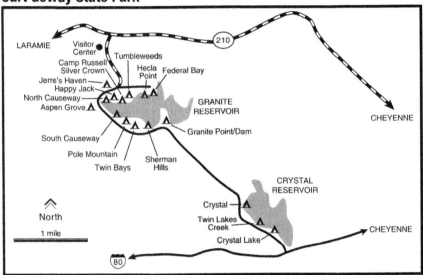

The first few campgrounds near the visitor center offer electric hookups, including Jerre's Haven, Happy Jack, Camp Russel, and Tumbleweeds. These sites mostly occupy an open slope above Granite Reservoir with few trees, but they offer easy access to the boat ramp and better parking for long trailers and RVs. Tumbleweeds and Hecla Point Campgrounds have paved parking spurs, fire rings, and water hydrants at most sites.

Aspen Grove Campground, on the west side of Granite Reservoir, is set a little farther away from the shoreline, close to trails, the corral, and the archery range. The South Causeway, Pole Mountain, Twin Bays, Sherman Hills, and Granite Point/Dam camps line the southern shoreline and have a little more shade (still not much) due to a peppering of evergreens and cottonwoods. These camps are better suited for short trailers, vans, or tents. Not all camps have close-by pit toilets or potable water, so you may need to go for a short drive or walk. Several reservable group sites, cabins, and picnic shelters are divided among these campgrounds.

Crystal Reservoir has three more campgrounds including Crystal (with a few electric hookups), Twin Lakes Creek (includes a group site), and Crystal Lake. Some cottonwoods can be found near the dam, but many of the sites are exposed under the open Wyoming sky.

Archery Range: An archery range on the west side of the park hosts a number of archery events each year including the State Field Archery Tournament and Bow Hunters' Weekend.

Natural Attractions: There is an overlook at each reservoir. The overlook at Granite Reservoir is located on the southeast side. The overlook at Crystal Reservoir is located on the southern shoreline.

Curt Gowdy State Park

Trails/Mountain Biking: There are more than 41 miles of trails throughout the park and they include highly-rated mountain bike routes. In fact, these tracks that wind between clear creeks and granite boulders have become regionally known. It really is an impressive trail system.

If you're a hiker, a good route is the 4-mile trek (round trip) to Hidden Falls that begins at the west end of Granite Reservoir. There is also Kate's Trail, a 1-mile handicap-accessible trail near the visitor center. Trail maps can also be picked up there.

Fishing/Boating: Fishing for rainbow and cutthroat trout is common and each reservoir has a boat ramp. Mon-motorized watercraft can be rented by a concessionaire during the peak season. Swimming is prohibited.

Picnicking/Group Lodge: The stone Hynds Lodge (north of the highway) is perfect for group gatherings and can be reserved. The lodge includes a covered porch, well-equipped kitchen, dining area, as well as a recreational area and sleeping quarters for thirty people. An amphitheater near the lodge provides the means for outdoor performances or concerts.

All areas are open for picnics. For kids, there are two playgrounds: on the north side of Granite Reservoir and on the south side of Crystal Reservoir.

Field Notes: Be prepared for strong winds at any time of the year. During late spring and summer, afternoon thunderstorms pound this area. However, unless a storm is severe, you're likely to welcome a little cloud cover at this sun-soaked state park. There are also a lot of raccoons so watch your food and trash!

Vedauwoo Campground

8,300 feet

Location/Map	Between Cheyenne and Laramie; Page 380
GPS Coordinates	N41° 9.412' W105° 22.684'
Sites/Spur Length	28 sites, Long spurs—over 30 feet
Cost	$10
Facilities/Services	Fire rings, grills, picnic tables, water, pit toilets, trash containers
Managing Agency	USDA Forest Service (Medicine Bow National Forest); A host is often present
Reservations	Not accepted—first come, first served
Season/Usage	Open late May through October; High use

Directions: From Laramie, head east on I-80 for 13 miles and take Exit 329. Drive east just over 1 mile to the Vedauwoo Recreation Area. Take a short left and drive to the camp on the right side of the road.

Description: Vedauwoo (pronounced "Vee-da-voo") is the closest campground to the Turtle Rock and Devils Playground areas—popular places for rock climbing and hiking. Sites are spacious and are distributed along two paved, dust-free loops. Trees are sparse but are substituted by massive boulders and rock piles. RVs and trailers are easily accommodated in several long and level parking spurs and tent campers will find seven walk-in sites. This is a high traffic area so arrive early on summer weekends.

Vedauwoo Campground

Scenic Driving: For a scenic backroad, follow FR 700 east from the camp for 7 miles to where it ends at HWY 210 (Happy Jack Road). The road travels through fascinating rock structures and has numerous spurs where you can park and explore by foot or have a picnic.

Trails: The most heavily-used hiking route in the area is the 2.5-mile Turtle Rock Trail just north of the campground. This route loops around a massive rock structure as it travels through a pine and aspen forest as well as a riparian area sculpted by beavers. The trail is rated as easy and can be started from a trail at the campground.

Rock Climbing/Bouldering: Vedauwoo is nationally known for its incredible rock climbing. Routes range from 5.0 to 5.14 in difficulty, but even novices can have fun scrambling over boulders.

Picnicking: There may be no better place in Wyoming for a picnic area than here at Vedauwoo. Shady aspens, scenic rock formations, and dozens of ponds make this a great escape from monotonous Interstate driving. Several designated picnic areas are found throughout the area, but the closest is just north of the campground at the recreation site.

Field Notes: This family-friendly camp has a lot going for it; easy Interstate access, intriguing scenery, and lots of places to explore. It does get busy, though, and summertime thunderstorms can be severe.

Vedauwoo Designated Dispersed Camping Zone

Vedauwoo Road (FR 700)—the 7.5-mile gravel road that runs between Exit 329 at I-80 and HWY 210—has 85 designated dispersed campsites along it and its peripheral roads. Some of these side roads are rough and require high clearance and four-wheel drive. A map of the sites can be found on Forest Service maps as well as on information boards in the area.

Upon finding a site, park within 50 feet of the numbered site marker. Groups that have more than 8 people or two vehicles must use one of the group sites that are indicated by the letter "G" on the marker. As dispersed camping, there are no picnic tables, trash containers, pit toilets, or water, but some sites have rough fire rings. Stays are limited to 16 days.

Dispersed camping can also be found in other areas of Pole Mountain. Popular areas include Headquarters Road (FR 707) as well as the rougher secondary roads north of HWY 210.

Yellow Pine Campground

8,400 feet

Location/Map	Between Cheyenne and Laramie; Page 380
GPS Coordinates	N41° 15.250' W105° 24.6'
Sites/Spur Length	19 sites, Medium spurs—up to 30 feet
Cost	$10
Facilities/Services	Fire rings, grills, picnic tables, water, pit toilets, trash containers
Managing Agency	USDA Forest Service (Medicine Bow National Forest)
Reservations	Not accepted—first come, first served
Season/Usage	Open late May through October; High use

Directions: From Laramie, head east on I-80 for 7 miles and take Exit 323 (Summit Rest Area). Drive 2 miles on HWY 210 (Happy Jack Road) and then turn right into the Happy Jack Recreation Area. Drive 1.4 miles from the turnoff.

Description: Yellow Pine is an open camp just a few miles from the nation's longest Interstate highway. It makes a great weekend destination or it can be used as a quick overnighter on your way to bigger attractions. Over half of the sites are pull-throughs that are decently spread out and will fit longer trailers. But you won't have much privacy here as the camp's pine trees were removed after a pine beetle outbreak.

Scenic Driving: Much of this area is known as Vedauwoo, a land of awkwardly balanced rocks. For a nice scenic drive, follow HWY 210 (Happy Jack Road) east for 9 miles and turn south on FR 700. The 7.5-mile forest road travels through the fascinating Vedauwoo area and has numerous spurs where you can park and explore by foot or have a picnic.

Trails: Hiking and mountain biking are the biggest draws to this area. The Happy Jack-Tie City trail system is comprised of over a dozen fun miles of tangled routes. The large Happy Jack Trailhead is passed on your way to the camp.

Field Notes: This hidden-away encampment seems like a place that nobody would find, but it's often pretty busy with both locals and out-of-state Interstate travelers. Without the trees, you'll get a broad view of the sky allowing you to watch tall cumulonimbus clouds build over the Cheyenne area during summer afternoons. Then when it clears and cools off in the evening, you'll have a great spot for stargazing.

Tie City Campground

8,600 feet

Location/Map	Between Cheyenne and Laramie; Page 380
GPS Coordinates	N41° 15.092' W105° 26.165'
Sites/Spur Length	18 sites, Medium spurs—up to 30 feet
Cost	$10
Facilities/Services	Fire rings, grills, picnic tables, water, pit toilets, trash containers
Managing Agency	USDA Forest Service (Medicine Bow National Forest)
Reservations	Not accepted—first come, first served
Season/Usage	Open late May through October; Moderate use

Directions: From Laramie, head east on I-80 for 7 miles and take Exit 323 (Summit Rest Area). Drive 1 mile on HWY 210 (Happy Jack Road) and then turn right into the Tie City Recreation Area.

Description: This popular campground is located on Pole Mountain near the I-80 Summit Rest Area, making it very accessible. The Interstate is so close that you can hear road noise, but fortunately, the camp feels more remote than it is. Sites are found in a light forest of aspen and pine. Overgrown understory helps provide decent privacy between campers. There are six pull-through sites, but they are fairly unlevel.

Scenic Driving: Much of this area is known as Vedauwoo, a land of awkwardly balanced rocks. For a short scenic drive, follow HWY 210 (Happy Jack Road) east for 10 miles and turn south on FR 700. The 7-mile forest road travels through the fascinating Vedauwoo area and has numerous spurs where you can park and explore by foot or have a picnic.

Trails: Hiking and mountain biking are the biggest draws to this area and the busy Tie City Trailhead is located at the campground's entrance. The Happy Jack-Tie City trail system is comprised of over a dozen fun miles of tangled routes.

Field Notes: This camp was closed for a few seasons and could use some maintenance, but it's still a beautiful spot that fills quickly in the summer with families and trail users. Day time traffic is high as people drive through the trailhead and camp.

Contacts

National Park Service
http://www.nps.gov

Grand Teton National Park
http://www.nps.gov/grte
307-739-3399
P.O. Box 170
Moose, WY 83012

Yellowstone National Park
http://www.nps.gov/yell
307-344-7381
P.O. Box 168
Yellowstone National Park, WY 82190

Devils Tower National Monument
http://www.nps.gov/deto
307-467-5283
P.O. Box 10
Devils Tower, WY 82714

Bighorn Canyon NRA
http://www.nps.gov/bica
307-548-5406
20 Highway 14A East
Lovell, WY 82431

USDA Forest Service
http://www.fs.fed.us

Medicine Bow National Forest
http://www.fs.usda.gov/mbr

Supervisor's Office
Laramie District
307-745-2300
2468 Jackson Street
Laramie, WY 82070

Douglas Ranger District
307-358-4690
2250 East Richards Street
Douglas, WY 82633

Brush Creek - Hayden
Ranger District
307-326-5258
2171 Highway 130, Box 249
Saratoga, WY 82331

Bighorn National Forest
http://www.fs.usda.gov/bighorn

Supervisor's Office
Tongue Ranger District
307-674-2600
2013 Eastside 2nd Street
Sheridan, WY 82801

Powder River Ranger District
307-684-7806
1415 Fort Street
Buffalo, WY 82834

Medicine Wheel Ranger District
307-765-4435
95 HWY 16/20
Greybull, WY 82426

Shoshone National Forest
http://www.fs.usda.gov/shoshone

Supervisor's Office
307-527-6241
808 Meadow Lane
Cody, WY 82414

Clarks Fork, Greybull, Wapiti Districts
307-527-6921
203A Yellowstone Ave
Cody, WY 82414

Wind River Ranger District
307-455-2466
1403 W Ramshorn
Dubois, WY 82513

Washakie Ranger District
307-332-5460
333 East Main St
Lander, WY 82520

Black Hills National Forest
http://www.fs.usda.gov/blackhills

Supervisor's Office
605-673-9200
1019 N. 5th Street
Custer, SD 57730

Bearlodge Ranger District
307-283-1361
121 South 21st Street, Box 680
Sundance, WY 82729

Hell Canyon Ranger District
307-746-2782
1225 Washington
Newcastle, WY 82701

Bridger-Teton National Forest
http://www.fs.usda.gov/btnf

Supervisor's Office
307-739-5500
P.O. Box 1888
Jackson, WY 83001

Kemmerer Ranger District
307-828-5100
308 Hwy 189
Kemmerer, WY 83101

Greys River Ranger District
307-886-5300
671 North Washington Street
Afton, WY 83110

Blackrock Ranger District
307-543-2386
Highway 26/287, Box 278
Moran, WY 83013

Jackson Hole Visitor Center
532 N. Cache Street
Jackson, WY 83001

Jackson Ranger District
307-739-5400
25 Rosencrans Lane, P.O. Box 1689
Jackson, WY 83001

Big Piney Ranger District
307-276-5800
10418 South US HWY 189, P.O. Box 218
Big Piney, WY 83113

Pinedale Ranger District
307-367-4326
29 East Fremont Lake Road, Box 220
Pinedale, WY 82941

Ashley National Forest
http://www.fs.usda.gov/ashley

Flaming Gorge National Rec Area
435-784-3445
25 West Highway 43, Box 279
Manila, UT 84046

Green River Office
307-875-2871
1155 West Flaming Gorge Way
Green River, WY 82635

Caribou-Targhee National Forest
http://www.fs.usda.gov/ctnf

Supervisor's Office
208-557-5900
1405 Hollipark Dr
Idaho Falls, ID 83401

Ashton-Island Park Ranger District
208-558-7301
3726 HWY 20
Island Park, ID 83429

Teton-Basin Ranger District
208-354-2312
515 South Main, Driggs, ID 83422

Uinta-Wasatch-Cache National Forest
http://www.fs.usda.gov/uwcnf

Supervisor's Office
801-999-2103
857 West South Jordan Parkway
South Jordan, UT 84095

Evanston-Mountain View Ranger District
307-789-3194
1565 Highway 150, Suite A
Evanston, WY 82930

Evanston-Mountain View Ranger District
307-782-6555
321 Highway 414
Mountain View, WY 82939

Bureau of Land Management (BLM)
http://www.blm.gov/wyoming

Wyoming State Office
307-775-6256
5353 Yellowstone Road, Box 1828
Cheyenne, WY 82009

Rawlins Office
307-328-4200
1300 N Third Street
Rawlins, WY 82301

Buffalo Field Office
307-684-1100
1425 Fort Street
Buffalo, WY 82834

Lander Field Office
307-332-8400
1335 Main, Box 589
Lander, WY 82520

Pinedale Field Office
307-367-5300
1625 West Pine Street
Pinedale, WY 82941

Worland Field Office
307-347-5100
101 South 23rd
Worland, WY 82401

Casper Field Office
307-261-7600
2987 Prospector Drive
Casper, WY 82604

Cody Field Office
307-578-5900
1002 Blackburn Avenue
Cody, WY 82414

Kemmerer Field Office
307-828-4500
430 N Highway 189
Kemmerer, WY 83101

Newcastle Field Office
307-746-6600
1101 Washington Boulevard
Newcastle, WY 82701

Rock Springs Field Office
307-352-0256
280 Hwy. 191 North
Rock Springs, WY 82901

Wyoming Game and Fish
http://wgfd.wyo.gov/

Wyoming Game and Fish Department
307-777-4600
5400 Bishop Blvd.
Cheyenne, WY 82006

Casper Regional Office
307-473-3400
3030 Energy Lane, Suite 100
Casper, WY 82604

Cody Regional Office
307-527-7125
2820 State Highway 120
Cody, WY 82414

Laramie Regional Office
307-745-4046
1212 S. Adams
Laramie, WY 82070

Pinedale Regional Office
307-367-4353
432 E. Mill Street
Pinedale, WY 82941

Green River Regional Office
307-875-3223
351 Astle Ave
Green River, WY 82935

Jackson Regional Office
307-733-2321
420 North Cache
Jackson, WY 83001

Lander Regional Office
307-332-2688
260 Buena Vista
Lander, WY 82520

Sheridan Regional Office
307-672-7418
700 Valley View Drive
Sheridan, WY 82801

Wyoming County Contacts
This list includes Tourism Boards, Chamber of Commerces, Information Centers, and Recreation & Parks Departments

Albany County: 800-445-5303
Bighorn County: 307-568-2381
Campbell County: 307-686-3851
Carbon County: 800-228-3547
Converse County: 307-358-2244
Crook County: 307-283-2440
Fremont County: 307-645-6233
Goshen County: 800-577-3555
Hot Springs County: 877-864-3192
Johnson County: 800-227-5122
Laramie County: 800-426-5009
Lincoln County: 888-300-3413

Natrona County: (See information below)
Niobrara County: 307-334-2950
Park County: 800-393-2639
Platte County: 307-322-2322
Sheridan County: 307-672-2485
Sublette County: 888-285-7282
Sweetwater County: 800-354-6743
Teton County: 307-733-3316
Uinta County: 307-783-0301
Washakie County: 307-347-3226
Weston County: 307-746-2739

Natrona County Road, Bridges, and Parks
http://www.natrona.net
307-235-9200

Wyoming Office of Tourism
http://www.travelwyoming.com

Wyoming Office of Tourism
307-777-7777
5611 High Plains Road
Cheyenne, Wyoming 82002

Index

A
Absaroka Range (north), 82
Absaroka Range (south), 114
Alcova Reservoir, 243
   Black Beach Campground, 243
   Cottonwood Beach Campground, 243
   County RV Campground, 243
   Fremont Campground, 243
   Okie Beach Campground, 243
   Westside Campground, 243
Allred Flat Campground, 296
Alpine Campground, 280
Amsden Creek WHMA, 143
Aspen Campground, 356
Atherton Creek Campground, 71
Atlantic City Campground, 226
Ayres Natural Bridge Campground, 265

B
Baker's Hole Campground, 46
Bald Mountain Campground, 148
Battle Creek (dispersed), 347
Bearlodge Campground, 197
Beartooth Lake Campground, 86
Beartooth Scenic Byway, 82
Beartrap Meadows Campground, 239
Belle Fourche Campground, 201
Bennett Peak Campground, 375
Big Atlantic Gulch Campground, 229
Big Game Campground, 104
Big Sandy Recreation Area, 323
Big Sandy Wilderness Campground, 302
Bighorn Canyon NRA, 152
Bighorn Mountains (north), 138
Bighorn Mountains (south), 168
Bighorn Scenic Byway, 138
Black Hills, 194
Boars Tusk, 320
Bottle Creek Campground, 344
Boulder Lake Campground, 305
Boulder Park Campground, 186
Bow River Campground, 354
Boysen State Park, 211
   Brannon Campground, 213
   Fremont Bay Campground, 213
   Lower Wind River Campground, 213
   North Muddy Campground, 213
   Poison Creek Campground, 213
   Sand Mesa Campground, 213
   South Muddy Campground, 213
   Tamarask Campground, 213
   Tough Creek Campground, 213
   Upper Wind River Campground, 213
Bridge Bay Campground, 49

Brooklyn Lake Campground, 362
Brooks Lake Campground, 130
Brown Mountain Campground, 120
Buckboard Crossing Campground, 329
Bucking Mule Falls, 151
Buffalo Bill Cody Scenic Highway, 99
Buffalo Bill State Park, 102
   North Fork, 103
   North Shore Bay Campground, 103
   Trout Creek Campground, 103
   Trout Creek Natural Trail, 103
Buffalo Creek Campground, 234

C
Campbell Creek Campground, 269
Canyon Campground, 42
Casper Mountain Campgrounds, 239
Cave Falls Campground, 57
Chief Joseph Scenic Byway, 82
Circle Park Campground, 175
Clearwater Campground, 108
Cloud Peak Skyway, 168
Colter Bay Campground, 63
Colter Campground, 92
Connor Battlefield State Park, 142
Continental Divide Trail, 225, 349
Cook Lake Campground, 198
Corral Creek Campground, 374
Cottonwood Campground, 249
Cottonwood Lake Campground, 295
Crazy Creek Campground, 89
Crazy Woman Canyon, 179
Cross Creek Campground, 161
Crystal Creek Campground, 73
Curt Gowdy State Park, 381
   Aspen Grove Campground, 382
   Camp Russell Campground, 382
   Crystal Campground, 382
   Crystal Lakes Campground, 382
   Federal Bay Campground, 382
   Granite Point/Dam Campground, 382
   Happy Jack Campground, 382
   Hecla Point Campground, 382
   Jerre's Haven Campground, 382
   North Causeway Campground, 382
   Pole Mountain Campground, 382
   Sherman Hills Campground, 382
   Silver Crown Campground, 382
   South Causeway Campground, 382
   Tumbleweeds Campground, 382
   Twin Bays Campground, 382
   Twin Lakes Creek Campground, 382

Curtis Canyon Campground, 74
Curtis Gulch Campground, 268

D
Dead Indian Campground, 95
Dead Swede Campground, 156
Deadhorse Trailhead Campground, 334
Deep Creek Campground, 355
Deer Creek Campground, 116
Deer Park Campground, 187
Devils Tower National Monument, 201
Dickinson Creek Campground, 215
Double Cabin Campground, 127
Doyle Campground, 181
Dugway Campground, 253

E
Eagle Creek Campground, 111
East Fork Campground, 158
East Table Creek Campground, 276
Elk Fork Campground, 106
Encampment River Campground, 343
Esterbrook Campground, 266

F
Falls Campground, 128
Fiddlers Lake Campground, 221
Firehole Campground, 331
Fishing Bridge RV Park, 47
Five Springs Falls Campground, 151
Flagg Ranch, 56
Flaming Gorge NRA, 329
    Boat Campgrounds, 330
    Buckboard Crossing Campground, 329
    Firehole Campground, 331
    Utah Campgrounds, 333
Fontenelle Creek Campground, 324
Fontenelle Reservoir Campgrounds, 325
Forest Park Campground, 289
Fossil Butte National Monument, 320
Fox Creek Campground, 91
Fremont Canyon, 237
Fremont Lake Campground, 307
French Creek Campground, 373
Friend Park Campground, 267

G
Glendo State Park, 262
    Broken Arrow Campground, 263
    Burnt Wagon Campground, 263
    Cottonwood Creek Campground, 263
    Custer Cove Campground, 263
    Dune Campground, 263
    Indian Point Campground, 263
    Red Hills Campground, 263
    Reno Cove Campground, 263
    Sagebrush Campground, 263
    Sandy Beach Campground, 263
    Shelter Point Campground, 263
    Two Moon Campground, 263
    Whiskey Gulch Campground, 263
Grand Canyon of the Snake River, 274
Grand Encampment Museum, 340
Grand Teton National Park, 59
    Colter Bay Campground, 63
    Gros Ventre Campground, 69
    Jenny Lake Campground, 67
    Lizard Creek Campground, 62
    Pacific Creek Campground, 64
    Signal Mountain Campground, 65
Granite Creek Campground, 79
Granite Creek Hot Springs, 79
Granite Reservoir, 386
Grant Village Campground, 51
Grave Springs Campground, 234
Grayrocks Reservoir WHMA, 258
Green Mountain, 249
Green River Lakes Campground, 315
Grizzly & Wolf Discovery Center, 46
Gros Ventre Campground, 69
Guernsey State Park, 258
    Black Canyon Cove Campground, 260
    Black Canyon Point Campground, 260
    Cottonwood Cove Campground, 260
    Davis Bay Campground, 259
    Deadmans Gulch Campground, 260
    Fish Canyon Campground, 260
    Fish Canyon Cove Campground, 260
    Long Canyon East Campground, 260
    Long Canyon West Campground, 260
    Newell Bay Campground, 259
    Red Cloud Campground, 260
    Sandy Beach Campground, 260
    Sandy Cove Campground, 260
    Sandy Point Campground, 260
    Skyline Drive Campground, 259
    Spotted Tail Campground, 260

H
Half Moon Campground, 308
Hams Fork Campground, 292
Hatchet Campground, 133
Hawk Springs State Park, 257
Headwaters Campground, 56
Hettinger Group Campground, 174
Hoback Campground, 81
Hobble Creek Campground, 290
Hog Park Campground, 345
Hogan and Luce Campground, 98
Hole in the Wall, 228
Horse Creek Campground, 126
Hunter Campground, 172
Hunter Peak Campground, 94

I
Indian Creek Campground, 41
Intermittent Spring, 294
Island Lake Campground, 84
Island Park Campground, 187

J
Jack Creek Campground, 117, 348
Jenny Lake Campground, 67

K
Keyhole State Park, 203
    Arch Rock Campground, 204
    Beach Campground, 204
    Cottonwood Campground, 204
    Coulter Bay Campground, 204
    Homestead Campground, 204
    Pat's Point Campground, 204
    Pronghorn Campground, 204
    Rocky Point Campground, 204
    Tatanka Campground, 204
    Wind Creek Campground, 204
Killpecker Sand Dunes, 320
Kirk Inberg/Kevin Roy WHMA, 124
Kirwin, 119
Kozy Campground, 78

L
Lake Alice, 291
Lake Creek Campground, 93
Lake DeSmet, 171
Lake Hattie, 354
Lake Owen Campground, 370
Lakeview Campground, 182
Laramie Peak, 267
Laramie Plains Lakes, 353
Laramie Range, 254
Leigh Creek Campground, 190
Lewis Lake Campground, 52
Lily Lake Camping Area, 88
Lincoln Park Campground, 369
Little Cottonwood Group Campground, 279
Little Goose Campground, 160
Little Popo Agie Campground, 222
Little Sunlight Campground, 97
Lizard Creek Campground, 62
Lodgepole Campground, 241
Lost Cabin Campground, 180
Lost Creek Campground, 347
Louis Lake Campground, 223
Louis Lake Road, 220
Lower Bear Creek Campground, 124
Lower Paint Rock Lake Campground, 167
Lucerne Campground, 333

M
Madison Campground, 45
Mammoth Campground, 39
McCoy Creek Campground, 280
Medicine Bow Mountains, 351
Medicine Lodge Archaeological Site, 191
Medicine Lodge Lake Campground, 165
Medicine Wheel National Hist. Landmark, 150
Meeks Cabin Campground, 335
Middle Fork Campground, 173, 233
Middle Piney Lake Campground, 284
Mikesell-Potts Recreation Area, 171
Miller Lake Dispersed Camping Area, 377
Miracle Mile, 251
Montana Campgrounds
    Baker's Hole Campground, 46
    Colter Campground, 92
    Soda Butte Campground, 92

Moose Flat Campground, 287
Muddy Mountain
    Lodgepole Campground, 241
    Rim Campground, 242
Murphy Creek Campground, 286

N
Narrows Campground, 312
Nash Fork Campground, 361
New Fork Lake Campground, 311
New Fork River Campground, 322
Newton Creek Campground, 110
Norris Campground, 44
North Boulder Lake Campground, 306
North Fork Campground, 360
North Tongue Campground, 147

O
Ocean Lake WHMA, 216
Old Faithful, 50
Outlaw Cave Campground, 231
Owen Creek Campground, 154

P
Pacific Creek Campground, 64
Pathfinder Reservoir, 246
    Bishops Point Campground, 248
    Diabase Campground, 248
    Sage Campground, 248
    Weiss Campground, 248
    Wolf Point Camping Area, 248
Pebble Creek Campground, 36
Pelton Creek Campground, 377
Periodic Spring, 294
Pickaroon Campground, 376
Pilot Butte, 320

Pine Campground, 357
Pine Island Group Campground, 146
Pinnacles Campground, 129
Porcupine Campground, 149
Prior Flat Campground, 250
Prune Creek Campground, 145

R

Ranger Creek Campground, 157, 164
Red Canyon, 224
Red Canyon (Utah), 333
Red Desert, 320
Reunion Flats Campground, 76
Reuter Campground, 200
Rex Hale Campground, 109
Rim Campground, 242
Rob Roy Campground, 372
Ryan Park Campground, 367

S

Sacajawea Campground, 283
Salt River Range, 281
Sand Creek Public Access Area, 196
Scab Creek Campground, 304
Seedskadee Wildlife Refuge, 325
Seminoe-Alcova Backcountry Byway, 251
Seminoe State Park, 251
  North Red Hills Campground, 251
  South Red Hills Campground, 251
  Sunshine Beach Campground, 251
Sheffield Creek Campground, 55
Shell Creek Campground, 163
Sibley Lake Campground, 142
Sierra Madre Range, 340
Signal Mountain Campground, 65
Silver Lake Campground, 365
Sinks Canyon Campground, 218
Sinks Canyon State Park, 217
  Popo Agie Campground, 217
  Sawmill Campground, 217
Sitting Bull Campground, 183
Six Mile Campground, 378
Slate Creek Campground, 325
Slough Creek Campground, 37
Snake River Range, 274
Snake River Recreation Area, 54
Snowy Range, 367
Snowy Range Scenic Byway, 351
Soda Butte Campground, 92
Soda Lake WHMA, 311
South Brush Creek Campground, 368
South Fork Campground, 178
South Pass City Historic Site, 227
Spence/Moriarity WHMA, 124
Spruce Campground, 359
Station Creek Campground, 277

Sugarloaf Campground, 364
Sundance Horse Campground, 199
Sunlight WHMA, 98
Sweetwater Bridge Campground, 301
Sweetwater Guard Station
  Campground, 300
Swift Creek Campground, 293

T

Tail Race Campground, 325
Teton Canyon Campground, 77
Teton Reservoir Campground, 349
Three Mile Campground, 112
Three Patches Campground, 328
Tie City Campground, 387
Tie Flume Campground, 155
Tie Hack Campground, 176
Tom Thorne/Beth Williams WHMA, 270
Tower Fall Campground, 38
Trail Creek Campground, 75
Trails End Campground, 309
Turpin Meadows Campground, 132

U

Uinta Mountains, 320
Upper Campground, 125
Utah Campgrounds, 333
  Antelope Flat Campground, 333
  Arch Dam Campground, 333
  Canyon Rim Campground, 333
  Cedar Springs Campground, 333
  Deer Run Campground, 333
  Dipping Springs Campground, 333
  Firefighters Memorial Campground, 333
  Green Lakes Campground, 333
  Greendale Campground, 333
  Lucerne, 333
  Mann Campground, 333
  Mustang Ridge Campground, 333
  Skull Creek Campground, 333
  Willow Campground, 333

V

Vedauwoo, 384
Vedauwoo Campground, 384
Vedauwoo Dispersed Camping Zone, 385
Viva Naughton Reservoir, 293

W

Wapiti Campground, 105
Warren Bridge Campground, 319
Warren Bridge Recreation Area, 317
Weeping Rock Campground, 325
West Tensleep Lake Campground, 188
Whiskey Basin WHMA, 125

Whiskey Grove Campground, 314
White Mountain, 320
Wick/Beumee WHMA, 354
Wiggins Fork Campground, 125
Willow Campground, 358
Willow Lake Campground, 310
Willow Park Group Campground, 184
Wind River Range, 297
Wolf Creek Campground, 278
Wood River Campground, 119
Worthen Meadows Campground, 220
Wyoming Range, 281

Y

Yellow Pine Campground, 386
Yellowstone, 32
    Bridge Bay Campground, 49
    Canyon Campground, 42
    Fishing Bridge RV Park, 47
    Grant Village Campground, 51
    Indian Creek Campground, 41
    Lewis Lake Campground, 52
    Madison Campground, 45
    Mammoth Campground, 39
    Norris Campground, 44
    Pebble Creek Campground, 36
    Slough Creek Campground, 37
    Tower Fall Campground, 38
Yellowtail WHMA, 154

Acknowledgments and Afterword

My earliest memories involve camping; it was a staple in my childhood. It's the fear I remember most from the early years. At night, I'd flinch when a crack of lightning illuminated the sky. The thunder would echo off the mountains, amplifying the sound and my worry. Then there were the bears. How many hours I stayed awake wondering if a giant bear would get me I'll never know. There were some scary moments, but the good ones were innumerable. Camping was wonderful—there were rocks to climb, chipmunks to chase, s'mores to eat, and lots of campfires. It's all a kid could want.

Unrealized at the time, my mountain-loving parents, Merrill and Jo Ann, were instilling a passion for the outdoors in me. They showed me how camping and being in nature add focus to what's important in life. It's a passion I have carried from the backyard to the backcountry and I'm now trying to instill the same enthusiasm for nature into my own kids. Access to the outdoors, in whatever capacity possible, is one of the best gifts a parent can give. Thanks Mom and Dad!

Conversely, a kid's unique perspective of the outdoors is a pretty good gift back to the parent. My kids have a way of turning dull places into family favorites. That desolate reservoir way out in the dusty, windy desert was never a fun place to visit. But it now serves up fond memories of where we flew a kite like it was caught in the jet stream for way too long. It was just us and a lot of pelicans. Another place we'd normally blast past became a trip highlight when we stopped to watch an antelope fawn learn how to dart across the sage flats. Of course, any wildlife sighting (butterflies to bears) is more fun with kids, and in Wyoming, there is no shortage of these sightings. So for this new view on old places and things, I have my daughters to thank. My wife also deserves much credit for keeping us all going in the same direction with minimal fuss. She's been instrumental in helping me get these books completed.

Julie Cornia, thanks again for your creativity. My favorite part of this project (besides the camping) is seeing your skills at work. Judi Wright, your rich understanding of the English language saved me many an embarrassment. I am filled with gratitude for the help you both provided.

The Fifth Edition of this book represents more than two decades of ongoing research. I've logged well over 150,000 miles on Wyoming roads and trails and try to visit each campground in this book on a regular basis. It's probably a bit much, but the exploring never gets old. However, I'm certainly not alone in being enamored with Wyoming's wide open spaces and wild places and there is a good chance that you are too (or soon will be). Thank you for choosing this book—I hope it leads you to new adventures and many good memories. -Marc

About the Author

When Marc Smith isn't sitting at a desk working as a technical writer for the USDA Forest Service, he's out exploring Wyoming and the rest of the Rocky Mountain West with his family. He also stays busy by serving on a search and rescue team. Aside from the book you are holding, Marc has written four others including Black Hills Camping, Wyoming Backroads, Hiking Wyoming's Medicine Bow National Forest, and Rocky Mountain National Park with Kids (ebook).

Open Space Publications

Updates, current conditions, corrections, and additional photos can be found at: www.WyomingCampingGuide.com

If you have a question, need another book, or just want to share your trip notes, you can contact us by letter or email.

Open Space Publications, LLC
PO Box 50133
Casper, WY 82605-0133

Email: info@openspacepublications.com
Website: www.OpenSpacePublications.com